The Complete Analyst

COMPLETE INVESTMENT BANKER

Part I: Accounting and Valuation Analytics

FitchLearning

Published by Fitch Learning Publishing
4 Chiswell Street, London, EC1Y 4UP
www.fitchlearning.com
Edited by David Mignano and Caroline Herbert

Fourth edition

FitchLearning

Preface

After the success of the first edition of the *Complete Investment Banker* in 2010, Fitch Learning's IBD team were determined to build on its content to provide bankers with more at-the-desk practical reference material. This manual is an invaluable resource for those who are interested in, new to, or experienced in investment banking and is written with the benefit of 100 combined year's experience of training and working in the investment banking sector.

The fourth edition has been organized as a two-book volume seies to enhance portability.

Book I includes topics such as:

- Accounting and analysis from a banker's perspective
- Financial statement DNA
- Cash flow derivation and analysis
- Financial statement integration
- Ratio analysis and metric identification
- Introduction to valuation
- Trading comparables
- Transaction comparables
- Discounted cash flow valuation
- Football field summaries

The fourth edition of the *Complete Investment Banker* is up-to-date for IFRS and US GAAP. It also includes new content provided by FactSet, Bloomberg and Thomson Reuters – to further fuse technical knowledge with the necessary desktop skills bankers need.

Like previous editions, the **CA Tip** concept is a cornerstone of the manual, providing practical tips and advice that are relevant to the job – rather than, as much of the industry's training material does, merely reiterating academic content without context.

The *Complete Investment Banker* series will also be launched as an eBook version in 2014 as part of our online portal offering. The eBook is supported by 200+ HD videos that examine some of the more conceptual and technical topics within the manual. The portal will act as an online repository of IBD technical knowledge, worked examples and on-the-job technical support.

The *Complete Investment Banker,* along with other components of the Complete Analyst series can now be purchased online at www.TheCompleteAnalyst.com

Foreword

The *Complete Investment Banker* volume series covers a substantial range of topics – from the conceptual basics of accounting and finance, to the practical skills of Excel modeling, and creating PowerPoint presentations. What sets this manual apart from other reference books is the clear attention the authors have given to tailoring this book to investment bankers.

The material in the guide is presented in a way that links each topic to the practical analysis that Analysts will be asked to perform in an investment bank. These linkages are both implicitly and explicitly formed. Implicitly, the accounting concepts covered at the beginning of the book are presented with the clear purpose of helping new bankers develop a basic understanding of accounting, so they can use these core skills to engage with in-depth financial analysis. The focus of this section is not only to teach basic accounting rules, but to help bankers understand the linkages that exist between the three financial statements.

The series also offers explicit explanations of how the subjects covered in the manual (such as income statement earnings metrics) have relevance to IBD-specific financial analysis, such as normalizing EBIT. These practical points are clearly labeled as 'CA Tips' making it easy for the reader to distinguish these crucial analysis skills.

The beauty of this guide is that it does not assume the incoming banker has any prior financial training. Starting with an emphasis on the fundamentals of accounting and finance, it creates an almost narrative-like progression, which presents more detailed topics in the context of the conceptual framework established at the outset of the volume series.

Personally, I came into a Fitch Learning Training program with no prior background in accounting or financial analysis. I have found the *Complete Investment Banker Parts I and II* to be extremely helpful because it clearly explains the most basic accounting concepts as they relate to the analysis I now use at my desk. I found the progression of the content to be quite effective as the concepts taught are continually reinforced throughout the chapters, as each new skill presented builds on prior knowledge covered in the series.

The *Complete Investment Banker* series has been an invaluable reference since starting work on the desk, as the manual includes a wealth of practical references on topics ranging from Excel and PowerPoint to Bloomberg.

SO, Analyst, Top Tier Investment Bank

About Fitch Learning

Fitch Learning is a global provider of learning and development solutions for the financial services industry. We train nine out of ten of each of the largest Investment Banks, Asset Managers and Global Banks, delivering in-house, public and online training.

Fitch Learning operates worldwide with trainers based in Europe, the US and Asia. We have trained in over 80 cities globally. Our public (open enrolment) courses are now offered in 16 locations across EMEA, US, Canada and Asia Pacific, and also delivering training in French and Mandarin, as well as in English.

Fitch Learning has over thirty years of experience delivering high quality training which enhances and hones the skills of experienced professionals. Our ability to consistently deliver this level and quality of training is intrinsically linked to our dedicated trainers who train only for us.

In 2015, we offer over 250 courses as we continue expanding our course offerings, our locations and our language capabilities to ensure we can respond to the needs of our clients.

About Fitch Learning

Contents

Introduction

The *Complete Investment Banker (both Books I and II)* are technical reference manuals that are fully integrated into Fitch Learning's investment banking training offering. Both *Books I and II* are designed to act as reference guides for Analysts on your initial program and equally as importantly, when you arrive at your desks.

Theese manuals are not just a collection of technical notes. They have been written by experienced investment banking trainers at Fitch Learning who have applied their wealth of knowledge to produce the clearest explanation and application of the technical skills required by today's Analysts. Each chapter is carefully crafted to ensure that the technical content is pitched at the correct level.

Both *Books I and II manuals* are packed with application notes (or 'CA Tips') that take the technical issues and provide clear and digestible angles that are directly applicable for day-to-day tasks.

The CA Tips include:

- Analysis implications
- Real world examples
- Research issues
- Metric adjustments
- Modeling tricks
- Key review points and practical tips
- Practical advice from senior bankers

Watch out for the CA Tip icon!

Both manuals have been created to guide Analysts in the early stages of their careers. It is a practical and up-to-date source of advice.

Content across the *Complete Investment Banker* series covers:

- Accounting for Analysts
- Valuation
- Financial modeling
- Merger and LBO modeling
- Capital markets

The series is based on Microsoft Excel 2007® (with reference and comparisons to earlier versions and Excel 2010® where relevant), IFRS and US GAAP.

What is an investment bank?

The investment bank

Traditionally, banks have either operated as commercial, or investment banks. Commercial banking focuses on the savings and loans model, while investment banking focuses on the provision of transaction advice, the underwriting of acquisition finance, risk, and liquidity management.

In the US it was illegal to operate as both an investment and commercial bank. In 1999, the Gramm-Leach-Bliley Act legalized the idea of a universal bank that could operate as both an investment bank and a commercial bank.

Investment banks are large enterprises, although somewhat smaller as a result of the credit crunch. They are complicated businesses who will service the needs of a wide variety of clients such as:

- Corporates (listed and unlisted)
- Institutions such as insurance companies, pension and private equity funds
- Charities
- Governments

Investment banking is a widely used term but lacks a precise definition. These investment banks have a much wider remit than they had even ten years ago. One of the reasons the remit has changed over the years is due to the consolidation that has taken place in the industry.

For example Barclays Capital, the investment banking division of Barclays Bank, is a significantly different operation compared to what it was at the beginning of the millennia. Back then, Barclays Capital ('BarCap') was largely a debt advisory and rates, sales and trading business. Now, with the acquisition of the Lehman Brothers business in the US and its strategic growth path, the services that BarCap can provide to its clients is much wider. Likewise, the credit crunch has seen the disappearance/swallowing up of a number of banks into other institutions. For instance, JP Morgan has absorbed Bear Stearns and Washington Mutual. Their service provision and operating model has evolved as a result.

Therefore, traditional definitions or outlines of what an investment bank does must evolve and be clarified.

The investment banking terminology is used to cover a variety of different roles within the world's investment banks. However, it can refer to the provision of services such as:

- Corporate finance advisory covering M&A advisory and finance underwriting
- Banking for corporate entities and governments
- Investment management
- Securities trading
- Treasury services

The term 'investment bank' is often used to generically cover the full spectrum of banking services. Due to the consolidation in the industry, most banking institutions will provide advisory services to its clients. For instance, many members of the general public will look at The Royal Bank of Scotland (RBS) as a typical retail, or high street bank dealing in savings and loans. Many are oblivious to the fact that RBS Global banking and markets is a significant part of their business and RBS is very much an investment bank.

Most institutions will separate the investment banking activities into divisions.

A typical structure is illustrated below:

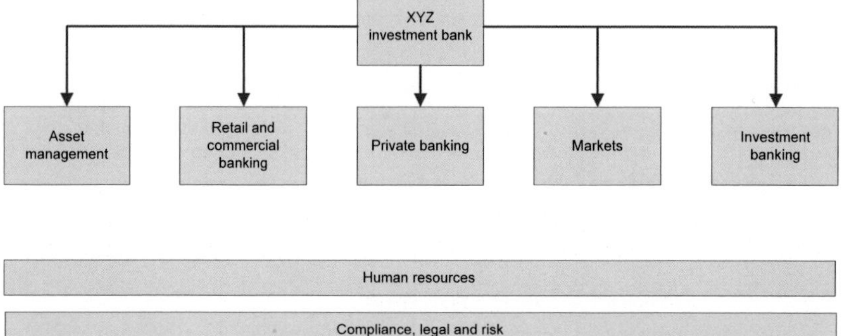

Human resources

Compliance, legal and risk

Technology and operations

The structure above highlights the typical business divisions within an investment bank. Each division will be supported by cross-divisional units such as human resources and operations etc.

What do these teams do?

We will examine some of these activities later in further detail, but as an overview:

Asset management

Asset managers provide advice and products for clients with cash to invest. Essentially an asset manager is managing another client's cash. Asset or fund managers will invest in a variety of assets ranging from equities to fixed income and commodities. The asset manager's objective is to increase the value of a client's investments within the constraints of the client's desired risk exposure.

Retail and commercial banking

Retail banking focuses on the provision of traditional savings and loans services to individuals directly. Typical services include savings and loans, credit cards and mortgages.

Commercial or corporate banking is the provision of banking services such as lending, treasury services, investment banking and management to corporates.

Private banking

Private banking is the term for the provision of banking services to high net worth individuals ('HNWI'). The hurdle rate for what makes someone a HNWI varies from bank to bank.

Unless you have liquid assets in excess of seven figures, consider yourself outside the remit; private banking is providing a personal retail banking service to these clients. Most of the major banks have successful private banking businesses.

The key areas of wealth management that a private banker will provide advice around are:

- Investment management
- Liquidity management
- Tax planning
- Estate management and planning

Markets

Markets or global markets at many institutions have changed noticeably over the last 20 years. To the uninitiated, there is disappointment when the trading floor is not full of traders screaming '*buy*' or '*sell*' at each other. 'Open outcry' trading still exists in small pockets around the globe – for instance on the Chicago Mercantile Exchange or the London Metal Exchange – however the trading floor these days is generally a much quieter place, with rows of computer screens – something more akin to the Matrix.

The markets business is normally split into 'desks' covering defined markets or regions.

A typical structure for the markets division is illustrated below:

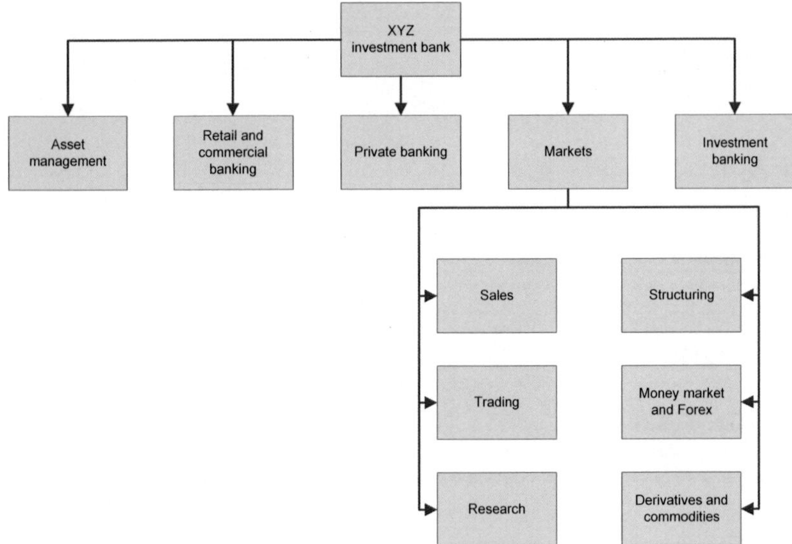

- **Sales**

  The sales people are responsible for making sure that clients are fully up-to-date with investment opportunities, potential trading strategies, and products.

  The sales team must be in constant contact with the traders and research teams to ensure they are in touch with the market, strategy, exposure and current trading book risk.

  Sales will also work with capital market origination teams (equity and debt capital markets – see later), in terms of placing new issues into the market with investors.

- **Trading**

  Traders will make markets (give prices) and book trades for clients. They will work with the sales teams to ensure they understand the client's requirements and risk appetite, as well as relying on the sales teams for ideas and market appetite information.

- **Research**

  Research can be equity, credit or economic in terms of focus. They are the intellectual and academic engine of the bank, presenting views on the markets, economic outlook and individual stock recommendations.

- **Structuring**

  Structurers create complex and tailored financial instruments for clients, e.g. to achieve a required risk profile, particular cash flow patterns or satisfy certain regulatory requirements.

- **Money markets and forex**

  The money market provides short-term liquidity to clients offering short-term lending/borrowing services. The money market tends to focus on instruments of up to three months maturity.

  Banks also offer clients forex services to buy and sell foreign currency now (spot) or through the use of derivatives (in the future).

- **Derivatives and commodities**

  Derivatives are complicated instruments that are used by clients to manage and transfer risk. The markets division is able to structure, trade, and sell these instruments to clients. Derivatives can be structured around:

  - Equities
  - Credit
  - Commodities
  - Foreign exchange

Investment banking division (IBD)

The structure of the investment banking business within 'an investment bank' varies from bank to bank. This terminology creates a great deal of confusion as an investment bank and an investment banking division are quite different terms.

An investment bank is a collective term for the wide range of activities that an investment bank may engage in. For instance, JP Morgan is termed as an investment bank. Its activities cover:

- Private banking
- Investment banking
- Commercial banking
- Markets
- Retail banking
- Security services

IBD (investment banking or just banking at some institutions) typically services the needs of large corporates and multinationals. Traditionally, investment banking focused on advisory services and acted as an intermediary between potential debt and equity investors. However as the banking model has evolved, IBD will often enter into lending activities with its clients.

IBD covers the provision of advice to clients on mergers and acquisitions (M&A advisory), as well as assisting in the raising of funds in the equity and debt capital markets. The term 'corporate finance' is often used to describe these activities.

IBD is typically structured along industry and product lines. This can sometimes create an overlap of responsibilities and can create confusion.

IBD advisory assignments can include:

- Acquisition searches
- Balance sheet advisory (capital structure advice)
- Business portfolio review
- Buy-side advisory
- Sell-side advisory
- Corporate governance
- Dividend policy making
- Fairness opinions (second opinions on a valuation)
- Financing advisory
- Public takeovers

An overview of the investment banking division:

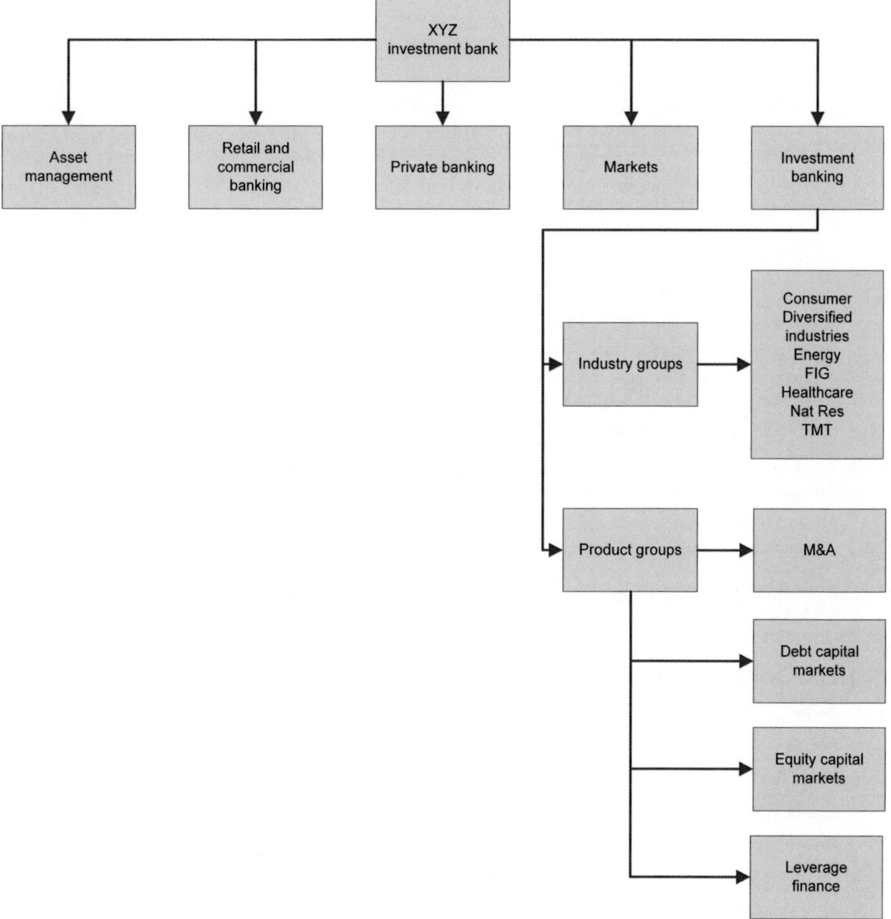

Industry/client coverage

Industry or client coverage groups will focus on specific industries such as technology, media and telecoms (TMT), healthcare, natural resources, and industrials. Industry groups will provide a broad range of services to key industry clients.

Coverage groups can be geographically defined as well.

The bankers in these groups are industry specialists. This allows the clients access to experienced bankers who have a deep understanding of their markets and business models. Once a coverage team has identified a particular need for a client, they will call on specialist product advice from the product coverage teams.

Product coverage

Some banks will collectively refer to these groups as 'corporate finance'.

Product coverage groups include:

- **Mergers and acquisitions (M&A)**

  An M&A transaction is a critical moment in the life of a client. The transaction can be an acquisition, a disposal, a restructuring, an initial public offering ('IPO'), or a spin-off. These transactions carry significant risks and are critical to the development and strategic growth of the client. Therefore clients will pay large fees for high quality advice concerning valuations, financing and buy, and sell-side options.

- **Equity capital markets ('ECM') and debt capital markets ('DCM)**

  ECM and DCM (sometimes referred to as global finance or capital market origination) are the capital raising divisions working to raise capital for clients.

  A strong capital markets business requires origination strength and the ability to structure the products according to the needs of the client and the desires of the investor base. These strengths then need to be coupled with the ability to distribute the product.

Typical origination capabilities are:

- IPOs
- Follow-on issues
- Block trades and accelerated equity issues
- Equity linked issues such as convertibles
- Private placement
- Loan origination
- Syndication
- Bond issues
- Leverage finance origination

Detail around these origination capabilities are discussed in the technical linked sections of the manual.

Interactions between IBD and markets

The relationship between IBD and markets is interesting. The relationship is controlled and monitored with a 'Chinese wall'. A Chinese wall is a barrier that is created to separate parties who make investment decisions from parties that are party to material inside information that may influence these decisions. The aim of the Chinese wall is to avoid conflicts of interest.

IBD and markets represents such a conflict of interest. Suppose there is a potential transaction in the deal pipeline of an M&A team. The transaction could be a material change and improve the fortunes of a listed client. If this information was to fall into the hands of the traders, there is a risk the information would be used to take a position in the market using information that is not freely available to all. The traders would be trading on the basis of 'insider information'.

Investment banks will create a Chinese wall between IBD and markets.

The wall can take the form of:

- Physical restrictions – where investment bankers cannot get access to trading floors where the sales, trading and research teams may sit.
- Information restrictions – restrictions can be systems-driven, in terms of restriction of access to networks, servers and files.

Illustration of how the various divisions within a bank can interact on a deal:

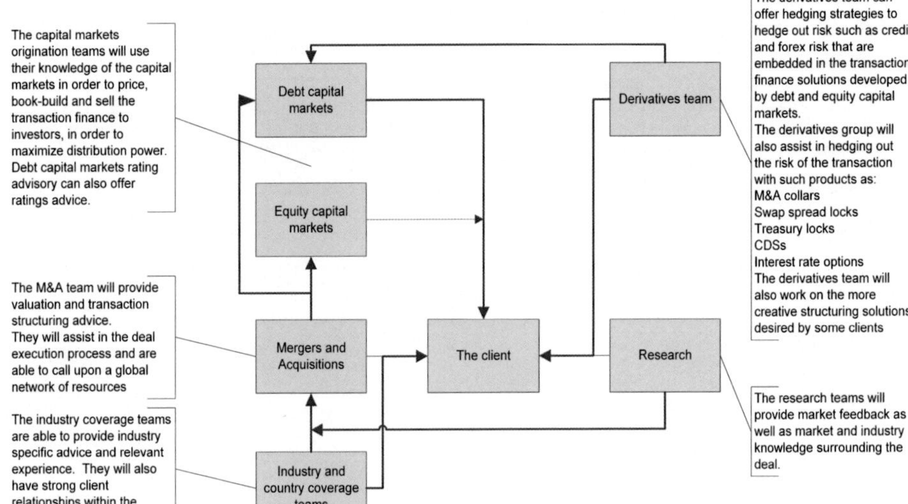

What to expect as an Analyst within a bank

Pursuing a career within a bank or any profession for that matter is an important decision – a crucial life-changing decision. It is a decision to be taken with as much information as possible to hand – high quality and relevant information should make for a better informed decision.

Banking is a tough job whether it is markets, corporate, origination, or IBD. The jobs are different, and so are the stresses, strains and rewards.

So what to expect:

- Challenging hard work
- To be stretched
- To learn, grow and develop
- To react
- A lot of jargon
- Intense competition and an ambitious working environment
- To be flexible in terms of your work, your social life and your career
- To work long hours
- Diversity in terms of your work, your clients and the people you work with/for
- To enjoy it – otherwise what is the point?
- To be rewarded for good work

And what not to expect:

- A pat on the back every time you do something well
- A stress-free existence
- A padded 'cotton ball' working environment
- An easy ride

The role of an Analyst

Most Analysts are new undergraduates coming in from some of the top universities around the globe. The hours are long and the work can initially be basic, but nonetheless crucial to the overall flow of the deal.

Key Analyst skills include:

- Extracting data from annual reports, research and other data sources
- Understanding the numbers that feed into valuations
- The ability to build and maintain financial models
- Keeping the models up-to-date
- Being a whiz on Bloomberg, FactSet and Thomson
- Keeping schedules up-to-date and booking meetings
- Generating prospectuses
- Liaising with printers
- Prepping parts of the pitch book
- Answering client phone calls
- Probably getting the lunches in for the team…

What makes a complete Analyst?

An interview with a director at a bank

Compliments for good work may seem few and far between for an Analyst. There is often a feeling of being at the bottom of a long corporate ladder and acting as a 'gopher' with a degree. However, one of the ultimate and most understated accolades an Analyst can receive from their associate is that they are deemed to be 'a good Analyst'.

What makes a 'good Analyst'?

We asked this question to a director at a large global bank:

A good Analyst has to demonstrate a wide range of qualities.

Most of these qualities are simple qualities but it's the range that poses the most challenges to these people as they come into the business. I guess if an Analyst helps me to get the job done and done well – she is a 'good Analyst'. I will then make sure we work together again and as the trust builds, so will responsibility.

From my perspective, the list of qualities or competencies of a good Analyst would certainly include (and I will take top rate intelligence and technical excellence as a given):

Attention to detail – Analysts will spend a significant amount of time putting pitch books and profiles together and running comps models. They will take responsibility for making sure that these documents are client ready, free from error and presented in line with the bank's presentation protocols.

Listen – they need to be good listeners. We know they are intelligent; otherwise they would not be here. However, a new Analyst will benefit from the knowledge of those around them as well as the client. It's an advisory role and often the best person to listen to is the client – they know the business they work in better than anyone else.

Think – we work in a tough industry, the time pressure can be immense and the hours can be long. In this environment, it's very easy for the job to become just a number crunching role. Crunching the numbers is necessary, as it then gives us the ability to think about the implications and the softer side of our work. Think – what are the implications of what I am doing? How does this fit into the deal? How do I sell the idea to the client? Don't just process your work – take time to think about it. I am the first to admit this is easier said than done at the Analyst level, when tiredness, deadlines and general workload can be serious issues. My advice is to find time to stop, push your work away, go for a walk, grab a coffee, and then come back to the desk and take a few minutes to stand back and view the bigger picture. This approach to work will also identify the majority of errors you may have made in your own work. Self-review is another key skill.

Ask questions and communicate – an Analyst needs to ask questions. They are surrounded by people who have more experience and they can learn from them. Asking questions from my perspective is reassuring; it shows thought, hopefully, and it provides comfort that they have the clarity to complete their work as efficiently as possible. It is very annoying to have an Analyst who is unclear about the task in hand and who then spends hours trying to work out what they are trying to do in isolation, when a quick question would have sorted the problem. We are all under time pressure at the best of times – a well thought-out question can ease this pressure significantly.

Judgment – this job does have a significant technical aspect to it, however it requires good judgment – it is an advisory role for the most part. For instance, a financial model provides a lot of numbers in the output, but that is not the answer.

The answer – for example the valuation, is a judgment call in terms of addressing the client's needs and the behavior of the market. A good banker will demonstrate excellent judgment throughout their career. Too often I see Analysts so set in the numbers and the detail that they cannot see the big picture. Without the bigger picture, judgment is impossible.

Desktop applications – become a whiz-kid with the firm's desktop tools. Being able to quickly navigate through Bloomberg, FactSet and Thomson as examples, is a great skill.

Hit your deadlines.

Know when to keep a low profile.

A bit of flair, humility and charm doesn't go amiss either! ”

RLM – Director Global Bank

The Analyst's technical skill set

Numbers are the cornerstone of the Analyst's technical skill set. Without an excellent command of the numbers, analysis, valuation and modeling become impossible tasks. The diagram below illustrates how the technical skills an Analyst requires interact and flow. The key point to appreciate is the skill set is based on a solid foundation of accounting and an excellent knowledge of how the numbers work.

The interaction of the IBD skill set

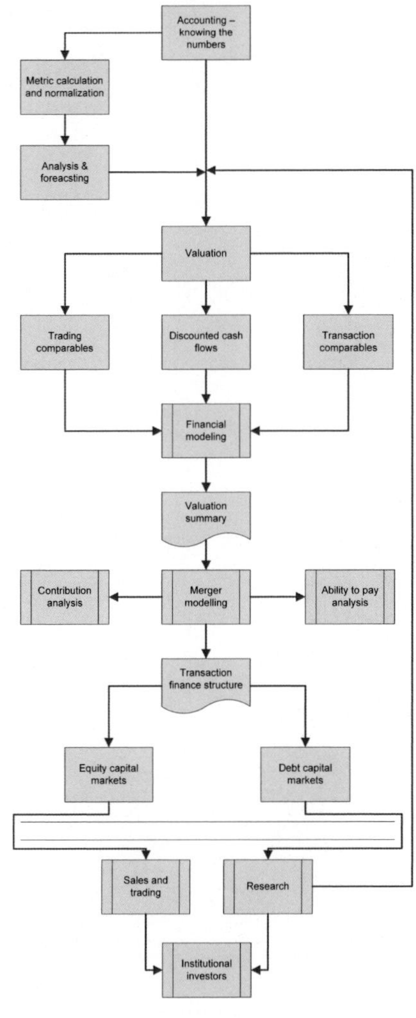

Introduction

Most investment banks will use data providers such as FactSet and Thomson Reuters to provide in-depth company and industry insight, with integrated data and investment analytics tools. These tools are designed specifically to improve the efficiency of a banker's workflow.

Bankers will use these tools to:

- Build models
- Create pitch book presentations
- Analyze markets, industries and companies
- Gain insight into the global deal market
- Identify new opportunities.

However as a banker, the main data provision services that will be used on a day-to-day basis are:

- As a cross-check against other sources of data
- As a source of research consensus estimates
- To embed Excel coding into internal models to download market information
- As a filing search
- Shareholder analysis information
- Accessing up-to-date share price data – current – 52 week highs and lows
- Company profiling information
- As a news source
- Raw financial information downloads
- Share price graph downloads
- Analyzing trading comparable information
- Analyzing precedent transactions for potential inclusion in a transactions comp valuation

This fourth edition of the *Complete Investment Banker* series has been produced in association with FactSet and Thomson Reuters. Both data providers have provided content to support this manual. Thus the technical and practical content of the manual is now better positioned to help bankers operate more effectively with their work flow.

These data providers are an invaluable resource for bankers. Time spent getting to know the product and navigating around the many menus will be time well spent.

The following CA Tips outline some of the key fundamentals required, in order to work effectively within the FactSet and Thomson Reuters environments.

Data Responsibility

Analysts and Associates will make extensive use of FactSet as a financial database. However, FactSet users must be fully aware that they are fully responsible for the integrity of the data. If errors occur in the downloading or exporting of the data into models, valuations or presentations, it is the responsibility of the preparer to spot these errors. It is no defence to state, “I got it from FactSet”.

Information from data aggregators, such as FactSet, must be cross-checked against alternative sources and sanity checked for reasonableness. If information is used in presentations, the source must be footnoted.

The following pages establish how to get started with the FactSet and Thomson Reuters applications.

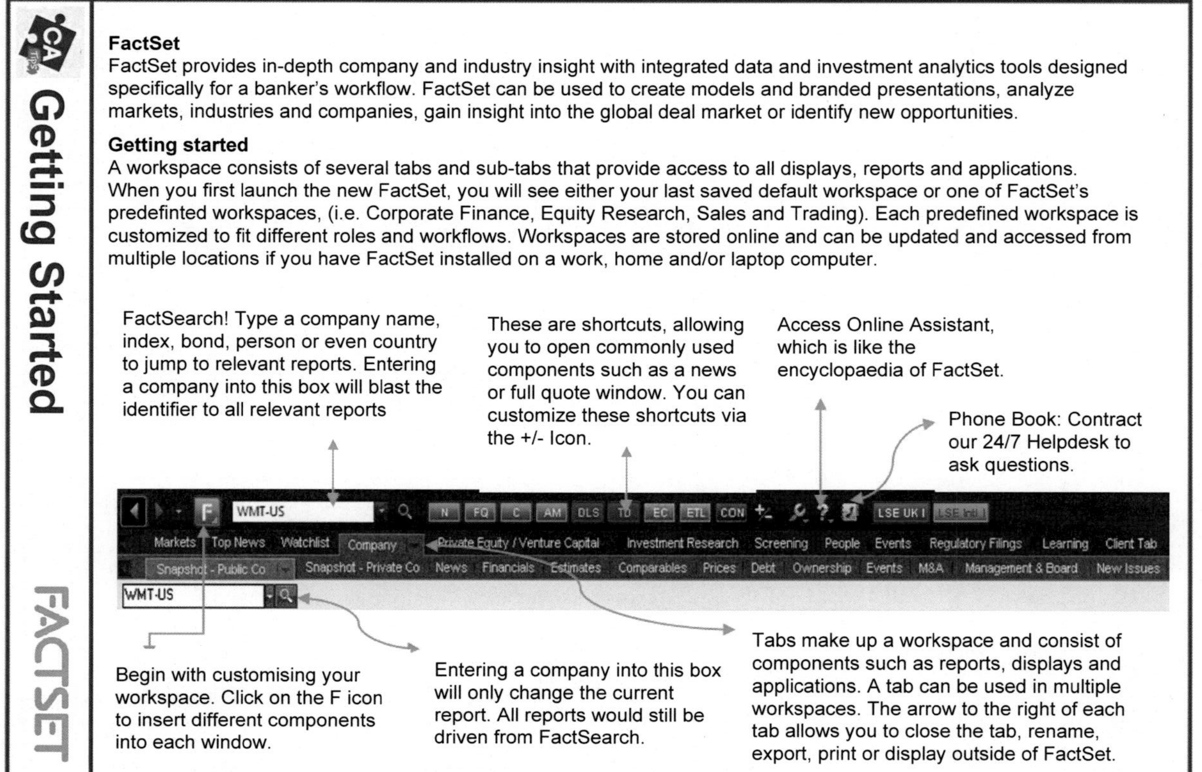

Source: FactSet

Application Shortcuts

- To hide/show the identifier toolbar, press ALT+A
- To hide/show scroll bars, press ALT+B
- To hide/show a component's title bar, press ALT+C
- To activate the FactSet Insert menu, press ALT+F
- To find text within a component, press CTRL+F
- To tile the components horizontally within a tab, press CTRL+SHIFT+ALT+H
- To tile the components vertically within a tab, press CTRL+SHIFT+ALT+V
- To activate channel audit, press ALT+I
- To add a new tab/sub-tab, press CTRL+N
- To open a tab, press CTRL+O
- To revert back to the last saved version of a tab, press CTRL+R or the ~ key

- To save a workspace and document (i.e. settings) press CTRL+S
- To activate Fact Search or the Master Identifier box, press CTRL+T
- To select the next component in a tab, press CTRL+TAB
- To select the previous component in a tab, press CTRL+ SHIFT+ TAB
- To navigate to the lowest tab layer, press ALT+[1-9]
- To toggle up/down through the tab layers, press CTRL+Up Arrow or Down Arrow
- To move the cursor left in a tab layer press CTRL+ Left Arrow or Page Up
- To move the cursor right in a tab layer press CTRL+ Right Arrow or Page Down
- To close the active component, press CTRL+F4

Source: FactSet

Company Identifiers FACTSET

Most of the data on FactSet is driven by company identifiers. Throughout the FactSet platform, two main identifier lookups are available to find and enter company identifiers.

To launch these identifier lookups, click the **Lookup** button.

As an alternative to using the Identifier Lookup utility, you can use 'FactSearch' searching to find identifiers on FactSet.

FactSearch (To the right of the F menu)

Additional features:

- FactSearch allows you to quickly search for and navigate to securities, reports and components within FactSet
- Select the 'Broadcast ID' option which allows you to send the security selected in Fact Search to multiple components, throughout the tabs in your workspace
- Hover over an equity or people security type to see an info box with a brief company description or bio
- You can quickly 'jump' to a component or filing by using shortcuts in FactSearch

Source: FactSet

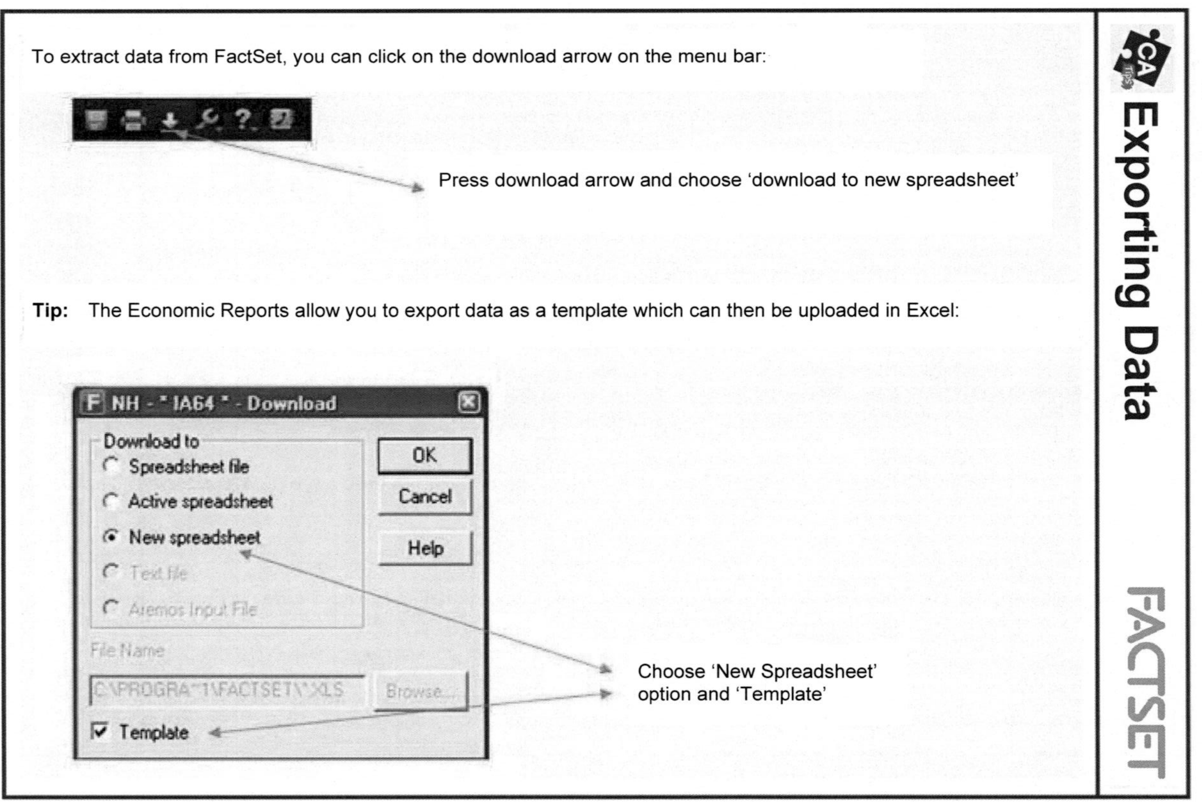

Source: FactSet

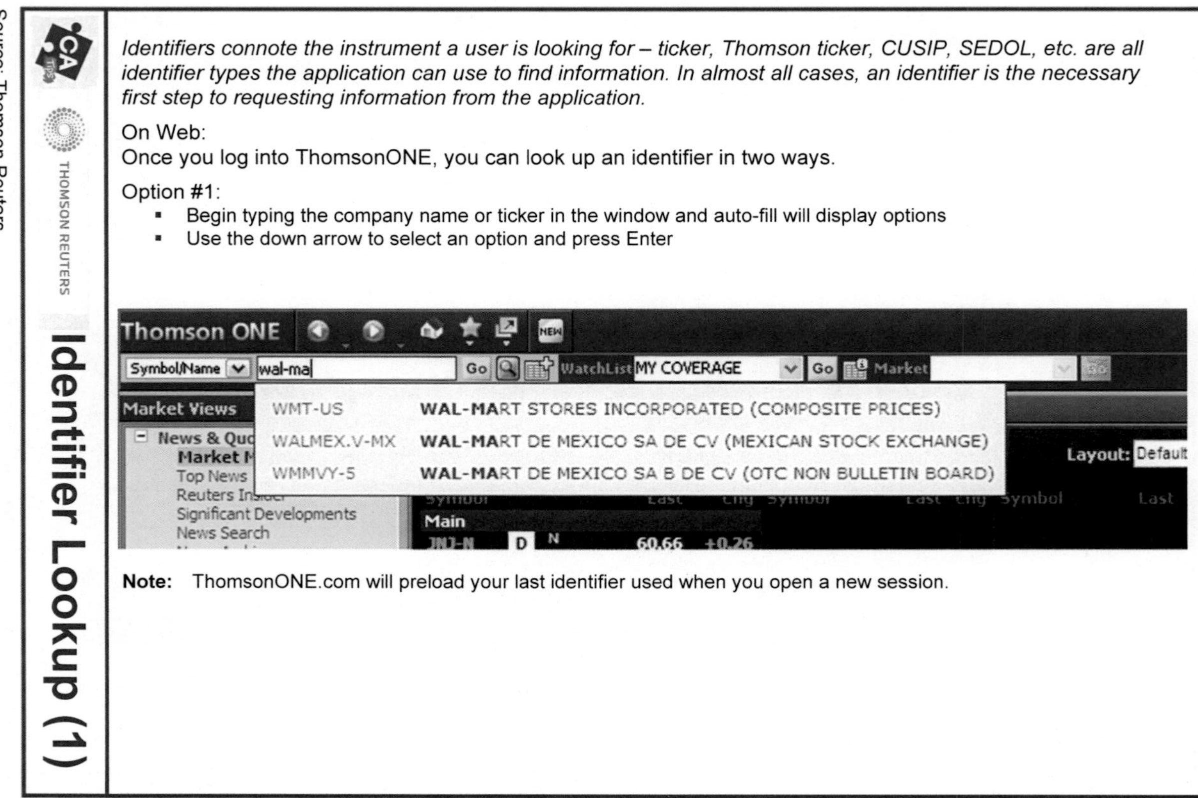

Source: Thomson Reuters

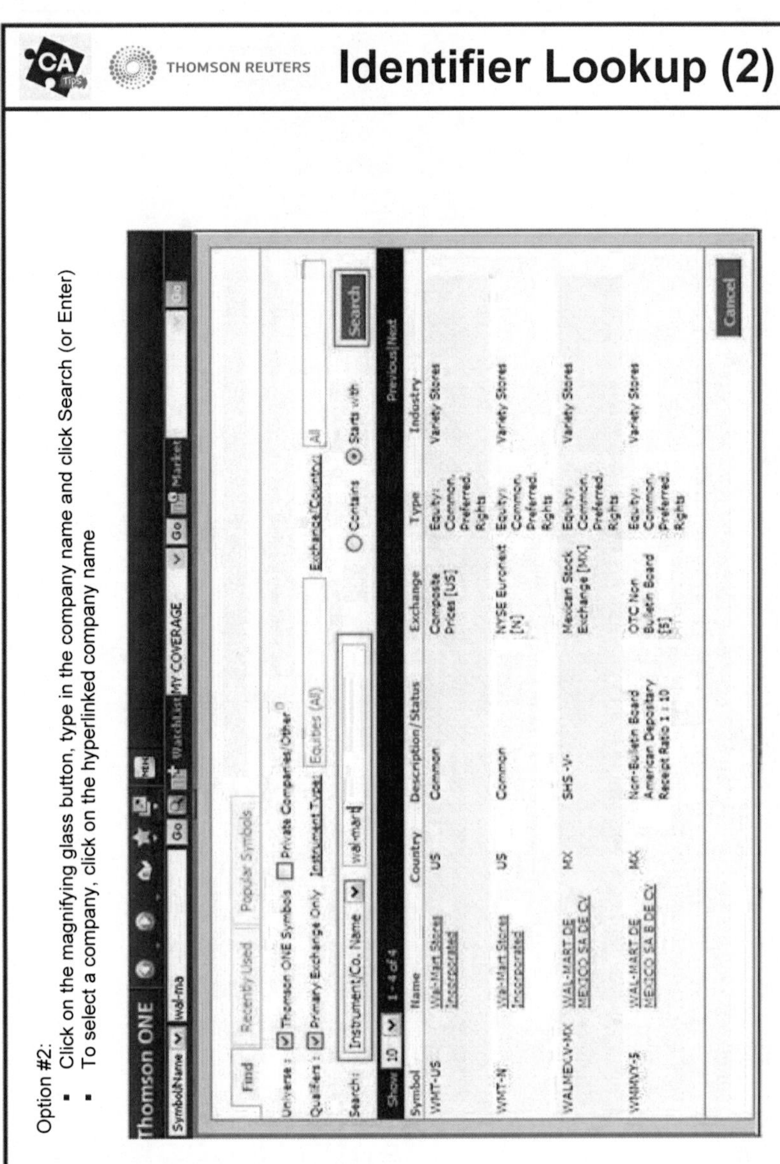

Source: Thomson Reuters

Identifier Lookup in Excel

THOMSON REUTERS

- Click on the Thomson Reuters tab → Identifiers (ALT + S + I)
- Select the Entity Type (Public or Private Company, Equity Index, FX Rate or IBES Global Aggregate)
- Keyword: Search by Company Name or identifier type (like ticker, etc.)
- Input your search information and click on Show Results (or press Enter)

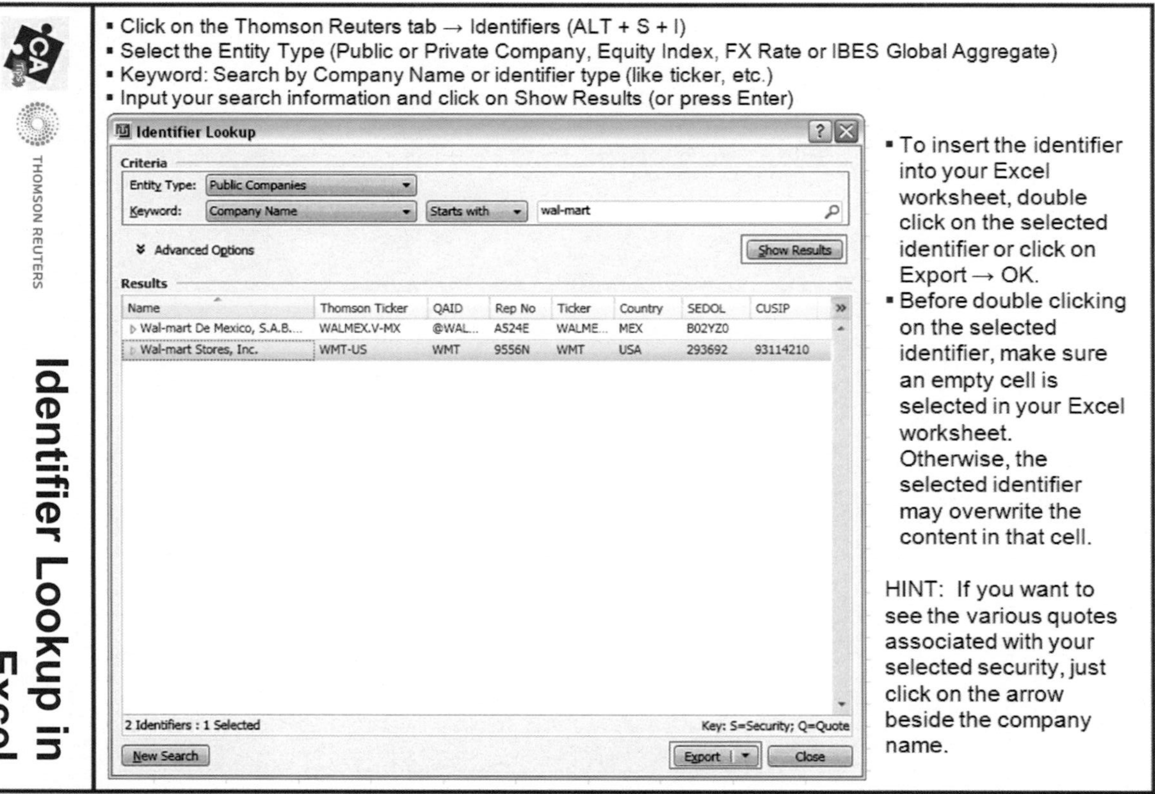

- To insert the identifier into your Excel worksheet, double click on the selected identifier or click on Export → OK.
- Before double clicking on the selected identifier, make sure an empty cell is selected in your Excel worksheet. Otherwise, the selected identifier may overwrite the content in that cell.

HINT: If you want to see the various quotes associated with your selected security, just click on the arrow beside the company name.

Source: Thomson Reuters

Introduction

Analysts do not need to be accountants – however they must have an excellent command of the numbers that are reported in a set of financial statements, as well as those that are analyzed by research brokers.

The numbers will be used to:

- Extract and normalize financials for analysis
- Analyze performance, leverage, liquidity and efficiency
- Forecast the financials, often under different scenarios, going forward
- Assess the financial impacts of a proposed investment, acquisition, disposal, divestment, refinancing, etc.
- Build consistent multiples for comps purposes
- Derive forecast cash flows for DCF valuation purposes
- Combine bidder and target entities in order to assess the EPS, return on investment and credit rating impacts of an acquisition
- Assess risk and price that risk into the financial products offered on behalf of clients

We will examine the DNA of a set of financials, building the ideas from the 'bottom up'.

Financial statement DNA

A set of financial statements will include the three key financial statements:

- Balance sheet
- Income statement
- Cash flow statement

Before any of these statements can be examined in detail, the DNA of the financial statements must be picked apart. A set of financials is derived from five key fragments, which, when sequenced together, produce the financial statements.

The five financial statement DNA fragments are:

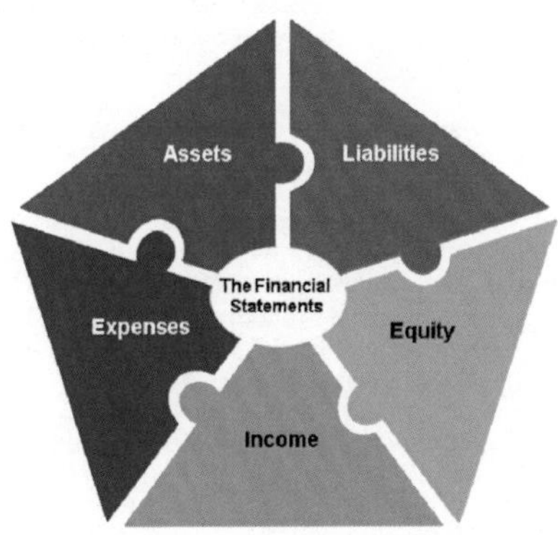

The DNA fragments interact with each other to produce a full set of financials. However, before any interaction can be analyzed, the fragments must be examined.

Assets

An asset is a store of future benefit that is controlled by an entity.

Assets can be tangible; they have a physical substance. Or they can be intangible; they lack physical substance.

Examples of tangible and intangible assets could be:

Tangible assets	Intangible assets
Property, plant and equipment (PPE)	Goodwill
Investments in joint ventures	Brands
Investment in associates	Licenses
Inventories	Research and development
Receivables	Software
Investments	
Cash	

It is worth noting that not all the assets of an entity will be recognized in the financial statements. The term 'recognized' is accounting terminology meaning 'to place an item onto the financial statements'.

The key considerations when attempting to determine recognition will be:

- Assessing whether the control of the asset does actually rest with the entity
- Whether the benefits of the asset can be reliably measured

Recognition issues are often clear-cut. For example, when an entity makes some sales on credit to a customer, the customer owes the entity money. Normally, this is treated as an asset as the entity has the future benefit that the cash will flow into the business when the customer settles the outstanding account. The future cash flow receipt is relatively easy to measure – it is the outstanding amount owed. The outstanding amount is the asset.

Issues will arise when the assessment of whether there is control of the asset becomes blurred or the measurement of the benefits becomes too subjective.

Extending the above example, the entity making the credit sales then decides to sell the amount it is owed to a third party agency – the third party takes on the collection of the outstanding amount. Depending on the terms of the agreement, the entity may continue to recognize the asset on its financial statements or it may be forced to remove or de-recognize the asset. The decision will take into account issues such as which party is exposed to the risks and rewards of the asset. The decision can become difficult very quickly as the issues get blurred.

Analysts should have an awareness of these issues, but ultimately when the lines are blurred, the bank will seek professional advice.

Assets are also classified according to the purpose for which they are held:

- Non-current assets (also known as long-lived or fixed assets)
- Current assets

Current assets are assets that the entity will be seeking to realize into cash within the next year or within the entity's operating cycle. Non-current assets are those assets where the entity's intention is to hold them for the longer-term. They are typically those assets with which the entity runs the operations and which generate cash flows.

Using the previous asset examples and now reallocating them according to whether they are current or non-current assets, we get quite a different allocation of assets:

Current assets	Non-current assets
Inventories	Property, plant and equipment (PPE)
Receivables	Investments in joint ventures
Short-term investments	Investment in associates
Cash	Goodwill
	Brands
	Licenses
	Research and development
	Software
	Long term investments

The classification of an asset can have a significant impact on how that asset is accounted for. In the illustration above, depending on the entity's intention with their investments, some will be treated as long-term whilst others are short-term. The accounting treatment will then vary accordingly.

Liabilities

Liabilities are amounts owed to third parties as a result of a past event.

Typical examples are:

- Accounts payable
- Taxes payable
- Pension deficits
- Provisions
- Amounts owed to banks (loans)
- Amounts owed to debt investors (debt)

Liabilities are classified between amounts that fall due within one year and amounts falling due after more than one year.

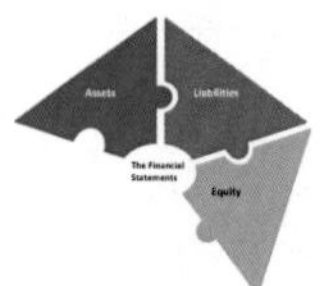

Equity

Equity can be thought of as amounts that are owned by the shareholders of the business. Equity is not a liability as the amounts are not obligations; rather they are the residual interest in the business.

The balance sheet

The balance sheet is a financial statement that discloses information about an entity's financial position. It is a 'snapshot' of the assets, liabilities and equity. All balance sheets must balance – that's a given. The reason they balance is due to the nature of how accountants record an entity's transactions. The joys of double-entry bookkeeping will be visited later.

Irrespective of the entity's country of incorporation, all balance sheets adhere to the same basic equation – the accounting equation:

Assets - Liabilities = Equity

Again this is a product of double-entry bookkeeping. As with any equation, the elements of the equation can be rearranged:

Assets = Liabilities + Equity

Both equations are perfectly acceptable ways to present a balance sheet, the latter form being the most prevalent in Europe and the US.

The income statement

The numbers on the balance sheet will change from one period to the next. The majority of this movement is driven by the financial performance of the entity. Financial performance is captured in the income statement. It is the income statement that presents an entity's ability to generate income and incur expenses. The net result of income less expenses is profit or earnings. The type of profit (earnings) is dependent on the nature of the expenses deducted against income and is presented at a number of different levels:

- Gross profit
- Operating profit
- EBIT (earnings before interest and tax)
- EBITDA (earnings before interest, tax, depreciation and amortization)
- EBITDAR (earnings before interest, tax, depreciation, amortization and rent)
- PBT or EBT (profit, or earnings, before tax)
- PAT or EAT (profit, or earnings, after tax)
- Net income (earnings)

These various profit metrics will be discussed as we examine the income statement in more detail. However to understand the income statement, we must understand the components – the last two fragments of financial statement DNA – income and expenses.

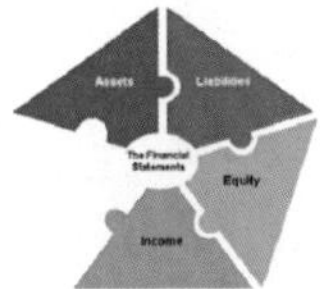

Income

Income is the measure of the increase in an entity's economic benefit over a period. This definition does not normally mean much to the non-accountant. Most Analysts will simply view income as the revenue or sales generated by an entity's operations (net of any sales taxes). This income can be described as trading income.

An entity can also have non-trading income:

- Income from investments
- Interest income
- Income from non-core operations

Income may not be directly correlated with cash generation. Income is generally recognized in a set of financials in the period that the transaction generating the income takes place, not on the basis of when the physical cash is received. Therefore entities can be income rich, but cash poor.

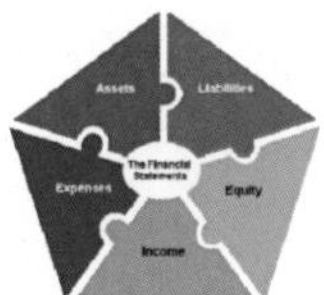

Expenses

Expenses are the costs of using up benefits during a period. Like income, the expense incurred may not be recognized at the same time as the cash is paid out. Expenses are recognized in a set of financials on the basis of when the expense was incurred or the asset was used up, rather than when the cash cost was made.

Examples of expenses are:

- Costs of sales
- Selling, general and administration costs
- Depreciation
- Amortization

The above expenses would be classed as operating expense.

Non-operating expenses would be:

- Interest and other financial expenses
- Tax

The cash flow statement

The cash flow statement is a refreshing change for non-accountants. It is a clear statement of what cash the entity generated from operations, how that cash was allocated to investing activities and what cash financing demands resulted. It is a clean statement, almost free from the distortions of accounting policies. It is important that the cash flow statement is understood by the investment banker as it is the basis for discounted cash flow valuations and is a cornerstone for analysis.
It will be examined in detail later.

Accounting frameworks

Accountants are governed by sets of rules that detail how the numbers should be presented in the financial statements. These rules historically have varied between countries reflecting each country's unique legal and regulatory framework evolution.

Generally accepted accounting principles (GAAP) refers to the standard set of rules and guidelines used within a particular country. Over the years, the term has become Americanized in the sense that 'GAAP' is often synonymous with US GAAP to US bankers.

It was not too long ago that bankers would have to deal with UK GAAP, German GAAP or French GAAP to mention just a few examples. One country's rules could be quite different to another's due to economic and political forces. Many European GAAPs were heavily influenced by the development of their country's commercial and tax codes, as well as historical legacy.

This made the life of an investment banker rather difficult. Comparability was difficult to achieve when analyzing results across different geographies as these would have arisen from different rules and guidelines. However, it could be described as being a little easier now.

There are now two dominant sets of rules that govern the accounting world:

- International Financial Reporting Standards (IFRS)
- US GAAP

IFRS

International standards have been around since the 1970s, however the adoption of these international rules was limited. The turning point was 2005.
In 2005, the European Commission required that all European Union (EU) companies listed with the European Economic Area (EEA) on a regulated stock exchange had to adopt IFRS. This captured around 8,000 companies in total.

In December 2008, for non-EU companies listed on an EU stock exchange, the EU designated the GAAPs of the following countries to be IFRS equivalent, for the purpose of filing of accounts:

- US
- Canada
- Japan
- India
- South Korea

Companies from any other country listed on the EU stock exchange from 2009 must either use IFRS as adopted by the EU or IFRS as adopted by the International Accounting Standards Board (IASB). These requirements apply to listed companies.

EU states at their own discretion can extend the IFRS requirements to unlisted companies if they wish. The vast majority of EU member states permit the use of IFRS.

IFRS are often referred to as principle-based standards. This is because they:

- Are based on core principles
- Are linked to a conceptual framework
- Require judgment in their application
- Provide a minimum guidance, relying on judgment to provide adaptability in their application

Around the world with IFRS

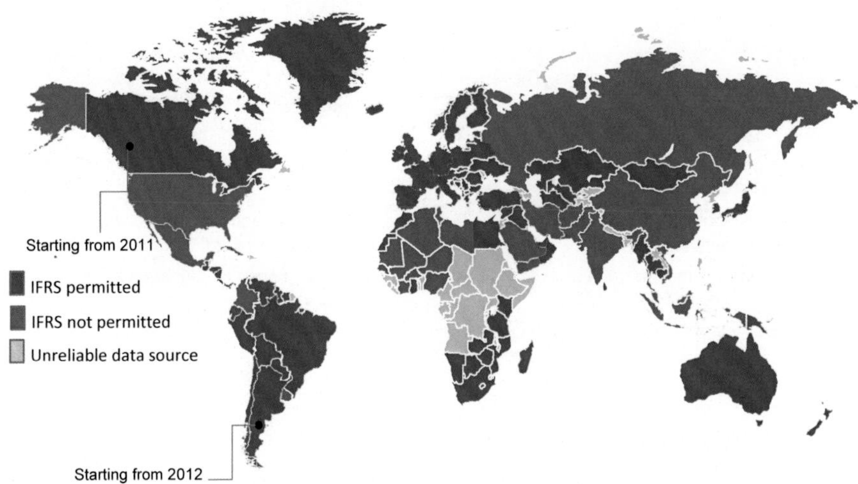

US GAAP

There are over 13,000 companies registered with the US Securities and Exchanges Commission (SEC). Domestic US companies produce their accounts in accordance with US GAAP –which is a rule-based framework built on a legal foundation. That is:

- There are many, many rules
- The rules are prescriptive and legalistic
- The rules do not rely on judgment
- There is an emphasis on enforcing consistency

US GAAP conversion

Of the 13,000 companies registered with the SEC, some 1,500 of these are non-US issuers. Prior to November 2007, these companies were required to submit a US GAAP reconciliation of net income and net assets if their financials were submitted using non-US GAAP standards.

Since November 2007, the SEC has allowed non-US issuers to submit IFRS prepared financial statements without having to reconcile the numbers to US GAAP.

The SEC has set out a roadmap for adopting IFRS by 2014. However, there are a number of potential adoption issues such as:

- The two frameworks are starting from very different places
- There are significant differences in the regulatory, business, cultural and institutional environments
- Political resistance
- US GAAP users are accustomed to detailed guidance

However, given the signals by the SEC, conversion from US GAAP to IFRS has certain inevitability. Analysts used to predominantly dealing with US GAAP financial statements must gain fluency in the IFRS rules.

Strong evidence of the convergence has been seen with the issuing of new standards addressing business combinations and pensions. These new rules under IFRS and US GAAP, whilst not identical, are closely aligned. The accounting bodies are getting closer to issuing truly global standards.

Even if the conversion was not inevitable, US Analysts must still have working fluency in IFRS for a number of significant reasons:

- US entities acquire and dispose of entities that use IFRS. Analysis and interpretation of the valuations using IFRS numbers will be essential in order to negotiate the deal
- US entities may look to raise finance in foreign capital markets. These capital markets may require the use of IFRS numbers
- When compiling comparables databases, a significant number of the companies and transactions will be from non-US GAAP jurisdictions

Accounting principles

A set of financials are prepared using a number of core accounting principles. Analysts should be aware of these principles when analyzing the numbers:

Going concern

This is an assumption that the entity has the ability to continue functioning operationally for the foreseeable future. This assumption will impact how assets and liabilities are valued in the financials. For instance, an entity where there are concerns about its ability to continue as a going concern may see its assets valued on a break-up basis i.e. the assets would be valued at their realizable value.

Accruals

Under this basis, revenues and costs are recognized as they are earned or incurred rather than when the cash is received or paid. The accruals basis is used to prepare income statements and balance sheet information.

Consistency

The financials should be prepared on the same basis from one period to another, unless there has been a change in the accounting rules or a significant change in the nature of the entity's operations such that a change in the application of the rules would provide a more appropriate result.

Offsetting

Offsetting is the action of netting off an asset against a liability or an income against an expense and thus just disclosing the net number. Offsetting is deemed acceptable only if required or permitted by an accounting rule.

Financial Statement DNA Tick Sheet

How does a good understanding of the numbers help a banker?

It enables the banker to:

- Extract and normalize
- Analyze the performance, leverage, liquidity and efficiency
- Forecase the financials, often under different scenarios, going forward
- Assess the fianancial impacts of a proposed investment, acquisition, disposal, divestment, refinancing etc.
- Build consistent multiples for comp purposes
- Derive forecast cash flows for DCF valuation purposes
- Combine bidder and target entities in order to assess the EPS, return on investment and credit rating impacts of an acquisition
- Assess risk – and then price that risk into the financial products offered on behalf of clients

Financial statements DNA – the DNA fragments:

- Assets – benefits
- Liabilities – obligations
- Equity – ownership
- Income – earned
- Expense – incurred

The primary statements are:

- Balance sheet
- Income statement
- Cash flow statement

The two main accounting frameworks are:

- IFRS
- US GAAP

IFRS must be used by EEA listed companies.

IFRS can be used in over 100 countries.

US GAAP aims for transition to IFRS by 2014.

Introduction

The balance sheet is a snapshot of an entity's assets, liabilities and equity at a particular moment in time. The majority of the movement in the balance sheet numbers from one period to another is driven by the entity's trading operations as captured in the income statement.

Financial statement integration

The balance sheet is a snapshot of an entity's financial position (its assets and liabilities.) The entity's financial performance as disclosed in the income statement will drive the movement in the balance sheet from one period to another.

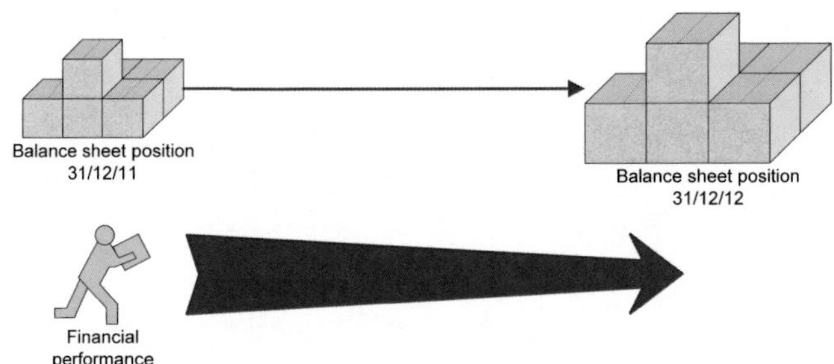

Many of the numbers included in the balance sheet can be misleading and it is important to have a good grasp of what the numbers in the balance sheet mean. There can be certain numbers that are under or over-stated. There are even assets an entity may have that are not even included on the balance sheet. The Analyst must be fully aware of the weaknesses inherent in the balance sheet and be able to adjust for them.

The balance sheet does have its plus points. It is a useful starting point for:

- Debt numbers
- Net debt calculations
- Working capital numbers

But the caveat must be added – faithful reliance on a balance sheet is dangerous.
This section of the manual will examine the key balance sheet line items in more detail.

Balance sheet formats

A set of financial statements will include the three key financial statements:

- A balance sheet
- An income statement
- A cash flow statement

The Balance Sheet Assets

Balance sheet formats vary across the globe, although they are essentially disclosing the same line items. The main differences in the formats are centered on rearranging the accounting equation.

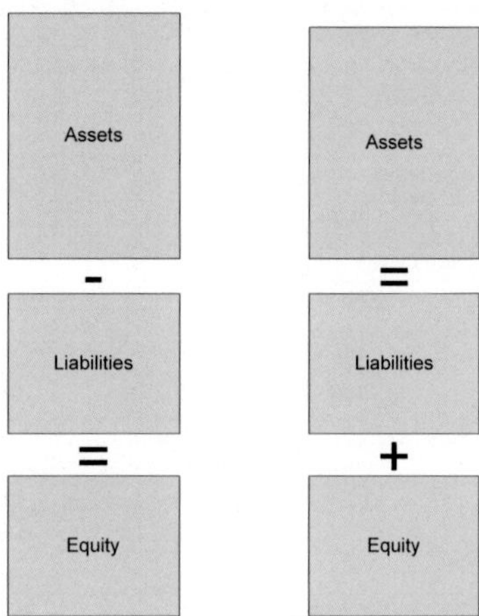

The balance sheet format of choice tends to be Assets = Liabilities + Equity. This format is used on both sides of the Atlantic. The terminology and order of disclosure of the individual line items does vary between countries.

Entities using US GAAP disclose the balance sheet assets in descending order of liquidity. The Wal-Mart balance sheet extract is a typical example of the US asset disclosure. Cash and cash equivalents are the most common liquid balance sheet asset. In the US, these assets appear first on the balance sheet. As the user wanders down the list of assets on the Wal-Mart Inc balance sheet, the asset liquidity falls.

(Amounts in millions except per share data)	January 31,	
Assets		
Current assets:		
Cash and cash equivalents	$ 7,275	$ 5,492
Receivables	3,905	3,642
Inventories	34,511	35,159
Prepaid expenses and other	3,063	2,760
Current assets of discontinued operations	195	967
Total current assets	48,949	48,020
Property and equipment, at cost:		
Land	19,852	19,879
Buildings and improvements	73,810	72,141
Fixtures and equipment	29,851	28,026
Transportation equipment	2,307	2,210
Property and equipment, at cost	125,820	122,256
Less accumulated depreciation	(32,964)	(28,531)
Property and equipment, net	92,856	93,725
Property under capital lease:		
Property under capital lease	5,341	5,736
Less accumulated amortization	(2,544)	(2,594)
Property under capital lease, net	2,797	3,142
Goodwill	15,260	15,879
Other assets and deferred charges	3,567	2,748
Total assets	$163,429	$163,514

Source: Wal-Mart Inc 10K

The Cadbury plc extract below is a typical European balance sheet and as you can see, the asset order is the reverse of the US disclosures. Non-current assets appear first, followed by the current assets. The current assets are disclosed in ascending order of liquidity. A very liquid asset, cash and cash equivalents is disclosed quite far down in the asset list.

		Group	
Notes		£m	£m
	Assets		
	Non-current assets		
14	Goodwill	2,288	2,805
15	Acquisition intangibles	1,598	3,378
15	Software intangibles	87	149
16	Property, plant and equipment	1,761	1,904
17	Investment in associates	28	32
17	Investment in subsidiaries	–	–
24	Deferred tax assets	181	124
25	Retirement benefit assets	17	223
20	Trade and other receivables	28	50
18	Other investments	2	2
		5,990	8,667
	Current assets		
19	Inventories	767	821
	Short-term investments	247	2
20	Trade and other receivables	1,067	1,197
	Tax recoverable	35	41
	Cash and cash equivalents	251	493
27	Derivative financial instruments	268	46
		2,635	2,600
21	Assets held for sale	270	71
	Total assets	8,895	11,338

Source: Cadbury annual report

Finding Financial Information – Filings and Annual Reports

Investment bankers need to have a full and thorough understanding of the numbers reported by corporates and financial institutions for analysis, valuation and financial modeling purposes. These reported numbers will be used to formulate expectations of the future performance of the businesses under examination.

Common locations to find these filings are:

- Internal library service (within the investment bank)
- A standard Google search
- Company websites – usually as part of the investor relations section of the corporate web or group websites
- FactSet company filings (see CA Tip below)
- FactSet Global filings (see CA Tip below)
- The Financial Times annual shares services
- EDGAR online
- Annual reports – www.annualreports.com
- www.orderannualreports.com

When using the company filing services, make sure you use financial information from the source document. Do not rely on reproduced information and assume that it has been correctly extracted from the reported numbers.

The FactSet company filings tool (see CA Tip following) allows the user to click through to the source filing document directly from the FactSet screen.

FACTSET Company Identifiers

Most of the data on FactSet is driven by company identifiers. Throughout the FactSet platform, two main identifier lookups are available to find and enter company identifiers.

To launch these identifier lookups, click the **Lookup** button. 

As an alternative to using the Identifier Lookup utility, you can use 'FactSearch' searching to find identifiers on FactSet.

FactSearch (To the right of the F menu)

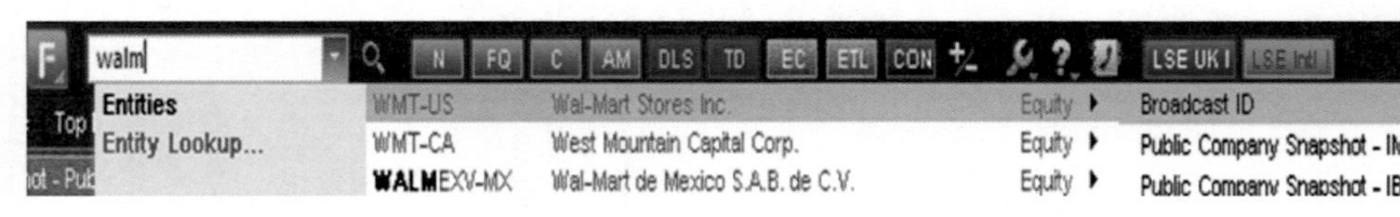

Additional features:

- FactSearch allows you to quickly search for and navigate to securities, reports and components within FactSet
- Select the 'Broadcast ID' option which allows you to send the security selected in Fact Search to multiple components, throughout the tabs in your workspace
- Hover over an equity or people security type to see an info box with a brief company description or bio
- You can quickly 'jump' to a component or filing by using shortcuts in FactSearch

Source: FactSet

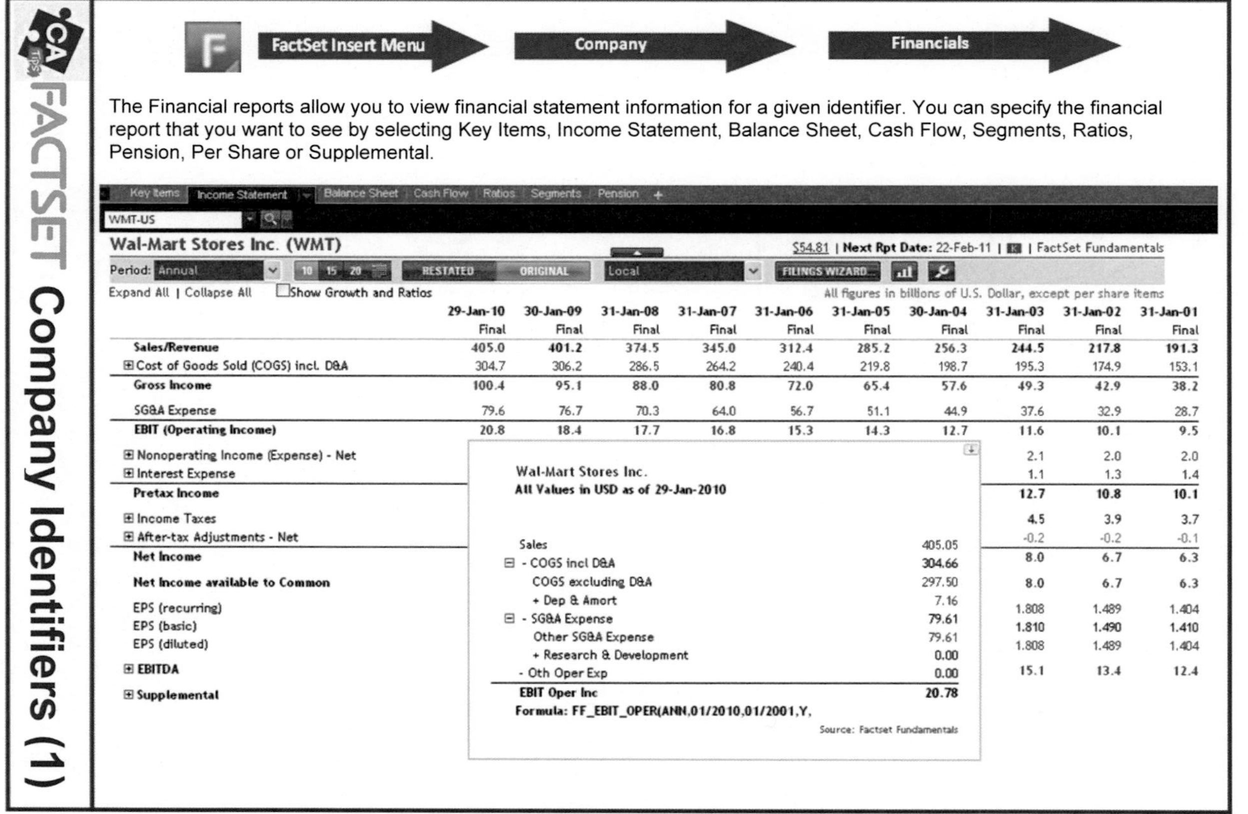

	29-Jan-10	30-Jan-09	31-Jan-08	31-Jan-07	31-Jan-06	31-Jan-05	30-Jan-04	31-Jan-03	31-Jan-02	31-Jan-01
	Final	Final	Final	Final	Final	Final	Final	Final	Final	Final
Sales/Revenue	405.0	401.2	374.5	345.0	312.4	285.2	256.3	244.5	217.8	191.3
Cost of Goods Sold (COGS) incl. D&A	304.7	306.2	286.5	264.2	240.4	219.8	198.7	195.3	174.9	153.1
Gross Income	100.4	95.1	88.0	80.8	72.0	65.4	57.6	49.3	42.9	38.2
SG&A Expense	79.6	76.7	70.3	64.0	56.7	51.1	44.9	37.6	32.9	28.7
EBIT (Operating Income)	20.8	18.4	17.7	16.8	15.3	14.3	12.7	11.6	10.1	9.5
Nonoperating Income (Expense) - Net								2.1	2.0	2.0
Interest Expense								1.1	1.3	1.4
Pretax Income								12.7	10.8	10.1
Income Taxes								4.5	3.9	3.7
After-tax Adjustments - Net								-0.2	-0.2	-0.1
Net Income								8.0	6.7	6.3
Net Income available to Common								8.0	6.7	6.3
EPS (recurring)								1.808	1.489	1.404
EPS (basic)								1.810	1.490	1.410
EPS (diluted)								1.808	1.489	1.404
EBITDA								15.1	13.4	12.4
Supplemental										

Wal-Mart Stores Inc.
All Values in USD as of 29-Jan-2010

Sales	405.05
- COGS incl D&A	304.66
COGS excluding D&A	297.50
+ Dep & Amort	7.16
- SG&A Expense	79.61
Other SG&A Expense	79.61
+ Research & Development	0.00
- Oth Oper Exp	0.00
EBIT Oper Inc	**20.78**

Formula: FF_EBIT_OPER(ANN,01/2010,01/2001,Y,

Source: Factset Fundamentals

Source: FactSet

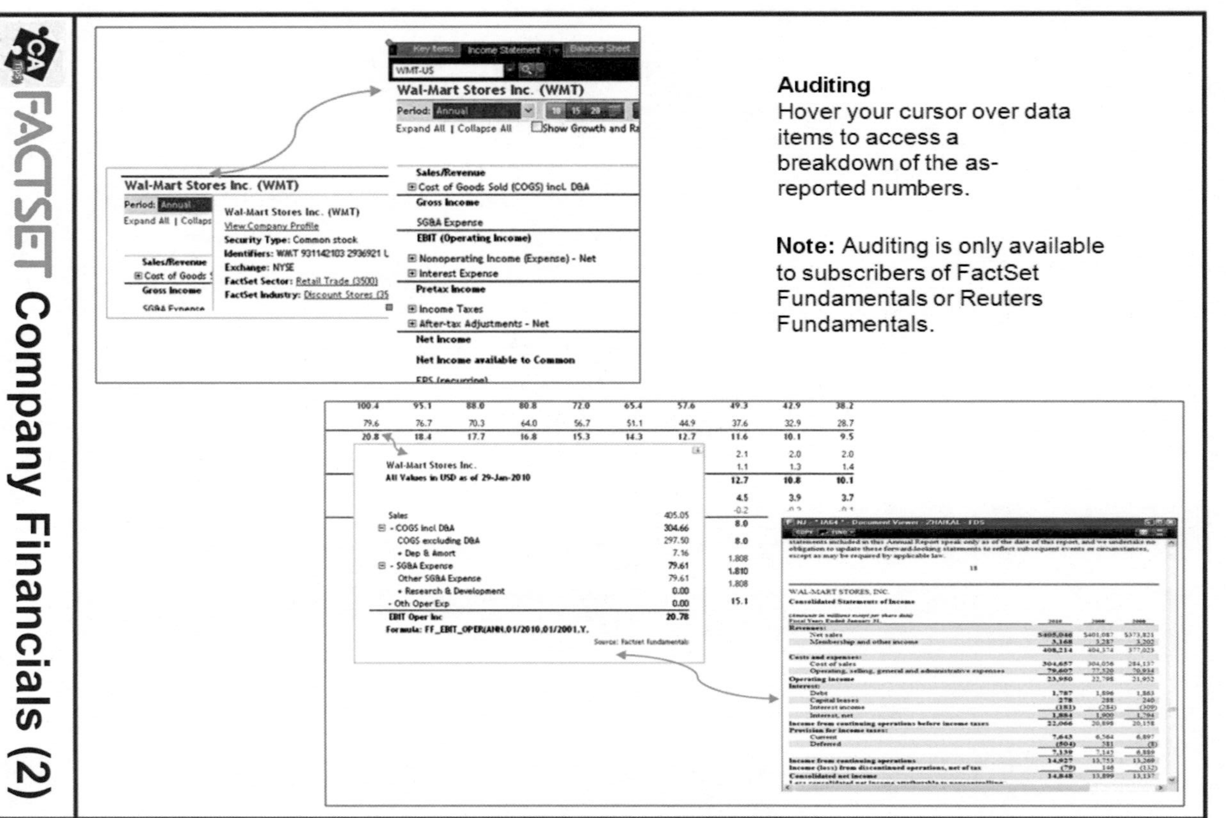

Source: FactSet

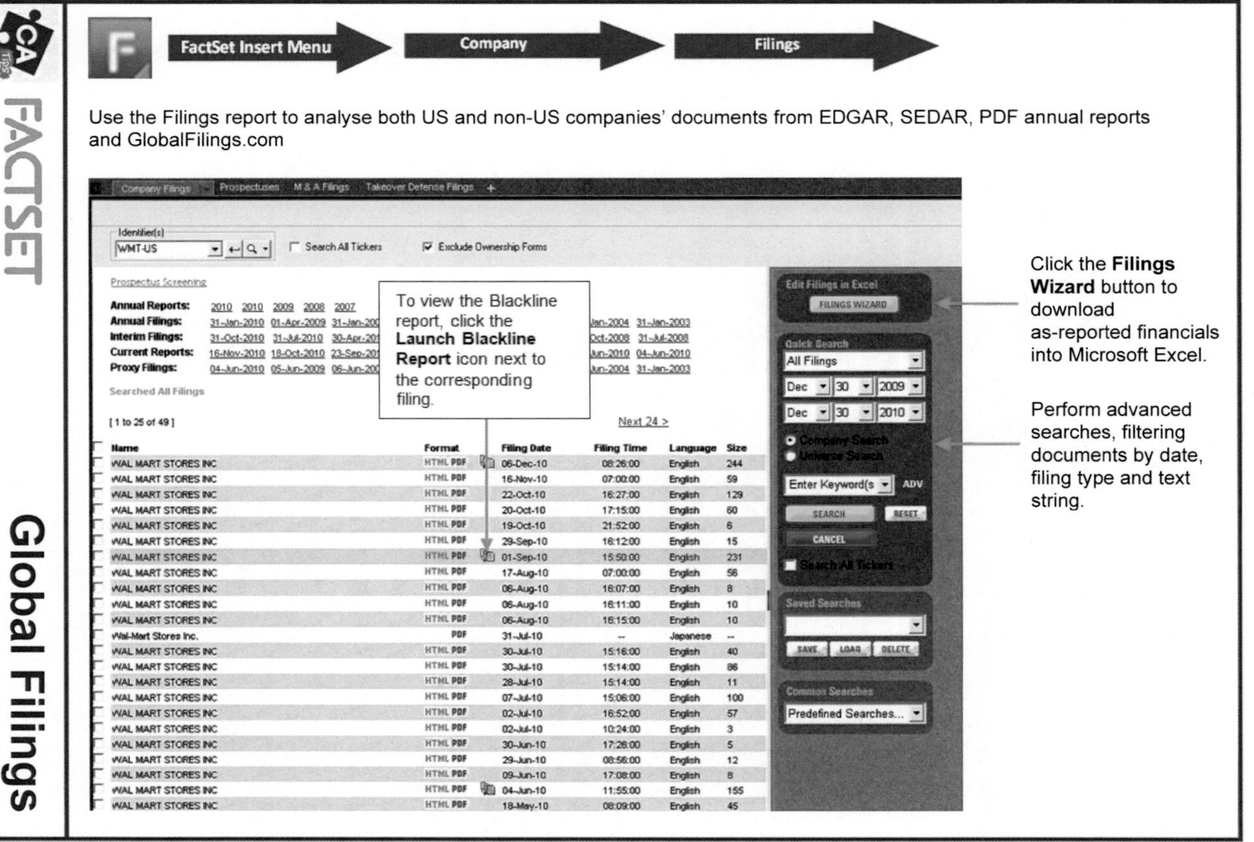

Source: FactSet

Non-current assets vs. current assets

The distinction between current and non-current assets is a useful distinction as it allows the Analyst to determine which assets are used as part of the long-term operations and those which are circulating as part of the working capital of the entity.

The split between current and non-current assets is industry specific and can be a matter of judgment.

Entities make the distinction between current and non-current on the basis of either:

- **A fixed length of time**
  In many industries, a one year time period is used as a cut-off point between assets being classified as current, or non-current. However, this simply does not work well for certain industries, such as property development and construction. These industries have assets held for re-sale that have long gestation periods between asset acquisition and the final realization into cash. A one year arbitrary cut-off point would potentially result in assets that are really working capital and therefore by nature, current assets being classified as non-current.

- **The length of the operating cycle**
  A more flexible alternative is to classify the assets on the basis of the length of the operating cycle, being the period from acquiring an asset to realizing it as cash. Assets consumed by the entity within one operating cycle would be classified as current assets, whereas assets held for more than one operating cycle would be classified as non-current assets.

  The distinction in practical terms requires judgment and will be industry specific.

Some general concepts

As with any basic concepts, there will be exceptions. The intention here is to outline some general concepts that apply to most (but not all) non-current assets[1]:

- Non-current assets are recognized initially on the balance sheet at cost
- Non-current assets can be impaired, that is their values can be reduced on the balance sheet
- The cost of the non-current asset is normally spread into the income statement over the life of the asset in the form of depreciation or amortization

Depreciation and amortization

Depreciation and amortization (D&A) are almost synonymous concepts. Both are accounting mechanisms used to spread the cost of tangible and intangible assets through the income statement over the asset's useful life.

Depreciation relates to the spreading of a tangible asset cost.

Amortization relates to the spreading of an intangible asset cost.

The purpose of D&A is two-fold:

- It represents the consumption of an asset's benefits over its useful life
- It matches the cost of the asset to the benefits generated by the asset

[1] The most notable exceptions would be non-current asset investments (financial assets, property, joint ventures and associates) and goodwill

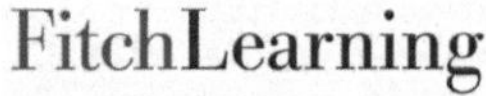

If the whole cost of the asset was to immediately hit the income statement, it would be hit with a significant expense each time an entity bought a new asset. In subsequent periods, the asset would be realizing benefits without an associated cost being matched to it. This would result in a profit profile that would be erratic and uncorrelated to the entity's underlying trading performance. D&A therefore matches the benefit and cost of tangible and intangible assets together in the same reporting period.

D&A are non-cash expenses and are charged in arriving at earnings before interest and tax (EBIT).

D&A methods

There are a variety of acceptable D&A methods. The preparers of financials should choose a method that best reflects the asset's consumption over time. For instance, cars tend to lose much of their value in the early years of their life. Therefore, the chosen depreciation method should load the depreciation expense in the earlier years of the asset's life.

The two most common depreciation methods are:

- Straight line
- Reducing balance

The extract below is a typical example of the depreciation policy an entity might adopt:

Depreciation
Land is not depreciated. Depreciation on other assets is calculated using the straight-line method to allocate their cost or revalued amounts to their residual values over their estimated useful lives, as follows:

Building core	50 years or lease term if shorter
Building surfaces and finishes	30 years or lease term if shorter
Plant and machinery	15-20 years
Furniture and equipment	10 years
Soft furnishings	5-7 years
Computer equipment	5 years
Motor vehicles	4 years

No residual values are ascribed to building surfaces and finishes. Residual values ascribed to building core depend on the nature, location and tenure of each property. Residual values are reassessed annually.

Straight line depreciation is a constant annual charge to the income statement. It is the most common depreciation method used in practice and should be used when there is uncertainty about how the asset's benefits are consumed over time.

The calculation of straight line depreciation is straightforward – it is: **Cost of the asset ÷ Asset life**.

The balance sheet value of an asset that has been depreciated and/or amortized is called net book value (NBV):

Initial asset cost	X
Less: accumulated D&A	(X)
Net book value (NBV)	X

Accumulated D&A is the total D&A charged to-date on an asset. D&A will be charged to the income statement as an operating expense. NBV is also referred to as carrying value or book value.

Reducing balance depreciation is slightly more involved. The method is designed to accelerate the depreciation charge (and would be appropriate for cars, as mentioned earlier). For instance, a car is bought for €12,000. Reducing balance depreciation policies are normally expressed in terms of a percentage. The reducing balance depreciation policy on this asset is 25%.

The depreciation charges will be calculated as follows:

	€
Initial cost	12,000
1st year charge (25%)	(3,000)
NBV at end of 1st year	**9,000**
2nd year charge (25%)	(2,250)
NBV at end of 2nd year	**6,750**
3rd year charge (25%)	(1,688)
NBV at end of 3rd year	**5,062**

Reducing balance depreciation theoretically continues into perpetuity.

D&A methods and the NBV profiles

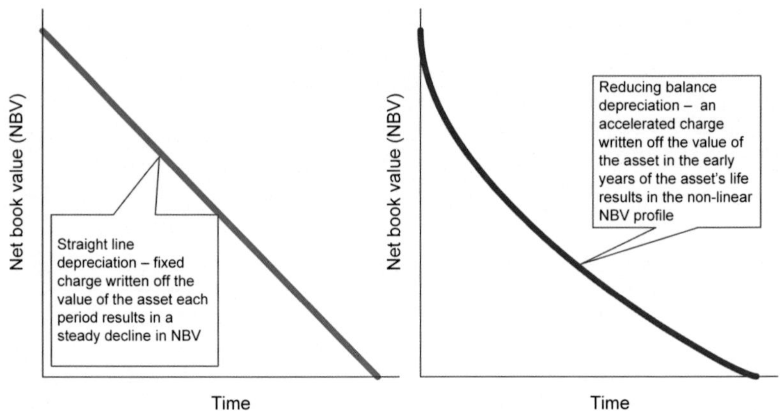

Depreciation and Amortization Numbers

D&A numbers are subject to manipulation. The motivation is driven by the desire to manage the earnings number in the income statement. D&A numbers are charged in arriving at operating profit or EBIT. Given EBIT is a key metric for analysis, valuation and modeling purposes, the weaknesses in the D&A numbers must be fully appreciated.

The key variables required to calculate D&A are:

- Initial cost
- Useful life

Both of these variables can be manipulated. The simplest form of manipulation is the ease with which the useful life can be extended or reduced. Take a £600 laptop. There are no prescriptive accounting rules that state a laptop should be depreciated over X number of years. It is relatively easy to justify that a laptop should be depreciated over two years – hence we have a depreciation charge of £300, on a straight line basis. Three years can also be easily justified. The depreciation charge then is £200. EBIT has been managed upwards by £100. Apply a 10x EBIT valuation multiple to this and the valuation has been altered by £1,000. Bear in mind this is just one asset and it's a small number.

D&A can also be manipulated in the financials through the choice of D&A method. An entity wishing to suppress current earnings may opt for a reducing balance D&A method, thus accelerating the charge to the income statement and reducing the short-term earnings profile.

D&A numbers are also non-cash numbers – they are pure accounting numbers, which widens the disconnect between earnings and cash.

There are no prescriptive requirements in the accounting rules for particular assets to be depreciated in a particular way. Therefore it is common for similar assets on the balance sheets of similar entities in the same peer group to be depreciated differently.

Depending on the jurisdiction, D&A policy can also be driven by local tax policy. In some countries, the D&A numbers may be tax deductible. Therefore there is a motivation to accelerate the D&A in order to secure the tax deductions at the earliest opportunity.

Comparability for analysis and valuation purposes therefore becomes a potential issue.

In summary, D&A numbers pose issues for Analysts. D&A numbers are:

- Easily manipulated
- Non-cash items
- Inconsistently applied between peer group entities
- Inconsistently applied internationally

As a result of this, Analysts often strip out the D&A numbers from the EBIT. This produces an earnings number before interest, tax, depreciation and amortization (EBITDA).

Asset Disposals

When an entity disposes of an asset, there will normally be an associated profit or loss on disposal. If there is a significant profit or loss on disposal in relation to the asset's NBV, it could suggest that the depreciation policy in relation to the asset was inappropriate.

If a significant profit is made, this means the NBV was significantly lower than the disposal proceeds. This suggests that the asset may have been over depreciated over its life and its NBV consequently too low. Hence the large profit on disposal.

The reverse is true for significant losses.

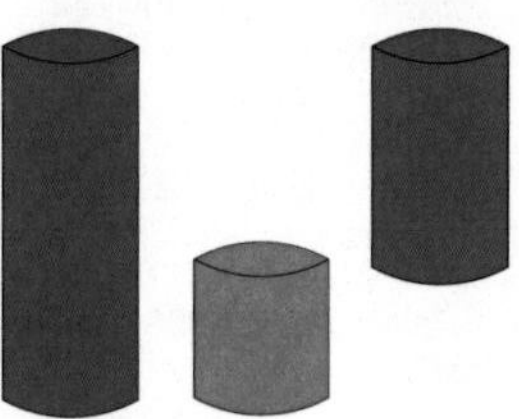

Large profits – potential over depreciation

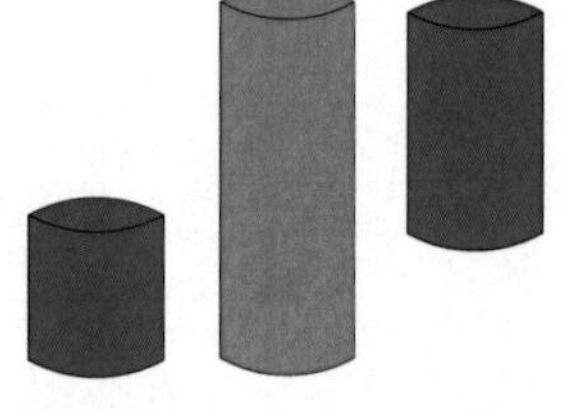

Large losses – potential under depreciation

Revaluations

Intangible (with the exception of goodwill) and tangible assets (in practice normally Property, Plant and Equipment (PPE)), can be revalued.

Once a revaluation policy is adopted, it must be kept up-to-date.

A revaluation results in an increase in the balance sheet value of the asset. In order for the balance sheet to balance, a revaluation reserve is set up in equity. The reserve represents an unrealized gain which cannot go to the income statement as it is unrealized.

In some jurisdictions, the gain on the revaluation becomes immediately chargeable to tax. Depending on the company law of the entity's incorporation, the revaluation reserve might be treated as a non-distributable reserve. It is not possible to distribute a dividend out of the reserve.

If the asset is sold, any remaining revaluation reserve can be transferred to equity, as the gain has become realized. The reserve transfer then becomes distributable.

Revaluation treatment

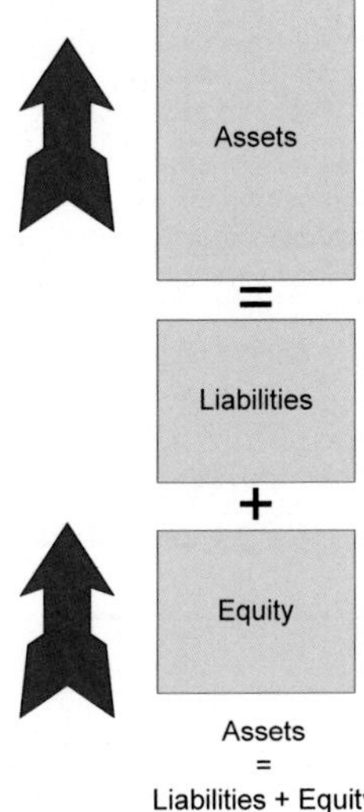

Assets
=
Liabilities + Equity

Revaluations are not permitted

US GAAP does not allow revaluation of PPE.

Why Revalue?
What is the Analysis Impact?

Revaluations are not that common in practice. Although intuitively it might be thought that bigger asset values are better, revaluations have the effect of harming measures of performance, such as return on assets and return on capital employed.

However, when revaluations do happen, it is worth investigating to see if there is a background story that drives the policy.

Why revalue?

- To reflect a better fair value of the entity
- To increase collateral for a loan
- Prior to pricing a sale and leaseback transaction
- Prior to commencing a disposal strategy
- To reduce leverage ratios
- Can help to prevent debt covenant violations
- As a bid defence – reflect a better fair value for the entity
- To strengthen the position as part of bid negotiations
- Can be used to manage dividend policy. A revaluation will increase the depreciation charge and hence reduce the profits available for distribution to shareholders.

Analysis impacts:

- Increase in the depreciation charge
- Dilution of EBIT
- There is no impact on EBITDA
- In some countries, there may be an immediate tax impact as a result of the revaluation

Impairments

Impairment is a downward adjustment to an asset's value. The impairment will be in response to an indication that the asset's realizable value has fallen below the current NBV.

Indicators of impairment:

- A decline in market value
- Changes in technological, market, economic or legal environment
- Net assets greater than the market capitalization
- Obsolescence or physical damage
- Change in use of asset

If an asset is impaired, it must be written down. The write down is a charge to the income statement and can be thought of as 'emergency' depreciation or amortization. The asset's NBV catches up with its true value.

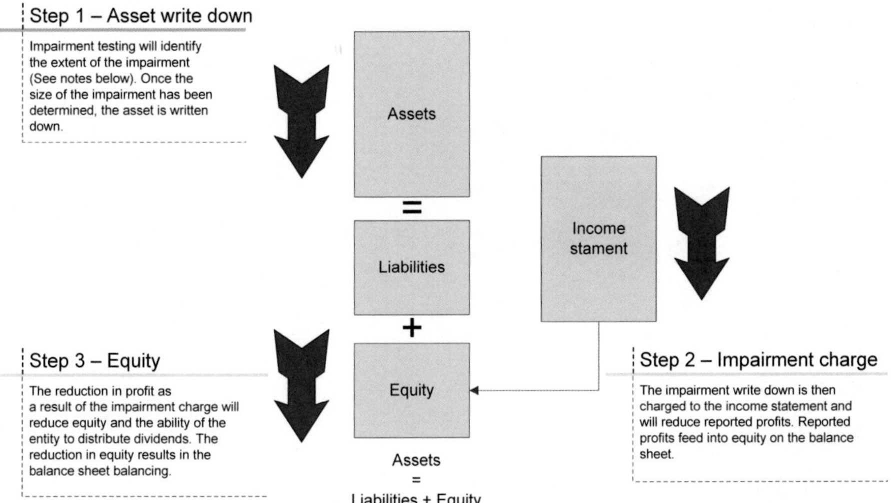

There are significant differences concerning the testing for impairment between IFRS vs. US GAAP.

Impairment Testing

IFRS uses a one step impairment test. The size of the impairment is the difference between the asset's NBV and its recoverable amount.

The recoverable amount has two reference points:

- How much the asset could be sold for in an arm's length transaction (fair value)
- The present value of the asset's cash flows using a pre-tax discount rate (i.e. what the asset is worth to the business)

The asset is impaired down to the higher of these two amounts. The reason the recoverable amount is the higher of the two reference points is based purely on logic. Suppose an entity holds an impaired asset. It can either dispose of the asset at fair value or it can hold the asset and secure the cash flows generated by the item. Logically, the entity will take the action that maximizes the cash flow benefit – hence the higher of the fair value or the present value of the asset's cash flows.

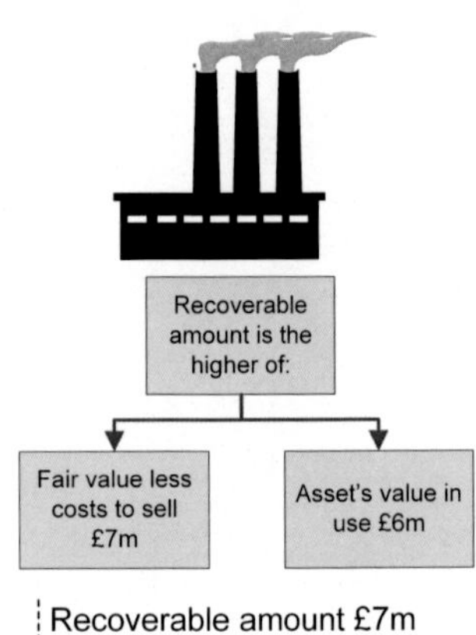

Current NBV £10m

The current NBV is £10m. There is an indication that the asset is impaired. An impairment test needs to be applied to the asset

Recoverable amount £7m

The asset will be written down by £3m The impairment will be charged to the income statement.

Impairment Testing

US GAAP has a two stage impairment test.

Stage 1:

The NBV of the asset is compared to its undiscounted forecast cash flows.
If the NBV is lower than the undiscounted cash flows, there is no impairment.
If the NBV is higher than the undiscounted cash flows, there has been an impairment.

Stage 2:

The asset is then written down to its fair value.

Current NBV $10m

The current NBV is $10m.
There is an indication that the asset is impaired. An impairment test needs to be applied to the asset.

Stage 1

The undiscounted cash flows are estimated at $8m. This is lower than the NBV.
The asset is impaired.
Go to Stage 2 and measure the impairment with reference to the asset's fair value

Stage 2

The asset's fair value is $7m. The asset will be impaired by $3m and the amount charged to the income statement as an expense.

Impairment Write Down

The term 'impairment' has found a place in everyday language as a result of the credit crisis. Since September 2008, impairments seem to have been an almost everyday occurrence in the financial press.

Impairments provide important information to Analysts. An impairment adjusts bloated financials for assets that were often acquired during the boom times at inflated prices. Regular impairments by an entity may provide additional information concerning management's decision-making abilities or lack thereof. Another impairment could be interpreted as another admission of a poor investment decision.

Impairment rules can be weak. The accounting rules do allow a degree of discretion in the impairment testing. The notes above referred to fair values and value in use. These numbers are often estimates and estimated numbers can be manipluated. Many directors and senior managers are incentivised through EPS or earnings metrics. This often gives rise to a reluctance to impair assets because of the direct hit to earnings.

As mentioned, impairments reduce profit and equity. This can have a detrimental impact on credit covenants (most lenders require companies to maintain certain ratios in order to minimise the possibility of default). The possibility of breaching covenants is therefore another reason that an impairment could be artificially delayed due to the 'discretion' in the accounting rules.

AOL – Time Warner – $54bn impairment write down

In April 2002, AOL-Time Warner reported a $54bn impairment write down in its income statement. At the time, this was the largest write down in US corporate history. To put into perspective, the write down was 64% of the company's market capitalisation and it was larger than the GDP of Ecuador.

The impairment related to goodwill – the premium paid on the combination of AOL and Time Warner towards the end of the dot-com bubble in the late 1990s. At the time, the value of the combined entity was in the region of $290bn. Much of the premium was driven by the bubble uplift in the AOL share price. When the bubble burst, the driver of the premium – AOL's share price – had come back down to earth with a bump. AOL-Time Warner was forced by the rules under US GAAP to confess to the drop in value and impair their goodwill.

The question is, should Analysts take much notice of these impairment write downs. Is it bad news? Is it bad news that the markets already know about? Should an Analyst react and panic? To a certain extent the market anticipated the impairment. The accounting to a certain extent was catching up with reality. However, an impairment is often an acknowledgement of a mistake. In terms of AOL-Time Warner, they had a bloated balance sheet, driven by over paying for acquisitions during the dot-com bubble. They overpaid with shareholders' money and that exuberance came back to haunt them.

From an analytical point of view, a single impairment could be casting light on bigger issues. Enron started with a single impairment and look where that company ended up...

Intangible assets

An intangible asset is a non-monetary asset without physical substance.

Examples of intangible assets are:

- Goodwill
- Brands, licenses and copyrights
- Web site development costs
- Software
- Music libraries
- Aircraft landing rights
- Research and development

The accounting is governed by a number of different accounting rules. However, the general principles will be covered now. Goodwill is examined in more detail in *Chapter 10: M&A Transaction Accouting.*

Control

One of the key ingredients in order to recognize an asset is to have control of that asset. Control is the ability to have power and restrict access to an asset's benefits. In terms of intangible assets, this could be in the form of a legal right, a document of ownership or purely through secrecy.

Control does become a tricky issue when considering intangible 'assets' such as an entity's workforce or customer relationships. Workforce recognition on the balance sheet is unlikely as it is difficult (given employment law) for an entity to suggest it has sufficient control or power over its employees. Similar types of issue arise with customer relationships. Unless there are legal rights to protect the client relationship, it is difficult to justify sufficient control to allow asset recognition on the balance sheet.

Lack of physical substance

The issue of physical substance can cause conceptual problems when trying to determine if an asset is tangible or intangible. Intangible assets are often contained in or recorded on an item that has physical substance. For example:

- Software recorded on a DVD
- Legal notes that provide evidence of patents or copyrights
- Music saved on CD

Judgment is required to assess which elements of the asset (tangible vs. intangible) are more significant. If the intangible elements are the most significant then the asset should be accounted for as an intangible asset.

Identifiability

An intangible asset must be identifiable – such as separable (can be sold, transferred, licensed, rented or exchanged) or arises from contractual or legal rights.

Assuming that the entity has control of the asset's benefits and those benefits are probably going to flow to the entity, the intangible asset should be recognized on the balance sheet.

As far as the idea of a 'probable' flow of benefits is concerned, probable is generally assumed to mean 'more likely than not'. This is not the most helpful guidance, so think in terms of probabilities greater than 50% as a guideline.

Intangibles in an M&A Transaction

If an intangible asset is purchased in isolation, the price paid reflects the economic benefits that are expected to be generated by the asset.
The issues of control and the probability of the benefit are clearer to see.
A purchased intangible will normally be recognised immediately on the balance sheet.

M&A transactions involving intangibles are a different case. The consideration paid for an entity will reflect the profitability expectations for the entity as a whole. The amounts paid do not relate directly to individual assets.
The task of identifying what intangibles are recognised on the balance sheet of the acquirer is made easier by guidance that appears in IFRS and US GAAP.

Examples of intangible assets that can be recognized on acquisition:

- Intellectual property
- Client relationships
- Internally generated brands
- R&D projects

The following 'intangible assets' are examples of items that are not permitted to be recognised on an acquirer's balance sheet, as a result of M&A transactions:

- Employees
- A geographic market presence
- Strong credit or equity ratings

M&A accounting is reviewed in detail in *Chapter 10*.

Initial measurement

Intangible assets are initially recognized on the balance sheet at cost. Cost being the cash cost of the asset or the fair value of consideration given in order to acquire the asset.

The cost of the asset can include:

- The purchase cost
- Import duties
- Professional fees
- Costs of testing the asset in order to have it ready for use

The asset cost must not include:

- Advertising and promotional costs
- Any overheads

Once the asset is ready for use, the inclusion (capitalization) of further costs into the asset must stop.

Income Statement Manipulation

Cost capitalization into assets is an area of the financials to be acutely aware of. By capitalizing a cost into an asset, the income statement is protected from an immediate hit to earnings. This in itself is enough motivation for people preparing financials to manage the earnings line in the income statement.

Be aware of changes in accounting policies and earnings margins, as this could be evidence of earnings manipulation.

Specific intangible asset issues

Amortization, revaluation and impairments were covered earlier in this chapter. However, there are a number of intangible asset specific issues to address.

Goodwill

See *Chaper 10: M&A Transaction Accounting*.

Internally generated assets

Internally generated assets struggle to be recognized on the balance sheet due to:

- Difficulties measuring the asset's benefits reliably
- Problems in separating the asset from the business as a whole

For instance, Diageo does not recognize the brand value of Guinness. The Coca Cola brand does not appear on the balance sheet of Coca Cola Inc. These are assets of the businesses, however there are real difficulties measuring the assets' benefits reliably, as the assets were generated internally by the business. Their fair values have never been verified by acquisition. If the assets' values cannot be measured reliably, they will not be recognized on the balance sheet.

Brand Recognition

Balance sheet brand recognition can be one of the main areas of the balance sheet where assets are 'undervalued'. Brands are only recognized on the balance sheet if they are purchased. Hence for a number of companies, significant amounts of company value are not reflected on the balance sheet.

Cadbury's brand accounting policy extract below highlights a number of key issues:

- Only major brands purchased after 1985 are recognized on the balance sheet
- The Cadbury brand is not on the balance sheet because it is internally generated
- 95% of their brands are not amortized. This is common with brand companies as many established brands are believed to have indefinite lives.
- A KPMG study noted that on average only 35% of a company's brand value was recognized on the balance sheet.

(o) Acquisition intangibles
Brands
The main economic and competitive assets of the Group are its brands, including the Cadbury brand, some of which are not on the balance sheet as these are internally generated. The Group carries assets in the balance sheet only for major brands that have been acquired since 1986. Acquired brand values are calculated based on the Group's valuation methodology, which is based on valuations of discounted cash flows. Intangible assets are treated as local currency assets and are retranslated to the exchange rate in effect at the end of the financial year. Where the Group licenses the use of a brand then there is no value recognised in the Group's accounts.

No amortisation is charged on over 95% of brand intangibles, as the Group believes that the value of these brands is maintained indefinitely. The factors that result in the durability of brands capitalised is that there are no material legal, regulatory, contractual, competitive, economic or other factors that limit the useful life of these intangibles. Furthermore:

> The Group is a brands business and expects to acquire, hold and support brands for an indefinite period. The Group supports these brands through spending on consumer marketing across the business and through significant investment in promotional support. The brands capitalised are expected to be in longstanding and profitable market sectors.

> The likelihood that market based factors could truncate a brand's life is relatively remote because of the size, diversification and market share of the brands in question.

> The Group owns the trademark for all brands valued on the balance sheet and renews these for nominal cost at regular intervals. The Group has never experienced problems with such renewals.

Where a brand's life is not deemed to be indefinite it is written off over its expected useful life on a straight-line basis, with the lives reviewed annually.

Source: Cadbury annual report

In terms of valuation, the intangible asset numbers and especially the brand numbers are often significantly understated. This is a major reason why the balance sheet is not a good basis for generating valuation metrics for most companies.

Research and development

Research and development expenditure is an important issue in industries such as pharmaceuticals, engineering and technology. It is however another example of a major IFRS/US GAAP difference.

R&D Costs

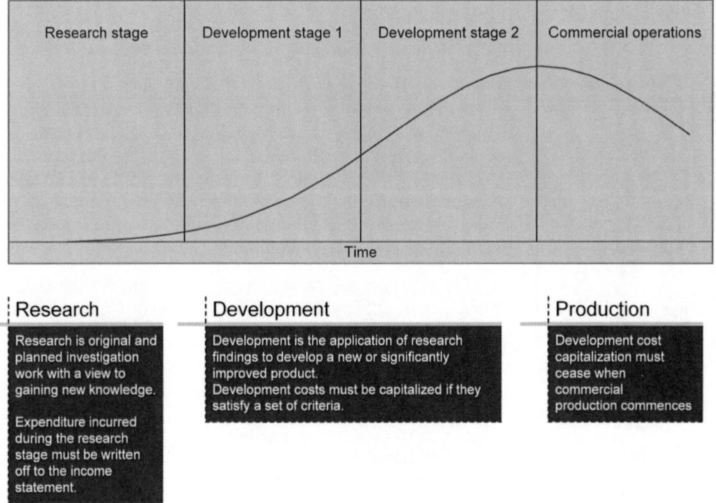

Research and development (R&D) expenditure is an example of an internally generated asset that must be recognized on the balance sheet as an intangible asset, if a number of criteria are satisfied.

Any expenditure classified as research expenditure must be written off as incurred.

Expenditure classified as development expenditure must be capitalized if all of the following six criteria are satisfied:

- The project is technically feasible
- There is an intention to complete the project and then use or sell the asset
- There must be the ability to use or sell the asset
- There must be a probable future economic benefit of the project
- Resources are available to complete the project
- The project expenditure can be measured reliably during the development

Once the R&D project is ready for commercial production, the capitalized R&D expenses will be amortized through the income statement over the project's expected life.

US GAAP generally prohibits the capitalization of development costs. There are some very limited exceptions to this (e.g. the development of software for sale to third parties).

Capitalization in practice is very rare.

<table>
<tr>
<td>

Research and Development</td>
<td>There is often a reluctance to satisfy the IFRS R&D capitalization criteria, even though the cost capitalization protects the income statement.

If an entity (let us say a pharmaceutical company) capitalizes drug development costs, it will give the impression to Analysts that the company has a strong R&D pipeline. This may lead to an increase in valuations as multiples improve and cash flow forecasts become more bullish.

In the pharmaceutical industry it is common for drugs to look very promising and then fail certain regulatory hurdles late in the development. If the company had initially capitalized drug development costs and then failed a regulatory test that 'mothballed' the project, the capitalized costs would have to be written off immediately. Earnings would be hit. Valuations would be adjusted downwards, the equity market would probably overreact and we would see equity price volatility as a result of a mismanagement of expectations driven by accounting.

As a result, many companies try not to capitalize their R&D costs if possible. Better to give unexpected good news than unexpected bad news.</td>
</tr>
</table>

Tangible assets

A tangible asset is a non-monetary asset with physical substance that is controlled by the entity.

Examples of tangible assets are:

- Property, plant and equipment (PPE)
- Investments in joint ventures and associates
- Investment property

PPE for many entities is the largest class of asset.

PPE

PPE are tangible assets held for use in an entity's business and are expected to be used for more than one period. PPE is normally:

- Depreciated
- Subject to impairment
- Able to be revalued

These issues were covered in the earlier non-current assets notes.

Initial measurement

PPE is initially recognized on the balance sheet at cost. Cost is generally easy to measure as it is normally the price paid for the asset. However with more complicated acquisitions or assets constructed internally for use, the cost element can comprise:

- Purchase price
- Import duties
- Delivery costs
- Site preparation
- Professional fees
- Commissioning costs
- Installation costs

Only costs that are directly attributable to the asset can be capitalized into the cost. General operating costs must not be capitalized into the asset.

The capitalization of costs must cease once the asset is ready for its intended use. The asset is then depreciated over its useful life.

Capitalization of borrowing costs

There are differing opinions on whether finance costs should be capitalized into PPE. Some argue that it is a cost of getting an asset ready for its intended use. Arguably without the financing, it would not be possible to get the asset ready for use. Hence the financing cost can be argued to be a directly attributable cost. Others argue that the financing cost is an expense in relation to the period and should be expensed as such through the income statement.

Under IFRS and US GAAP, borrowing costs in relation to PPE must be capitalized as part of the asset cost.

The capitalization of borrowing costs is not limited to PPE. The policy is also applied to any asset that requires a substantial period of time to bring it to a saleable condition. Inventories are an example of where this policy can apply.

Only directly attributable borrowings costs (i.e. borrowing costs that were incurred as a result of the asset expenditure) should be capitalized. When a specific debt instrument is issued in order to fund an asset acquisition, the capitalization of the borrowing cost is straightforward as there is a clear link between the instrument, the cost and the asset. If the borrowings are sourced from a general funding pool, the entity must estimate a capitalization rate (a weighted average interest rate or capitalization rate in reality) that is used to capitalize the borrowing costs.

The borrowing costs will be capitalized during the period of construction of the asset and will cease once the asset is ready for its intended use of sale.

Borrowing Costs

US GAAP allows more judgement in the determination of the capitalization rate used to capitalize the borrowing costs into PPE. The US standard states that a reasonable measure of the cost of finance should be used to capitalize the borrowing costs. This could lead to differences in the amounts capitalized when compared to IFRS.

Tesco plc capitalizes relevant borrowing costs into PPE. The impact of this policy is to reduce the interest charge to the income statement. The PPE number in the balance sheet will increase as a result. The borrowing costs capitalized into PPE will eventually hit the income statement as the PPE number is depreciated over time. So capitalizing interest is a deferral and spreading of the charge, rather than a 100% removal of the cost from the income statement.

The capitalization policy has the impact of artificially understating the interest charge in the income statement. Below is an example of Tesco plc:

Group income statement

	notes		
Continuing operations			
	2	**54,327**	47,298
Cost of sales		**(50,109)**	(43,668)
Gross profit		**4,218**	3,630
Administrative expenses		**(1,248)**	(1,027)
Profit arising on property-related items	2/3	**236**	188
Operating profit	2	**3,206**	2,791
Share of post-tax profits of joint ventures and associates	13	**110**	75
Finance income	5	**116**	187
Finance costs	5	**(478)**	(250)
Profit before tax	3	**2,954**	2,803
Taxation	6	**(788)**	(673)
Profit for the year		**2,166**	2,130

Source: Tesco Annual Report

The income statement discloses a finance cost of £478m. However, this is after capitalizing interest of £152m. A fairer number for analysis for finance costs would be £630m, whereby the interest capitalized is added back to the income statement charge.

Finance cost per income statement	£478m
Add back: Interest capitalized	£152m
Adjusted finance cost	£630m

This type of adjustment has a significant impact on analysis.
For instance, a basic interest cover calculation based on operating profit is materially affected by the capitalisation of the borrowing cost:

Finance cost per income statement	£478m	£478m
Add back: Interest capitalized		£152m
Adjusted finance cost	£478m	£630m
Operating profit (EBIT)	£3,206	£3,206m
Basic EBIT interest cover	**6.71x**	**5.09x**

It is very useful to add back the interest capitalized in order to appreciate the full impact of the entity's capital structure.

Borrowing Costs

Maintenance and improvement expenditure

There is a fine line separating the treatment of maintenance and improvement expenditure. If the cost can be justified as an improvement – which the expenditure leads to an improvement of the asset's benefits (e.g. enhanced life, enhanced revenue generating ability), then those costs may be capitalized into the asset.

However, day-to-day maintenance costs do not improve the asset's benefit, they merely allow the benefits to be fully utilized by the entity. These costs should be written off as incurred to the income statement.

Spare parts

Spare parts are normally treated as inventory and are expensed as they are used. However, if the spare parts are major items or stand-by items of equipment, they may be included as part of the PPE number in non-current assets. These items would then be depreciated.

Non-depreciation of assets

There are arguments that not all items of PPE should be depreciated. Often this argument is in relation to buildings. The argument is often justified if the residual value of the asset is similar to the original cost. This may be evidenced by high levels of maintenance in relation to the asset. Some luxury hotel groups adopt non-depreciation policies for their hotel properties.

Investment property

An investment property is a property held in order to generate a capital and rental return.

The recognition of an investment property asset is in line with the standard asset recognition requirements, that is that the:

- Asset must be controlled by the entity
- Benefits will flow from the asset
- Benefits can be reliably measured

The investment property will initially be measured at cost. Cost is the purchase price including direct attributable costs, such as legal fees and property taxes.

Subsequent measurement can adopt either:

- A fair value model
- A cost model

If the fair value model is adopted, any gains and losses arising from a revaluation to fair value should be recognized in the income statement for the period. Investment properties valued at fair value are not depreciated.

The cost model will treat the investment property just like an item of PPE. The asset will be depreciated and disclosed on the balance sheet at its net book value. The property will be subject to the impairment rules as required.

Investment Property

US GAAP does not have a specific rule for investment properties. Most entities holding investment properties use the historic cost model and will depreciate the assets over their useful lives.

Associates and joint ventures

See *Chaper 10: M&A Transaction Accounting*.

Current assets

A current asset is an asset that is generally expected to be used within one year or within one operating cycle.

Typical current assets are:

- Inventories – items bought with a view to being resold
- Receivables – sales made on credit, but where no cash has been received from the customers
- Cash and cash equivalents

These items are often referred to as components of working capital.

Working capital is an entity's operating capital. That is, the assets and liabilities that are used to operate the business on a day-to-day basis. Working capital is usually expressed as net when the operating liabilities are included in the working capital definition.

A basic definition of working capital can be:

- Inventories
- Receivables
- Cash and cash equivalents
- Less: trade payables

Net Working Capital

An understanding of working capital is essential for:

- Analysing an entity's liquidity and cash management situation
- Deriving cash flows for analysis and valuation purposes

The term 'working capital' is widely used but unfortunately there are many definitions. Care must be taken when using the term.

Some standard 'university' textbook working capital definitions are too simplistic. For instance, the definition of net working capital as current assets – current liabilities is arguably an adequate quick and dirty definition, but it can capture items that are current by definition but not operating by nature. For instance, Analysts often exclude tax liabilities, surplus assets or excess cash from the net working capital definition.

One definition of net working capital is:

- Inventories
- Receivables
- Less: trade payables

An increase in net working capital means that the working capital assets have increased in relation to the working capital liabilities.This means more cash is tied up in the working capital assets of the entity. This type of understanding is key in relation to the later work on cash flow analysis and valuation. An increase in net working capital is poor for cash (when viewed in isolation) though it might be vital for the business in order to support additional activity.

Depending on the use to which the working capital definition is being put, it may be relevant to include that part of the cash and cash equivalents which is essential for the proper operation of the business.

Current assets are valued at the lower of their cost and their net realizable value (the value the assets can be sold for net of any realization costs).

Cash and cash equivalents

Cash and cash equivalents require a more detailed examination because of the item's use in net debt definitions and subsequently in valuation metrics, capital employed and firm (or enterprise) value breakdowns.

Cash is cash on-hand and on-demand deposits. A demand deposit is a deposit with financial institutions that is repayable on demand and available within 24 hours or one working day.

A cash equivalent is a short-term and highly liquid investment. The investment is readily convertible to a known amount of cash that has an insignificant risk of change in value. A cash equivalent would normally have a short maturity which is normally a period of no more than three months, as measured from the date of the acquisition of the investment.

Typical examples of cash equivalents are short-term:

- Money market investments
- Corporate bonds
- Certificates of deposits
- Government bill/stock investments

Cash and Cash Equivalents

Cash may include bank overdrafts. Short-term bank borrowings are not included in cash or cash equivalents.

Cash and Cash Equivalents

Bank overdrafts are not included in the US GAAP definition of cash and cash equivalents. US 10K annual financials often define the cash equivalents maturity period as 90 days or less maturity from date of acquisition of the asset.

The extract below illustrates a typical definition of cash equivalents. The extract is taken from Pfizer's 10K annual report.

'**Cash Equivalents and Statement of Cash Flows**
Cash equivalents include items almost as liquid as cash, such as certificates of deposit and time deposits with maturity periods of three months or less when purchased. If items meeting this definition are part of a larger investment pool, we classify them as *short-term investments*.'

Assessing Short-term Investment Liquidity

It is often difficult to determine from balance sheet disclosures whether an item should be treated as a liquid investment for net debt (see later notes) purposes. Without going into too much detail, net debt is the entity's total borrowing, net of cash and liquid resources. The liquid resource element will include cash equivalents and short-term liquid investments that are readily disposable into known amounts of cash.

The Tesco extract below is typical of the issues faced when assessing the liquidity of current assets. Firstly the disclosure is typically European. The current assets are disclosed in ascending order of liquidity – least liquid asset first.

Cash and cash equivalents being the most liquid are disclosed last in the list. Issues however arise when attempting to analyze the liquidity of current asset short-term investments, especially, as is the case with Tesco, when there is no associated note providing further detail on the number.

Current assets			
Inventories	15	**2,669**	2,430
Trade and other receivables	16	**1,798**	1,311
Loans and advances to customers	17	**1,918**	–
Loans and advances to banks and other financial assets	18	**2,129**	–
Derivative financial instruments	22	**382**	97
Current tax assets		**9**	6
Short-term investments		**1,233**	360
Cash and cash equivalents	19	**3,509**	1,788
		13,647	5,992

Source: Tesco Annual Report

Tesco has £1,233m of short-term investments. This is a large number with no associated note. So how can we assess the liquidity of the asset? Without any further notes, the liquidity can only been assessed by considering the position of the short-term investment disclosure. A short-term investment line item disclosed in close proximity to the cash and cash equivalents line can be analyzed as being sufficiently liquid to include in a net debt calculation. Short-term investments disclosed nearer the inventories line are looking less liquid and therefore more unlikely to be classified as liquid resources for net debt purposes.

Consolidated Balance Sheets
Pfizer Inc and Subsidiary Companies

(MILLIONS, EXCEPT PREFERRED STOCK ISSUED AND PER COMMON SHARE DATA)	2008	2007
Assets		
Cash and cash equivalents	$ 2,122	$ 3,406
Short-term investments	21,609	22,069
Accounts receivable, less allowance for doubtful accounts: 2008—$190; 2007—$223	8,958	9,843
Short-term loans	824	617
Inventories	4,381	5,302
Taxes and other current assets	5,034	5,498
Assets held for sale	148	114
Total current assets	43,076	46,849

Source: Pfizer 10K

Note the difference in the US GAAP order of disclosure for the current assets. The disclosure is in descending order of liquidity with the most liquid asset first.

Tick Sheet – Non-current Assets

Intangible assets:

- A cost or fair value model can be adopted
- Revaluations are permitted but are very rare
- Intangible assets are normally amortized over their useful lives
- A useful life can be indefinite
- Amortization is an operating cost charged to the income statement above EBIT
- Amortization is a non-cash expense
- Impairment rules apply
- Internally generated intangible assets (with the exception of R&D) are not capitalized
- R&D costs may be capitalized subject to recognition criteria under IFRS
- US GAAP is very restrictive with respect to internally generated intangible assets

Tangible assets:

- A cost or fair value model can be adopted
- Revaluations are permitted
- Borrowing costs can be capitalized during the construction of the asset
- Tangible assets are normally depreciated over their useful lives
- A useful life can be indefinite
- Depreciation is an operating cost charged to the income statement above EBIT
- Depreciation is a non-cash cost
- US GAAP does not allow revaluations of PPE

Depreciation and amortisation

D&A numbers are:

- Easily manipulated
- Non-cash items
- Inconsistently applied between peer group entities
- Inconsistently applied internationally

Revaluations

Analysis impacts:

- Increase in the depreciation charge
- Dilution of EBIT
- There is no impact on EBITDA
- In some countries, there may be an immediate tax impact as a result of the revaluation
- Return on capital employed (profit/capital employed) is reduced as profits are reduced by the increase in the depreciation charge and capital employed is increased by the creation of a revaluation reserve.

Tick Sheet (cont.)

Current assets:

- Valued at lower of cost or net realizable value
- Components of current assets will form part of the working capital definition
- A basic working capital definition is:
  - Inventories +
  - Receivables +
  - Less: trade payables

Cash is an immediately liquid cash asset – access is immediate or within one day.

Cash equivalents are short-term, highly liquid investments. The instruments are considered to have a maturity of < 90 days.

Introduction

Liabilities are obligations owed by the entity to third parties. The liabilities section of the balance sheet is a key area as it provides important information for:

- Net debt metrics
- Working capital metrics
- Leverage ratios

The liabilities section in the balance sheet is normally split into liabilities:

- Falling due within one year
- Falling due after one year

Liabilities and equity

The distinction between liabilities and equity seems an elementary one at a basic level. Liabilities are amounts owed to third parties. Equity is a residual claim the equity holders have on the net assets of the entity.

However, as modern day financial products have evolved, the distinction between an equity instrument and a liability have become increasingly blurred. Capital markets bankers have become adept at developing products that are treated as equity for credit purposes, but the distributions from which are treated as interest in the hands of the payer and are deductible for corporate tax purposes.

The accounting rules do venture into very detailed territory when considering the distinction. However, one of the key considerations when assessing the classification as either debt or equity is the concept of obligation.

In simple terms, liabilities have an obligation to deliver or to exchange – whether it is cash, or another financial asset. Equity does not. Ordinary share capital or common stock has no dividend or principal obligation and hence does not meet the definition of a liability. There is no obligation.

The liability/equity distinction is illustrated below:

4% preference share with a fixed dividend and a mandatory redemption

A preference share is an instrument that ranks above ordinary share capital or common stock in terms of priority of dividend payment and on a distribution of capital on a winding up. The preference dividend is normally calculated as a fixed percentage of the nominal value of the instrument and the instrument is referred to as a share.

However, because the dividends are fixed and there is a mandatory redemption feature, there exists an obligation to deliver cash that cannot be avoided. This instrument would therefore meet the definition of a liability (a financial liability).

4% non-redeemable preference share with a fixed dividend

A non-redemption feature further blurs the liability/equity distinction. The instrument has equity characteristics in terms of the principal, however, the payment of a fixed dividend has an obligation feature. The instrument therefore seems part equity and part liability. This is when the bankers start to call in the accountants, because depending on the detail in the features of the instrument, the accounting treatment could swing either way.

Irredeemable debt

Irredeemable debt is an instrument that pays out interest into perpetuity without the requirement to return the principal. The instrument has no obligation to return the principal, but there is an obligation to pay interest into perpetuity. This obligation meets with the definition of a financial liability.

Liability – equity definitions

US GAAP has narrower definitions of what qualifies as a liability. The difference in the definitions leads to more instruments being classified as equity under US GAAP compared to under IFRS.

Operating payables

Operating payables such as...

- Trade or accounts payable – amounts owed to suppliers
- Accruals – amounts owed to suppliers where the amount has not been invoiced (these amounts are often estimated in practice)
- Deferred income – monies received from customers in advance of the goods or services being supplied
- Tax payable – amounts owed to the tax authorities

...are liabilities as they all create obligations to deliver or exchange.

These operating payables can form part of the working capital definitions for analysis and indirect cash flow derivation purposes.

Net debt

Net debt is a metric that is widely used by Analysts.

It is used in:

- Credit analysis
- Return on capital employed calculations
- Enterprise (or firm) value numbers
- Comparable company and transaction analysis
- The move from enterprise (or firm) to equity value
- Assessing the credit implications in a merger model
- Leverage multiples in LBO models

As an Analyst, not knowing how to extract a net debt metric from a set of financials quickly should be considered a sin.

Basic net debt definition

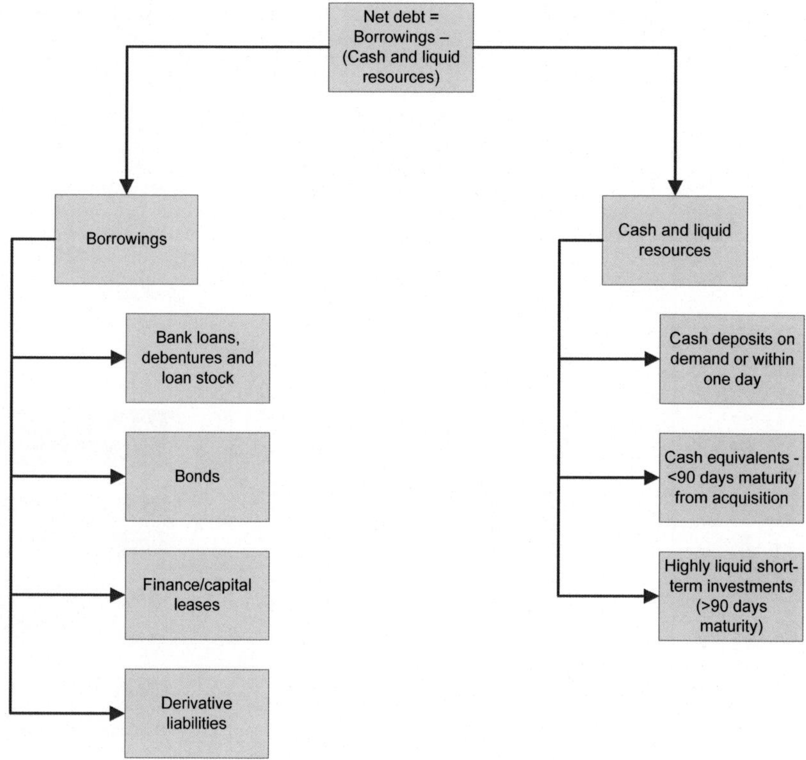

Pulling out a Basic Net Debt Metric From the Financials: Part 1

The basic net debt definition is borrowings – (Cash + Liquid resources). More often than not, these numbers can be picked up straight off the face of the balance sheet. It is however, a worthwhile exercise to check out the notes to the financials that support these key balance sheet numbers. Often the notes will reveal additional information that will add support to the calculation of the metric.

The Cadbury Annual Report balance sheet extract below is a good illustration of a basic net debt calculation that still requires some thought in terms of which numbers to include. The balance sheet as you can see is reasonably detailed with all the key numbers that would feed into a net debt calculation, disclosed on the face of the statement.

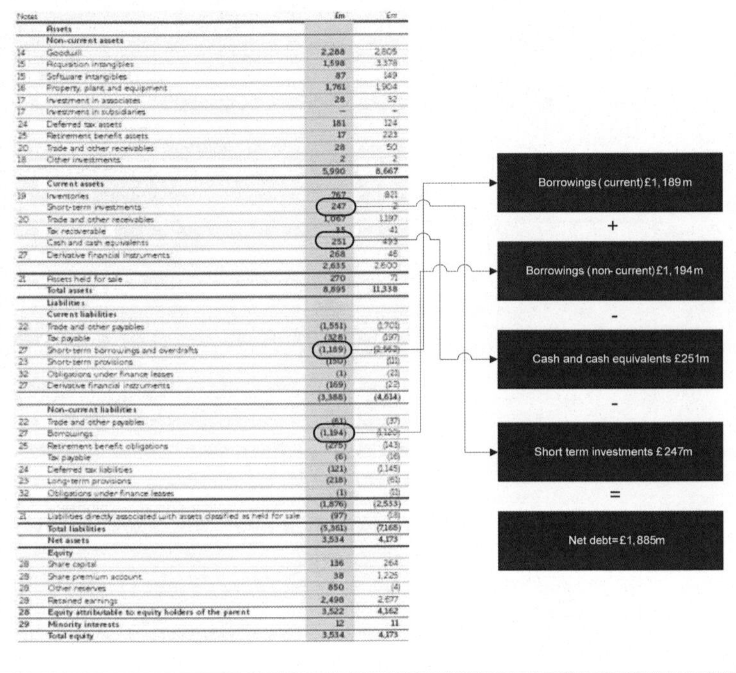

Notes		£m	£m
	Assets		
	Non-current assets		
14	Goodwill	2,288	2,805
15	Acquisition intangibles	1,598	3,378
15	Software intangibles	87	149
16	Property, plant and equipment	1,761	1,904
17	Investment in associates	28	32
17	Investment in subsidiaries	–	–
24	Deferred tax assets	181	124
25	Retirement benefit assets	17	223
20	Trade and other receivables	28	50
18	Other investments	2	2
		5,990	8,667
	Current assets		
19	Inventories	767	821
	Short-term investments	247	2
20	Trade and other receivables	1,067	1,197
	Tax recoverable	[illegible]	41
	Cash and cash equivalents	251	[illegible]
27	Derivative financial instruments	268	46
		2,635	2,600
21	Assets held for sale	270	71
	Total assets	8,895	11,338
	Liabilities		
	Current liabilities		
22	Trade and other payables	(1,551)	(1,705)
	Tax payable	(328)	(197)
27	Short-term borrowings and overdrafts	(1,189)	[illegible]
23	Short-term provisions	(150)	(111)
32	Obligations under finance leases	(1)	(21)
27	Derivative financial instruments	(169)	(22)
		(3,388)	(4,614)
	Non-current liabilities		
22	Trade and other payables	(61)	(37)
27	Borrowings	(1,194)	[illegible]
25	Retirement benefit obligations	(275)	(143)
	Tax payable	(6)	(16)
24	Deferred tax liabilities	(121)	(1,145)
23	Long-term provisions	(218)	(61)
32	Obligations under finance leases	(1)	(11)
		(1,876)	(2,533)
21	Liabilities directly associated with assets classified as held for sale	(97)	(18)
	Total liabilities	(5,361)	(7,168)
	Net assets	3,534	4,173
	Equity		
28	Share capital	136	264
28	Share premium account	38	1,225
28	Other reserves	850	(4)
28	Retained earnings	2,498	2,677
28	**Equity attributable to equity holders of the parent**	3,522	4,162
29	**Minority interests**	12	11
	Total equity	3,534	4,173

Pulling out a Basic Net Debt Metric From the Financials: Part 2

However, even this basic calculation posed a few problems.

Firstly, the short-term investments (£247m) disclosed within current assets appear to be liquid due to the line item description. However, the position of the line item disclosure, just below inventories, seems to contradict the belief that the investments are sufficiently liquid to be included in the net debt calculation. In addition to this there appears to be no cross-referenced notes in the financials that could provide some additional information concerning the liquidity of the line item.

Before making assumptions as to the extent of the item's liquidity, a search of the document should be made for the words 'short-term investments'. This is very easy to do if the document is available in a PDF version. Using the find function (Control F within Adobe Reader) in the Cadbury Annual Report, a reference to short-term investments is found that states that the investments are money market deposits. The money market deposits may have maturities longer than 90 days (the cash equivalents maturity cut off) but still be considered liquid investments. Hence the short-term investments were included in the net debt calculation above.

The second issue concerns the treatment of derivatives in the net debt calculation. There are a number of issues, and hence options available in terms of the net debt treatment:

- The derivatives can comprise a number of instruments. For most corporate entities, the derivatives are instruments to hedge the operational risk of the business. Such risks could relate to:
  - Interest rates
  - Commodity prices
  - Foreign exchange rates
- Not all of these derivatives are directly related to the risks inherent in net debt. Hence some Analysts will review the derivative instruments and only include those instruments that hedge out risks associated with net debt. For instance, a commodity derivative hedging the risk of a rise in the price of coffee beans is unlikely to be related to a net debt number (unless the entity had commodity linked bonds where the redemption price was linked into the price of coffee). However, an interest rate swap does hedge the interest rate risk associated with bonds and loans. The interest rate swap (a derivative) would therefore be included in the net debt calculation.
- An easier option, followed by a number of Analysts, is the all or nothing approach. Either include all derivatives or exclude them all. Consistency of treatment is the key issue. For ease, the net debt illustration above adopted the 'exclude all the derivatives' approach.

Debt

Having examined probably one of the key metrics – net debt – it is now necessary to understand the debt numbers and how they are accounted for on the balance sheet.

Debt instruments are financial liabilities, as they are contractual obligations to deliver cash or financial assets. The contractual obligation can also arise out of a requirement to exchange financial assets and liabilities.

Financial liabilities can be classified as one of the two following categories:

- At fair value through profit or loss (AFVTPL)
- All other financial liabilities

AFVTPL is restricted to financial liabilities that are held for trading or have been designated as such at initial recognition.

Most entities will categorize their own issued debt instruments as other financial liabilities.

Debt instruments classified as other financial liabilities are accounted for at amortized cost.

Common examples of financial liabilities accounted for at amortized cost are:

- Bonds
- Bank loans
- Debentures
- Loan stock

Amortized cost

Amortized cost is an accounting mechanism that spreads the full interest cost (including transaction costs) of the instrument over the instrument's life.

The fair value of the instrument is not taken into consideration during the instrument's life. Therefore there can be valuation differences between the balance sheet book value of the instrument (its amortized cost) and the fair value of the instrument.

The spreading mechanism of the instrument's interest (and transaction) cost is called the effective interest rate method.

Basic amortized cost

The example below illustrates how the method works.

A debt instrument is issued at par of 10,000. There are no transaction costs. The coupon is 5.00%. The instrument will be redeemed at par. As the instrument was issued with no transaction costs and there is no discount or premium on issue or on redemption, the effective interest rate (or the yield to maturity at issue) is also 5%. There are no further costs to spread over the life of the instrument, other than the basic cash coupon.

Accounting for debt instruments

Par	10,000
Proceeds	10,000
Redemption	10,000
Coupon rate	5.00%
Effective rate	5.00%

Period	Start BS	Interest IS	Coupon CFS	End BS
1	10,000	500	(500)	10,000
2	10,000	500	(500)	10,000
3	10,000	500	(500)	10,000
4	10,000	500	(500)	10,000
5	10,000	500	(500)	10,000
Total interest charge to IS		**2,500**		
Total cash coupon paid			**(2,500)**	

Cash coupon rate

The cash coupon rate is the amount of cash interest paid per year. It is calculated as a percentage of the nominal value of the bond.

A 5% cash coupon rate on a 10,000 nominal (par or face value) bond gives a cash interest payment of 500 per year.

Effective rate calculation

Period	CF
--	10,000
1	(500)
2	(500)
3	(500)
4	(500)
5	(10,500)
Effective rate	**5.00%**

Effective rate of interest

The effective rate of interest is the rate of interest that captures the full interest cost of the bond.

The full interest cost of the bonds includes:

- The cash coupon rate paid
- Any premiums or discounts on issue
- Transaction costs

The effective rate of interest is the internal rate of return (IRR) of the instrument's cash flow stream. In this example, there are no transaction costs and the instrument was issued and redeemed at par. Therefore the coupon and the effective rate are identical.

Basic amortized cost with transaction costs

Continuing with the above example, the same instrument is issued with identical terms, except that there is a transaction cost of 750. This transaction cost is classified as part of the interest cost of the instrument. The cost will be spread (or amortized) and charged to the income statement over the instrument's life using the effective rate of interest. The effective rate of interest now comprises two elements:

- The cash coupon
- The transaction cost

Therefore the effective rate of interest will be bigger than the 5% cash coupon rate.

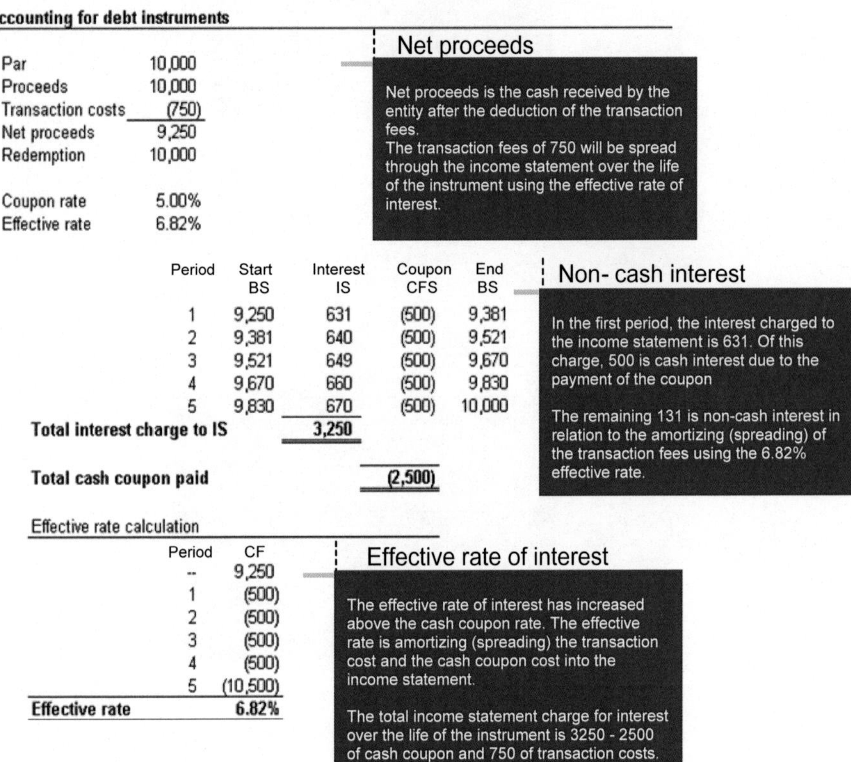

Accounting for debt instruments

Par	10,000
Proceeds	10,000
Transaction costs	(750)
Net proceeds	9,250
Redemption	10,000
Coupon rate	5.00%
Effective rate	6.82%

Period	Start BS	Interest IS	Coupon CFS	End BS
1	9,250	631	(500)	9,381
2	9,381	640	(500)	9,521
3	9,521	649	(500)	9,670
4	9,670	660	(500)	9,830
5	9,830	670	(500)	10,000
Total interest charge to IS		**3,250**		
Total cash coupon paid			**(2,500)**	

Effective rate calculation

Period	CF
--	9,250
1	(500)
2	(500)
3	(500)
4	(500)
5	(10,500)
Effective rate	**6.82%**

Transaction costs

Transaction costs are costs and fees that are integral to the issuing of the instrument.

They are the incremental costs associated with issuance and can include:

- Advisory fees
- Broker fees
- Dealer fees
- Regulatory levies
- Security exchange payments
- Transfer taxes and duties

Transaction costs do not include internal administration or holding costs.

Transaction Cost Treatment

Under US GAAP, when the instrument is accounted for at amortized cost, the transaction costs are accounted for as a deferred asset – usually deferred financing fees. The deferred fees are then amortized to the income statement over the life of the instrument.

Under IFRS, the debt amount in the balance sheet is shown net of the transaction costs.

Transaction costs are expensed immediately if the instrument is carried at fair value. This is consistent with IFRS.

Amortized cost with a discount on issue and transaction costs

Continuing with the above example, the same instrument is issued with identical terms, except for the fact that there is a transaction cost of 750 and a 1,000 discount on issue. The discount on issue and the transaction cost are classified as part of the interest cost of the instrument. The cost will be spread and charged to the income statement over the instrument's life using the effective rate of interest.

The effective rate of interest now comprises three elements:

- The cash coupon
- The discount on issue
- The transaction cost

Therefore the effective rate of interest has increased to 9.57% in order to capture the full cost of the instrument.

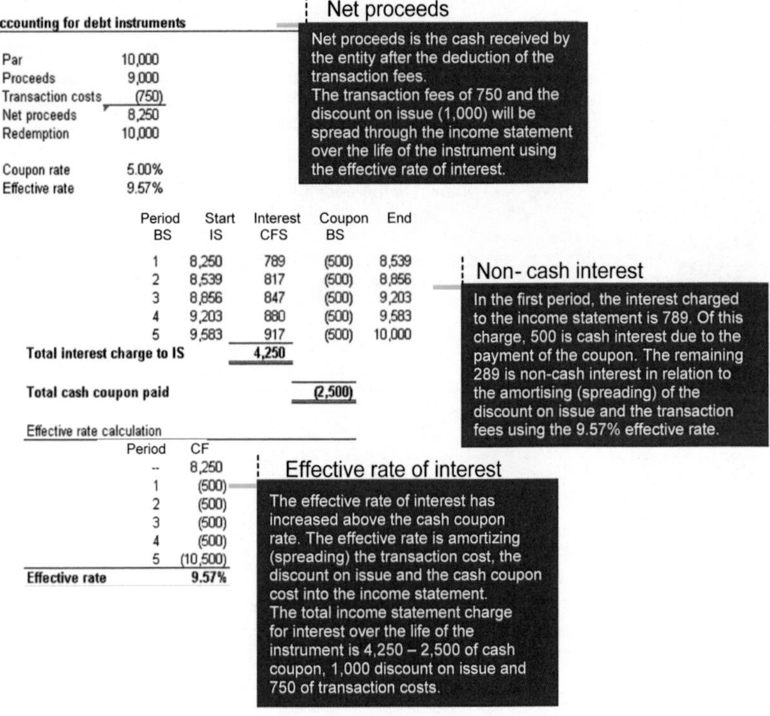

Accounting for debt instruments

Par	10,000
Proceeds	9,000
Transaction costs	(750)
Net proceeds	8,250
Redemption	10,000
Coupon rate	5.00%
Effective rate	9.57%

	Period BS	Start IS	Interest CFS	Coupon BS	End
	1	8,250	789	(500)	8,539
	2	8,539	817	(500)	8,856
	3	8,856	847	(500)	9,203
	4	9,203	880	(500)	9,583
	5	9,583	917	(500)	10,000
Total interest charge to IS			**4,250**		
Total cash coupon paid				**(2,500)**	

Effective rate calculation

	Period	CF
	--	8,250
	1	(500)
	2	(500)
	3	(500)
	4	(500)
	5	(10,500)
Effective rate		**9.57%**

Amortized cost with a zero coupon and a deep discount

In this example a similar instrument is issued, however there is no cash coupon and the issue is at a significant discount to par. The discount on issue and the transaction cost are classified as part of the interest cost of the instrument. The cost will be spread and charged to the income statement over the instrument's life using the effective rate of interest.

The effective rate of interest now comprises two elements:

- The discount on issue
- The transaction cost

Therefore the effective rate of interest has increased to 8.18% in order to capture the full cost of the instrument. The greater the discount on issue, the higher the effective interest rate will become.

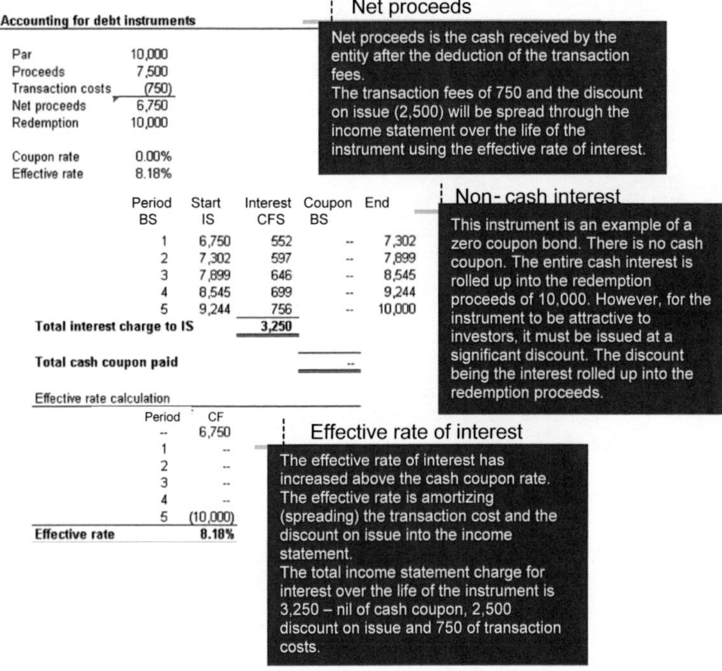

Accounting for debt instruments

Par	10,000
Proceeds	7,500
Transaction costs	(750)
Net proceeds	6,750
Redemption	10,000
Coupon rate	0.00%
Effective rate	8.18%

Period	Start	Interest	Coupon	End
BS	IS	CFS	BS	
1	6,750	552	--	7,302
2	7,302	597	--	7,899
3	7,899	646	--	8,545
4	8,545	699	--	9,244
5	9,244	756	--	10,000
Total interest charge to IS		**3,250**		
Total cash coupon paid			--	

Effective rate calculation

Period	CF
--	6,750
1	--
2	--
3	--
4	--
5	(10,000)
Effective rate	**8.18%**

Floating rate notes (FRN)

The effective rate method as described above is ideal for fixed rate debt instruments. However, when the future cash flows of the instrument are uncertain, matters are a little more complicated.

A FRN is an instrument that has a variable cash interest payment. The amount paid is often linked to an underlying benchmark interest rate such as LIBOR. Often the interest rates are expressed as LIBOR + a number of bps (basis points). The number of bps are often referred to as the credit spread. The higher the credit risk associated with the instrument, the larger the credit spread will be in order to compensate for the additional risk. The interest rate on a FRN is re-set periodically to reflect changes in the benchmark rate and the credit risk.

If a FRN is issued and redeemed at par with no transaction costs, the cash interest paid is simply charged to the income statement. In this case the treatment of the instrument is identical to the plain vanilla instrument (no discount, premium or transaction costs) as outlined earlier.

However, if the instrument is issued at a discount or premium and/or there are associated transaction costs, there is the issue regarding what period these amounts should be amortized over:

- The life of the instrument
- To the next re-set date (re-pricing date)

The answer depends on the nature of the premium or discount and the instrument's relationship with prevailing market rates.

For instance, if an instrument is issued at a discount and the discount is determined with reference to market rates, the discount should be amortized over the life of the instrument.

Amortised Cost vs. Fair Value

Most corporate entities will account for debt on the balance sheet using amortized cost. The reason being, this method avoids adding fair value volatility to the financials, especially the income statement. If issued debt was classified as AFVTPL, the fair value gains and losses would flow through to the income statement.

However, Analysts must be aware that the amortized cost number could be materially different to the fair value of the debt. This is particularly important if there have been significant changes to the entity's credit rating since the instrument was issued.

For example:

- An entity issues debt when the credit rating is AA (high quality credit instrument)
- The instrument is accounted for using the amortized cost method
- Subsequently, the credit rating falls to non-investment grade (BB)
- The impact of the credit rating adjustment is to increase the instrument's yield to maturity
- The increase in the yield to maturity discounts the future cash flows of the instrument more aggressively, leading to a decline in its fair value. The decline in the fair value is not recognized in the financials.

This issue is far more serious when an entity takes the decision to fair value its own debt using the AFVTPL option (see later financial instrument notes). A number of financial institutions have used this option with their own debt. A US institution booked a $30m gain on its own debt, essentially profiting from its own credit rating deterioration. The institution's credit rating fell, so therefore did the fair value of its debt. The fair value adjustment was then booked to the balance sheet with a corresponding gain to the income statement. From a layman's perspective, the debt was worth less and ultimately this was a gain to the shareholders.

Issues will arise as the credit rating recovers and the institutions have to take hits due to the fair value uplifts on their own issued debt instruments, just as the earnings profile starts to show recovery.

The issue is summed up perfectly by Dennis Jullens UBS research:

> "...clearly demonstrates the absurdity of an entity booking gains when its credit quality worsens and reporting losses when creditworthiness improves. We feel that the financial sector earnings boosted by large fair value gains on own debt may not truthfully represent the actual performance of the sector. Looking forward, if the credit markets recover significantly during 2009, falling corporate bond yields could translate into material losses for banks, and even more than reverse gains from previous periods....would introduce substantial and unwarranted volatility in earnings..."

Debt with embedded derivatives

It is very common for debt instruments to have additional terms and conditions embedded into the documentation of the contract.

For instance:

- Equity options that provide debt instruments with an equity upside
- Principal repayments that are linked into an underlying asset's performance.
- Interest rate caps, floors and collars

The objective of these additional terms and conditions is to alter the cash flow profile of the instrument as well as manage risk between parties.

Many of these terms and conditions are structured through the use of derivatives. A derivative is an instrument that derives its value from an underlying asset. A simple example is an option to buy equity. If you hold an option to buy some Apple stock at $175 and the stock price rises to $210, but you still have the right to buy at $175 – your equity option has increased in value. The option's increase in value is driven by the value of the underlying Apple equity.

Derivatives are used to structure these contracts (host contracts). A host contract with an embedded derivative is often called a hybrid instrument.

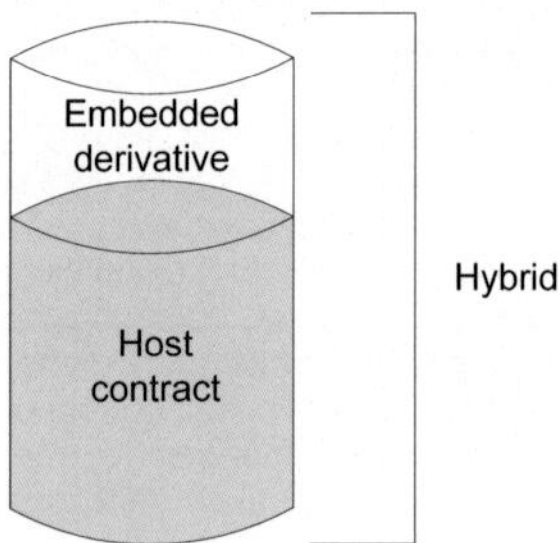

Not so long ago these embedded derivatives were not accounted for until the host contract either matured or was sold on. Hence there was no disclosure of the risks of the embedded derivatives. Historically this has caused some market shocks.

For example, a derivative embedded in a host contract that structures the redemption price of a bond to an underlying foreign currency would not make an appearance in the financials until the host contract matured. Suppose that the underlying currency moved in such a way over the life of the instrument, that the derivative in the host contract resulted in a significant increase in the redemption price of the bond. Again this information would only come to light at maturity or disposal of the instrument.

The embedding of the derivative would hide the risks associated with the product.

Separation

Both US GAAP and IFRS consider the idea of separation. That is, under certain circumstances embedded derivatives are separated from their host contracts. However, there are significant differences in the rules and their application. The principle behind the separation of the host contract and the embedded derivative is disclosure of risks. Better disclosure hopefully leads to better and more informed decision-making.

Separation

IFRS requires that an embedded derivative should be separated from the host contract and accounted for as a separate instrument if:

- Its economics are not closely related to those of the host contract
- A separate instrument with the same terms as the embedded derivative would meet with the definition of a derivative. A derivative is a financial instrument that demonstrates all of the following characteristics:
  - Its value changes in response to changes in an underlying price or index

    It requires no initial investment or an initial net investment that is smaller than would be required to purchase the underlying instrument
  - It is settled at a future date
- The contract is not carried at fair value through profit or loss (AFVTPL)

Typical instruments where embedded derivatives are separated under IFRS are:

- Convertible debt instruments with equity options
- Debt instruments with interest and principal repayments linked into an underlying equity or commodity
- Debt instruments with embedded credit derivatives

Examples of embedded derivatives that are not separated under IFRS are:

- Foreign currency denominated debt instruments
- Debt instruments with interest rate caps, floors or collars
- Dual currency bonds

Separation

US GAAP does contain provisions to separate embedded derivatives. However the mechanics involved under US GAAP can give rise to significant differences compared to IFRS.

US GAAP has recently been updated with ASC 470-20 'Debt with conversion and other options' which states that 'if the convertibles can be potentially cash settled, then the convertible must be split into debt and equity'. This split is done using the same approach as the IFRS rules above.

Leasing

Leasing is a rental agreement for the use of an asset over a period of time. The terms of the lease agreement will determine how the lease is classified and consequently how it will be treated in the financials.

The most significant benefit leasing provides is that the asset's use can be 'acquired' without having to bear the upfront capital cost. As a result, leasing can be used as an effective way to manage financing.

There are two types of lease from an accounting perspective:

- Operating leases
- Finance or capital leases

Capital lease is the US terminology for a finance lease.

Lease classification

Almost immediately we have US GAAP/IFRS differences. Lease classification is a good example of how different the two GAAPs can be. US GAAP is very much rules-driven whereas the IFRS rules are based on conceptual foundations.

Lease Classification

IFRS guidance focuses on the substance of the transaction. The classification relies on whether the risks and rewards of ownership have been substantially transferred to the lessee.

An easy way to think about the rules is to consider whether the leased asset in the hands of the lessee feels like it belongs to the lessee. If it does, the lease agreement should be classified as a finance (or capital) lease.

Indicators that the leased asset feels like it is owned by the lessee (that the risks and rewards of ownership have been substantially transferred) could be:

- There is a transfer of legal ownership by the end of the lease term
- The length of the lease is a significant proportion of the asset's life
- The lease payments in present value terms account for a significant proportion of the asset's cost
- There is a very favorable option to buy the leased asset
- The leased assets are very specialized in nature
- Insurance costs are the responsibility of the lessee
- Maintenance costs are the responsibility of the lessee
- There are no lease break clauses or they are towards the end of a long lease term

Lease Classification

US GAAP lease classification is based on satisfying one of four specific criteria. A lease will be classified as a capital lease if one of the following criteria is satisfied:

- The legal title to the asset transfers to the lessee
- The lease contains a bargain purchase option
- The lease term is >75% of the asset's life
- The present value of the minimum lease payments is >90% of the asset's fair value

As you can see two of the four rules have quantitative breakpoints, which can give rise to a lease agreement being structured to achieve a desired lease classification.

Lease accounting

Finance (capital) leases

The accounting for a finance (capital) lease is debt-driven. The lease commitment is valued in present value terms using the interest rate implicit in the lease agreement and this amount is then recognized as the debt commitment and asset value.

The debt will then be treated like any other vanilla instrument and accounted for using the amortized cost method. The asset is normally depreciated over the term of the lease or the life of the asset, whichever is shorter.

Therefore, there are two charges to the income statement:

- Depreciation (above EBIT)
- Interest (below EBIT)

Both charges have no impact on EBITDA metrics, as EBITDA is before depreciation and interest. This is one of a number of weaknesses of the EBITDA metric – it ignores the charges associated with finance leases.

The finance lease cash payment (rental) has two elements:

- Interest cash payment (an operating cash flow)
- Principal cash repayment (a financing cash flow)

Operating leases

The accounting for operating leases is very straightforward. No debt or asset is recognized on the balance sheet. The only accounting is the charging of an operating lease rental expense to the income statement.

The rental expense is a charge to EBIT and EBITDA.

The cash flow is classified as an operating cash flow.

Finance/capital lease illustration

An entity enters into a new lease agreement
The lease term is 5 years with annual lease rental payments of €34,000
The lease payments are made in arrears
The interest rate implicit in the lease is 8%

Finance lease accounting - year 1 of the lease:

Step 1

Calculate the present value of the minimum lease payment (MLP)

Period		8.00%	
1	34,000	0.926	31,481
2	34,000	0.857	29,150
3	34,000	0.794	26,990
4	34,000	0.735	24,991
5	34,000	0.681	23,140
PV of the MLPs			**135,752**

Finance/capital lease

The finance lease is treated as a financing commitment because the lease agreement is a claim on the future cash flows of the business.
The valuation of the commitment uses a present value approach that follows the basics of bond valuation.

Step 2

Capitalise the lease debt and asset (assumed to be PPE)

	Inception
PPE	135,752
Net assets	135,752
Debt	135,752
Liabilities & equity	135,752

Debt & asset recognition

At the inception of the lease, the present value of the lease commitment is recognized on the balance sheet as both debt and the corresponding asset.

Step 3

The leased asset is depreciated over 5 years and interest accrues on the debt at a rate of 8% on the outstanding balance

	Inception	**Interest**	**Depn**
PPE	135,752		(27,150)
Net assets	135,752	--	(27,150)
Debt	135,752	10,860	
Retained earnings		(10,860)	(27,150)
Liabilities & equity	135,752	--	(27,150)

Debt & asset accounting – year 1

The debt is accounted for using an amortized cost calculation. Interest charged at 8% on the outstanding balance of €135,752 gives an interest charge of €10,860 in the first year. The interest is charged to the income statement below EBIT.

The asset (normally part of PPE) is depreciated over the lease term, or if shorter the asset's useful life. The PPE valuation is €135,752 – this is spread over the 5 year lease term and gives an annual depreciation charge of €27,150. The depreciation is charged to the income statement above EBIT

Step 4

The cash lease rental payment of €34,000 is made at the end of the period

	Inception	**Interest**	**Depn**	**Cash**	**BS**
PPE	135,752		(27,150)		108,602
				(34,000)	(34,000)
Net assets	135,752	--	(27,150)	(34,000)	74,602
Debt	135,752	10,860		(34,000)	112,612
Retained earnings		(10,860)	(27,150)		(38,011)
Liabilities & equity	135,752	--	(27,150)	(34,000)	74,602

Cash payment treatment - year 1

The cash payment of €34,000 comprises two elements.
The payment conceptually first services the finance – paying the interest on the debt that has accrued over the period. The residual €23,140 pays down the debt principal. This split will be different in subsequent years as the debt principal reduces and hence the interest element.

In the cash flow statement the €34,000 payment in the first year will be split on this basis between operating (the interest of €10,860) and financing (the principal €23,140) cash flows.

Leasing and EBITDA Comparability

EBITDA is a widely used metric in equity and credit research, as well as for valuation purposes. However, the metric does pose some problems when trying to compare entities that account for their leases in different ways.

Given the accounting rules, entities in the same peer group could quite easily account for these leases differently, i.e. as operating in one entity and finance/capital in another. This gives rise to substantially different numbers in the financials. Not only will the debt and asset numbers, and therefore the capital employed numbers, be inconsistent, but the profit metrics will also not be comparable.

Entities classifying their leases as finance lease will suffer no hit to EBITDA whereas entities classifying the leases as operating will see the full rental charge hit EBITDA. Two identical operating entities who classify their leases differently would report very different EBITDAs.

In order to present a level playing field, Analysts have created the EBITDAR metric. The 'R' relates to operating lease rentals. Thus this metric ignores all charges in relation to leasing – interest, depreciation and operating lease rentals.

New standard due – US GAAP and IFRS joint project

FASB & IASB have a joint project to produce a new leasing standard which began in 2010. The proposal is that all leases will be brought onto the balance sheet. There has been further discussion in 2011. As at the start of 2012, there is no agreement but the IASB (unilaterally) intends that from 1 January 2013, all leases will come on to the balance sheet.

The credit rating agencies support the development of the new accounting rules:

- Lease accounting is incongruent with other standards
- Clarity is needed for the accounting for lease-like arrangements
- Disclosures are improving but still lacking—especially for non-SEC registrants and foreign companies not reporting under IFRS
- International convergence and greater consistency among issuers would be beneficial to Analysts

The common question that crops up now is will the accounting changes lead to changes in credit ratings. Material changes in credit ratings are not anticipated. However with better disclosure will come better numbers. This may lead to a change in the disclosed numbers that may give rise to the following issues:

- Covenant and regulatory compliance matters (reported leverage will increase)
- New accounting or disclosures could reveal new information or risks not previously known to Analysts
- Adverse market reaction to the new numbers
- Changes in business practices due to the accounting treatment

Operating Lease Conversion

Credit rating agencies have the fundamental belief that operating lease commitments are simply a form of financing that have claims on the future cash flows of the entity. The fact that the accounting rules have historically made a distinction between operating and financing cash flows is largely a matter for the accountants – the distinction is artificial.

According to the SEC approximately $1.25 trillion in non-cancelable future operating lease commitments are disclosed and are off-balance sheet. These commitments should be recognized on the balance sheet for a number of reasons:

- Enable more meaningful peer and period-over-period comparisons
- Better reflect underlying economics
- Better reflect creditors' risks, rights and benefits
- Facilitate more robust financial forecasts

Credit rating agencies, when doing their own analysis, convert operating leases into finance leases.

This operating lease conversion practice will be relevant until new rules on leasing are introduced.

Each credit rating agency has its own operating lease conversion model.

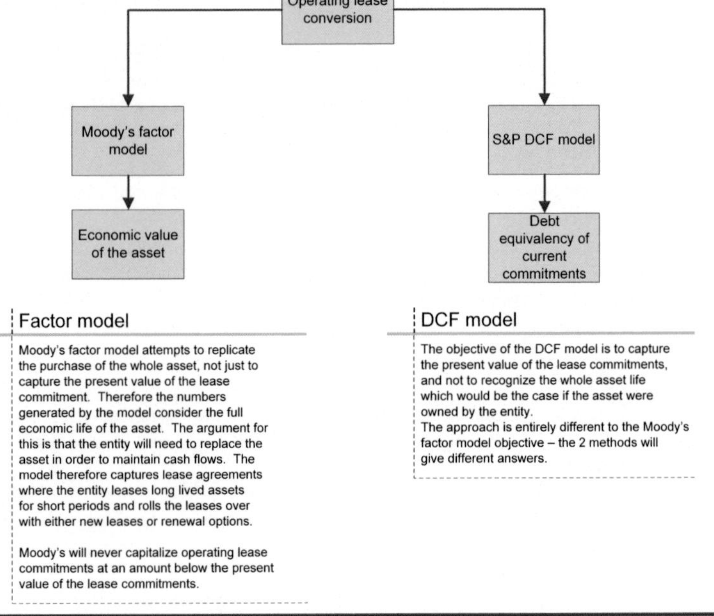

The Factor model

The Factor model works on the assumption of replicating the purchase of the asset, financed with a like amount of debt. The method is designed not just to capture the present value of the lease commitments, but to recognize the full life of the asset (not just the lease term).

The value of the capitalized debt is calculated as follows:

Capitalized debt = Current lease rental charge x Appropriate lease multiple

The size of the lease multiple depends on:

- The industry
- The type of asset leased
- The length of the lease term

Many Analysts are used to an 8x lease multiple. The 'magic number eight' is a term often heard. This reflects the fact that the 8x lease multiple is often used, but possibly not properly understood. The multiple must be understood and justified, as clients will want an explanation of how and why you have loaded their balance sheets with additional debt.

Moody's do provide guidance on suitable lease multiples for particular industries. See the extract (later in this section). Moody's will apply industry specific lease multiples of 5x, 6x, 8x and 10x in their operating lease conversion calculations.

In order to provide a benchmark, the 8x multiple assumes a lease term of 15 years and an interest rate implicit in the lease of 6%. In industries such as shipping, utilities or where commercial property leases are used, larger multiples tend to be used.

In any event, Moody's will not capitalize leases at an amount lower than the present value of the operating lease commitments.

The Factor model is also very useful for GAAPs that provide poor lease commitment disclosure, especially when there is a lack of information in relation to annual cash flow commitments.

Illustration: Cadbury plc – Factor model approach

(b) Operating leases

At the balance sheet date, the Group had outstanding commitments for future minimum lease payments under non-cancellable operating leases, which fall due as follows:

	£m	£m
Within one year	44	35
Between one and five years	140	104
After five years	94	98
	278	237

	£m	£m
Operating lease expenses charged in the income statement	45	53

Source: Cadbury plc annual report

Capitalized debt = Current lease rental charge x Appropriate lease multiple
= £45m x 6 (Moody's consumer products lease multiple)
= £270m

Balance Sheet Liabilities

Given that the total operating lease commitments are £278m in the above extract, it is highly unlikely that the present value of the operating lease commitment will be above £270m. Therefore £270m will be the debt and PPE numbers on the 'adjusted' balance sheet.

The income statement will also be adjusted. The operating lease rental charge needs to be converted into its finance lease elements. That is, the charge now needs to be split into its two elements – interest and depreciation. Moody's convention for splitting into the two elements is to allocate 1/3 of the charge to interest and the remaining 2/3 to depreciation.

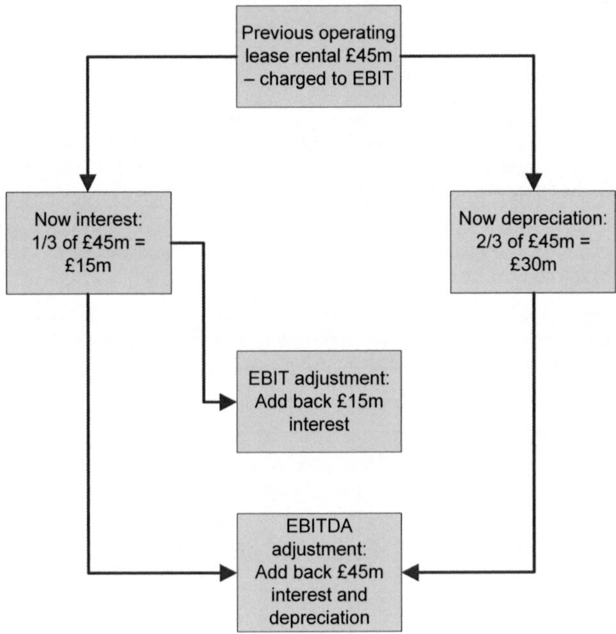

Table 2 - Multiples of Current Rent Expense by Industry

Industry	Multiple of Rent Expense
Aerospace / Defense	6
Automotive	6
Chemicals	6
Consumer Products	6
Energy: Electricity Cooperative	6
Energy: Electricity - Project Finance	6
Energy: Electricity - Non Project Finance	8
Energy: Oil & Gas - Drilling	5
Energy: Oil & Gas - Exploration & Production	6
Energy: Oil & Gas - Integrated	6
Energy: Oil & Gas - Merchant Energy	6
Energy: Oil & Gas - Midstream	6
Energy: Oil & Gas - Project Finance	6
Energy: Oil & Gas - Refining & Marketing	6
Energy: Oil & Gas - Services	5
Environment	6
Forest Products	5
Gaming / Lodging	8
Healthcare - Hospitals and Services	6
Healthcare - Medical Devices	6
Homebuilding	5
Leisure & Entertainment	8
Manufacturing	6
Media: Advertising & Broadcasting	6
Media: Diversified, Paid TV & Subscription Radio	6
Media: Printing & Publishing	6
Metals & Mining	5
Natural Products Processor	6
Packaging	5
Pharmaceuticals	5
Public Utility	6
Public Utility - Gas Distribution	8
Public Utility - Gas Transmission	8
Restaurants	8
Retail	8
Services - Business	6
Services - Consumer	6
Services - Contractors	5
Services - Processors	5
Services - Rental	5
Services - Towers & Satellites	5
Technology	5
Telecommunications	5
Transportation Services	6
Airline	8
Maritime Shipping	8
Transportation Services - Airports & Toll Roads	6
Wholesale Distribution	6

Source: Guideline Rent Expense Multiples for Use with Moody's Global Standard Adjustment to Capitalize Operating Leases – Moody's Investor Service Revised March 2006

DCF model

The DCF model is S&P's model of choice. The objective of the DCF model is to capture the present value of the operating lease commitments. No adjustment is made to reflect the fact that a particular lease might not be for the whole life of the asset.

This is conceptually a very different approach to Moody's factor model.

The method estimates the entity's operating lease commitments using the commitments notes available in US GAAP and IFRS and then discounts the cash flows using a rate estimated to reflect the entity's actual borrowing costs.

The borrowing cost can be estimated by:

- Adding a credit spread to a benchmark risk-free rate
- Reviewing comparable company financials
- Calculating an average interest rate = Interest expense ÷ Average debt outstanding
- Reviewing the notes – sometimes entities will disclose the rates implicit in their finance leases

S&P will revert to a factor model if the lease disclosures are insufficient to complete the DCF approach.

Illustration: Cadbury plc – DCF model approach

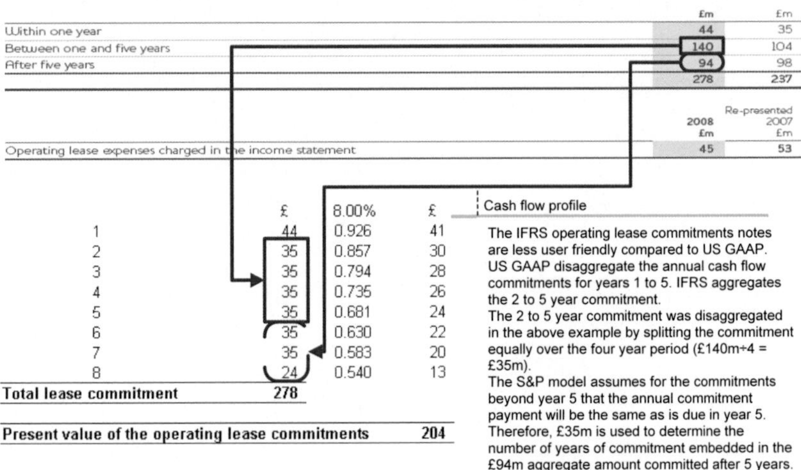

(b) Operating leases

At the balance sheet date, the Group had outstanding commitments for future minimum lease payments under non-cancellable operating leases, which fall due as follows:

	£m	£m
Within one year	44	35
Between one and five years	140	104
After five years	94	98
	278	237

	2008 £m	Re-presented 2007 £m
Operating lease expenses charged in the income statement	45	53

	£	8.00%	£
1	44	0.926	41
2	35	0.857	30
3	35	0.794	28
4	35	0.735	26
5	35	0.681	24
6	35	0.630	22
7	35	0.583	20
8	24	0.540	13
Total lease commitment	**278**		
Present value of the operating lease commitments			**204**

Source: Cadbury plc annual report

The S&P estimate of the capitalized debt is £204m, assuming that the appropriate discount rate for the operating lease commitments was 8%.

S&P will also adjust EBIT and EBITDA.

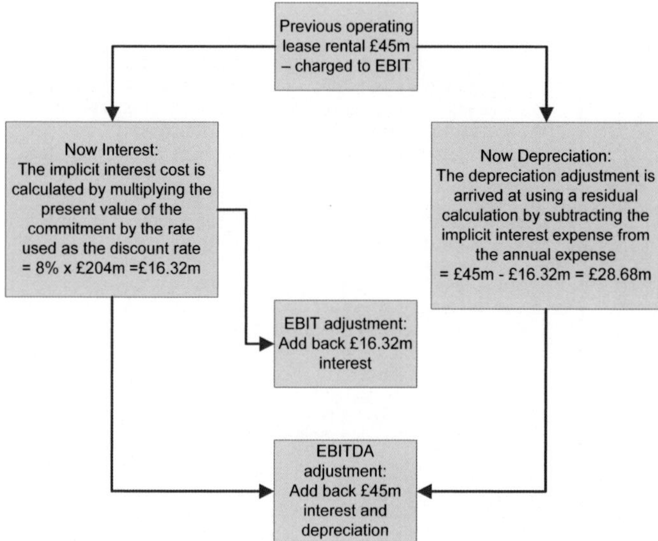

Limitations with the conversion models

In many cases, the DCF model significantly understates the true debt figure, because the capitalization calculation is based on the disclosed minimum future rental payments. Possible or contingent lease payments are not included.

The DCF model does not attempt to capture the scenario where the asset is acquired for its full life. It attempts to capture only the debt equivalent of the lease contracts in place. The model therefore only adjusts for the rent associated with the primary lease term of an asset and not its full productive life.

Leases differ significantly in structure and in features such as:

- Purchase options
- Renewal options
- Contingent rent and
- Responsibility for executory costs

Most of this information is not usually disclosed in the financials. This makes complete conversion of the operating lease commitment almost impossible. Both models are therefore probably still understating the true commitment.

Pulling out a Net Debt Metric from the Financials: Part 3

Earlier in this chapter, Cadbury's net debt was calculated. The on-balance sheet net debt was £1,885m. This net debt is purely a starting point for analysis purposes. As the above notes have mentioned, the credit rating agencies treat operating leases as off-balance sheet debt-like commitments and they will adjust their ratios accordingly.

Using the above calculations, the net debt adjusted for operating lease commitments for Cadbury would be:

	£m
On-balance sheet net debt	1,885
Plus: capitalized operating lease commitment	270*
Net debt adjusted	2,155

*Assuming the operating leases are capitalized using Moody's factor model.

Sale and leaseback transactions

Sale and leaseback transactions are usually structured to unlock equity an entity has in its assets – converting the value locked up in the asset into cash. The crystallization of the cash is normally accomplished by transferring the legal title of the asset to the investing entity, in return for an upfront cash lump sum. The investing entity then leases the asset back to the original owner.

Historically these structures were treated as a last resort source of borrowing and the act of a desperate entity whose traditional lines of credit were dry. The act was perceived as attempting to sell the 'family silver' in order to keep the entity's financial head above water.

However, in recent years attitudes have softened towards these structures. In fact, whilst commercial property values have increased, many entities have considered it of little sense to continue holding such assets when there are investors willing to unlock the value. The unlocked value results in an immediate cash inflow for the business. If this cash inflow can be invested to generate a return in excess of the cost of capital, value is created.

There are a number of advantages to these structures:

- The cash lump sum can be used to invest (capital expenditure, M&A activity, restructuring)
- Depending on the tax jurisdiction there could be tax benefits:
  - The lease costs can be tax deductible
  - Gains crystallized on disposal might be able to absorb group operating losses, hence minimizing any tax payable
- The seller maintains day to day control of the asset
- Cash is a more liquid asset than property
- Property price risk is transferred to a third party

From an accounting perspective, a sale and leaseback can either be:

- An operating leaseback
- A finance leaseback

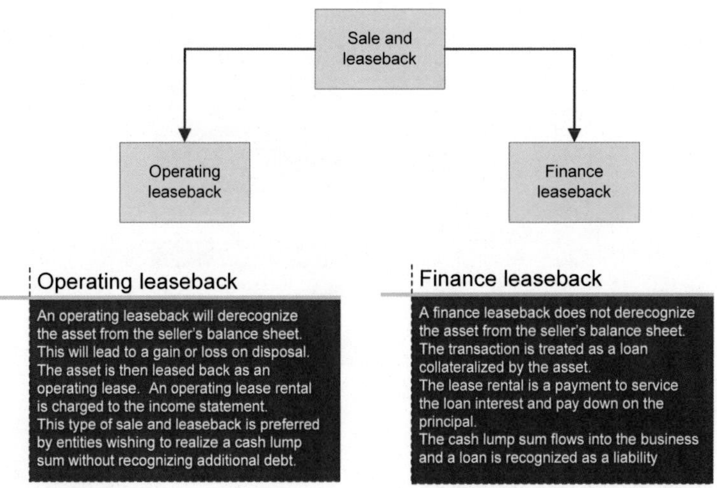

The 2009 HSBC Canada Square transaction is an excellent example of a sale and leaseback transaction. The transaction crystallized a £772.5m cash lump sum for HSBC. The details are outlined below.

2009 HSBC sale and leaseback of 8 Canada Square – Canary Wharf

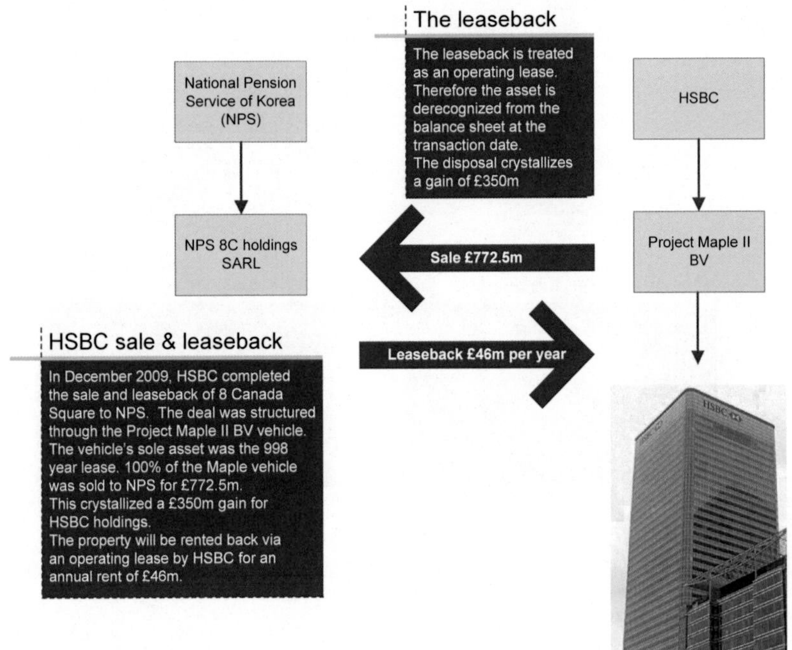

Pensions

A pension is a regular income received when somebody retires. There are a number of different types of pension scheme.

However, the most common forms are:

- Defined benefit schemes
- Defined contribution schemes

The key to understanding the pension numbers in a set of financials isn't the vast array of rules used by US GAAP or IFRS, but an appreciation of the terminology and what it means.

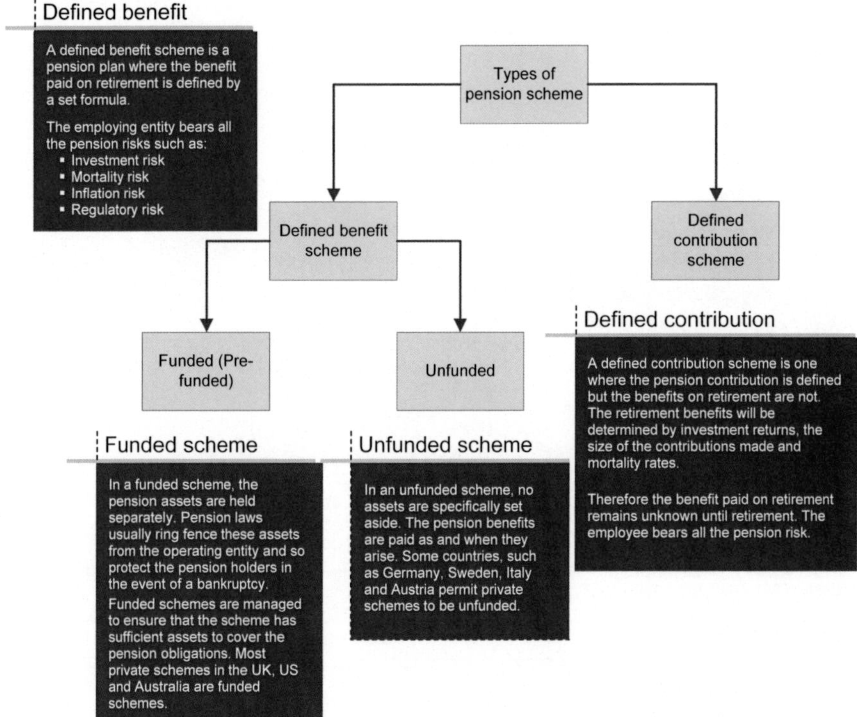

A defined benefit scheme can be under-funded or over-funded. An under-funded scheme is a defined benefit scheme that has insufficient pension assets to cover the pension obligations. This is more often known as a pension deficit.

An over-funded scheme has pension assets in excess of the pension obligations.

Pension accounting – defined contribution scheme

The accounting for a defined contribution scheme is straightforward. The employing entity's contributions to the employee's pension account are charged to the income statement in the same way as any other salary or wage. The contribution is merely an expense.

Pension accounting – defined benefit scheme

The accounting for a defined benefit scheme is more complicated. A significant issue is the global inconsistency of the accounting rules. From an Analyst's perspective, a detailed knowledge of the 'world's' accounting rules isn't of great assistance in a practical situation. The detailed knowledge is not the key skill – the Analyst's key skill is the ability to manage the pension disclosure in the financials and pick out and adjust the key metrics.

What are the key issues?

A defined benefit scheme guarantees a pension to its employees on retirement. This obligation accrues over the employee's service period. The value of the obligation is normally calculated by an actuary.

This valuation is a discounted cash flow valuation driven by a number of assumptions such as:

- Discount rates
- Wage inflation
- Rates of investment return
- Anticipated mortality rates during and after employment
- Rates of employee turnover
- Age, sex and marital status of the members

Funded defined benefit schemes will invest in assets normally managed by an asset manager in order to satisfy the pension obligation. The asset manager will hold a portfolio of assets such as:

- Equities
- Bonds
- Property
- Cash

The key issue for a number of entities running defined benefit schemes is that the pension assets are insufficient to cover the pension obligations. The pension schemes are under-funded or are in deficit.

The schemes may be in deficit due to:

- The assets being hit hard as a result of overweight equity portfolios during an equity bear market
- An increase in life expectancies
- Falling interest rates which reduce investment returns, whilst also increasing the present value of obligations

Current accounting rules around the globe often fail to recognize in full on the balance sheet the economic position or funded status of the defined benefit pension scheme. A number of accounting frameworks artificially attempt to smooth the volatility associated with the pension numbers. The impact of the smoothing often distorts the numbers in the income statement and the balance sheet.

The table below summarizes the key accounting rules and treatments currently in use:

	UK FRS 17	Old US FAS 87	New US FAS 158	IFRS IAS 19
Is the deficit on balance sheet in full?	☑	X	☑	☑ X
Is the service cost the only pension cost above EBIT?	☑	X	X	☑ X
Is the interest cost charged to the interest line?	☑	X	X	☑ X
What is the level of analysis risk?	☺	⚠	⚠	⚠

IFRS IAS 19 has a number of acceptable pension treatments.

An Analyst is not expected to know all of these rules. As the table above outlines, most accounting frameworks carry some level of analysis risk.

A good knowledge of the terminology and the pension disclosures is more than sufficient to allow Analysts to adjust the required metrics.

A review of the terminology in the financials

The pension terminology is best illustrated with a real set of financials. Cadbury plc has an excellent set of pension disclosures in their financials.

The key terms to appreciate are:

- Current service cost
- Interest cost
- Actuarial gains and losses
- Benefits paid
- Expected returns on plan assets

The Cadbury pension extract below is the movement on the pension (or benefit) obligation and the plan assets. This format of disclosure is reasonably consistent globally and will normally be found in the notes to the accounts.

25. Retirement benefit obligations continued

Changes in the present value of the defined benefit obligation are as follows:

	£m	£m
Opening defined benefit obligation	(2,665)	(2,744)
Current service cost	(62)	(76)
Curtailment gain	10	1
Interest cost	(146)	(143)
Actuarial gains	197	207
Contributions by employees	(5)	(6)
Liabilities extinguished on settlements	–	6
Demerger of Americas Beverages	261	–
Exchange differences	(233)	(40)
Benefits paid	116	130
Closing defined benefit obligation	**(2,527)**	**(2,665)**

The current service cost is the present value of the pension benefits earned during the period by the active employees. It is the operating cost of the pension scheme for the period.

The interest cost represents the unwinding of the discount on the pension obligation. The obligation is 1 period closer to settlement and hence the value of the obligation increases. This is a financial cost.

Actuarial gains or losses are gains and losses arising from changes in actuarial assumptions and differences between these assumptions and what actually occurred during the period. Actuarial gains and losses affect the pension obligation and the asset.

Benefits paid to current pensioners reduce the pension obligation and require a corresponding liquidation of pension assets.

Of the £2,527 million of defined benefit obligations above, £114 million (2007: £94 million) are in respect of unfunded schemes. Of the remaining obligation of £2,413 million, assets of £2,269 million are held.

Changes in the fair value of these scheme assets are as follows:

Opening fair value of scheme assets	2,745	2,540
Expected return	172	172
Actuarial (losses)/gains	(585)	11
Contributions by employees	5	6
Contributions by employer – normal	54	72
Contributions by employer – additional	30	48
Assets utilised in settlements	–	(6)
Demerger of Americas Beverages	(224)	–
Exchange differences	188	32
Benefits paid	(116)	(130)
Closing fair value of scheme assets	**2,269**	**2,745**

The expected return is the expected income derived from the plan assets (interest, dividend etc). The difference between the expected return and the actual return is captured in the actuarial gain or loss.

Source: Cadbury plc Annual Report

Treatment of the income statement pension numbers

Whilst the disclosure of the fair value of plan assets and the pension obligation are relatively consistent internationally, the income statement disclosure can be inconsistent.

A defined benefit scheme will generate three key income statement numbers:

- Current service cost
- Interest cost
- Expected returns on plan assets

Intuitively these numbers should be dealt with as follows:

- Current service cost – above EBIT as an operating expense
- Interest cost – below EBIT as part of financial expense
- Expected returns on plan assets – below EBIT as part of financial income

However, intuition is not an assumption to be made with the financials. There are two generally accepted treatments for these pension numbers:

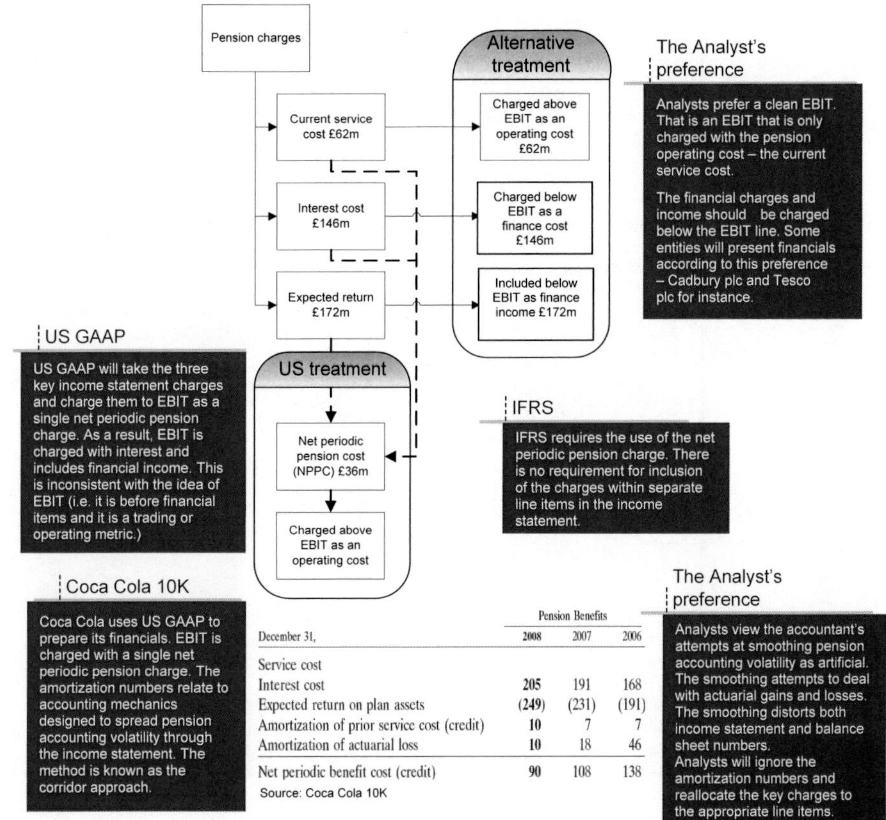

	Pension Benefits		
December 31,	**2008**	2007	2006
Service cost			
Interest cost	**205**	191	168
Expected return on plan assets	**(249)**	(231)	(191)
Amortization of prior service cost (credit)	**10**	7	7
Amortization of actuarial loss	**10**	18	46
Net periodic benefit cost (credit)	**90**	108	138

Source: Coca Cola 10K

Adjusting Metrics for Pensions

As outlined above, financials often do not recognize the funded or economic status of the pension scheme on the balance sheet. Most Analysts believe that the actual pension status should be included in the financials. If it is not, then the metrics extracted from the financials should be adjusted for the pension status when necessary.

To what extent the pension deficit should be included in the metrics for analysis, depends on the type of scheme (funded or unfunded) operated by the company. Cadbury operates both funded and unfunded pension schemes.

A funded scheme

The previous Cadbury's pension example discloses that Cadbury runs funded and unfunded schemes (see the written narrative below the pension obligation table). This narrative allows us to isolate the pension deficit in relation to each scheme. The funded scheme details are below:

	£m
Pension assets	2,269
Pension obligation with respect to funded schemes	2,413
Pension deficit (funded scheme)	£144

If there is a funded pension deficit (i.e. the plan assets are insufficient to cover the pension obligations), the number should be treated as debt-like due to the contractual obligations the entity will have to its employees.

Some Analysts will anticipate a deferred tax benefit in relation to this adjustment. The decision whether to include the deferred tax benefit depends on the Analyst's view surrounding the time and certainty of the tax adjustment. A prudent approach would be to include the pension adjustment before any tax adjustment.

Analysts will then ensure that the income statement numbers (especially EBIT) are correctly stated – that is EBIT is only charged with the current service cost.

EBIT	X
Add back: all pension costs charged to EBIT	X
Less: Current service cost	(X)
EBIT (pension adjusted)	X

This adjustment is only necessary if EBIT has been charged or credited with non-operating charges. This is usually the case when the entity has charged a net periodic pension cost to EBIT.

Reviewing the notes to Cadbury's accounts it is clear that the entity has charged the pension charges to the appropriate line items in the income statement.

Adjusting Metrics for Pensions (cont.)

An unfunded scheme

£114m of the Cadbury pension obligation is in relation to unfunded schemes. There are no pension assets set aside in relation to this obligation. Most Analysts will treat this pension obligation as part debt-like.

Even though there are no pension assets set aside to fund the scheme, the payment requirements are normally sufficiently predictable to allow entities enough time to raise the necessary finance to fund the obligation. Assuming that entities have open access to the capital markets to raise this finance, Analysts can assume that the obligation will be funded using the entity's target debt to equity mix. If the entity has excess liquid resources, Analysts can assume these resources will be used to fund the unfunded pension obligation prior to calling on the capital markets for funding.

Using Cadbury's unfunded obligation as an example:

The unfunded obligation	£114m
Excess liquid resources (estimated)	£48m
Unfunded obligation to fund	£66m
Cadbury estimated target debt /(debt + equity) mix	23%
Unfunded obligation treated as debt-like	£15.18m

The £15.18m will then be used as a basis to adjust the income statement interest charge.

Pulling out a Net Debt Metric from the Financials: Part 4

Continuing with the background net debt example for Cadbury – if the pension deficit is treated as debt-like it should be included in the adjusted net debt metrics.

Using the above calculations, the net debt adjusted for operating lease commitments and the pension deficits for Cadbury would be:

	£m
On-balance sheet net debt	1,885
Plus: capitalized operating lease commitment	270
Plus: pension deficit (funded)	144
Plus: pension deficit (unfunded)	15
Net debt adjusted	2,314

Funded pension surplus

No adjustment should be made to net debt if an entity has a pension surplus. These excess plan assets cannot be used to pay down existing debt, as these assets are normally ring-fenced from the company.

Balance Sheet Liabilities

Pension issues – where are the problems?

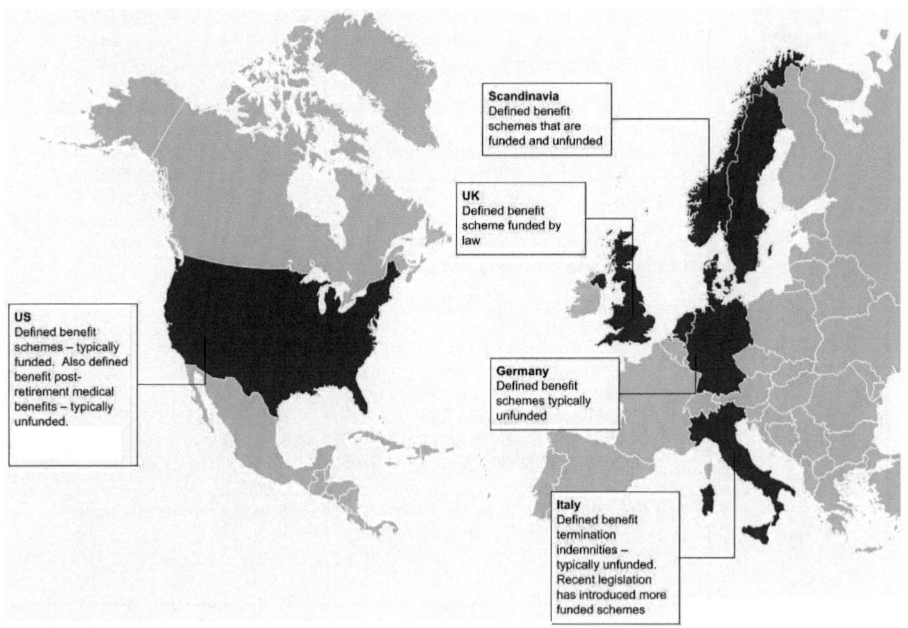

Pensions can be Deal Breakers in M&A

Pensions can become central issues in M&A deals.The Alliance Boots/ KKR deal in 2007 is a good example of pension issues causing real headaches for bankers in a deal. The KKR deal had been approved by the shareholders. However there had been no real consideration of the pension scheme. The pension scheme at the time was running a surplus and was not seen as a particularly significant issue. The pension scheme argued for a £1bn injection. KKR as you can imagine argued a £1bn injection for a scheme already in surplus was unreasonable. Arguments and negotiations followed. Eventually the deal cleared, but only after KKR agreed to inject £418m over ten years.

The pension scheme has power. Their upfront demands can be material in terms of the deal size.

Deferred tax

Deferred tax is an important concept for an Analyst to understand. However the rules are complicated and detailed and professional advice should be sought before advising a client on potential tax issues.

Therefore this section focuses on the concept of deferred tax and the circumstances when deferred tax issues may arise.

Most transactions that an entity makes will have a tax consequence. The tax consequence can be immediate or it can happen in the future (deferred). For instance, if an entity purchases some PPE, it will receive a tax deduction over an extended period of time. Some of the tax impact is deferred to later periods. However if the entity makes a sale the tax consequences are probably immediate.

If an entity enters into a transaction that results in a deferred tax consequence, whether it is a future benefit or cost, the financials will often attempt to account for the consequence.

For instance:

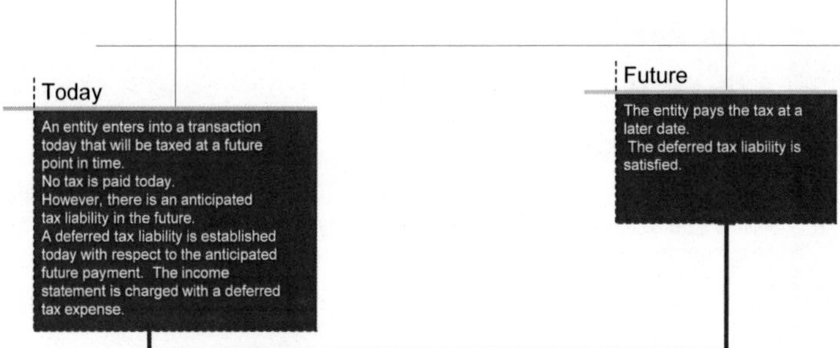

When Should Deferred Tax Issues be Anticipated?

Deferred tax issues potentially arise:

- On an M&A transaction when the target entity's balance sheet is revalued to fair value.
- When entities recognize provisions (see later notes) in their financials. Provisions normally do not qualify for tax deductions until the expenditure is actually incurred.
- If an entity has made tax losses and the tax losses can be carried forward to set off against future taxable earnings.
- If an entity purchases PPE and is able to claim accelerated capital allowances (tax depreciation allowances).
- If an entity enters into new finance lease arrangements.
- If an entity runs a pension scheme.

Provisions

A provision is a liability where there is uncertainty surrounding the amount and/or the timing.

A provision must satisfy the following criteria:

- There must be a past event
- That creates an obligation
- That leads to a probable outflow

When a provision is recognized in the financials, it leads to a charge to the income statement and hence reduces earnings.

Probable Definitions

US GAAP defines probable as likely to occur.

In practice, this is taken as meaning a probability of >75%. IFRS defines probable as more likely than not to occur. In practice this is taken to be a probability in excess of 50%.

The US GAAP probable definition is narrower than IFRS. The IFRS definition could lead to situations where a provision might be recorded (and hence expense recognition) earlier than under the US GAAP rules.

Typical provisions found in the financials could be related to:

- Litigation
- Warranties
- Restructuring
- Decommissioning
- Environmental issues

Earnings Management with Provisions

Provisions can be used to manage earnings. Establishing a provision in the financials will result in an increase in liabilities and an earnings reducing charge to the income statement.

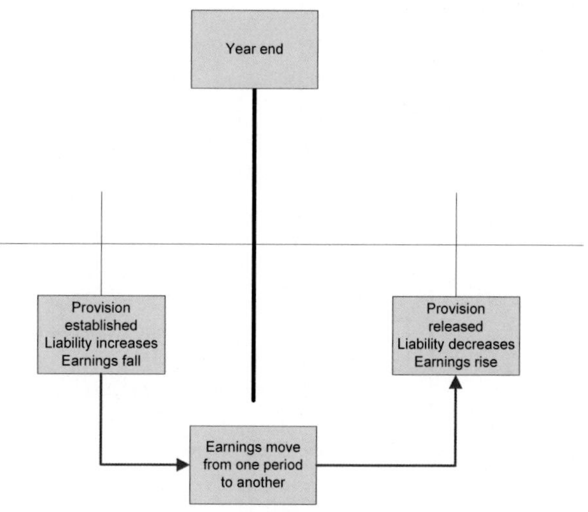

If the same provision is then reversed in the following year, the liability would be removed and there would be an enhancement to earnings. Earnings have been moved from one period to another, purely through the use of some basic accounting.

The recognition requirements for there to be a past event that creates an obligation has greatly reduced the abuse of this area in the financials. However, its use to smooth earnings between periods is still prevalent.

The method is used in good years for instance to reduce excess earnings and to hold these excess earnings on the balance sheet in the form of a provision. A possible reason for this may be a desire to reduce current earnings, so that broker and shareholder expectations are not exceeded. The earnings held on the balance sheet can be released if and when earnings take a downward turn at some stage in the future.

Provisioning is also an issue in the bad years. If an entity is going to miss expectations materially, there is an argument that all the bad news stored up in the business should be released to the market in one period. If the news is going to be bad, it may as well be very bad. Provisions in this context are used to clean up the financials. At least all the bad news is out in one period and the next period starts with a clean slate.

Tick-sheet – Liabilities

Liabilities:

- Obligations arising from past events to third parties

Net debt:

- Net debt = Borrowings - (Cash + Liquid resources)
- Borrowings include:
  - Debt and bank loans
  - Financial (capital) leases
- Cash – highly liquid demand deposits (< 1 working day / 24 hours)
- Liquid resources include:
  - Cash equivalents – maturity < 90 days
  - Highly liquid short-term investments
- Net debt can be adjusted for:
  - Present value of operating lease commitments
  - Funded pension deficits
  - Unfunded pension deficits (at target debt/debt+equity mix)

Debt:

- Normally accounted for at amortized cost (can be held AFVTPL)
- Full interest cost is spread through the income statement using the effective interest rate
- Embedded derivatives may be separated from host contracts

Leasing:

- Operating and finance (capital) leases
- Finance (capital) leases:
  - Asset and debt recognition
  - Interest and depreciation charge to the income statement
  - No impact on EBITDA
- Operating leases:
  - No asset and debt recognition
  - Operating lease charge to the income statement
  - Analysts convert into debt-like obligations.
  - Often adjusted in net debt metrics
- Two methods:
  - Factor model
  - DCF model

Tick-sheet – Liabilities (cont.)

Pensions:

- Defined benefit and contribution schemes
- Key Analyst skills:
  - Ability to interpret the notes to the financials
  - Identify the funded/economic status of the schemes
  - Only current service costs deducted from EBIT
- Defined benefit deficits often treated as debt-like obligations
- Often adjusted in net debt metrics
- Pensions can be a key deal issue in M&A transactions

Deferred taxes:

- Future tax issues arising from current transactions
- Key issue in M&A transactions – fair value revaluations

Provisions:

- Liabilities where there is uncertainty as to the amount and timing of the outflow
- Can be used to smooth earnings

Introduction

Equity is a widely used term that has several meanings. It can simply refer to investing in shares or common stocks and it can be used within a valuation context to refer to the book value or market value of shares. In a set of financials, equity refers to the numbers that appear normally at the bottom of the balance sheet. Equity in a balance sheet will encompass an entity's equity instruments and its reserves.

This area is referred to under a variety of names:

- Equity
- Shareholders' funds
- Shareholders' equity
- Stockholders' equity
- Capital and reserves

Reserves can include:

- Revaluation reserves
- Translation reserves
- Buyback reserves
- Legal reserves
- Retained earnings

From an accounting perspective, equity is a residual claim that the equity holders have on the net assets of an entity.

Issued equity is initially recorded at proceeds less transaction cost and is not revalued to fair value.

Types of equity

There are many different types of equity instrument an entity can issue. For instance, a company can issue:

- Ordinary shares or common stocks
- Preferred shares
- Redeemable shares
- Non-redeemable shares

Whether the instrument is classified as equity depends on whether there is an obligation to transfer economic benefits. If there is an obligation, the likelihood is that the instrument will be classified as a liability, rather than equity. For instance, ordinary shares or common stocks have no obligation to pay to a dividend and therefore will be classified as equity.

However, redeemable preferred stocks that have a mandatory dividend will be classified as liabilities.

Paid-in capital/additional paid-in capital

Paid-in capital refers to the value of the shareholder investment injected into the entity. If an entity issues, say, £1m equity for cash, the cash received will be recorded as an asset. However, the dual effect is that £1m belongs to the shareholders and so is recorded in equity as paid-in capital.

Equity shares can be issued at amounts greater than their face or nominal value. If an entity issues an equity share for £10 with a nominal (or par) value of £1, the £1 is recorded in the share capital or common stock account and the premium, £9, is recorded in the share premium or additional paid-in capital account ('premium accounts'). If this was the case with the £1m equity issue, £100,000 would be recorded within share capital or common stock and £900,000 would be recoded within the share premium or additional paid-in capital account.

Commercial law will govern the use of the share premium or additional paid-in capital account.

Bonus issues

A bonus issue is an issue of free shares to existing shareholders. There is no cash inflow arising from the share issue. Bonus issues are also known as scrip or capitalization issues.

The bonus issue is capitalizing part of the entity's distributable reserves, usually retained earnings.

Entities may have a bonus issue in order to:

- Manage the share price
- Improve the liquidity of its shares

Number of outstanding shares (NOSH)

The number of outstanding shares, commonly abbreviated to NOSH, is a key metric for computing the market capitalization, enterprise value and various multiple calculations. Although it would seem to be a straightforward figure to find or calculate, it can be a tricky metric to pick up in practice. There are two particular issues that give rise to the difficulty:

- Getting an up-to-date number. Most calculations involving NOSH require an up-to-date number. The issue is financials are only published periodically. In the US, entities report on a quarterly basis. For many parts of the world, the frequency of reporting is at best twice a year.
- The variety of terminology. There are a number of 'NOSH' numbers in the financials. The key skill is navigating the myriad of terminology and picking up the appropriate metric.

28. Capital and reserves
(a) Share capital of Cadbury plc

	£m
Authorised share capital:	
Ordinary shares (2008: 2,500 million of 10p each, 2007: 3,200 million of 12.5p each)	250
Allotted, called up and fully paid share capital:	
Ordinary shares (2008: 1,361 million of 10p each, 2007: 2,109 million of 12.5p each)	136

Source: Cadbury plc Annual Report

Shareholders' equity:		
Preferred stock ($0.10 par value; 100 shares authorized, none issued)	—	—
Common stock ($0.10 par value; 11,000 shares authorized, 3,925 and 3,973 issued and outstanding at January 31, 2009 and January 31, 2008, respectively)	393	397
Capital in excess of par value	3,920	3,028
Retained earnings	63,660	57,319
Accumulated other comprehensive (loss) income	(2,688)	3,864
Total shareholders' equity	65,285	64,608
Total liabilities and shareholders' equity	$163,429	$163,514

Source: Wal-Mart Stores, Inc. 10K

Share capital information can be found either on the face of the balance sheet (typically under US GAAP) or in the notes to the accounts (IFRS). Either way the following terms are likely to be disclosed:

Authorized

Authorized shares refer to the maximum number of shares an entity can issue.

Issued

Issued share capital is the actual number of shares the entity has issued. It includes all the shares that are in public hands as well as shares that are restricted. Restricted shares or stock have transaction restrictions placed on them. Although the rights to these shares are restricted, they are still classified as issued.

The issued number of shares will fluctuate over time as the entity issues new shares or buys back existing shares. New shares issued can take the form of:

- Equity placements
- Rights issues
- Exercise of share options and warrants

The issued number of shares is a key number that is often used in various per share metrics. The most accurate analysis will require the actual number of issued shares on any given day. The problem is the number in the financials is likely to be out of date for analysis purposes. However, the issued number of shares in the financials acts as an excellent starting point for the analysis.

Outstanding

Not all issued shares are classed as outstanding.

The outstanding number of shares is the issued number of shares, net of treasury shares which are those shares that have been bought back by the entity. See below.

Treasury shares

Treasury shares (or stock) are shares that have been acquired by the entity. The shares have not been canceled and so could be re-issued in the future. Entities may acquire shares:

- As part of a buyback programmed
- To satisfy the exercise of equity share options
- To return surplus cash to shareholders
- To manage their capital structure

If an entity acquires its own equity instruments, the instruments are presented as a deduction against equity. No profit or loss is recognized in the income statement.

Treasury shares are described as issued, but not outstanding shares.

Weighted average NOSH

The weighted average NOSH is a number that is only relevant for earnings per share calculations.

Market capitalization calculations and valuations require an up-to-date number of shares for an accurate result. The published financials are normally out of date for this purpose.

Current NOSH numbers can be sourced from data service providers like Bloomberg, FactSet, CAPIQ and Thomson. Care should be taken with these numbers as they are not always kept sufficiently up-to-date. Reliance on these numbers is risky. They should only be relied on if the calculations will be used for quick and dirty estimates. In any case, if the data service number is to be relied upon, it is advisable to cross-check the numbers against a second data source.

If the NOSH number is being used for a client presentation or a deal deliverable, then it may be worth rolling forward the NOSH number from the financials to the calculation date, using stock exchange announcements. The published NOSH will be correct per the date of the financial's period end.

Most stock exchanges will announce equity issues and buybacks. The information is public and normally easily accessible. A print-off of these announcements will provide sufficient information to roll forward the NOSH number to the calculation date.

NOSH M&A

NOSH for a standard market capitalization calculation needs to be the outstanding shares for a particular date. The NOSH number in the financials will be the issued and outstanding shares, including restricted shares but net of treasury shares.

In a valuation situation the NOSH will usually capture the impact of the in-the-money options dilution. That is, the current share price will be used to estimate the number of in-the-money options that would be exercised. These extra in-the-money shares will then be used in the diluted market capitalization calculation.

In an M&A situation the NOSH will capture the in-the-money options (whether vested or not – i.e. capable of exercise). The extension of this definition attempts to capture the impact of change of control clauses (and therefore the in-the-money options which would also have to be bought out) that would be invoked on acquisition.

NOSH Summary

NOSH summary

The correct number of outstanding shares (often referred to as the 'NOSH') is a key number in comps and DCF valuations when attempting to quantify the equity value per share. Many Analysts make serious and material errors with this number – it seems like it should be an easy number to identify – it isn't:

Authorized share capital	The maximum number of shares issued by a company
Issued share capital	The number of shares issued by the company
Outstanding share capital	The issued number of shares net of treasury shares
Outstanding (public valuation)	Includes potential dilutive securities (outstanding and ITM)
Outstanding (M&A)	Includes potential dilutive securities (change of control capture) Include whether or not vested/exercisable

Types of reserves

Distributable vs. non-distributable reserves

Distributable refers to whether a dividend can be paid out of a reserve. The non-distributable reserve forms part of the creditor protection rules. The idea is that if a reserve is non-distributable and cannot be paid out to shareholders, there must be net asset value left in the entity that can be liquidated in the event of a bankruptcy. This offers some credit protection to preferential creditors of the entity.

These rules are country specific and are based on commercial law.

Revaluation reserves

An upward revaluation of PPE results in an increase in PPE. However, the gain cannot be disclosed in the income statement as it is unrealized. Instead the gain is recognized as a revaluation reserve within equity. The reserve is non-distributable.

Only when the revalued asset is sold will the revaluation reserve become distributable. At this point, the revaluation reserve is transferred to retained earnings.

Retained earnings

Retained earnings are the accumulated net earnings of an entity that have been reinvested back into the entity (after dividend payments).

Retained earnings are also known as:

- Reinvested earnings
- Retained profit
- Revenue reserves
- Profit and loss reserve or account

Retained earnings are a distributable reserve.

Dividends

Dividends are distributions to equity holders. Broadly speaking, dividends can only be paid if there are sufficient distributable reserves.

Legal (or statutory) reserves

Legal reserves are used by a number of countries to offer additional creditor protection in the event of a bankruptcy.

In Sweden for example, incorporated companies are required to allocate 10% of the profits per year as legal reserves until the legal reserves are at least 20% of the start-up capital.

In the Czech Republic, limited liability companies must set up a reserve fund of at least 10% of the share capital.

Mexican incorporated companies must allocate 5% of annual profits to a reserve until the reserve totals 20% of the capital.

Non-controlling interests

Non-controlling interests are relevant only to group financials. They are a component of equity and represent that part of the net assets of a subsidiary that is not own by the parent company.
A non-controlling interest only arises when a parent does not own the entirety of the subsidiary.

Non-controlling interests are also known as minority interests.

See later M&A accounting notes in Chapter 10.

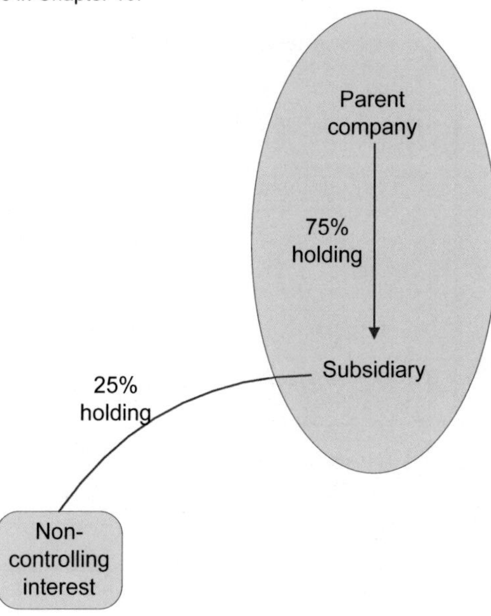

The equity section of the balance sheet masquerades as a number of different terms:

- Equity
- Shareholders' funds
- Shareholders' equity
- Stockholders' equity
- Capital and reserves

The important NOSH terms:

- Authorized
- Issued
- Outstanding
- Treasury shares
- NOSH M&A

Typical reserves can include:

- Revaluation reserves
- Translation reserves
- Buyback reserves
- Legal reserves

Introduction

The income statement is a statement of financial performance. It discloses the income generated and expenses incurred by an entity over a period.

The income statement is a key statement for Analysts to fully understand:

- As it provides the basis for many of the metrics used in analysis
- A number of income statement metrics are used for valuation multiples
- The income statement is used in the initial stages of a DCF valuation

The income statement is constructed on the foundations of the accruals concept. That is revenues are matched with the costs associated with the revenue generation and as far as possible, recognized in the period when revenue is earned or expense incurred. There is no necessary direct relationship with cash flow.

Revenue recognition

Revenue is defined by accountants with reference to inflows of economic benefit arising during the course of the ordinary activities. This type of definition is not that helpful to Analysts. In this context, revenue is best thought of in terms of examples.

Revenues are generated by:

- Providing products
- The provision of services

Revenue has a variety of names such as:

- Sales
- Turnover
- Fees

The most significant issue concerning revenue is how to determine when to recognize in the income statement. That is, when is the revenue actually earned?

When an entity sells a product to a customer, it is normally clear that the revenue is earned at the point of sale. However, it does become a more involved task if there is a longer-term contract and the revenue is earned over a longer period. Should the revenue be recognized in the income statement at the start of the contract, as the contract progresses or at the end of the contract?

There is a whole raft of issues that arise with revenue recognition.

Rather than examine a multitude of possible examples, Analysts should consider some key revenue recognition concepts. Revenue should be recognized in the income statement if:

- Work has been performed
- The revenue can be measured reliably
- Recoverability is reasonably assured

The substance of the transaction should be the focus of recognition rather than the legal form. Cash received in advance of the performance of work cannot be recognized as revenue. The cash will be recognized as an asset, but performance is still owed. Therefore a liability for this 'owed' performance will be recognized on the balance sheet. The liability is often called deferred income.

Earnings metrics

An earnings metric is a key earnings line within the income statement. Metrics are used extensively in analysis and valuation. Examples of earnings metrics are:

- Gross profit
- Operating profit / EBIT – often used interchangeably but beware of brokers and others treating them in different ways
- EBITA
- EBITDA
- EBITDAR

Analysts must have a strong understanding of these metrics, their definitions and inherent weaknesses.

Types of earnings metrics

Gross profit

Gross profit is defined as:

Revenues	X
Costs of sales	(X)
Gross profit	**X**

Gross profit is not a commonly used metric in analysis and valuation as it ignores significant operating costs such as selling, general and administration costs (SG&A). However, it does provide a quick view on the direct profitability of the entity.

Operating profit (EBIT)

Operating profit is defined as:

Revenues	X
Costs of sales	(X)
SG&A	(X)
Operating profit (EBIT)	**X**

Operating profit or EBIT (Earnings before interest and tax) as it is more commonly known by Analysts is a very common metric. It provides profitability information about an entity's trading operations. How much does an entity make from its normal trading operations? The metric takes into consideration all operating expenses including overheads.

A major weakness with the EBIT metric is that it is after the deduction of depreciation and amortization. Hence the metric is open to manipulation and leads to comparability issues between different time periods and between entities.

What is EBITA?

Some Analysts will make reference to EBITA, where they treat 'A' as the amortization of goodwill. Given that goodwill is no longer systematically amortized, the 'A' is largely redundant and therefore the metric can be treated as the same as EBIT. Many Analysts will classify any amortization associated with other intangibles as depreciation. Therefore, EBITA is only before the amortization of goodwill – which as mentioned is normally zero.

EBITDA

EBITDA is defined as earnings before interest, tax, depreciation and amortization.

Revenues	X
Costs of sales	(X)
SG&A	(X)
Operating profit (EBIT)	**X**
Add back: Depreciation	X
Add back: Amortization	X
EBITDA	**X**

EBITDA is a very commonly used metric in analysis and valuation. The popularity of the metric is due to the fact it ignores the noise created by D&A. As mentioned in the chapter on balance sheet assets, D&A are accounting mechanics that can be easily manipulated in the financials. This leads to comparability issues. Focusing on EBITDA makes it easier to compare the performance of different entities.

EBITDA is often described as a proxy for operating cash flow. Although this is a risky assumption to make, it does have elements of truth. D&A are non-cash items and EBITDA does ignore them. Hence the metric is closer to operating cash flow than to EBIT. However, EBITDA is not operating cash flow as it ignores the movements in working capital and other possible non-cash items.

EBITDAR

EBITDAR is defined as earnings before interest, tax, depreciation, amortization and operating lease rentals.

Revenues	X
Costs of sales	(X)
SG&A	(X)
Operating profit (EBIT)	**X**
Add back: Depreciation	X
Add back: Amortization	X
Add back: Rentals (on operating leases)	X
EBITDAR	**X**

EBITDAR is a metric associated with entities that lease assets. The chapter on balance sheet liabilities discussed the accounting and analysis issues surrounding leasing. The existence of operating and finance lease accounting treatments creates comparability difficulties in the income statement.

EBITDA is where the main issues arises. EBITDA ignores the full impact of finance (or capital) leases in the income statement, namely depreciation and interest. However EBITDA is still calculated after the deduction of operating lease rentals.

In order to present a comparable metric between entities, EBITDAR is before deducting operating lease rentals. The EBITDAR metric is therefore before any leasing charges, irrespective of the nature of the lease.

Non-recurring items

A non-recurring or exceptional item is an item that is normally recorded in the income statement that falls outside the normal activities of the business. The definitions of these items and the terminology used are inconsistent between US GAAP and IFRS – see below.

However, from an Analyst's perspective, whether a term is classified by accountants as exceptional or non-recurring is less important. What is important is to make a judgment as to whether a metric should be adjusted or normalized to remove items that are unlikely to recur.

Common examples of non-recurring items are:

- Asset write downs or impairments
- Restructuring costs
- Profits and losses on disposals of PPE
- Litigation expenses

Ten Critical Failings of EBITDA

The use of EBITDA has become so popular over the years that there is a tendency for Analysts to over rely on the metric. One metric cannot cover all forms of analysis. The metric is also best analyzed by looking at each of the components of the metric:

EBIT

D

A

EBITDA

For instance, the greater the proportion of EBITDA derived from EBIT, the stronger the operating cash flows will be.

Moody's has produced some excellent research that examines EBITDA and outlined ten critical failings with the metric.

The ten critical failings of EBITDA:

1. Ignores changes in working capital and overstates cash flow in periods of working capital growth
2. Can be a misleading measure of liquidity
3. Does not consider the amount of required reinvestment – especially for companies with short-lived assets
4. Says nothing about the quality of earnings
5. Is an inadequate standalone measure for comparing acquisition multiples
6. Ignores distinctions in the quality of cash flow resulting from differing accounting policies – *not* all revenues are cash
7. Is not a common denominator for cross-border accounting conventions
8. Offers limited protection when used in indenture covenants
9. Can drift from the realm of reality
10. Is not well suited for the analysis of many industries because it ignores their unique attributes

Source: *Putting EBITDA in Perspective – Ten Critical Failings of EBITDA* Moody's June 2000

Warren Buffet has for a long time been a strong critic of EBITDA. His view was quite nicely summed up by Charlie Munger, Buffet's long-term business partner, as follows:

> Whenever you read or hear the term EBITDA, you should substitute 'bulls**t accounting'

A little strong, but when it comes from someone involved with such a strong investment fund as Berkshire Hathaway, investors tend to take some notice.

Exceptional Items

IFRS requires that entities that disclose EBIT should include all items of an operating nature. This includes items which are infrequent, irregular or unusual, in other words, items that most Analysts would refer to as being exceptional or non-recurring by nature.

The term exceptional is not actually used or defined in IFRS. However, if an item is sufficiently large to be considered material to the financials, it should be disclosed separately on the face of the income statement.

There is no such thing as an extraordinary item under IFRS.

Exceptional Items

US GAAP does not use the term exceptional items.

Unusual items or infrequently occurring items are reported as part of the income statement below operating profit from continuing operations.

US GAAP does use the term extraordinary items for those items that are infrequent and unusual in nature. They very rarely occur in practice.

Normalizing Earnings Metrics

If an Analyst picks EBIT or operating profit straight from a set of financials, there is a strong possibility that the number will include non-recurring or exceptional items. This poses an analytical issue as the peer group and previous time period data may not be comparable.

Analysts will be required to normalize metrics on a regular basis. Normalizing refers to the stripping out of non-recurring or exceptional items from metrics. The normalizing procedure can be subjective and dependent on an Analyst's own views, but it does improve the comparable qualities of the metric.

Accountants will assist the process of normalization by disclosing what they believe to be material non-recurring items on the face of the income statement. However, Analysts must not just be led by the view of the accountants. Analysts must be prepared to review the notes to the accounts in order to discover additional items that may be considered as non-recurring or exceptional.

Normalizing earnings metrics will also focus attention on whether the numbers are considered core to the entity's operations.

Cadbury provides a good example for normalizing EBIT:

Consolidated income statement for the year ended 31 December 2008

Notes		2008 Underlying[1] £m	2008 Non-underlying[2] £m	2008 Total £m
	Continuing operations			
2	Revenue	5,384	–	5,384
3	Trading costs	(4,746)	(57)	(4,803)
4	Restructuring costs	–	(194)	(194)
5	Non-trading items	–	1	1
	Profit from operations	638	(250)	388
17	Share of result in associates	10	–	10
	Profit before financing and taxation	648	(250)	398

Cadbury plc Annual Report

At first glance, Cadbury discloses two profits from operations. These can be described as EBIT metrics. However, there is a significant difference between the total EBIT of £388m and the underlying EBIT of £638m.
An Analyst must never blindly rely on a metric just because it is described as 'underlying'. The adjustments must be analyzed.

Normalizing Earnings Metrics (cont.)

There are three sets of 'non-underlying' adjustments made to this EBIT number:

- Trading adjustments
- Restructuring adjustments
- Non-trading adjustments

These adjustments amount to £250m in total and so are material to the overall EBIT number.

The next step would be to review the notes to the accounts in order to determine the nature and context of the adjustments.

Note 4 to the income statement provides background detail on the £194m restructuring adjustment. It is clear from the review of the note that these items are not part of the ordinary activities of the business and are sufficiently unusual. An Analyst might reasonably conclude that these numbers should be stripped out of an EBIT metric.

4. Restructuring costs

During 2008, the Group incurred £200 million (2007: £200 million) of restructuring costs. Of this total charge £6 million (2007: £35 million) relates to discontinued operations as disclosed in Note 31(g) and £194 million (2007: £165 million) relates to continuing operations as disclosed below. The Group initiated a restructuring programme in 2007 "Vision into Action", in pursuit of mid-teen margins. The third party supply contract with Gumlink became onerous in 2007 and net penalties payable have been recognised. The costs incurred to effect the separation and creation of a stand-alone confectionery business following the demerger of the Americas Beverages business and the announced sale of Australia Beverages have been classified as restructuring in 2007 and 2008.

	2008 £m	Re-presented 2007 £m
Vision into Action	142	151
Integration costs	9	–
Onerous contract and penalties payable – Gumlink	27	9
Separation and creation of stand-alone confectionery business costs	16	5
	194	165

Of this total charge of £194 million (2007: £165 million), £82 million (2007: £83 million) was redundancy related, £13 million (2007: £19 million) related to external consulting costs and £45 million (2007: £24 million) was associated with onerous contracts. The remaining costs consisted of asset write-offs, site closure costs, relocation costs, distribution contract termination payments and acquisition integration costs. The analysis of these costs by segment is shown below:

A similar exercise must be conducted for the trading and non-trading adjustments.

The adjustments necessary to normalize EBIT would therefore be:

	£m
EBIT per financials	388
Add: Restructuring costs	194
Add: Trading costs	57
Less: Non-trading items	(1)
EBIT (normalized)	638

Care must be taken with the signs on these adjustments. The reversal of an expense from a metric will always be a positive adjustment. The opposite is the case for the reversal of an income item.

Pro-forma Numbers

The term 'pro-forma numbers' has a wide variety of meanings. Pro-forma comes from the Latin 'as a matter of form'. The numbers are prepared in addition to the entity's standard reporting numbers. There is no uniform template for what is a pro-forma number. It is therefore difficult to provide much confidence that pro-forma numbers are comparable with other numbers produced by an entity. Pro-forma numbers are normally in the form of research or press releases. As a result they often (depending on the jurisdiction) do not fall under the remit of regulatory rules. This can lead to the claim that pro-forma numbers 'window dress' the true accounting numbers. During the dot.com boom many tech companies used pro-forma numbers to present an enhanced view of their earnings profiles.

Pro-forma numbers are often adjusted for:

- Exceptional or non-recurring items
- Like-for-like items
- New acquisitions to reflect a full year's worth of earnings from the new acquisitions

Share-based payments

For a number of years entities have issued equity options to their employees as part of their remuneration packages. Historically these schemes have been focused more on rewarding senior management and board level staff. In recent years, this type of remuneration policy has made its way further down the corporate hierarchy.

The majority of schemes are based on the employees satisfying specific performance criteria. Most equity options are issued either at or possibly just out of the money; that is, the option's exercise price is equal to or just above the current market price of the equity at the date of grant. The attraction to the employee is that, for no capital outlay, there is the opportunity to make money if the share price appreciates. Historically equity options have been accounted for by charging the intrinsic value of the option (the excess of the market price over the exercise price of the share at the date of the grant) to the income statement. At the date of grant, most equity options have a zero intrinsic value. Hence the charge to the income statement would be zero.

This view became increasingly dated. Again, a view beautifully summed up by Warren Buffet:

"If options aren't a form of compensation, what are they? If compensation isn't an expense, what is it? And if expenses shouldn't go into the calculations of earnings, where in the world should they go?"

There has been a great deal of resistance to the introduction of accounting rules that charge an expense to the income statement in relation to the issuing of share options. The resisters to these changes have used every argument in the book. Their main arguments are:

- Options do not affect current earnings. The impact on future earnings is subjective. Why introduce more uncertainty and subjective estimation to the financials?
- Option pricing models do not provide sufficiently accurate estimates.
- Expensing the option values will add more volatility to the financial statements over time.
- Expensing options will suppress entrepreneurship. Start-up firms attract talent by offering them an upside on the equity success of the entity. Associate an expense with this mechanism to attract staff and new start-ups will struggle. They will be charging expenses to weak or negative earnings numbers.

Income Statement

The general principle of the accounting now (IFRS and US GAAP) is that the fair value of the option is valued at the grant date (using an option pricing model) and this value is amortized into the income statement over the vesting period of the option. This will result in a non-cash charge above EBIT.

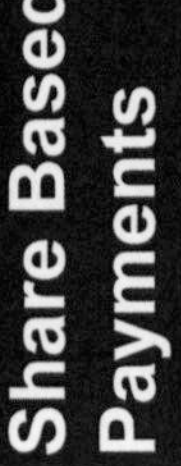

IFRS has a much wider scope for share based payments compared to US GAAP. The IFRS rules scope three key types of transaction:

Equity-settled share-based payment transactions, in which the entity receives goods or services (such as employee services) as consideration for equity instruments of the entity (including shares or share options).

Cash-settled share based payment transactions, in which the entity acquires goods or services by incurring liabilities to the supplier of those goods or services (e.g. employees) for amounts that are based on the price (or value) of the entity's shares or other equity instruments of the entity. Transactions involving share appreciation rights (SARs) fall into this category.

Transactions in which the entity receives or acquires goods or services and the terms of the arrangement provide either the entity or the supplier of those goods or services with a choice of whether the entity settles the transaction in cash (or other assets) or by issuing equity instruments.

There are separate measurement issues with each type of transaction.

From an Analyst's perspective, the most common form of share-based payment is an equity-settled share based payment. The fair value of the options at the date of grant is amortized over the vesting period into the income statement. There will be a corresponding increase in equity as a result.

Share Based Payments

Public companies must use the fair value model to value its options awards as at the grant date.

Earnings per share (EPS)

EPS is a key metric that is used by Analysts across the industry. It is the earnings per ordinary share or common stock. That is the earnings that belong to the ordinary shareholders of the business. Naturally it is a focal point for shareholders.

It is used:

- As a comparison tool between peers (not the most robust tool it must be said)
- To calculate payout ratios and dividend cover
- As a key valuation metric by research brokers
- To quantify earnings growth between periods
- As a variable to calculate P/E multiples
- In merger models to perform EPS accretion/dilution analysis

The metric is however inherently weak and it should be used with care and as a high level analytical tool.

The metric is calculated using information at the very bottom of the income statement. Therefore it is open to manipulation at every level above this bottom line earnings measure. This leads to real issues of comparability between peers and over time.

There are two forms of EPS calculation Analysts must be aware of:

- Basic EPS
- Diluted EPS

In simple terms, EPS is the earnings belonging to the equity shareholders divided by the number of equity shares. The calculation can become increasingly complicated depending on the range and complexity of instruments held by the entity.

Basic EPS

Basic EPS is calculated as follows:

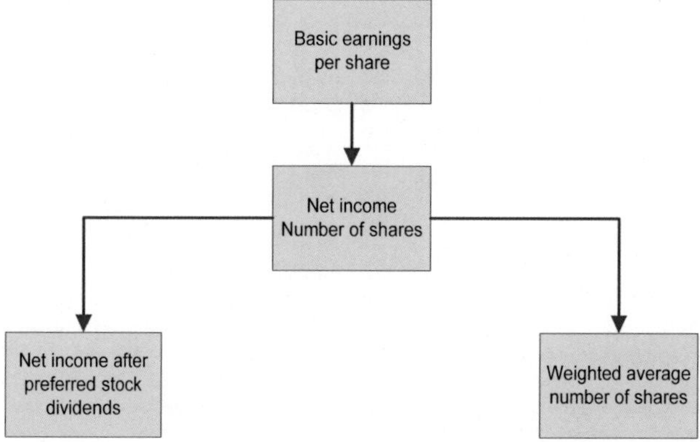

The calculation looks like it should be straightforward; however there are a few complications. The calculation of the net income is reasonably straightforward. The net income is purely the income belonging to equity shareholders or common stockholders of the business.

The complications arise with the weighted average number of shares.

Equity issues during the period

If there are no changes in the equity capital structure during the period, the number of shares included in the EPS calculation will be the number of shares outstanding at the end of the year. However, it is unlikely that an entity will have a static equity capital structure over a period. Small amounts of equity capital can be issued during a period. For instance, share options might be exercised during the period.

If the equity capital does change, it would not be fair to allocate the earnings for the period over the enlarged equity capital base. This is because the equity capital injected into the business as a result of the issue was only available to generate a return for part of the period.

The same thought process is applied to equity bought back during the period.

In order to foster comparability and also to produce a fairer representation of the availability of resources and the generation of earnings over the period, the number of shares included in the EPS calculation is weighted.

This is most effectively demonstrated with an illustration:

An entity has 100,000 equity shares outstanding on January,1. It issues 15,000 new shares to the market on April, 1. Later that year on the November, 1 – it buys back 8,000 shares from the market.

The weighted average number of shares is:

			Weighted average
January 1 to March 31	3/12	100,000	25,000
April 1 to October 31	7/12	115,000	67,083
November 1 to December 31	2/12	107,000	17,833
Weighted average number of shares			109,916

Shares are included in the weighted average calculation from the date consideration is receivable. However the date depends on the circumstances surrounding the issue of the equity:

Equity issue in exchange for cash	Date cash is receivable
Conversion of a debt instrument into shares	Date interest stops accruing
As consideration for an acquisition	Date on which the acquisition is recognized

Bonus issues

A bonus issue is an issue of free shares by the entity. There is no injection of capital into the business or change in resource. The only impact of the issue is to increase the number of shares outstanding. Earnings will therefore not change as a result of the issue. The EPS calculation (and the rules are universal) treats the new bonus shares issued as if they had always been outstanding. This essentially strips out the impact of the bonus issue.

Bonus issue illustration

An entity has 100,000 equity shares outstanding on January, 1. It issues 15,000 new shares to the market on April,1. Later that year on the November, 1 the entity has a bonus issue of one new share for every four existing shares (a 1 for 4 bonus issue).

Earnings are €250,000.

The weighted average number of shares and the EPS are calculated as follows:

		Bonus fraction		Weighted average
January 1 to March 31	3/12	1.25	100,000	31,250
April 1 to October 31	7/12	1.25	115,000	83,854
November 1 to December 31	2/12		143,750[2]	23,958
Weighted average number of shares				139,062
Earnings				250,000
EPS				1.80

A 1 for 4 bonus issue increases the number of shares by 25%. The bonus fraction of 1.25 (5 shares outstanding post-bonus issue ÷ 4 pre-bonus issue) is applied to the weighted average calculation pre-bonus issue, so treating the extra 25% as if they had been in issue for the whole of the period. It would also be necessary to adjust previous years' disclosed EPS calculations so that there is comparability between EPSs.

For example, if the previous year's EPS was 2.04, it would appear that the company's performance has deteriorated over the year. However, this previous EPS should also be adjusted, so treating the new bonus shares issued as if they had always been outstanding. 2.04/1.25 gives 1.63. A comparison of 1.8 (this year) with 1.63 last year shows a growth in EPS of just around 10%.

Rights issues

A rights issue is an issue of shares to existing shareholders at a price below the current market price. A rights issue is a right to buy the shares at a discount, it is not an obligation. The rights can be sold on to other investors.

Why do entities have rights issues? The following are a few possible reasons:

- To raise further finance without accessing the debt capital markets
- So existing shareholders are not diluted on a capital raising
- Cheaper than raising money from the equity capital markets generally
- If the need for further finance is acquisition related, existing shareholders might wish to participate
- A way to inject funds to prevent bankruptcy

As the shares are issued below the current market price, the issue has a bonus element. This bonus element must be identified and adjusted for in the EPS calculation.

The determination of the bonus element of a rights issue is calculated using the theoretical ex-rights price (TERP) method. The TERP is the theoretical price per share after the rights issue.

[2] 115,000 existing shares. A 1 for 4 bonus issue will lead to 28,750 new shares (115,000 ÷ 4). The total number of shares outstanding after the bonus issue is 143,750.

Rights issue illustration:

An entity has 140,000 equity shares outstanding on January, 1. It issues 14,000 new shares to the market on April, 1. Later that year on the August, 1 the entity has a rights issue of one new share for every three existing shares (a 1 for 3 rights issue).

The share price immediately before the rights issue was €40.

The rights issue price is €24.

Earnings for the year are €450,000.

The weighted average number of shares is calculated as follows:

		Bonus fraction		Weighted average
January 1 to March 31	3/12	1.11	140,000	38,889
April 1 to July 31	4/12	1.11	154,000	57,037
August 1 to December 31	5/12		205,333	85,556
Weighted average number of shares				181,481
Earnings				450,000
EPS				€2.48

Ex-rights price:

Value of a 3 share portfolio before the rights issue (pre-rights price €40)	€120
1 new rights issue share value	€24
Therefore ex-rights price per share is (€120+€24) ÷ 4 shares	€36

The bonus fraction = Pre-rights price ÷ Ex-rights price
= €40 ÷ €36
= 1.11

The bonus fraction is applied to all share numbers prior to the rights issue.

It would also be necessary to adjust previous years' disclosed EPS calculations so that there is comparability between EPSs.

Rights Issue Bonus Fraction and Merger Modeling

The bonus fraction calculation is most relevant for Analysts when merger modeling. Merger modeling is covered later. A merger model will run different transaction finance scenarios with a view to producing an optimal capital structure that maximizes EPS accretion whilst maintaining a credible credit rating.

Equity will form part of the transaction finance structure. This equity can be raised in a variety of ways:

- Share for share exchange
- Share placing
- Rights issue

If the merger model runs a rights issue scenario, the bonus fraction on the rights issue may have to be applied to the EPS accretion/dilution analysis.

The bonus fraction is only relevant if the model is set up and:

- It is a mid-year acquisition
- Pro-forma numbers are not used
- It is the initial year of forecast

Rights issues are very rare in the US.

De Beers $1bn Rights Issue

In 2010, De Beers completed a $1bn rights issue. The recession had a major impact on De Beers with earnings falling 99%, net debt increasing to $4bn together with an impending refinancing in March 2010. The rights issue offered a timely cash injection in order to manage these problems.

A De Beers press release stated "By reducing De Beers' level of external debt and improving its capital structure, this investment would better enable the company to take advantage of new opportunities...as the recession gives way to recovery". This was a positive spin on a quite desperate situation.

Diluted EPS

Diluted EPS is a calculation that anticipates the impact of potentially dilutive securities on the EPS number. Diluted EPS acts as a warning to shareholders of the potential earnings dilution.

Typically a diluted EPS calculation is anticipating the impact of:

- Convertible debt
- Convertible preference shares
- Options
- Restricted stocks
- Warrants

A diluted EPS calculation adjusts the basic EPS. Both the earnings numerator and weighted average number of shares denominator must be adjusted.

Earnings dilution

The basic EPS earnings metric is typically adjusted for:

- Dividends on convertible preference shares – if preference shares are converted, more earnings will be available in the numerator in the EPS calculation.
- Interest on convertible debt – if this debt is converted, then less interest hits the income statement. However, less interest means more tax payable, so the adjustment to the earnings number in the numerator is post-tax.

Weighted average number of shares

The basic EPS weighted average number of shares metric is typically adjusted for:

- Shares that may be issued on an anticipated conversion of convertible debt into ordinary shares or common stock.
- Share options if they are currently in-the-money.

The impact of convertible debt on diluted EPS

Claimant 4 SA has a basic EPS of €1.40. This is based on earnings of €140,000 and a basic weighted average number of shares of 100,000. Claimant 4 SA also has a €45,000 5% convertible debt instrument in issue. The instrument is convertible in four years time at a rate of five shares per €10 of convertible debt.

The corporate tax rate is 35%.

The number of new shares that would be issued on conversion would be:

= €45,000 ÷ €10 x 5 shares

= 22,500 potential shares

The conversion would then save interest post-tax of:

= €45,000 x 5% x (1 - 35%)

= £1,463

Therefore the diluted earnings is restated at €141,463.

The diluted EPS is 141,463/122,500 = €1.15.

The impact of share options on diluted EPS

Both IFRS and US GAAP require the use of the treasury stock method to establish the impact of dilution on the EPS.

The treasury stock method assumes that the proceeds an entity receives from the exercise of outstanding in-the-money share options are used to buy back shares at full market price. Therefore the dilution is the difference between the number of shares before the exercise and the number of shares after the exercise (after the theoretical buy back at full market price).

This is most easily demonstrated with an illustration.

Illustration

Claimant 3 Inc has a basic EPS of $3.89. This is based on earnings of $764,400 and a basic weighted average number of shares of 196,600. Claimant 3 Inc has 15,000 stock options outstanding. The options have an exercise (or strike) price of $12.75. The current stock price is $16.00, hence the options are in-the-money.

The treasury stock calculation:

Proceeds received from the option exercise	= Number of options x Exercise price
	= 15,000 x $12.75
	= $191,250

The proceeds are then assumed to be used to buy back shares on the market at the current stock price.

Number of shares bought back	= Options proceeds ÷ Current market price
	= $191,250 ÷ $16.00
	= 11,953

Therefore if 15,000 new shares are issued under the option exercise, but this is followed by a buy back of 11,953 shares at full market value, the net dilution as a result of the anticipated option dilution is 15,000 - 11,953 = 3,047 shares.

This number is added to the basic weighted average number of shares.

The diluted EPS is now therefore	= Earnings ÷ Diluted weighted average shares
	= $764,400 ÷ (196,600 + 3,047)
	= $3.82

Diluted Equity Value and the Treasury Method

The treasury method is a key calculation technique for Analysts to understand. It is also something that many Analysts fail to fully appreciate by the time they have completed the initial training program.

The method is applied when calculating metrics such as diluted equity value (or diluted market capitalization), when completing comparable company analysis and in DCF work.

Basic equity value = Current share price x Number of outstanding shares (NOSH)

Diluted equity value = Current share price x Diluted NOSH

The diluted NOSH is calculated by anticipating the dilutive impact of outstanding in-the-money share options.

No dilution to the current share price is assumed when calculating diluted equity values.

Restricted Stock Rights

Restricted stock rights have become increasingly popular in recent years as an alternative to share options as a way to compensate employees.

Restricted stock rights are also known as:

- Letter stock
- Restricted securities

A restricted stock is a stock which carries restrictions such as it cannot be transferred or sold until certain conditions (e.g. continued employment or some target being achieved) are fulfilled.

Advantages of restricted stock rights:

- Tax authorities might look favorably on their issue as, at the time of the issue of the restricted rights, there may be little value in the securities
- Voting and dividend rights can be attached to the instrument at the entity's discretion during the vesting period

A restricted stock right has an intrinsic value at all times, whereas options on the other hand are worthless if the share price falls below the option's exercise price. If the share price falls after the date of grant, a restricted stock right will always retain some value in the hands of the holder.

Restricted Stock Rights and EPS Dilution

Restricted stock rights have a number of different forms:

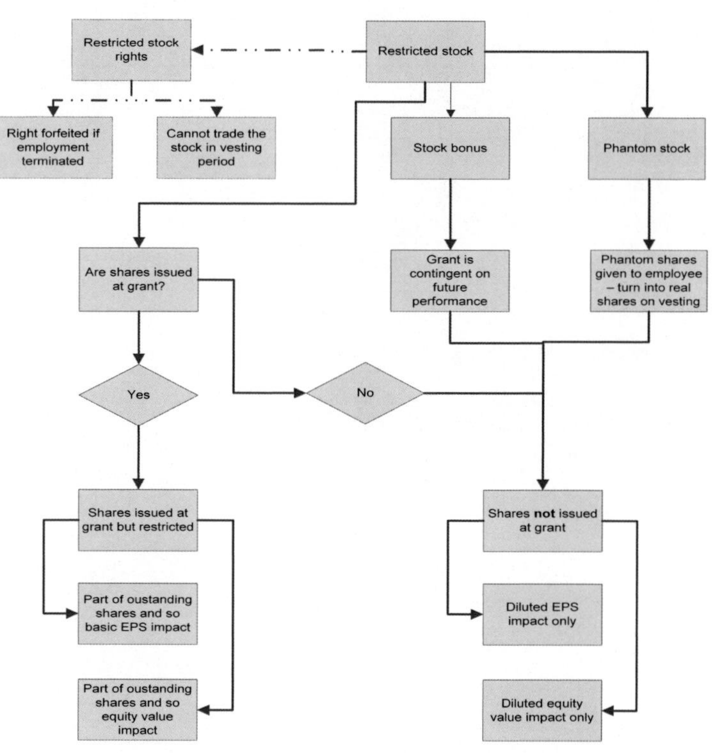

The form of the restricted stock rights impacts the treatment in the diluted EPS and equity value calculations. If a share is issued at grant, but the restriction comes in the form of a non-trading restriction and/or forfeiture on employment termination restriction, the share is classed as issued and outstanding. It is therefore included in the number of outstanding shares number for basic EPS and market capitalization purposes.

If the restricted stock right involves no share issue at the date of grant, the rights are dilutive and the impact should be quantified in the diluted EPS and diluted market capitalization calculations.

Restricted stock rights – Wal-Mart

Restricted stock rights

This is an extract from Walmart's 10K restricted stock note. When analyzing these notes, it is important to determine whether the restricted stock is issued at grant or when the vesting period finishes.

Often it is an interpretation of language. The phrase "Restricted stock rights are associate rights to Company stock after a specified service period" together with the information on the vesting post-granting, suggests that Walmart's restricted stock rights are shares issued at grant that provide full rights at the end of a vesting period.

Therefore, these restricted stock rights will be included in the NOSH number and should not be adjusted for in the diluted EPS calculation.

Source: Wal-Mart Stores, Inc. 10K

In fiscal 2007, the Company began issuing restricted stock rights to most associates in lieu of stock option awards. Restricted stock rights are associate rights to Company stock after a specified service period. Grants issued before fiscal 2009 typically vest over five years with 40% vesting three years from grant date and the remaining 60% vesting five years from grant date. Beginning in fiscal 2009, the vesting schedule was adjusted for new grants to 50% vesting three years from grant date and the remaining 50% vesting five years from grant date. The fair value of each restricted stock right is determined on the date of grant using the stock price discounted for the expected dividend yield through the vesting period. Expected dividend yield over the vesting period is based on the annual dividend rate at the time of grant. The weighted average discount for dividend yield used to determine the fair value of restricted stock rights granted in fiscal 2009, 2008, and 2007 was 6.8%, 8.4% and 6.9%, respectively.

CA Tick-sheet: Income Statement

The income statement:

- A statement of financial performance
- It provides the basis for many of the metrics used in analysis
- A number of income statement metrics are used for valuation multiples
- The income statement is used in the initial stages of a DCF valuation

Key earnings metrics:

- Gross profit
- Operating profit
- EBIT
- EBITA
- EBITDA
- EBITDAR
- Earnings metrics must be normalized for analysis and valuation purposes

Earnings per share:

- Basic vs. diluted EPS
  - EPS uses/aspects:
    - As a comparison tool between peers (not the most robust tool it must be said)
    - To calculate payout ratios and dividend cover
    - Key metric produced by research brokers
    - To quantify earnings growth
    - As a variable to calculate P/E multiples
    - In merger models to perform EPS accretion/dilution analysis
    - Weighted average number of shares
    - Bonus fraction used to adjust for bonus issues
    - Theoretical Ex-Rights Price (TERP) calculated bonus fractions used to adjust for rights issues
    - Right issue bonus fractions are used in merger models
- Diluted EPS:
  - Used to anticipate the potentially dilutive impact of:
    - Convertible debt
    - Convertible preference shares
    - Options
    - Restricted stocks
    - Warrants
  - The treasury method is used to calculate the dilutive impact of share options
  - Restricted stock rights may cause dilutive impacts

Introduction

The construction of the financial statements will be based around the financial statement DNA idea, constructed from five key fragments:

- Assets
- Liabilities
- Equity
- Income
- Expenses

At all times the accounting equation (see below) will be maintained:

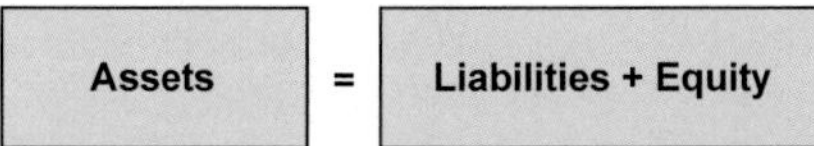

The equation will always be in balance because of the concept of double-entry bookkeeping. Every financial transaction will have two entries that will always balance the equation. The concepts of debit and credit bookkeeping, or T-accounts will not be used in this process as they are a technique more suited to accountants than Analysts.

Understanding the detail is crucial for Analysts as it provides:

- An excellent foundation to understanding the nature of the numbers in the financials and why they move
- Analysts with the detailed knowledge necessary to allow metric adjustment
- The skills necessary to create forecast financials
- The basis for deriving cash flows, which is the fundamental skill in DCF valuation

The remainder of this chapter is an annotated example of how a balance sheet and income statement is constructed. The example will run through a number of transactions for a start-up entity and construct a balance sheet and an income statement.

Sven SARL

Sven SARL is a recently incorporated entity. In the initial period of trading, the following transactions were recorded:

1. New equity shares were issued for €100,000 cash – par value of the shares was €20,000.
2. €60,000 of bank loan funding was received.
3. PPE was purchased for €52,000 cash. Depreciation of €10,000 was charged against this PPE during the period.
4. The company purchased on credit, inventories at a cost of €65,000. €60,000 of these inventories was used during the period to make sales. A cash payment of €55,000 was made to suppliers for the purchases made on credit.
5. Sven made sales on credit, of €120,000. €105,000 cash was received from customers.
6. SG&A (selling, general and administrative) expenses of €15,000 were incurred and paid during the period.
7. Interest on debt of €5,000 was incurred and paid during the period. €1,000 was then capitalized into PPE.
8. No taxes were paid during the period – however, the estimated tax charge was €11,000.
9. At the end of the period a dividend of €12,000 was paid.

Transaction 1

Sven issued equity share capital of €100,000. The shares issued had a par value of €20,000. The par value is recorded in the share capital account (common stock in the US). The excess over and above the par value is recorded in the share premium account (additional paid-in capital in the US).

The required double entries are:

Increase:	Cash (asset)	€100,000
Increase:	Share capital (equity)	€20,000
Increase:	Share premium (equity)	€80,000

The accounting equation impact is:

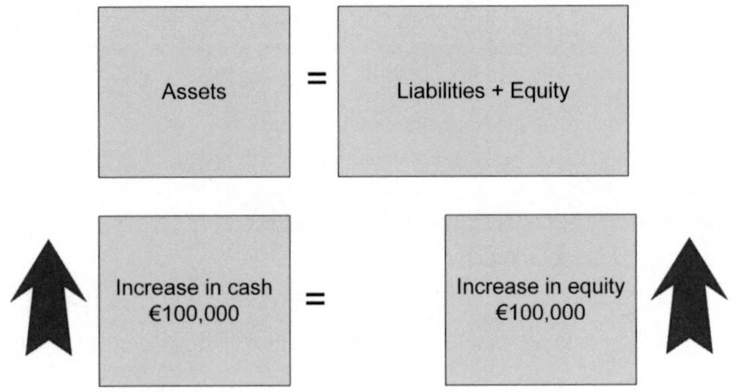

The balance sheet entries are:

Balance sheet	Start	1	2	3	4	5	6	7	8	9	End
PPE	--										--
Inventories	--										--
Trade receivables	--										--
Cash	--	100									100
Total assets	**--**	**100**	**--**	**--**	**--**	**--**	**--**	**--**	**--**	**--**	**100**
Trade payables	--										--
Taxes payable	--										--
Borrowings	--										--
Share capital	--	20									20
Share premium	--	80									80
Retained earnings	--										--
Total liabilities and equity	**--**	**100**	**--**	**--**	**--**	**--**	**--**	**--**	**--**	**--**	**100**

Transaction 2

Sven raised bank loan funding of €60,000. This cash injection into the business is recorded as a liability.

The required double entries are:

Increase:	Cash (asset)	€60,000
Increase:	Borrowings (liability)	€60,000

The accounting equation impact is:

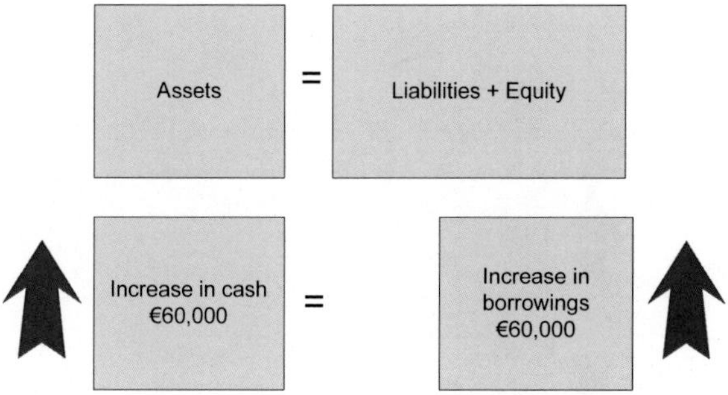

Assets	=	Liabilities + Equity
↑ Increase in cash €60,000	=	Increase in borrowings €60,000 ↑

The balance sheet entries are:

Balance sheet	Start	1	2	3	4	5	6	7	8	9	End
PPE	--										--
Inventories	--										--
Trade receivables	--										--
Cash	--	100	60								160
Total assets	**--**	**100**	**60**	**--**	**--**	**--**	**--**	**--**	**--**	**--**	**160**
Trade payables	--										--
Taxes payable	--										--
Borrowings	--		60								60
Share capital	--	20									20
Share premium	--	80									80
Retained earnings	--										--
Total liabilities and equity	**--**	**100**	**60**	**--**	**--**	**--**	**--**	**--**	**--**	**--**	**160**

Transaction 3

Sven had secured funding of €160,000 for the business up to this point. The company used €52,000 of this to purchase PPE. The PPE was depreciated by €10,000 over the period.

The required double entries for the PPE purchase are:

Increase:	PPE (asset)	€52,000
Decrease:	Cash (asset)	€52,000

The accounting equation impact is:

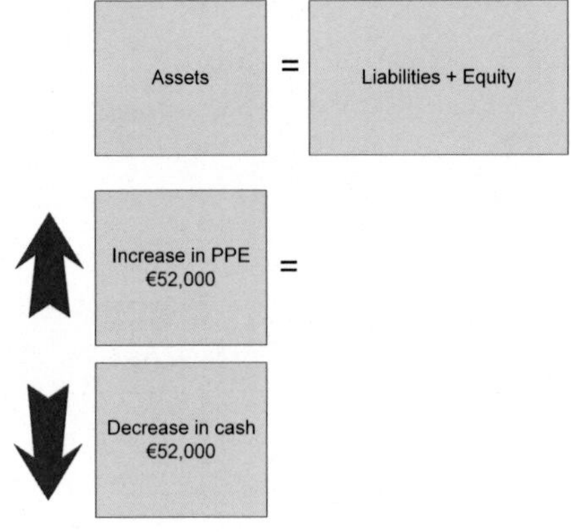

The balance sheet entries are:

Balance sheet	Start	1	2	3	4	5	6	7	8	9	End
PPE	--			52							52
Inventories	--										--
Trade receivables	--										--
Cash	--	100	60	(52)							108
Total assets	**--**	**100**	**60**	**--**	**--**	**--**	**--**	**--**	**--**	**--**	**160**
Trade payables	--										--
Taxes payable	--										--
Borrowings	--		60								60
Share capital	--	20									20
Share premium	--	80									80
Retained earnings	--										--
Total liabilities and equity	**--**	**100**	**60**	**--**	**--**	**--**	**--**	**--**	**--**	**--**	**160**

The PPE was depreciated by €10,000 over the period. Depreciation is an expense in the income statement. In this illustration, we will prepare the income statement once the balance sheet is completed.

All profits (and losses) created by the company are owned by (suffered by) the shareholders – with this ownership interest represented through the equity section of the balance sheet. The income statement (the home of the profits and losses) therefore must integrate into the balance sheet through the equity section if this ownership interest is to be shown. Retained earnings is the line in equity which records the cumulative profits, less losses which have not yet been paid to the shareholders.

The illustration below highlights this important link between the income statement and the equity component of the balance sheet. The depreciation of €10,000 is an expense. This expense will reduce the current period's earnings and therefore also the retained earnings by €10,000. As retained earnings forms part of the equity on the balance sheet then equity will be reduced by €10,000, as a result of the expense.

Another way to consider this impact is that equity is the residual claim shareholders have on the net assets of the business. Depreciation reduces the PPE number and therefore the net assets. This in turn reduces the residual claim – the equity – by €10,000.

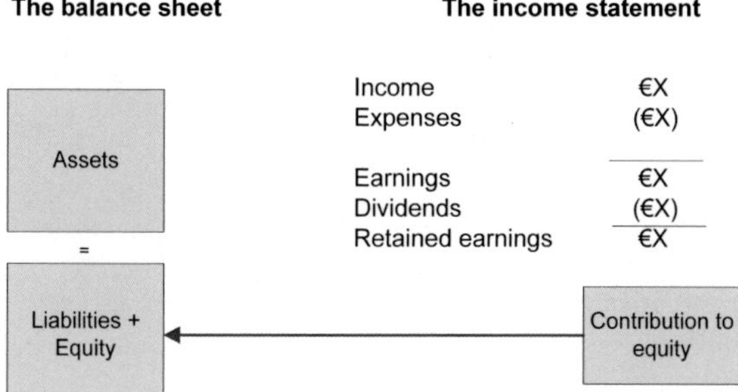

The required double entries for the depreciation are:

Decrease	PPE (asset)	€10,000
Decrease	Retained earnings (equity)	€10,000

The accounting equation impact:

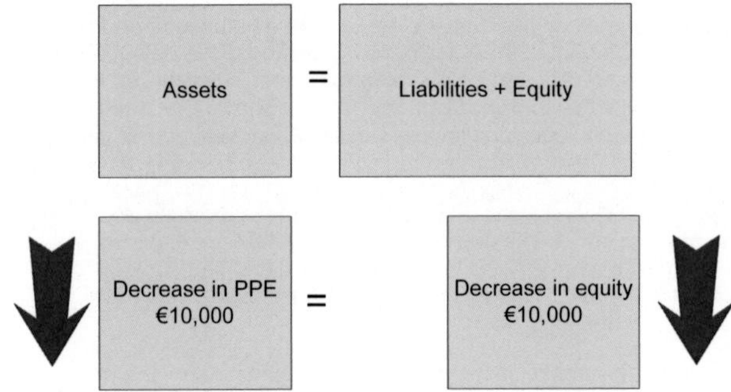

The balance sheet entries are:

Balance sheet	Start	1	2	3	4	5	6	7	8	9	End
PPE	--			42							42
Inventories	--										--
Trade receivables	--										--
Cash	--	100	60	(52)							108
Total assets	**--**	**100**	**60**	**(10)**	**--**	**--**	**--**	**--**	**--**	**--**	**150**
Trade payables	--										--
Taxes payable	--										--
Borrowings	--		60								60
Share capital	--	20									20
Share premium	--	80									80
Retained earnings	--			(10)							(10)
Total liabilities and equity	**--**	**100**	**60**	**(10)**	**--**	**--**	**--**	**--**	**--**	**--**	**150**

Income Statement Integration into Equity

The financials are an integrated set of statements. This integration needs to be fully understood not only to appreciate how the numbers change and flow through the financials, but also in terms of financial model building.

Analysts are expected to have the ability to construct fully integrated three-statement financial models. That is, models where the:

- Balance sheet
- Income statement
- Cash flow statement

...are fully integrated and robust.

There are three key integration conduits that will be built into a fully integrated model:

1. Income statement into equity
2. Income statement into the cash flow statement
3. Cash flow statement into the balance sheet

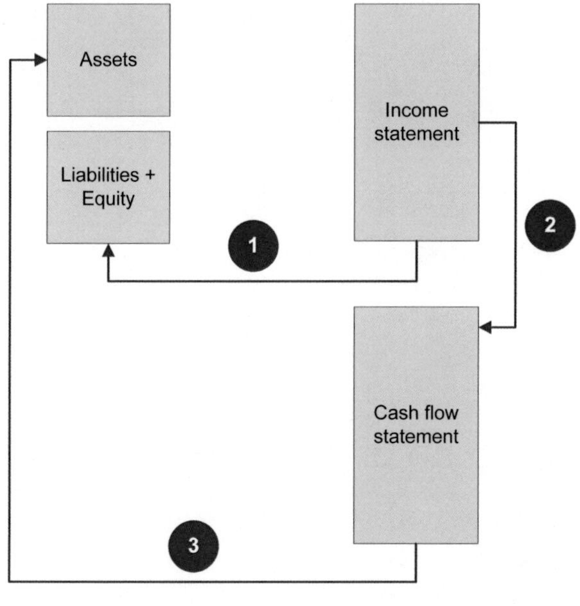

Transaction 4

The company purchased, on credit, inventories at a cost of €65,000. €60,000 of these inventories was used during the period to make sales. A cash payment of €55,000 was made to suppliers for the purchases made on credit.

These are Sven's first trading transactions. There are three separate transactions – each one will be dealt with in turn.

The required double entries for the credit purchase of the inventories are:

Increase	Inventories (asset)	€65,000
Increase	Trade payables (liability)	€65,000

The accounting equation impact is:

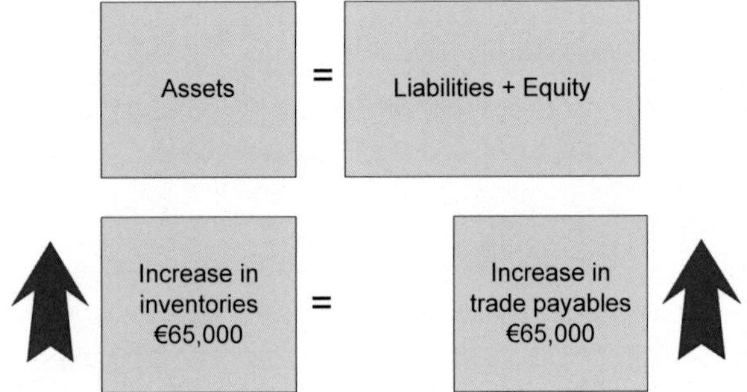

The balance sheet entries are:

Balance sheet	Start	1	2	3	4	5	6	7	8	9	End
PPE	--			42							42
Inventories	--				65						65
Trade receivables	--										--
Cash	--	100	60	(52)							108
Total assets	**--**	**100**	**60**	**(10)**	**65**	**--**	**--**	**--**	**--**	**--**	**215**
Trade payables	--				65						65
Taxes payable	--										--
Borrowings	--		60								60
Share capital	--	20									20
Share premium	--	80									80
Retained earnings	--			(10)							(10)
Total liabilities and equity	**--**	**100**	**60**	**(10)**	**65**	**--**	**--**	**--**	**--**	**--**	**215**

Once the inventories were purchased they were used to trade. The inventories were used to generate the company's revenues. The use of the inventories will be an expense (the cost of the goods sold) in the income statement. This expense reduces the retained earnings and therefore the equity number on the balance sheet.

The required double entries for the use of the inventories are:

Decrease	Inventories (asset)	€60,000
Decrease	Retained earnings (equity)	€60,000

The accounting equation impact is:

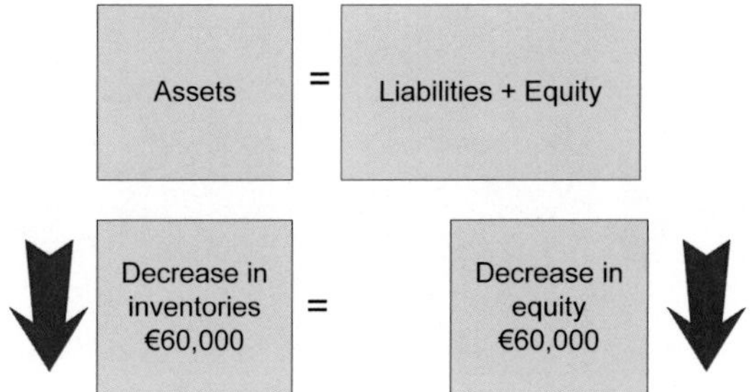

The balance sheet entries are:

Balance sheet	Start	1	2	3	4	5	6	7	8	9	End
PPE	--			42							42
Inventories	--				5						5
Trade receivables	--										--
Cash	--	100	60	(52)							108
Total assets	**--**	**100**	**60**	**(10)**	**5**	**--**	**--**	**--**	**--**	**--**	**155**
Trade payables	--				65						65
Taxes payable	--										--
Borrowings	--		60								60
Share capital	--	20									20
Share premium	--	80									80
Retained earnings	--			(10)	(60)						(70)
Total liabilities and equity	**--**	**100**	**60**	**(10)**	**5**	**--**	**--**	**--**	**--**	**--**	**155**

The inventories were purchased on credit. This liability will have to be settled. Sven made an initial cash payment of €55,000 towards the outstanding balance.

The required double entries for the part settlement of the liability are:

Decrease	Cash (asset)	€55,000
Decrease	Trade payables (liability)	€55,000

The accounting equation impact is:

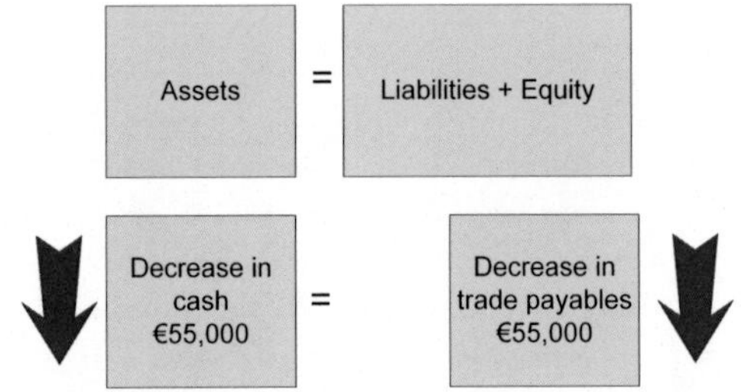

The balance sheet entries are:

Balance sheet	Start	1	2	3	4	5	6	7	8	9	End
PPE	--			42							42
Inventories	--				5						5
Trade receivables	--										--
Cash	--	100	60	(52)	(55)						53
Total assets	**--**	**100**	**60**	**(10)**	**(50)**	**--**	**--**	**--**	**--**	**--**	**100**
Trade payables	--				10						10
Taxes payable	--										--
Borrowings	--		60								60
Share capital	--	20									20
Share premium	--	80									80
Retained earnings	--			(10)	(60)						(70)
Total liabilities and equity	**--**	**100**	**60**	**(10)**	**(50)**	**--**	**--**	**--**	**--**	**--**	**100**

Transaction 5

Sven made sales on credit of €120,000, i.e. the company made the sales but did not receive the cash. The recognition of the sales (trading income) will increase earnings – this in turn will increase the retained earnings and the equity number on the balance sheet.

The required double entries for the sales made on credit are:

Increase	Receivables (asset)	€120,000
Increase	Retained earnings (equity)	€120,000

The accounting equation impact is:

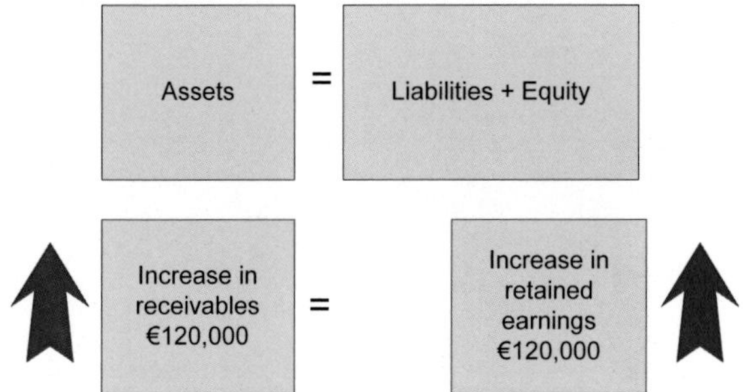

The balance sheet entries are:

Balance sheet	Start	1	2	3	4	5	6	7	8	9	End
PPE	--			42							42
Inventories	--				5						5
Trade receivables	--					120					120
Cash	--	100	60	(52)	(55)						53
Total assets	**--**	**100**	**60**	**(10)**	**(50)**	**120**	**--**	**--**	**--**	**--**	**220**
Trade payables	--				10						10
Taxes payable	--										--
Borrowings	--		60								60
Share capital	--	20									20
Share premium	--	80									80
Retained earnings	--			(10)	(60)	120					50
Total liabilities and equity	**--**	**100**	**60**	**(10)**	**(50)**	**120**	**--**	**--**	**--**	**--**	**220**

€105,000 cash was received from customers with respect to the credit sales.

The required double entries in relation to the cash collection of the sales made on credit are:

Increase	Cash (asset)	€105,000
Decrease	Receivables (asset)	€105,000

The accounting equation impact is:

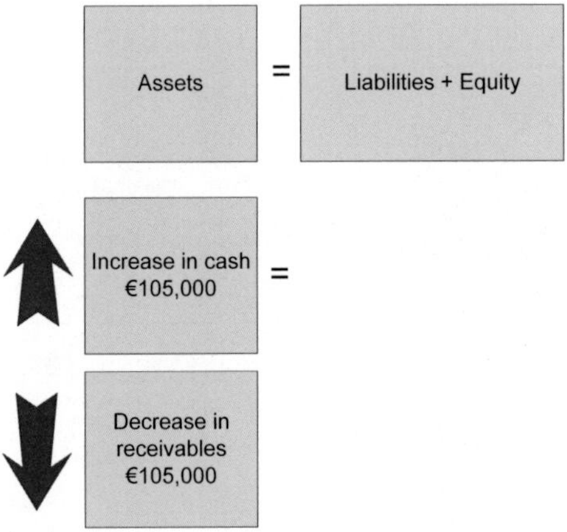

Assets = Liabilities + Equity

Increase in cash €105,000 =

Decrease in receivables €105,000

The balance sheet entries are:

Balance sheet	Start	1	2	3	4	5	6	7	8	9	End
PPE	--			42							42
Inventories	--				5						5
Trade receivables	--					15					15
Cash	--	100	60	(52)	(55)	105					158
Total assets	**--**	**100**	**60**	**(10)**	**(50)**	**120**	**--**	**--**	**--**	**--**	**220**
Trade payables	--				10						10
Taxes payable	--										--
Borrowings	--		60								60
Share capital	--	20									20
Share premium	--	80									80
Retained earnings	--			(10)	(60)	120					50
Total liabilities and equity	**--**	**100**	**60**	**(10)**	**(50)**	**120**	**--**	**--**	**--**	**--**	**220**

Transaction 6

SG&A (selling, general and administrative) expenses of €15,000 were incurred and paid during the period. The expenses are cash paid and so reduce the cash number. The incurred expenses will reduce earnings, retained earnings and therefore equity on the balance sheet.

The required double entries are:

Decrease	Cash (asset)	€15,000
Decrease	Retained earnings (equity)	€15,000

The accounting equation impact is:

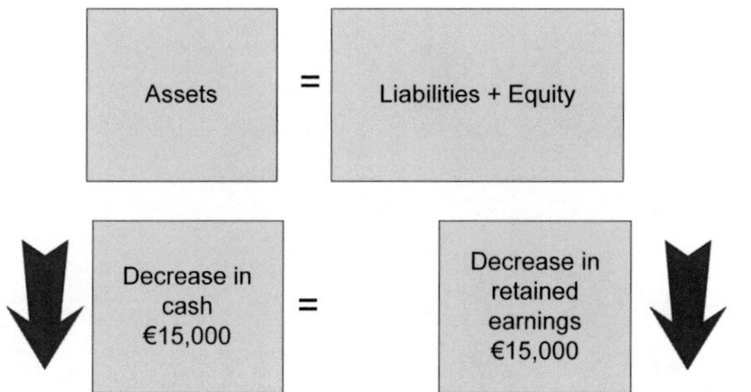

The balance sheet entries are:

Balance sheet	Start	1	2	3	4	5	6	7	8	9	End
PPE	--			42							42
Inventories	--				5						5
Trade receivables	--					15					15
Cash	--	100	60	(52)	(55)	105	(15)				143
Total assets	**--**	**100**	**60**	**(10)**	**(50)**	**120**	**(15)**	**--**	**--**	**--**	**205**
Trade payables	--				10						10
Taxes payable	--										--
Borrowings	--		60								60
Share capital	--	20									20
Share premium	--	80									80
Retained earnings	--			(10)	(60)	120	(15)				35
Total liabilities and equity	**--**	**100**	**60**	**(10)**	**(50)**	**120**	**(15)**	**--**	**--**	**--**	**205**

Transaction 7

Interest on debt of €5,000 was incurred and paid during the period. €1,000 was then capitalized into PPE.

Again we treat each bit in isolation. The interest is cash paid and so reduces the cash number. The incurred interest will reduce earnings, retained earnings and therefore equity on the balance sheet. The required double entries for the first part are:

Decrease	Cash (asset)	€5,000
Decrease	Retained earnings (equity)	€5,000

The accounting equation impact is:

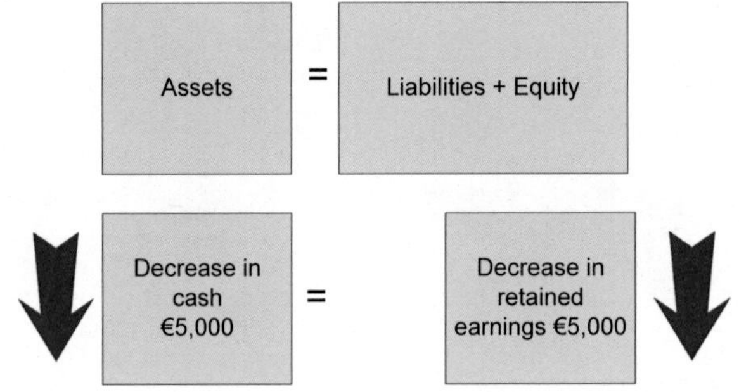

The balance sheet entries are:

Balance sheet	Start	1	2	3	4	5	6	7	8	9	End
PPE	--			42							42
Inventories	--				5						5
Trade receivables	--					15					15
Cash	--	100	60	(52)	(55)	105	(15)	(5)			138
Total assets	**--**	**100**	**60**	**(10)**	**(50)**	**120**	**(15)**	**(5)**	**--**	**--**	**200**
Trade payables	--				10						10
Taxes payable	--										--
Borrowings	--		60								60
Share capital	--	20									20
Share premium	--	80									80
Retained earnings	--			(10)	(60)	120	(15)	(5)			30
Total liabilities and equity	**--**	**100**	**60**	**(10)**	**(50)**	**120**	**(15)**	**(5)**	**--**	**--**	**200**

€1,000 was then capitalized into PPE. To capitalize something is to create an asset. Provided certain criteria are met (relating to what is being financed by the debt on which the interest arose) then a company must capitalize interest, i.e. call it an asset rather than an expense.
The capitalization of interest reduces the expense already charged to the income statement – the net interest charged to retained earnings is now only €4,000. This results in an increase in earnings, retained earnings and the equity number on the balance sheet.

The required double entries are:

Increase	PPE (asset)	€1,000
Increase	Retained earnings (equity)	€1,000

The accounting equation impact is:

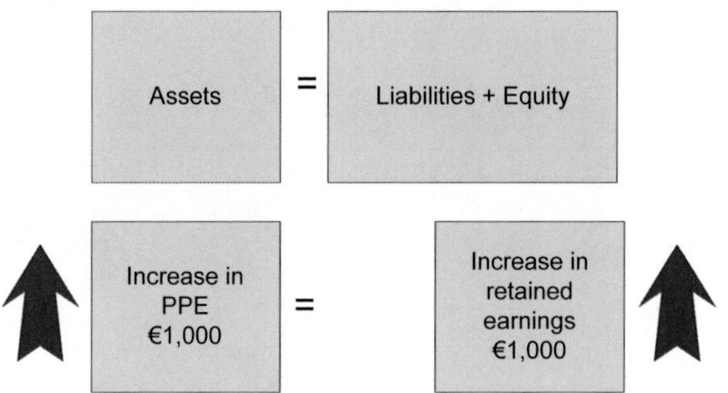

The balance sheet entries are:

Balance sheet	Start	1	2	3	4	5	6	7	8	9	End
PPE	--			42				1			43
Inventories	--				5						5
Trade receivables	--					15					15
Cash	--	100	60	(52)	(55)	105	(15)	(5)			138
Total assets	**--**	**100**	**60**	**(10)**	**(50)**	**120**	**(15)**	**(4)**	**--**	**--**	**201**
Trade payables	--				10						10
Taxes payable	--										--
Borrowings	--		60								60
Share capital	--	20									20
Share premium	--	80									80
Retained earnings	--			(10)	(60)	120	(15)	(4)			31
Total liabilities and equity	**--**	**100**	**60**	**(10)**	**(50)**	**120**	**(15)**	**(4)**	**--**	**--**	**201**

Transaction 8

No taxes were paid during the period (due to this being Sven's first period). However, the estimated tax charge was €11,000.

Despite this not being paid in the year, the tax charge relates to the profitability of the current period and so the expense must be recognized, together with the matching liability. The required double entries are:

Increase	Tax payables (liability)	€11,000
Decrease	Retained earnings (equity)	€11,000

The accounting equation impact is:

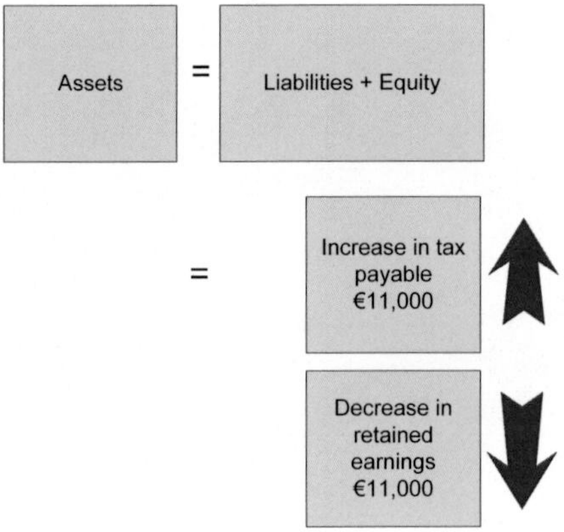

Assets = Liabilities + Equity

= Increase in tax payable €11,000

Decrease in retained earnings €11,000

The balance sheet entries are:

Balance sheet	Start	1	2	3	4	5	6	7	8	9	End
PPE	--			42				1			43
Inventories	--				5						5
Trade receivables	--					15					15
Cash	--	100	60	(52)	(55)	105	(15)	(5)			138
Total assets	**--**	**100**	**60**	**(10)**	**(50)**	**120**	**(15)**	**(4)**	**--**	**--**	**201**
Trade payables	--				10						10
Taxes payable	--								11		11
Borrowings	--		60								60
Share capital	--	20									20
Share premium	--	80									80
Retained earnings	--			(10)	(60)	120	(15)	(4)	(11)		20
Total liabilities and equity	**--**	**100**	**60**	**(10)**	**(50)**	**120**	**(15)**	**(4)**	**--**	**--**	**201**

Transaction 9

At the end of the period a dividend of €12,000 was paid.

This payment is not an expense but a distribution of the profits to the owners. Consequently, the cash payment reduces the amounts owed to shareholders (represented by equity), specifically the profits (represented by retained earnings). The required double entries are therefore:

Decrease	Cash (asset)	€12,000
Decrease	Retained earnings (equity)	€12,000

The accounting equation impact is:

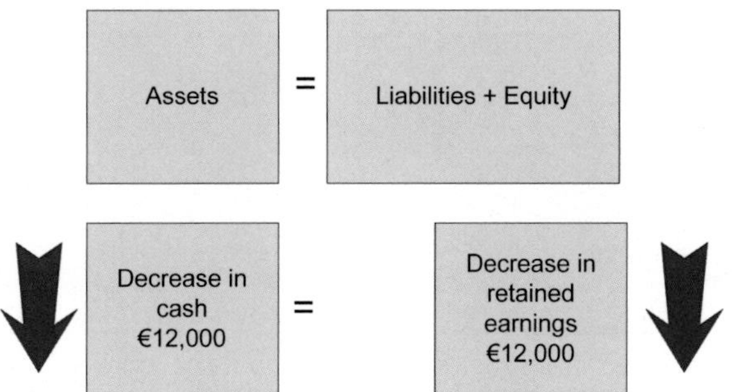

The balance sheet entries are:

Balance sheet	Start	1	2	3	4	5	6	7	8	9	End
PPE	--			42				1			43
Inventories	--				5						5
Trade receivables	--					15					15
Cash	--	100	60	(52)	(55)	105	(15)	(5)		(12)	126
Total assets	**--**	**100**	**60**	**(10)**	**(50)**	**120**	**(15)**	**(4)**	**--**	**(12)**	**189**
Trade payables	--				10						10
Taxes payable	--								11		11
Borrowings	--		60								60
Share capital	--	20									20
Share premium	--	80									80
Retained earnings	--			(10)	(60)	120	(15)	(4)	(11)	(12)	8
Total liabilities and equity	**--**	**100**	**60**	**(10)**	**(50)**	**120**	**(15)**	**(4)**	**--**	**(12)**	**189**

The complete balance sheet

The construction exercise illustrates how transactions are posted to the financials and how the balance sheet is gradually built up. The individual transaction disclosure does not appear in the financials in this form. However, the notes to the financials will provide some additional detail on the period's transactions.

Balance sheet	Start	1	2	3	4	5	6	7	8	9	End
PPE	--			42				1			43
Inventories	--				5						5
Trade receivables	--					15					15
Cash	--	100	60	(52)	(55)	105	(15)	(5)		(12)	126
Total assets	**--**	**100**	**60**	**(10)**	**(50)**	**120**	**(15)**	**(4)**	**--**	**(12)**	**189**
Trade payables	--				10						10
Taxes payable	--								11		11
Borrowings	--		60								60
Share capital	--	20									20
Share premium	--	80									80
Retained earnings	**--**			**(10)**	**(60)**	**120**	**(15)**	**(4)**	**(11)**	**(12)**	**8**
Total liabilities and equity	**--**	**100**	**60**	**(10)**	**(50)**	**120**	**(15)**	**(4)**	**--**	**(12)**	**189**

The financials will disclose a balance sheet on a year-on-year basis (see below).

Balance sheet	Start	End
PPE	--	43
Inventories	--	5
Trade receivables	--	15
Cash	--	126
Total assets	**--**	**189**
Trade payables	--	10
Taxes payable	--	11
Borrowings	--	60
Share capital	--	20
Share premium	--	80
Retained earnings	**--**	**8**
Total liabilities and equity	**--**	**189**

This disclosure is a snapshot of the entity's financial position at the start and end of the period.

Balance Sheet Numbers

Analysts must appreciate **how** the balance sheet numbers move from one period to another. This is an important skill for:

- Analysis purposes – knowing how the balance sheet numbers move will assist in analyzing any strengths and weaknesses of an entity.
- Building three-statement financial models – requires the builder to construct and integrate the financials. The conduits that link the financials together must be formulae-driven. Without a confident understanding of financial statement integration and where transactions hit the financials, a balancing balance sheet will be nothing more than a dream.
- Cash flow derivation is a skill built on a foundation of understanding the key balance sheet numbers and what drives the movements in the numbers

The cash and retained earnings lines have been highlighted on the balance sheet. The movement in the cash line on the balance sheet can be re-worked to create a cash flow statement in due course. Likewise, the income statement is a representation of the movements in the retained earnings line (ignoring the dividend paid).

In this simple financial construction example, the income statement is a detailed disclosure of the retained earnings line. In reality, the retained earnings will include additional entries that will not be included in the income statement.

The example on the next page illustrates how the retained earnings line is rearranged to produce an income statement and highlights why cash flow and profit may not be the same number.

In transaction 5, Sven SARL made sales on credit to its customers of €120,000. These sales were not immediately collected in cash. However, the retained earnings and income statement lines recognized the sales on the basis of work performed rather than the collection of cash.

Likewise, any expenses in the income statement are recognized on the basis of when the expense is incurred or used up rather than when it is paid.

Transaction 7 is an interesting example of the difference between the cash and income statement impacts of a transaction. Interest of €5,000 was paid during the period and this payment will flow through to the cash flow statement. However, the income statement below is disclosing a charge of only €4,000. The reduction in the interest charge was due to the interest capitalization policy followed by the company. Sven capitalized €1,000 of the interest paid into the balance sheet PPE number.

Financial Statement Construction

Balance sheet	Start	1	2	3	4	5	6	7	8	9	End
	€m	€m	€m	€m	€m	€m	€m	€m	€m	€m	€m
PPE	--			42				1			43
Inventories	--				5						5
Trade receivables	--					15					15
Cash	**--**	**100**	**60**	**(52)**	**(55)**	**105**	**(15)**	**(5)**		**(12)**	**126**
Total assets	--	**100**	**60**	**(10)**	**(50)**	**120**	**(15)**	**(4)**	--	**(12)**	**189**
Trade payables	--				10						10
Taxes payable	--								11		11
Borrowings	--		60								60
Share capital	--	20									20
Share premium	--	80									80
Retained earnings	--			(10)	(60)	120	(15)	(4)	(11)	(12)	8
Total liabilities and equity	--	**100**	**60**	**(10)**	**(50)**	**120**	**(15)**	**(4)**	--	**(12)**	**189**
	--	--	--	--	--	--	--	--	--	--	--

Income statement	€m
Revenues	120
Costs of sales	(60)
Depreciation	(10)
SGA	(15)
EBIT	35
Interest	(4)
Tax	(11)
Net income	20

Retained earnings	
Start of year	--
Net income	20
Dividends	(12)
End of year	8

Introduction

An entity's survival depends on its ability to generate cash as well as how well that cash is invested into the business. Cash is physical. It is an easy concept to identify with. It is free from the distortions of accounting principles and provides a clear picture of an entity's operations.

A cash flow statement brings together an entity's cash flow information. The statement is possibly the most important source of financial information for Analysts as it is:

- An excellent source of clean numbers to analyze from an equity and credit perspective
- A key source of information for DCF valuation purposes

Also, being able to create a cash flow statement from scratch is one of the key skills required in order to build robust financial models.

A cash flow statement provides excellent information on:

- Liquidity
- Viability
- Financial adaptability

Cash flow statement derivation

Cash flow statement derivation is a skill that must be based on a firm foundation of accounting knowledge. The skill will utilize balance sheet and income statement accounting knowledge.

The derivation of a cash flow statement will be demonstrated using the previous Sven SARL example.

Basic direct cash flow statement

As a recap, Sven SARL's balance sheet and income statement are below:

Balance sheet	Start	1	2	3	4	5	6	7	8	9	End
	€m	€m	€m	€m	€m	€m	€m	€m		€m	€m
PPE	--			42				1			43
Inventories	--				5						5
Trade receivables	--					15					15
Cash	**--**	**100**	**60**	**(52)**	**(55)**	**105**	**(15)**	**(5)**		**(12)**	**126**
Total assets	--	**100**	**60**	**(10)**	**(50)**	**120**	**(15)**	**(4)**	--	**(12)**	**189**
Trade payables	--				10						10
Taxes payable	--								11		11
Borrowings	--		60								60
Share capital	--	20									20
Share premium	--	80									80
Retained earnings	--			(10)	(60)	120	(15)	(4)	(11)	(12)	8
Total liabilities and equity	--	**100**	**60**	**(10)**	**(50)**	**120**	**(15)**	**(4)**	--	**(12)**	**189**

Cash Flow Statement

Income statement	€m
Revenues	120
Costs of sales	(60)
Depreciation	(10)
SGA	(15)
EBIT	35
Interest	(4)
Tax	(11)
Net income	20
Retained earnings	
Start of year	--
Net income	20
Dividends	(12)
End of year	8

A very basic cash flow statement can be derived from this information. The highlighted cash line is essentially a cash flow statement that can be converted into a list of cash inflows and outflows as you can see below:

Cash flow statement (basic direct method)		
Cash inflow		
Transaction 1	Cash rec'd from equity issue	100
Transaction 2	Cash rec'd from debt issue	60
Transaction 5	Cash red'd from customers	105
Cash outflow		
Transaction 3	Cash paid to acquire PPE	(52)
Transaction 4	Cash paid to purchase inventory	(55)
Transaction 6	Cash paid for SG&A	(15)
Transaction 7	Cash paid for interest	(5)
Transaction 9	Cash paid for dividends	(12)
Cash increase during the period		**126**
Cash at start		--
Cash increase during the period		126
Cash at end		**126**

This is a cash flow statement. It is a direct cash flow statement as it shows the direct source of cash receipts and payments.

Most cash flow statements around the world will classify the cash flows into one of three categories:

- Operating
- Investing
- Financing

The classification of a cash flow can be inconsistent between IFRS and US GAAP. The issues are limited to the classification of:

- Interest paid
- Dividends paid
- Taxes paid
- Interest received
- Dividends received

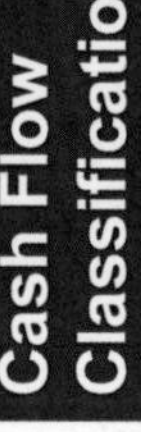

IFRS classification:

- Interest paid – classified either as operating or financing (normally operating)
- Dividends paid – classified either as operating or financing (normally financing)
- Taxes paid – classified as operating unless there is a specific investing or financing issue
- Interest received – classified either as operating or investing (normally investing)
- Dividends received – classified either as operating or investing (normally investing)

Cash Flow Classification

US GAAP classification:

- Interest paid – classified as operating
- Dividends paid – classified as financing
- Taxes paid – generally classified as operating
- Interest received – classified as operating
- Dividends received – classified as operating

So applying standard cash flow classifications, the Sven basic direct cash flow statement would now be disclosed as:

Cash flow statement (basic direct method)		
Operating cash flow		
Transaction 5	Cash red'd from customers	105
Transaction 4	Cash paid to purchase inventory	(55)
Transaction 6	Cash paid for SG&A	(15)
Transaction 7	Cash paid for interest	(5)
		30
Investing cash flow		
Transaction 3	Cash paid to acquire PPE	(52)
Financing cash flow		
Transaction 9	Cash paid for dividends	(12)
Transaction 1	Cash rec'd from equity issue	100
Transaction 2	Cash rec'd from debt issue	60
		148
Cash increase during the period		126.0

Transaction 8 has no cash impact as it was an estimated tax charge. The estimate was not paid during the period.

Sadly, this cash flow statement is not a cash flow statement format that Analysts will see a great deal of day today. Whilst some GAAPs allow the use of the direct cash flow statement it is rarely used.

Indirect cash flow statement

From a disclosure and financial modeling perspective, Analysts will have to be adept at deriving a cash flow statement using the indirect method. This method derives an operating cash flow from an earnings metric.

We should be clear now that profit does not equal cash flow. Why?

- Revenues are recognized when they are earned
- Costs are recognized on the basis of when incurred
- Depreciation and amortization are non-cash items
- Accounting will spread costs to match the generation of benefits

Operating cash flow derivation

The indirect method will start with an earnings metric and then strip out non-cash items in order to arrive at a cash flow number.

A number of companies will derive an operating cash flow from an EBIT number. The derivation strips out all non-cash items or influences from the metric.

The first non-cash adjustment to an earnings metric is normally a D&A adjustment. D&A is a non-cash expense that is charged in arriving at EBIT. Therefore D&A must be removed from the earnings metric. This eliminates the non-cash impact. The D&A numbers are added back (thus reversing the impact of the expense) to EBIT. The sub-total resulting from this add back is EBITDA.

Balance sheet	Start	End
	€m	
PPE	--	43
Inventories	--	5
Trade receivables	--	15
Cash	--	**126**
Total assets	--	**189**
Trade payables	--	10
Taxes payable	--	11
Borrowings	--	60
Share capital	--	20
Share premium	--	80
Retained earnings	--	8
Total liabilities and equity	--	**189**

Income statement	€m
Revenues	120
Costs of sales	(60)
Depreciation	(10)
SGA	(15)
EBIT	35
Interest	(4)
Tax	(11)
Net income	20

Cash flow statement	€m
EBIT	35
Depreciation	10
EBITDA	45

Working capital adjustments

The next adjustments to the earnings metric are usually the working capital adjustments. The working capital adjustments will strip out the non-cash elements of revenue and cost recognition policies. For instance, the Sven SARL extract above discloses revenues of €120m. However, we can see on the balance sheet that trade receivables have increased to €15m. Our accounting knowledge should therefore suggest that whilst €120m of revenues has been recognized in the income statement, only €105m of cash was received from customers. Therefore EBIT is overstated in cash terms by €15m.

An increase in receivables is 'bad for cash flow' – hence the adjustment to EBIT in the derivation of operating cash flow will be negative.

Cash Flow Statement

Cash flow statement	€m
EBIT	35
Depreciation	10
EBITDA	45
Increase in receivables	(15)
Operating cash flow	30

The same type of issue is applicable to the costs of sales number that feeds into EBIT. The number reflects the costs incurred during the period. However, not all of these costs were paid in cash. The trade payables number has increase by €10m. This suggests that if cost of sales were €60m, only €50m were paid. This leaves €10m outstanding as a payable at the end of the period. Therefore the EBIT number is understated by €10m when considering the cash flow implications.

Cash flow statement	€m
EBIT	35
Depreciation	10
EBITDA	45
Increase in receivables	(15)
Increase in payables	10
Operating cash flow	40

An increase in payables is 'good for cash flow' – hence the adjustment to EBIT in the derivation of operating cash flow will be positive.

The last standard working capital adjustment is usually inventories. Sven SARL saw inventories increase by €5m during the period. The inventories have been paid for during the period, but the charge would not have passed through the income statement, as the inventories have not been used.

An increase in inventories is 'bad for cash flow' – hence the adjustment to EBIT in the derivation of operating cash flow will be negative.

Cash flow statement	€m
EBIT	35
Depreciation	10
EBITDA	45
Increase in inventories	(5)
Increase in receivables	(15)
Increase in payables	10
Operating cash flow	35

The EBIT number has now been 'cleaned up' for non-cash items and we arrive at an operating cash flow. This operating cash flow derivation is pre-interest and tax as the cash flow statement started with a pre-interest and tax earnings metric – EBIT.

The standard working capital adjustments can be summarized as:

	Increase	Decrease
Inventories	Bad for cash	Good for cash
Receivables	Bad for cash	Good for cash
Payables	Good for cash	Bad for cash

Earnings Metric Starting Point

Not all companies will start the indirect operating cash flow derivation from EBIT. US companies for instance will always commence the derivation from net income. This has a number of implications. The skills required are the same as used in the Sven example; however the process is a little more involved when working from a net income starting point.

- Net income is a post-interest and tax metric. Therefore the operating cash flow derived is also post-interest and tax.
- The derivation will treat interest and tax as part of the working capital adjustment. This means that the non-cash elements of the interest and tax charges will be stripped out of the net income metric.

Analysts must be careful when using the operating cash flow metric. Operating cash flow metrics are post-tax and interest if starting the cash flow statement from net income, whilst cash flow statements using EBIT as the starting point will be inherently pre-interest and tax.

EBIT to Operating cash flow

An EBIT starting point will produce an operating cash flow that is pre-interest and tax.
Often companies reporting this type of derivation will also deduct interest and tax from operating cash flow and disclose a second post interest and tax cash flow. This second level of operating cash flow is very useful when comparing companies that produce cash flow statements.

Cash flow statement	€m
EBIT	
Depreciation	10
EBITDA	45
Increase in inventories	(5)
Increase in receivables	(15)
Increase in payables	10
Operating cash flow	35
Interest paid	(5)
Tax	--
Operating cash flow	30

Net Income to Operating cash flow

A net income starting point is post interest and tax. Therefore the operating cash flow will be post interest and tax.
This method of operating cash flow derivation is typical for US companies.

Cash flow statement	€m
Net income	
Depreciation	10
Increase in tax payables	11
Increase in inventories	(5)
Increase in receivables	(15)
Increase in payables	10
Non-cash interest	(1)
Operating cash flow	30

Operating cash flow

Analysts must make sure that they are confident with the definition of the operating cash flow metric they are using. Tax and interest can be significant numbers and a failure to appreciate what level of operating cash flow metric is bring analyzed will lead to poor analytical conclusions.

Deriving cash numbers

The extract below illustrates the three sections of an indirect cash flow statement; operating, investing and financing. The term indirect can be slightly misleading, as the 'indirect' element refers only to the derivation of operating cash flow from an earnings metric. The rest of the cash flows below operating cash flow are direct cash flows. That is they are actual cash flow line items.

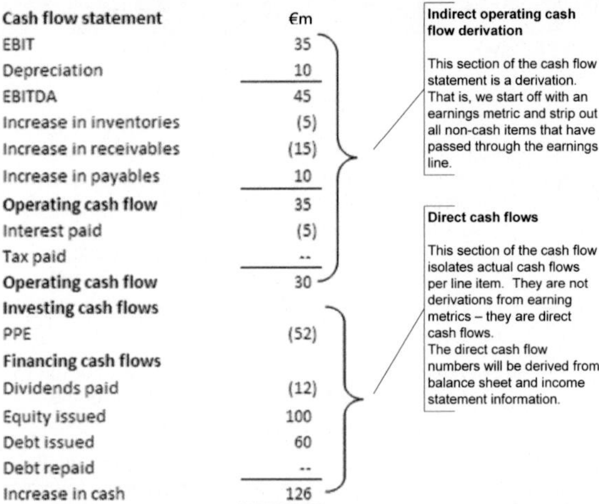

Cash flow statement	€m
EBIT	35
Depreciation	10
EBITDA	45
Increase in inventories	(5)
Increase in receivables	(15)
Increase in payables	10
Operating cash flow	35
Interest paid	(5)
Tax paid	--
Operating cash flow	30
Investing cash flows	
PPE	(52)
Financing cash flows	
Dividends paid	(12)
Equity issued	100
Debt issued	60
Debt repaid	--
Increase in cash	126

Indirect operating cash flow derivation

This section of the cash flow statement is a derivation. That is, we start off with an earnings metric and strip out all non-cash items that have passed through the earnings line.

Direct cash flows

This section of the cash flow isolates actual cash flows per line item. They are not derivations from earning metrics – they are direct cash flows.
The direct cash flow numbers will be derived from balance sheet and income statement information.

These direct cash flows will need to be calculated from available balance sheet and income statement information. The illustration below is an example of how the cash paid to acquire PPE can be derived from the available balance sheet and income statement information.

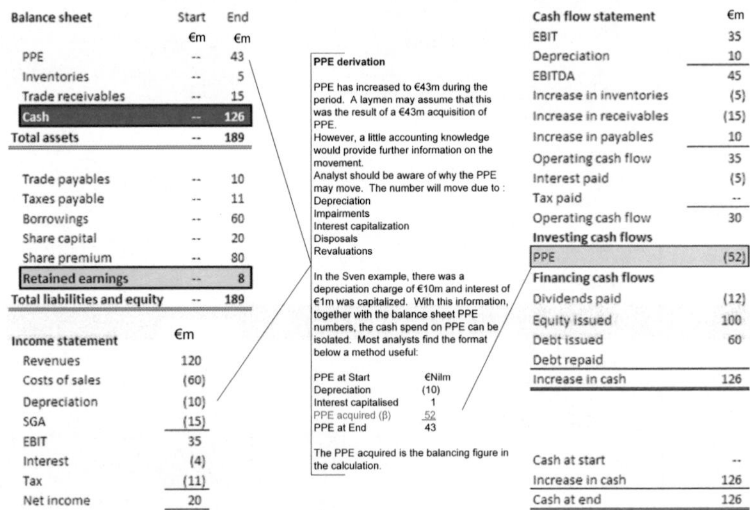

Balance sheet	Start €m	End €m
PPE	--	43
Inventories	--	5
Trade receivables	--	15
Cash	--	126
Total assets	--	**189**
Trade payables	--	10
Taxes payable	--	11
Borrowings	--	60
Share capital	--	20
Share premium	--	80
Retained earnings	--	8
Total liabilities and equity	--	**189**

Income statement	€m
Revenues	120
Costs of sales	(60)
Depreciation	(10)
SGA	(15)
EBIT	35
Interest	(4)
Tax	(11)
Net income	20

PPE derivation

PPE has increased to €43m during the period. A laymen may assume that this was the result of a €43m acquisition of PPE.
However, a little accounting knowledge would provide further information on the movement.
Analyst should be aware of why the PPE may move. The number will move due to :
Depreciation
Impairments
Interest capitalization
Disposals
Revaluations

In the Sven example, there was a depreciation charge of €10m and interest of €1m was capitalized. With this information, together with the balance sheet PPE numbers, the cash spend on PPE can be isolated. Most analysts find the format below a method useful:

PPE at Start	€Nilm
Depreciation	(10)
Interest capitalised	1
PPE acquired (β)	52
PPE at End	43

The PPE acquired is the balancing figure in the calculation.

Cash flow statement	€m
EBIT	35
Depreciation	10
EBITDA	45
Increase in inventories	(5)
Increase in receivables	(15)
Increase in payables	10
Operating cash flow	35
Interest paid	(5)
Tax paid	--
Operating cash flow	30
Investing cash flows	
PPE	(52)
Financing cash flows	
Dividends paid	(12)
Equity issued	100
Debt issued	60
Debt repaid	
Increase in cash	126

Cash at start	--
Increase in cash	126
Cash at end	126

Cash Flow Analysis

The cash flow statement is an excellent starting point for analysis, as it is a clean source of numbers, free from most types of accounting manipulation. An Analyst can pick up a 'story' from a quick review of a cash flow statement.

Continuing with the Sven SARL example:

Cash conversion (OCF/EBITDA) 1.3x

Cash flow statement	€m	
EBIT	35	
Depreciation	10	5.2x
EBITDA	45	1.3x
Increase in inventories	(5)	
Increase in receivables	(15)	
Increase in payables	10	
		1.3x
Operating cash flow	35	
Interest paid	(5)	7.0x
Tax	--	
Operating cash flow	30	
PPE	(52)	
Free cash flow		(22)
Dividends paid	(12)	
Free cash flow		(34)
Equity issued	100	
Debt issued	60	
Debt repaid	--	
Increase in cash	126	

1 Cash conversion 1.3x

Cash conversion is a measure of how well a company generates cash flow from its earnings. Cash conversion will quantify how well the entity's working capital is managed. Better working capital management will lead to better cash conversion and stronger operating cash flows.

2 Interest cover 7.0x

Cash based interest cover = operating cash (pre-interest & tax) ÷ cash interest paid. This is a measure of how many times the current interest commitment can be paid out of available operating cash flow. A low multiple suggests a high level of debt in relation to cash flow. However, a very high multiple is not necessarily a good sign. A high multiple may suggest an inefficient capital structure, where financing is weighted too much towards equity rather than debt.

3 Free cash flow (€22m)

Free cash flow (FCF) is a metric that quantifies how much cash is left in an entity for discretionary use. FCF can be calculated at various levels depending on what the analyst considers to be a default or discretionary cash flow.
If an entity operates in a capital intensive industry the capex line may be considered a default cash flow spend. Therefore the post-capex FCF may be the appropriate FCF metric.
In some cases, Analysts may not consider the dividend payment a discretionary cash flow and therefore calculate the FCF post dividend.
In the Sven case, FCF (post capex) is negative. This sugests that the capex spend is significant in relation to the operating cash flow and that it will require external financing. The capex spend will need to be compared to the Capex/Depn multiple (above) in order to get a feel for the relative size of the capex spend.

4 Capex/Depn 5.2x

Capex to Depn multiples are a quick and dirty assessment of the strength of the capex spend. Depreciation is used as a proxy for maintenance capex. If capex is greater than the depreciation, the capex in excess of depreciation can be considered investment capex.
The Sven multiple is strong. They are expanding their capex base aggressively. The expansion is given greater context when compared to FCF post capex.
The negative FCF reinforces the agreesive nature of the expansion.

5 Free cash flow (€34m)

FCF (post dividend) is often referred to as the net financing requirement. Sven is paying out a dividend from a negative FCF (post capex).
The dividend payment increases the negative FCF line.
The negative €34m FCF post dividend suggests that an external cash injection is required.

6 Context

Any analysis must be considered in context. Sven is a start up business. It will require considerable cash injections in the early years of its existence. The operating cash flows are unlikely to be mature enough to support an aggressive capex expansion. Its capital structure seems inefficient, as it is reliant on equity. The company has capacity to increase its debt as measured by the strong cash based interest cover. Whilst the analysis may seem negative towards the company, a long term investment view could be taken towards the conpany.

CA Tick-sheet: The Cash Flow Statement

The cash flow statement is possibly the most important source of financial information for bankers as it is:

- An excellent source of clean numbers to analyze from an equity and credit perspective
- A key source of information for DCF valuation purposes

A cash flow statement provides excellent information on:

- Liquidity
- Viability
- Financial adaptability

Most cash flow statements are prepared using the indirect method.

The indirect method will derive operating cash flow from an earnings metric.

Some companies (especially US ones) will derive operating cash flow from net income.

Other companies will derive the operating cash flow from EBIT.

The standard adjustments to the earnings metric to derive operating cash flows involve:

- Depreciation
- Amortization
- Changes in working capital (inventories, receivables and payables)

Working capital adjustments – thought process:

- Increase in inventories – 'bad for cash'
- Increase in receivables – 'bad for cash'
- Increase in payables – 'good for cash'

Operating cash flow definitions can be inconsistent internationally:

- Operating cash flow is post-interest and tax, if starting from net income
- Operating cash flow is normally pre-interest and tax, if starting from EBIT

Cash flows are classified into three broad categories:

- Operating
- Investing
- Financing

Cash flow classifications can be inconsistent internationally.

Cash flow statements are an excellent starting point for analysis.

Key cash flow ratios and metrics are:

- EBITDA/Cash conversion
- Net working capital changes
- Cash based interest cover

Introduction

This chapter deals with the consolidated financial statements (often called group accounts) that are produced for a group of entities that are controlled by a parent. In the majority of cases, it will be group accounts that are being analyzed and for which metrics and multiples will be calculated, so it is critical to understand how the numbers in the accounts are impacted by the acquisition of shares in another company. This accounting knowledge is also essential in order to fully understand the drivers and information flow for merger modeling purposes.

The method of accounting depends on the amount of control.

The spectrum of control

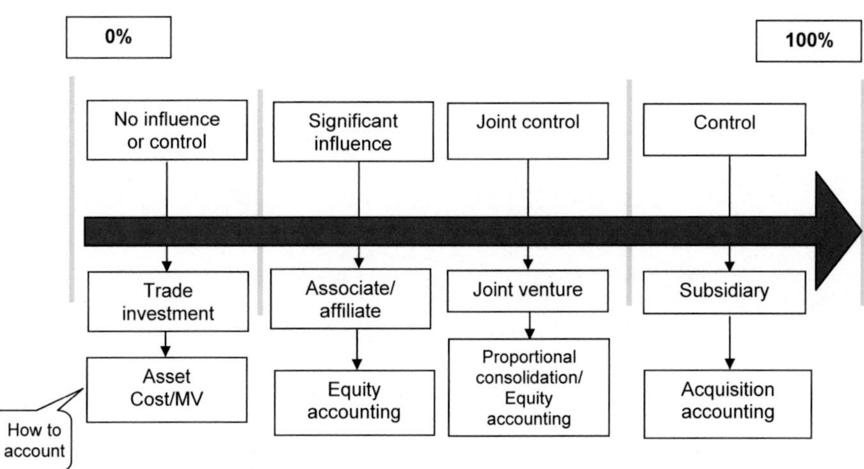

We will start by explaining the rules where the acquisition of shares gives the acquirer control over the other entity.

What is control?

Control is not based solely on legal ownership. The definition of control as it relates to the determination of parent and subsidiary relationships, is the power to govern the financial and operating policies of an entity so as to obtain benefit from its activities.

So the following questions need to be considered:

- Are the majority of the voting rights held?
- Is there power to appoint or remove directors holding a majority of the voting right?
- Is there power over more than half of the voting rights by virtue of an agreement with other investors?
- Is there power to govern the operating or financial policies by statute or under an agreement?
- Is there power to cast a majority of the votes at meetings of the board of directors

If control is not clearly apparent, an overall assessment of the relevant risk issues and factors will have to be considered. The determination of who is the controlling entity can be an arbitrary decision if the control question is unanswered.

IFRS – assessment of control

The IFRS control assessment model is based on a principles or conceptual framework. The nature and structure of the relationships in the group are assessed in order to determine the appropriate accounting.

Under IFRS, control is presumed if a parent owns (directly or indirectly) more than 50% of the voting rights of another entity. IFRS requires that potential voting rights must be included in any control assessment. So if an entity has currently exercisable or convertible instruments, these should be included in the control assessment. Note that options/warrants are excluded from the percentage if they are not currently exercisable/convertible.

US GAAP uses a two-level assessment model

Under US GAAP all entities are initially assessed to determine whether they are variable interest entities ('VIE'). A VIE is an entity that is financially controlled by one or more parties that do not hold a majority voting interest.

The second level of the VIE model attempts to determine which party is the primary beneficiary of a VIE. An entity will be determined as having a controlling interest in a VIE if:

- The entity has the power to direct activities of a VIE and this has a significant impact on the VIE's economic performance (this is called the 'power criteria')
- The entity has the right to receive the economic benefits of the VIE and the obligation to absorb the losses ('the benefit/loss criteria').

Part of this assessment process will consider why the VIE was established and for what purpose. Only one entity should be identified as having the controlling interest in relation to a VIE.

Entities that are not VIEs are assessed using voting rights ('the voting interest model'). Unlike IFRS, the US GAAP assessment focuses purely on the actual voting rights. Control can be assessed directly or indirectly, however in most instances the outcome will be the same as IFRS.

Special purpose entities

Special purpose entities entered common language due to the impact of the Enron financial crisis back in 2003. Special purposes entities ('SPE') were used to 'hive off' financial losses and hide debt from the Enron accounts. Losses and debt were transferred to these SPEs and due to the structure of these entities and the prevailing accounting rules, the losses disappeared from the consolidated financial statements. So when the losses/debt finally came out into the open, they came out all in one go and sent significant economic shocks through the financial system.

The accounting profession has made continued attempts to make sure that these SPEs are consolidated in the financial statements of the parent entities that control them. The biggest issue with SPEs is that they are often established where the presumed 'parent' owns little or none of the SPE's equity. SPEs are often referred to as thinly capitalized.

US GAAP assesses the control of a SPE using the VIE model.

If control is not clearly apparent with an SPE, IFRS will assess control not just on a risk and rewards basis, but it will also consider:

- The nature and purposes of the SPE in relation to the potential parent.
- The SPE's design – does the entity operate on an auto-pilot mechanism. An auto-pilot set-up makes it hard to establish day-to-day control – however, a party will have to have established the auto-pilot mechanism in the first place. This can often be a consideration for control.
- Which parties have rights of decision-making veto?
- Who can wind up the entity?
- Who has the residual claim on the SPE's net assets on a winding up?

Ultimately, there should be no SPE orphans. A parent should always be allocated to a SPE.

Parent vs. Group

A group is defined as a parent and all its subsidiaries. It is important to appreciate, at the outset, that accounting rules require a parent to present consolidated financial statements (i.e. group accounts) in which the accounts of the parent and subsidiary (or subsidiaries) are combined and presented as a single entity. However, the group is not considered an entity in law.

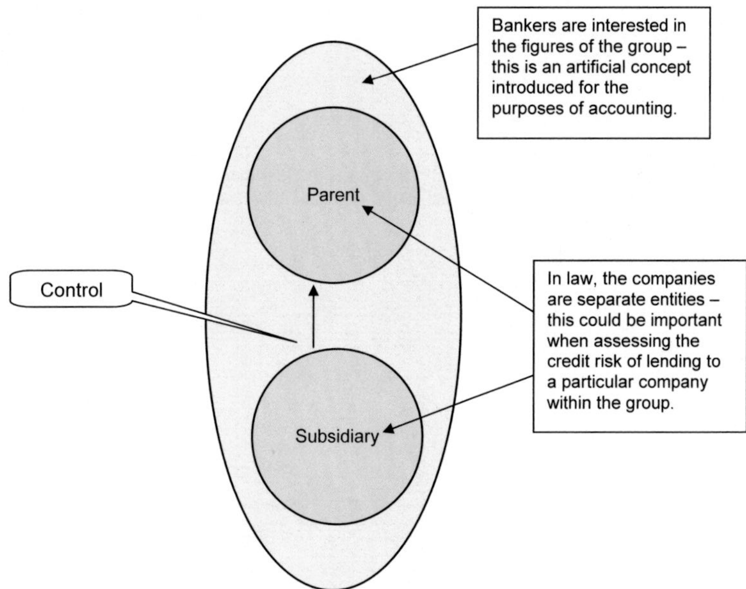

The group columns are what we will be most interested in

	Note	Group £m	Group £m	Company £m	Company restated £m
Non-current assets					
Property, plant and equipment	11	**7,821**	7,424	**42**	109
Intangible assets	12	**160**	165	**-**	-
Investments in subsidiaries	13	**-**	-	**7,262**	7,169
Investments in joint ventures	14	**288**	148	**91**	91
Available-for-sale financial assets	15	**97**	106	**7**	-
Other receivables	17	**45**	55	**1,050**	976
Derivative financial instruments	30	**31**	-	**31**	-
Deferred income tax asset	21	**-**	-	**1**	1
Retirement benefit asset	31	**-**	495	**-**	-
		8,442	8,393	**8,484**	8,346
Current assets					
Inventories	16	**689**	681	**-**	-
Trade and other receivables	17	**195**	206	**380**	359
Derivative financial instruments	30	**59**	4	**37**	-
Cash and cash equivalents	27	**627**	719	**460**	324
		1,570	1,610	**877**	683
Non-current assets held for sale	18	**21**	112	**-**	-
		1,591	1,722	**877**	683
Total assets		**10,033**	10,115	**9,361**	9,029

Source: J Sainsbury Annual Report

In the above extract from Sainsbury plc accounts, the last two columns are the accounts of the legal entity, J Sainsbury plc. However from a financial analysis and valuation perspective, it is the group numbers that are important.

Consolidation – the big picture

In essence, when one company controls another company, it controls 100% of the net assets. The accounting reflects this control aspect, therefore the consolidated balance sheet includes 100% of all the assets and liabilities of the subsidiary, on a line-by-line basis, even if not 100% owned. An adjustment, called non-controlling interest (NCI), is put in to reflect the fact that less than 100% is owned.

Similarly, in the income statement, the accounting reflects this control and so the consolidated income statement includes 100% of the subsidiary's profit after tax, on a line-by-line basis. Again, a NCI adjustment is put in to reflect the fact that less than 100% is owned.

Note that group accounts will have already eliminated the effects of any transactions between companies within the group – for example the impact of inter-company sales or dividends.

Balance sheet consolidation (at date of acquisition of subsidiary)			
Net assets	**P**	**S**	Group
Assets	X	X	P + 100% of S
Liabilities	X	X	P + 100% of S
Equity			
Shares	X	X	P + 0% of S
Retained earnings	X	X	P + 0% of S*
Non-controlling interest	X	X	P + (1 - acq'n %) of S

Income statement consolidation (post acquisition of subsidiary)			
	P	**S**	Group
Revenue	X	X	P + 100% of S
Operating costs	(X)	(X)	P + 100% of S
EBIT	X	X	
Interest	(X)	(X)	P + 100% of S
PBT	X	X	
Taxation	(X)	(X)	P + 100% of S
Profit for the year	X	X	
Attributable to the non-controlling interest	x	x	(1 - acq'n %) of S's PAT
Attributable to the equity holders of the parent	x	x	
Profit for the year	X	X	

* At date of acquisition. Group retained earnings will include post acquisition earnings of subsidiaries

Acquisition accounting

Where the acquisition results in control of an entity, the acquisition method of accounting must be used.

The key steps in the acquisition method of accounting are:

- Identification of the 'acquirer' – the combining entity that obtains control of the acquiree
- Determination of the 'acquisition date' – the date on which the acquirer obtains control of the acquiree
- Recognition and measurement of the identifiable assets acquired and the liabilities assumed in the acquiree
- Dealing with any non-controlling interest (NCI, formerly called minority interest)
- Recognition and measurement of goodwill

The easiest way to explain the accounting is to build up an example, adding more complexity as the chapter progresses.

Illustration 1 – 100% acquisition/100% cash finance

On December 31, P acquired 100% of the shares of S for a cash consideration of 620. M&A advisory fees of 30 were paid.

Both companies prepare accounts to December 31.

The summarized balance sheets of the two companies as at December 31, immediately prior to the transaction were as follows:

Acquisition accounting – Impact on balance sheet

	P	S
PPE	1,416	302
Net working capital	888	168
Net funds (net debt)	339	(70)
Net assets	2,643	400
Shares	2,100	335
Retained earnings	543	65
Total equity	2,643	400

The balance sheet of S must be restated at fair value for group accounting purposes – assumed to be fair values here

Note that for the purposes of group accounts all balance sheet items of the subsidiary must be restated at fair value (see later).

When merger modeling (modeling the acquisition accounting impact of one company acquiring another), the key control and engine for the model is the sources and uses of funds.

In this illustration, the sources and uses are as follows:

Sources and uses of funds			
	Sources		Uses
Cash	650	Share acquisition	620
		M&A advisory fees	30
Total sources	650	Total uses	650

The balance sheet of P, after the acquisition but before consolidating S, would be as follows:

	P
PPE	1,416
Investment in S	620
Net working capital	888
Net debt	(311)
Net assets	2,613
Shares	2,100
Retained earnings	513
Total equity	2,613
Balance sheet check	OK

It is essential that the balance sheet balances. Putting in a check helps to ensure the accounting is right.

Points to note:

1. The presentation format of the balance sheet has been chosen so that net assets are clearly identifiable
2. An asset, being the investment in shares in S, of 620 now appears
3. The net funds of 339 have become net debt of 311 as a result of the 620 cash to S's shareholders and the 30 spent on M&A advisory fees.
4. The 30 advisory fees are immediately written off to retained earnings which have been reduced from 543 to 513
5. The balance sheet balances immediately after the acquisition

However, of far more interest, is what the group accounts will look like.

In the above illustration, 620 has been paid for the acquisition, however the fair value of the net assets acquired is 400. The difference is goodwill.

Goodwill

Goodwill can be regarded as future economic benefits arising from assets that are not capable of being individually identified and separately recognized. Therefore, goodwill acquired in a business combination represents a payment made by the acquirer in anticipation of future economic benefits from assets that cannot be individually identified and separately recognized.

In practice, calculating goodwill is a big task, as it is first necessary to identify and separately recognize at fair value all identifiable assets in the company being acquired ('acquisition date fair value of net assets acquired').

Items such as:

- Copyrights
- Internet domain names
- Client lists
- Customer relationships
- Patents
- Marketing rights
- Brands
- Royalty agreements
- Construction permits
- Operating and broadcasting rights
- Franchise agreements
- Trade secrets
- Databases
- Computer software
- Other intangible assets (many of which might not have been recognized previously on the balance sheet)

...have to be separately identified and valued.

This goodwill is not amortized as it is considered to have an indefinite life – however, it must be tested annually for impairment.

The calculation of goodwill is as follows:

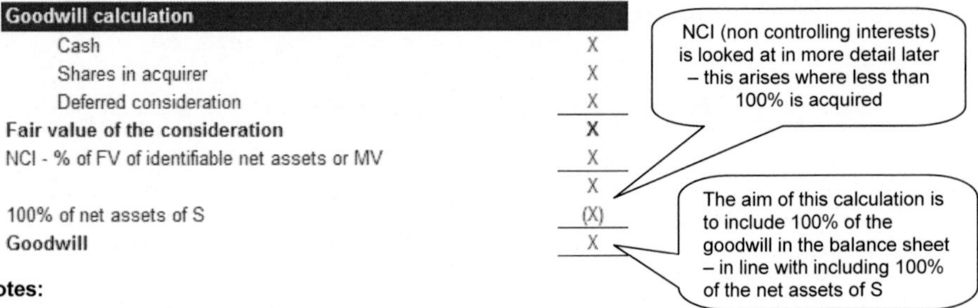

Goodwill calculation	
Cash	X
Shares in acquirer	X
Deferred consideration	X
Fair value of the consideration	**X**
NCI - % of FV of identifiable net assets or MV	X
	X
100% of net assets of S	(X)
Goodwill	X

Notes:

1. The consideration is made up of:
   a. Any cash consideration paid
   b. Shares in the parent offered as part of the consideration
   c. Deferred consideration/contingent consideration (commonly referred to as an 'earn-out') will be measured at its acquisition-date fair value, irrespective of the level of probability of being earned or measurement reliability
2. Where less than 100% of the shares are acquired (see later), the value of the NCI (the bit not acquired) is brought into the calculation – the reason for this is that the goodwill calculation relates to 100% of the business, rather than just the part of the business owned by the parent. However this can be calculated in one of two ways:
   a. Taking the non-controlling percentage of the fair value of the identifiable net assets (not allowed under US GAAP)
   b. Taking the fair value of the non-controlling interest (sometimes referred to as the full goodwill approach)
3. If the calculation of goodwill results in a negative amount, this is immediately written off in the income statement.

Contingent Consideration

Contingent consideration is a common element used in structuring transactions. The most common form of contingent consideration is an earn out. This is normally a cash payout that is structured around pre-defined financial performance hurdles.

Where contingent consideration forms part of the consideration, this usually creates an obligation to transfer assets to the previous owners of an acquiree as part of the deal. The transfer is normally contingent on the outcome of future events or by satisfying future performance criteria.

Contingent consideration is required to be recognized in the goodwill calculation at fair value even if the payment is not deemed to be probable at the date of the acquisition.

The consideration is then classified as either debt or equity. Cash based earn-out agreements will be classified as liabilities.

A key issue affecting deal structuring is the treatment of the contingent consideration between the transaction date and the resolution of the contingency. Consideration classified as a liability will be re-measured to fair value at each reporting date until the contingency is resolved. The fair value gains and losses will then pass through the income statement.

In contrast, equity classified contingent consideration is not re-measured.

Therefore a cash structured earn-out will add additional volatility to the post-acquisition income statement. This can lead to a preference for equity based contingent consideration.

IFRS and US GAAP are consistent on the treatment of contingent consideration.

These rules are recent changes and have changed the way transactions are structured.

M&A fess are those that are directly attributable to the acquisition.

They can include:

- Finder's fees
- IBD advisory fees
- Accounting fees
- Consultancy fees

M&A fees do not include general administrative costs or the cost of registering debt and equity securities.

M&A fees are written off as incurred to the income statement of the acquirer. This is a relatively new treatment. Previously, M&A fees were capitalized into goodwill.

Goodwill is recognized on the balance sheet and will only have an income statement impact if there is an impairment. Therefore when M&A fees were included in the goodwill calculations, the income statement was protected from dilution arising from the M&A fees.

Now that M&A fees are written off as incurred, clients must be made aware that the fees they are paying will have a dilutive effect on their income statements.

Negative Goodwill

Goodwill calculations can produce a negative number – negative goodwill – technically a 'bargain purchase'. This will happen if the fair value of identifiable net assets exceeds the fair value of consideration transferred and the value of the NCI.

A negative goodwill number can be the result of a forced sale where the seller is forced into selling its holding at a discount to its true fair value.

Negative goodwill is not recognized on the balance sheet. Rather it is shown as a 'gain' in the income statement.

An Analyst's initial reaction to a negative goodwill number in a model should be to review the formulas. Often the negative goodwill number is a formula error rather than a bargain purchase.

Bankers must make sure that they have:

- Picked up all the components of the consideration, not just the consideration transferred
- Included NCIs (and prior equity stakes if relevant)
- Revalued to fair value the target's identifiable net assets
- Checked the cell references that feed into the goodwill calculation

Illustration 1 – 100% acquisition / 100% cash finance (cont.)

In the above illustration, goodwill would be calculated as follows:

Goodwill calculation	
Cash	620
Shares in acquirer	n/a
Deferred consideration	n/a
Fair value of the consideration	**620**
NC	n/a
	620
100% of net assets of S	(400)
Goodwill	220

The group balance sheet, immediately after the acquisition would be as follows:

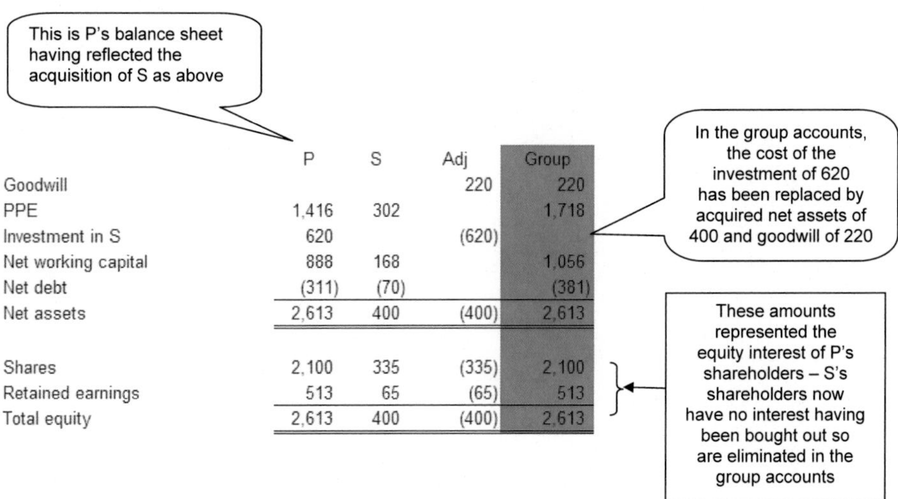

	P	S	Adj	Group
Goodwill			220	220
PPE	1,416	302		1,718
Investment in S	620		(620)	
Net working capital	888	168		1,056
Net debt	(311)	(70)		(381)
Net assets	2,613	400	(400)	2,613
Shares	2,100	335	(335)	2,100
Retained earnings	513	65	(65)	513
Total equity	2,613	400	(400)	2,613

Notes:

1. The first column is the Parent's balance sheet, adjusted for the acquisition as shown previously.
2. The adjustment column removes the investment in S, which only appears in the accounts of the parent as a separate entity, and brings in to the group balance sheet the goodwill calculated.
3. The shares and retained earnings in the group accounts are from the perspective of the parent's shareholders, so the shares and pre-acquisition retained earnings in S are eliminated.
4. The group balance sheet still balances.

Illustration 2 – 100% acquisition / equity and cash finance

On 31 December P acquired 100% of the shares of S, the total consideration of 620 being satisfied by an issue of shares in P with a fair value of 170 and a cash payment of 450. Advisory fees of 30 were paid. Equity and debt issue fees of 1 and 3 respectively were paid. Both companies prepare accounts to 31 December.

The summarized balance sheets of the two companies as at 31 December, immediately prior to the transaction were as before. The sources and uses of funds are as follows:

Sources and uses of funds			
	Sources		Uses
Cash	484	Share acquisition	620
Share issue	170	M&A advisory fees	30
		Equity issue fees	1
		Debt issue fees	3
Total sources	654	Total uses	654

The balance sheet of P, after the acquisition but before consolidating S, would be as follows:

	P	
PPE	1,416	
Investment in S	620	
Net working capital	888	
Net debt	(142)	=339-484+3
Net assets	2,782	
Shares	2,269	=2100+170-1
Retained earnings	513	=543-30
Total equity	2,782	
Balance sheet check	OK	

Points to note:

1. An asset, being the investment in shares in S, of 620 appears as before.
2. The net funds of 339 have become net debt of 142. This is as a result of the 484 (see sources of funds above) cash used and the capitalization of the 3 debt issue fees (see below).
3. Remember that, depending on the particular GAAP, the debt issue fees of 3 can be capitalized within the debt number or shown as a deferred asset (under US GAAP debt issue fees must be shown as a deferred asset).
4. The shares are increased by the fair value of the shares issued of 170, but reduced by the equity issue fees of 1.
5. The 30 advisory fees are immediately written off to retained earnings as before.
6. The balance sheet balances immediately after the acquisition.

Transaction costs relating to the issue of debt and equity

Under IFRS, when a financial liability is recognized initially, transaction costs that are directly attributable to the issue are deducted from the liability shown in the balance sheet.

Transaction costs are incremental costs that are directly attributable to the issue of a financial liability. An incremental cost is one that would not have been incurred if the entity had not issued the financial instrument. Transaction costs would include fees and commissions, levies to regulatory agencies and securities exchanges and transfer taxes and duties.

Under US GAAP the transaction costs are shown as a deferred asset.

Under IFRS and US GAAP, transaction costs that are directly attributable to the issue of the equity instrument should be accounted for as a deduction from the equity.

Illustration 2 – 100% acquisition / equity and cash finance (cont.)

Goodwill would be calculated as before.

The group balance sheet, immediately after the acquisition would be as follows:

	P	S	Adj	Group
Goodwill			220	220
PPE	1,416	302		1,718
Investment in S	620		(620)	
Net working capital	888	168		1,056
Net debt	(142)	(70)		(212)
Net assets	2,782	400	(400)	2,782
Shares	2,269	335	(335)	2,269
Retained earnings	513	65	(65)	513
Total equity	2,782	400	(400)	2,782

Notes:

1. The first column is the Parent's balance sheet, adjusted for the acquisition as shown previously.
2. The adjustment column removes the investment in S, which only appears in the accounts of the parent as a separate entity, and brings into the group balance sheet the goodwill calculated.
3. The shares and retained earnings in the group accounts are from the perspective of the parent's shareholders, so the shares and retained earnings in S are eliminated.
4. The group balance sheet still balances.

Illustration 3 – 80% acquisition / 100% cash finance

On December 31, P acquired 80% of the shares of S for a cash consideration of 450. Advisory fees of 30 were paid.

The market value of the 20% not acquired is 90 (see later for the significance of this).

Both companies prepare accounts to December 31.

The summarized balance sheets of the two companies as at December 31, immediately prior to the transaction were as follows:

	P	S
PPE	1,416	302
Net working capital	888	168
Net funds (net debt)	339	(70)
Net assets	2,643	400
Shares	2,100	335
Retained earnings	543	65
Total equity	2,643	400

Note that for the purposes of group accounts all balance sheet items of the subsidiary must be restated at fair value (assumed in this illustration).

The sources and uses of funds are as follows:

Sources and uses of funds			
	Sources		Uses
Cash	480	Share acquisition	450
		M&A advisory fees	30
Total sources	480	Total uses	480

The balance sheet of P, after the acquisition but before consolidating S, would be as follows:

	P
PPE	1,416
Investment in S	450
Net working capital	888
Net debt	(141)
Net assets	2,613
Shares	2,100
Retained earnings	513
Total equity	2,613

Points to note:

1. An asset, being the investment in shares in S, of 450 now appears.
2. The net funds of 339 have become net debt of 141 as a result of the 450 cash to S's shareholders and the 30 spent on advisory fees.
3. The 30 advisory fees are immediately written off to retained earnings which have been reduced from 543 to 513.
4. The balance sheet balances immediately after the acquisition.

However, of far more interest is what the group accounts will look like.

Non-controlling interest (NCI)

In the above illustration, 450 has been paid for the acquisition of S, but this is only for an 80% shareholding. The 20% not acquired is called the non-controlling interest (NCI).

Non-controlling interests in consolidated financial statements are presented as a component of equity, separate from the parent's shareholders' equity. The NCI is the part that the parent does not own.

Under IFRS NCI can be valued in two ways:

1. Using the fair value of the NCI
2. Using the NCI's proportionate share of the acquiree's identifiable net assets

Under US GAAP NCI must be valued at fair value. There is no net asset value option available.

NCI

NCI is the new term for minority interests. It is possible that bankers will continue to refer to this class of equity as a minority rather than follow the accounting NCI terminology.

The new terminology will be used in published financial statements. The NCI will be a component of equity on the balance sheet and will be disclosed at the bottom of the income statement.

Fair Valuation of NCI

The fair valuation of the NCI can be made with reference to an active equity market if the NCI is listed. If there is no available or liquid equity market price, the fair value of the NCI will have to be estimated using DCF and comps valuation techniques. If active market equity prices are used to value the NCI, care must be taken to ensure that the equity prices are not distorted by bid-speculation.

Under US GAAP, the NCI must be valued at fair value.

A choice exists in IFRS between fair value and the proportionate share of the acquiree's identifiable assets and liabilities.

Illustration 3 – 80% acquisition / 100% cash finance (cont.)

As covered earlier, the calculation of goodwill is as follows:

Goodwill calculation	
Cash	X
Shares in acquirer	X
Deferred consideration	X
Fair value of the consideration	**X**
NCI - % of FV of identifiable net assets or MV	X
	X
100% of net assets of S	(X)
Goodwill	X

In the above illustration, goodwill would be calculated in one of two ways as follows:

Goodwill – using % of net assets

This is 20% of the FV of the identifiable net assets of S (400) – this method is not allowed under US GAAP

Goodwill calculation - % of net assets approach	
Cash	450
Shares in acquirer	n/a
Deferred consideration	n/a
Fair value of the consideration	**450**
NCI (% of identifiable net assets)	80
	530
100% of net assets of S	(400)
Goodwill	130

The group balance sheet, immediately after the acquisition would be as follows:

	P	S	Adj	Group
Goodwill			130	130
PPE	1,416	302		1,718
Investment in S	450		(450)	
Net working capital	888	168		1,056
Net debt	(141)	(70)		(211)
Net assets	2,613	400	(320)	2,693
Shares	2,100	335	(335)	2,100
Retained earnings	513	65	(65)	513
Non-controlling interest			80	80
Total equity	2,613	400	(320)	2,693

These amounts represented the equity interest of P's shareholders – there is now a (residual) non controlling interest of 80, which is shown on a separate line within equity.

Notes:

1. The first column is the Parent's balance sheet, adjusted for the acquisition as shown previously.
2. The adjustment column removes the investment in S, which only appears in the accounts of the parent as a separate entity, and brings in to the group balance sheet the goodwill calculated of 130.
3. The shares and retained earnings in the group accounts are from the perspective of the parent's shareholders, so the shares and retained earnings in S are eliminated.
4. However as only 80% has been acquired, there is an NCI of 20% of 400 = 80 (using the % of net assets approach) – this is shown as a separate line within equity.
5. The group balance sheet still balances.

Goodwill – using FV

Under this approach, the NCI is valued at fair value (FV). It should be appreciated that it would probably be inappropriate to value a non-controlling interest on the same basis as a controlling interest due to the lack of control. For example, it is unlikely that a 20% shareholding would be valued at 20/80 of an 80% holding. In this illustration, the 20% shareholding is assumed to have a value of 90, which is less than 20/80 of 450 (the consideration for the 80% shareholding).

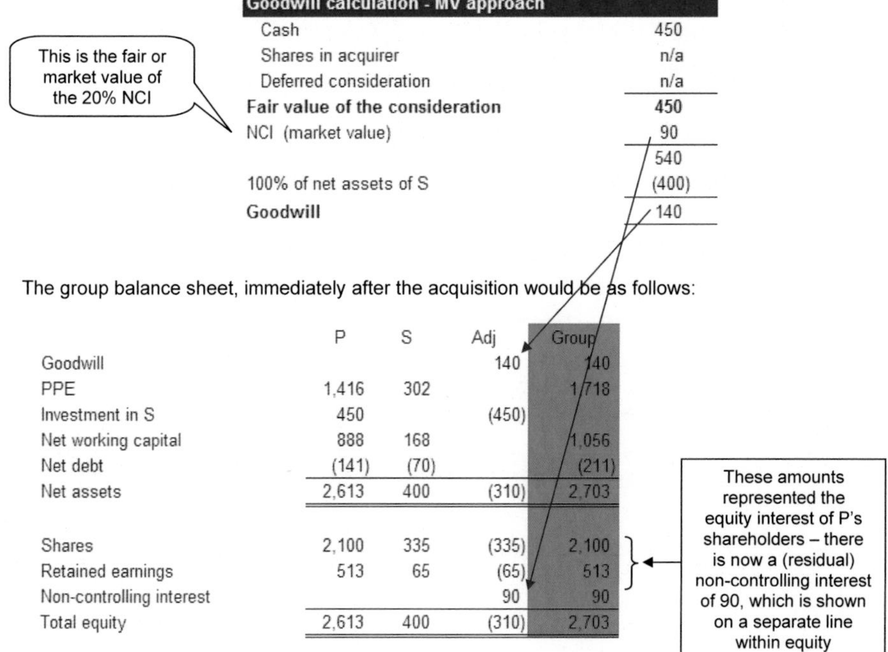

Goodwill calculation - MV approach	
Cash	450
Shares in acquirer	n/a
Deferred consideration	n/a
Fair value of the consideration	**450**
NCI (market value)	90
	540
100% of net assets of S	(400)
Goodwill	140

The group balance sheet, immediately after the acquisition would be as follows:

	P	S	Adj	Group
Goodwill			140	140
PPE	1,416	302		1,718
Investment in S	450		(450)	
Net working capital	888	168		1,056
Net debt	(141)	(70)		(211)
Net assets	2,613	400	(310)	2,703
Shares	2,100	335	(335)	2,100
Retained earnings	513	65	(65)	513
Non-controlling interest			90	90
Total equity	2,613	400	(310)	2,703

Notes:

1. The first column is the Parent's balance sheet, adjusted for the acquisition as shown previously.
2. The adjustment column removes the investment in S, which only appears in the accounts of the parent as a separate entity, and brings in to the group balance sheet the goodwill calculated of 140.
3. The shares and retained earnings in the group accounts are from the perspective of the parent's shareholders, so the shares and retained earnings in S are eliminated.
4. However as only 80% has been acquired, there is an NCI of 20% – however this time it is valued at 90 – this is shown as a separate line within equity.
5. The group balance sheet still balances.

Acquisition accounting – impact on the income statement

The income statement, following the acquisition, is the aggregate of the income statements of the combined entities, on a line-by-line basis. However there are a number of points to bear in mind:

1. The income statement of the acquired company (but not the parent) is based on the fair values, not the book values. Therefore if PPE or intangible assets have been re-valued, then depreciation and amortization respectively will be based on these revised amounts.
2. As with the balance sheet, where there is control, 100% of the subsidiary's income statement is added to the parent's on a line-by-line basis.
3. The net income has to be split into:
   a. Attributable to the non-controlling interest
   b. Attributable to the equity holders of the parent

Illustration 3 – 80% acquisition / 100% cash finance (cont.)

On December 31, P acquired 80% of the shares of S for a cash consideration of 450. Advisory fees of 30 were paid.

The market value of the 20% not acquired (the NCI) is 90.

Both companies prepare accounts to December 31.

It is anticipated that the interest cost of financing the 480 cash outlay (450 + 30 above) will be 25 in the year following the acquisition. It is also expected that synergies (cost savings from the elimination of duplicate processes and procedures etc) will be 150 in the first year. P pays corporation tax at a rate of 28%.

The forecast income statements for the two companies for the year following the acquisition are anticipated to be as follows:

	P	
Sales	2,500	1,000
Operating costs	(1,625)	(580)
EBIT	875	420
Interest (expense) / income	14	(4)
PBT	889	416
Tax	(311)	(116)
Profit for the year	578	300

The following will be assumed:

1. The figures for P have not yet reflected the impact of acquiring S.
2. The figures for S have already been adjusted to reflect fair values (for example any depreciation is based on the fair value of PPE).
3. The synergies will all arise within P.

The income statement of P, after adjusting for the interest, synergies and tax impacts, but before consolidating would be as follows:

	P	Adj	P adjusted
Sales	2,500	--	2,500
Operating costs	(1,625)	150	(1,475)
EBIT	875	150	1,025
Interest (expense) / income	14	(25)	(11)
PBT	889	125	1,014
Tax	(311)	(35)	(346)
Profit for the year	578	90	668

Points to note:

1. The anticipated synergies have reduced the forecast costs, and hence increased the forecast EBIT of P by 150.
2. The forecast interest cost of financing the 480 of 25 has turned what was originally anticipated to be net interest income of 14 into a net interest expense of 11.
3. The impact of the above two adjustments is to increase profit before tax by 125.
4. If PBT is expected to be 125 larger, then the tax, at 28%, will be 35 bigger, reducing net income accordingly.

The group income statement for the year following acquisition would be as follows:

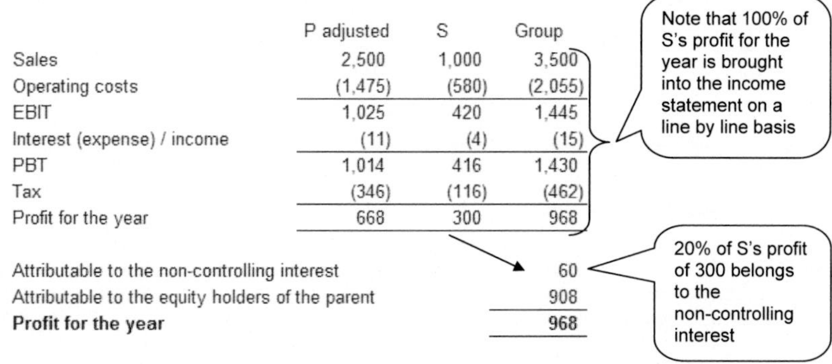

	P adjusted	S	Group
Sales	2,500	1,000	3,500
Operating costs	(1,475)	(580)	(2,055)
EBIT	1,025	420	1,445
Interest (expense) / income	(11)	(4)	(15)
PBT	1,014	416	1,430
Tax	(346)	(116)	(462)
Profit for the year	668	300	968
Attributable to the non-controlling interest			60
Attributable to the equity holders of the parent			908
Profit for the year			**968**

Points to note:

1. Despite owning 80% of S, 100% of S's profits are brought in on a line-by-line basis.
2. Of the profit for the year of 968, 60 (20% of 300) is attributable to the non-controlling interest.

Accounting for associates/affiliates

The key to the definition of an associate (or affiliate) is 'significant influence' which is the power to participate in the financial and operating decisions of the entity but which is not control or joint control over those policies.

It is presumed that where an investor holds 20% or more of the voting power of an entity, it has significant influence over that entity. However this presumption can be rebutted where an investor can demonstrate that it does not have significant influence.

An associate is accounted for using the equity method of accounting.

US GAAP – unconsolidated affiliates

US GAAP often refers to associates as unconsolidated affiliates or equity accounted investments. These investments will be accounted for using equity accounting rules.

Assessing Influence

Typically associates are investments where the investee holding is between 20-40% of the voting shares of the entity. In most cases, this level of shareholding and subsequent influence would lead to accounting for the investment as an associate.

However, an over-reliance on the shareholding percentage can lead to analytical issues.

For instance, Coca Cola owns 34% of Coca Cola Enterprises Inc (CCE) (listed on the NYSE). 93% of CCE's revenues were generated by Coca Cola products. Only 7% of the revenues were generated by non-Coca Cola products.

US GAAP treats this investment as an associate in the Coca Cola Inc accounts. However, given that the group supplies the vast majority of CCE's product, and much of this product has a 'secret' recipe it would not be a material leap of faith to argue that the group has effective control over CCE.

There is nothing to stop Analysts, who have this belief, treating CCE as a subsidiary and consolidating the business into a pro-forma set of Coca Cola Inc numbers for analysis purposes.

Equity method

Under the equity method, the investment is initially recorded in one line in the balance sheet at cost (strictly, share of net assets plus goodwill but it comes to the same thing as we will see). Thereafter the investment is increased or decreased to recognize the investor's share of the profit or loss of the associate after the date of acquisition.

The investor's share of the profit or loss of the associate after the date of acquisition is brought in to the investor's income statement in one line.

The equity method is often referred to as a 'one-line consolidation' since both the balance sheet and income statement disclose the impact of the associate in one line.

The easiest way to explain the accounting is to build up an example.

Equity accounting illustration

On December 31, P acquired 20% of the shares of A for a cash consideration of 90. Advisory fees of 5 were paid.

Both companies prepare accounts to December 31.

It is anticipated that the interest cost of financing the 95 cash outlay (90 + 5 above) will be 5 in the year following the acquisition. P pays corporation tax at a rate of 40%.

P expects to receive a dividend from A in the following year of 20.

The summarized balance sheets of the two companies as at December 31, immediately prior to the transaction were as follows:

	P	A
PPE	1,416	302
Net working capital	888	168
Net funds (net debt)	339	(70)
Net assets	2,643	400
Shares	2,100	335
Retained earnings	543	65
Total equity	2,643	400

Note that all balance sheet items of A must be restated at their fair values.

The sources and uses of funds are as follows:

Sources and uses of funds			
	Sources		Uses
Cash	95	Share acquisition	90
		M&A advisory fees	5
Total sources	95	Total uses	95

The balance sheet of P immediately after the acquisition of the associate would be as follows:

	P
PPE	1,416
Investment in Associate (A)	90
Net working capital	888
Net funds	244
Net assets	2,638
Shares	2,100
Retained earnings	538
Total equity	2,638

Points to note:

1. The investment is shown in one line as 90. However, it is important to break down this amount into its constituent parts:

Share of identifiable net assets	80
Goodwill (90 - 80)	10
Investment in Associate	90

The reason for the split is that the goodwill will need to be reviewed annually for impairment:

- Net funds have been reduced by 95 (90 cost of investment + 5 advisory fees)
- Retained earnings have been reduced by the 5 advisory fees
- Note that as it is a one line consolidation, and P only brings in its 20% share, there are no non-controlling interest issues

Credit Analysis of Net Debt

One of the major analytical issues arising out of equity accounting is how to assess net debt embedded in the associate. An associate can be structured to hold significant amounts of (net) debt. The lenders of this (net) debt often have no legal recourse to the parent company, however due possibly to the strategic nature of the associate's activities, the parent might not want the associate to fail. However, as a result of equity accounting, the associate's net debt does not get consolidated directly into the net debt line of the consolidated accounts.

For instance, Coca Cola structures most of its bottlers as associates. These associates hold a significant amount of net debt. Therefore when analyzing the accounts of Coca Cola Inc (the consolidated group accounts), the net debt line only captures the net debt of the parent and its subsidiaries. However, the bottlers are strategically crucial to the group as a whole. Therefore the credit risk carried in the net debt of the associates must be analyzed.

Analysts will have to pick up the accounts of the associates and calculate the net debt of these entities. The next issue is how much of the associate's net debt should be included in the overall net debt calculation.

The accounting would suggest that the Analysts should include the group's ownership proportion. However, strategically, for instance with Coca Cola's bottlers, there is an argument for including the full 100% of the associate's net debt in the analysis – as the associate itself is so crucial to the overall viability of the group.

S&P and Moody's will consider the net debt embedded in the associates of Coca Cola when determining its credit rating.

There can be a significant difference between the fair value and book value of the associate/affiliate. Failure to appreciate this issue can lead to materially mis-stated valuations.

Equity accounting illustration (cont.)

The forecast income statements for the two companies for the year following the acquisition are anticipated to be as follows:

	P	A
Sales	2,500	1,000
Operating costs	(1,625)	(580)
EBIT	875	420
Interest (expense) / income	14	(4)
PBT	889	416
Tax	(311)	(116)
Profit for the year	578	300

The group income statement for the year following acquisition would be as follows:

	P	Adj	P adjusted
Sales	2,500		2,500
Operating costs	(1,625)		(1,625)
EBIT	875		875
Interest (expense) / income	14	(5)	9
Share of profit of associate		60	60
PBT	889	55	944
Tax	(311)	2	(309)
Profit for the year	578	57	635

Points to note:

1. The forecast interest cost of financing the acquisition of 5 has reduced net interest income from 14 to 9.
2. P's share of A's profit for the year of 300 is 60 (20% of 300) and it is shown in one line, generally (but not always) somewhere below operating profit (EBIT). Note that this is already a post-tax number. It is important to realize that it is the share of A's profit for the year that goes into the income statement, not the dividends (if any) received in respect of the investment.
3. The tax line is adjusted by the tax saving (at 40%) on the interest of 5. Therefore the net of tax cost of the interest to finance the acquisition is 3.

The earnings generated by associates (and joint ventures – see later) are usually brought into the consolidated income statement just below the EBIT line (operating profit in the Tesco example below). This number is post-tax.

53 weeks ended 28 February 2009	notes	£m	£m
Continuing operations			
Revenue (sales excluding VAT)	2	**54,327**	47,298
Cost of sales		**(50,109)**	(43,668)
Gross profit		**4,218**	3,630
Administrative expenses		**(1,248)**	(1,027)
Profit arising on property-related items	2/3	**236**	188
Operating profit	2	**3,206**	2,791
Share of post-tax profits of joint ventures and associates	13	**110**	75
Finance income	5	**116**	187
Finance costs	5	**(478)**	(250)
Profit before tax	3	**2,954**	2,803
Taxation	6	**(788)**	(673)
Profit for the year		**2,166**	2,130

Source: Tesco accounts

A common mistake is to treat the earnings generated by the associate investments as pre-tax numbers – due to the location of the line item in the consolidated income statement. The share of joint ventures and associates number is often disclosed above the tax number, but it is a post-tax number.

Sometimes the associate result is mistakenly added to EBIT in an attempt to produce a core-operating metric. This type of adjustment is driven by the belief that the associate investments are part of the core operations of the group. Therefore adding their results into EBIT creates a core operating metric.

However, in reality this creates an inconsistent metric – EBIT metrics cannot be combined with post-tax (and interest) associate numbers.

For analysis and financial modeling purposes, it is useful to reclassify the earnings generated by the associates and disclose them below the tax line. This helps to prevent any pre/post-tax mismatch of metric components.

EBIT(DA) Metrics

Equity accounting illustration (cont.)
Investment in A – 1 year later

In one year's time, P will show its investment in A as follows:

At the start of the year	90
Share of profit of A	60
Dividend received from A	(20)
At the end of the year	130

Points to note:

1. The investment is increased by P's share of profit of 60. So the dual effect is quite apparent – the 60 increases profit (and hence equity) and it also increases the asset investment in the balance sheet.
2. The dividend received from A reduces the investment in the balance sheet. Again the dual effect is quite apparent – the 20 reduces the asset investment but increases the asset cash by 20 (the 20 would appear in the cash flow statement).

Joint ventures

A joint venture is a contractual arrangement whereby two or more parties undertake an economic activity that is subject to joint control. The key point here is that no one party has control but decisions require the unanimous consent of all the parties sharing control.

Under IFRS there are currently two allowable methods of accounting for joint ventures:

1. Equity accounting (already seen above)
2. Proportional consolidation (will probably be banned in the near future)

Proportional consolidation

Proportional consolidation is a method of accounting whereby an investor's share of the assets, liabilities, income and expenses of a jointly controlled entity is combined line by line with similar items in the investor's financial statements.

JVs – US GAAP

Proportional consolidation is an option under IFRS. However, its use is greatly limited under US GAAP. Proportional consolidation is allowed in very limited circumstances for unincorporated entities in certain industries.

US GAAP will first assess whether the JV entity is a VIE – a variable interest entity (discussed earlier in these notes). If the JV entity is deemed to be a VIE, the entity will be consolidated. If the JV is not deemed to be a VIE, it will be equity accounted, unless the entity is captured by the limited unincorporated entity exception.

Proportional consolidation illustration

The easiest way to explain the accounting is to build up an example. We will use the same numbers as we used for the associates example as it will be useful to compare the results.

On December 31, P acquired 20% of the shares of J for a cash consideration of 90. It is assumed that the other 80% of the company is equally owned by four other parties, such that J is jointly controlled by the five. Advisory fees of 5 were paid.

Both companies prepare accounts to December 31.

It is anticipated that the interest cost of financing the 95 cash outlay (90 + 5 above) will be 5 in the year following the acquisition. P pays corporation tax at a rate of 40%.

P expects to receive a dividend from J in the following year of 20.

The summarized balance sheets of the two companies as at December 31, immediately prior to the transaction, were as follows:

	P	J
PPE	1,416	302
Net working capital	888	168
Net funds (net debt)	339	(70)
Net assets	2,643	400
Shares	2,100	335
Retained earnings	543	65
Total equity	2,643	400

Note that all balance sheet items of J must be restated at their fair values.

The sources and uses of funds are as follows:

Sources and uses of funds			
	Sources		Uses
Cash	95	Share acquisition	90
		M&A advisory fees	5
Total sources	95	Total uses	95

The balance sheet of P immediately after the acquisition of 20% of J, but before proportionately consolidating J, would be:

	P
PPE	1,416
Investment in JV (J)	90
Net working capital	888
Net funds (net debt)	244
Net assets	2,638
Shares	2,100
Retained earnings	538
Total equity	2,638

Points to note:

1. An asset, being the investment in J, of 90 appears
2. Net funds have been reduced by 95 (90 cost of investment + 5 advisory fees)
3. Retained earnings have been reduced by the 5 advisory fees

The group balance sheet after proportionately consolidating would be as follows:

	P	J	Adj	Group
Goodwill			10	10
PPE	1,416	302		1,476
Investment in JV (J)	90		(90)	
Net working capital	888	168		922
Net funds (net debt)	244	(70)		230
Net assets	2,638	400	(80)	2,638
Shares	2,100	335	(67)	2,100
Retained earnings	538	65	(13)	538
Total equity	2,638	400	(80)	2,638

Points to note:

1. Goodwill would be calculated as follows:

Consideration	90
Share of net assets (20% of 400)	(80)
Goodwill	10

2. The final column for PPE, net working capital and net debt is P + 20% of J – for example the PPE is 1,416 + 60 (20% of 302) = 1,476
3. The 90 investment in J is eliminated in the group accounts, having been replaced, line by line, by the goodwill of 10 and the share of net assets of 80 (20% of 400)
4. There is no non-controlling interest as only the 20% share has been brought in.
5. The balance sheet still balances.

The forecast income statements for the two companies for the year following the acquisition are anticipated to be as follows:

	P	J
Sales	2,500	1,000
Operating costs	(1,625)	(580)
EBIT	875	420
Interest (expense) / income	14	(4)
PBT	889	416
Tax	(311)	(116)
Profit for the year	578	300

The group income statement for the year following acquisition would be as follows:

	P	Adj	P adjusted	J	Group
Sales	2,500		2,500	1,000	2,700
Operating costs	(1,625)		(1,625)	(580)	(1,741)
EBIT	875		875	420	959
Interest (expense) / income	14	(5)	9	(4)	8
PBT	889	(5)	884	416	967
Tax	(311)	2	(309)	(116)	(332)
Profit for the year	578	(3)	575	300	635

Points to note:

1. The forecast interest cost of financing the acquisition of 5 has reduced net interest income from 14 to 9.
2. The tax line is adjusted by the tax saving (at 40%) on the interest of 5. Therefore the net of tax cost of the interest to finance the acquisition is 3.
3. The Group column is the sum of the P adjusted column and 20% of J's column. For example, sales is 2,500 for P plus 20% of J's 1,000 = 2,700.
4. Note that the profit for the year of 635 is identical to that produced using equity accounting earlier. However, whereas under equity accounting, the share of profits of 60 was brought in in one line, under proportional consolidation it is done on a line-by-line basis.

Proportional Consolidation and Enterprise Value

"Is it included in enterprise value and associated earnings metrics?"

The 'it' often relates to associates and joint ventures. If a joint venture is proportionally consolidated, then the proportionate share of the JV's profits are implicitly within all profit metrics and the proportionate share of the JV's net debt (and other balance sheet constituents of enterprise value) are implicitly within the enterprise value. Consequently, both the numerator and denominator of EV multiples are implicitly consistent.

Comps

Trading and transactions comps will capture the value of joint ventures in the enterprise value through the calculation of market capitalization. This is because the equity prices used to calculate market capitalization will price in the value of these investments.

Multiples must be constructed consistently – the denominators and numerators must be consistent. If a joint venture is proportionally consolidated, the earnings impact of the joint venture will be included in the earnings metrics. As the value of the joint venture will be included in the enterprise value calculation, the multiple will be consistent as the denominator and numerator both pick up the impact of the investment.

In this case, Analysts must decide whether they wish to keep the joint venture in the multiple from a consistency perspective or whether the joint venture impact should be removed in order to present a 'clean' comparable multiple.

Cleaning up the multiple is difficult for proportionally consolidated JVs as we need to find and then remove the proportionate share of the JV's net debt, pensions, NCI, equity market value, etc. which are subsumed within the group numbers. Similar problems arise in trying to find (and then adjust) the appropriate adjustments for the profit metrics which are subsumed in the group numbers. For these reasons, such adjustments are rarely done.

The result is that EV multiples generally include the impact of proportionally consolidated JVs.

DCF

If a JV is proportionally consolidated, the cash flows generated by the investment will be included in the free cash flow to firm forecasts due to the line by line consolidation of the JV results. Therefore the EV produced by the DCF will capture the value of the JV.

Breakdown of EV

If the EV captures the value of the JV as a result of the proportional consolidation process, the breakdown of EV to equity value must not include a component adding the value of the JV back in order to arrive at the equity value number. Failure to achieve this level of consistency can lead to the double-counting of the JV value.

Who uses proportional consolidation?

Proportional consolidation is primarily an IFRS issue. The accounting technique is used in continental Europe, for instance in France and the Netherlands. The technique remains, in terms of use, more the exception to the rule but can be seen across some sectors such as Telecoms and Oil and Gas.

Disposals

When a parent disposes of a controlling interest, the gain or loss in the group accounts is calculated as follows:

Gain/loss on disposal of a controlling interest	
Fair value of consideration received	X
Fair value of residual interest	X
NCI at date of disposal - derecognised	X
Net assets and goodwill derecognised	(X)
Gain/(loss) on disposal	X/(X)

Illustration

Tiger purchased a 90% stake in Gazelle some years ago for 5,900. The fair value of Gazelle's net assets at that date was 5,500. The fair value of the NCI at that date was 1,400.

Goodwill on acquisition was as follows:

Goodwill	
Consideration	5,900
FV of NCI in Gazelle at acquisition	1,400
FV of net assets at acquisition	(5,500)
Goodwill	1,800

It is the group policy to use the full goodwill method (i.e. use FV) and there has been no impairment of goodwill since acquisition. Tiger has now decided to dispose of its entire holding in Gazelle.

The following facts are relevant:

- Sale proceeds of the 90% stake – 10,000
- Net assets of Gazelle at disposal date – 8,000

The net assets over the period of ownership have increased by 2,500 (8,000 – 5,500). 90% of that increase (2,250 being 90% x 2,500) will be reflected in the retained earnings of the parent and the NCI will have increased by the remaining 250.

The balance sheet of the Tiger group, immediately prior to the disposal, is as follows:

	Group
Goodwill	1,800
PPE	11,100
Net current assets	6,600
Net funds (debt)	(500)
	19,000
Shares	12,000
Retained earnings	5,350
NCI	1,650
	19,000

The breakdown of the net assets of Gazelle is as follows:

	Gazelle
PPE	3,700
Net current assets	3,400
Net funds (debt)	900
	8,000

The sources and uses of funds are as follows:

Sources and uses of funds			
	Sources		Uses
Sale of shares	10,000	Reduce net debt	10,000
Total sources	10,000	Total uses	10,000

The revised group balance sheet will be as follows:

	Group	Disposal	Group (revised)
Goodwill	1,800	(1,800)	--
PPE	11,100	(3,700)	7,400
Net current assets	6,600	(3,400)	3,200
Net funds (debt)	(500)	9,100	8,600
	19,000	200	19,200
Shares	12,000		12,000
Retained earnings	5,350	1,850	7,200
NCI	1,650	(1,650)	--
	19,000	200	19,200

Points to note:

1. Goodwill of 1,800 is eliminated as it all related to the acquisition of Gazelle
2. Net assets of 8,000 are stripped out, line by line (3,700 + 3,400 + 900)
3. Net funds are reduced by the 900 net funds of Gazelle but increased by the 10,000 proceeds
4. Retained earnings are increased by the gain on disposal of 1,850 (see below)
5. The NCI of 1,650 is removed as the subsidiary Gazelle has been disposed of

On disposal of the shares, the following gain will result:

Disposal	
Fair value of consideration received	10,000
Fair value of residual interest	--
NCI at date of disposal - derecognised	1,650
Goodwill - derecognised	(1,800)
FV of NA of Gazelle derecognised	(8,000)
Gain on disposal	1,850

Deferred taxation

In a business combination that is an acquisition, the identifiable assets and liabilities of the acquired business are recognized in the consolidated financial statements at their fair values at the date of acquisition.

If, for example, the carrying amount of PPE is increased by 100, this is an acknowledgement that additional future economic benefits of 100 are expected from that asset, on which tax will be payable at some time in the future. If the tax rate is 35%, additional tax of 35 will be payable in the future. A deferred tax liability of 35 should therefore be recognized in the financial statements.

In an acquisition context, the resulting deferred tax liability affects goodwill. Note that although goodwill arising on the acquisition could be argued to reflect future economic benefits and so could lead to a future tax liability, deferred taxation is not recognized on the goodwill itself as the calculations would become circular.

Illustration – deferred tax on an acquisition

On 31 December P acquired 100% of the shares of S for a cash consideration of 1,000. The balance sheets of P and S as at the date of the acquisition, before making any fair value adjustments to S's balance sheet, are as follows:

	P	S
PPE	1,416	423
Net working capital	888	235
Net funds (net debt)	339	(98)
Net assets	2,643	560
Shares	2,100	469
Retained earnings	543	91
Total equity	2,643	560

The balance sheet of P, following the acquisition of S, would be as follows:

	P
PPE	1,416
Investment in S	1,000
Net working capital	888
Net debt	(661)
Net assets	2,643
Shares	2,100
Retained earnings	543
Total equity	2,643

A fair value exercise is carried out on S with the following results:

Intangible assets (identified)	96	⬆
PPE	127	⬆
Net working capital	(23)	⬇
FV uplift	200	

The balance sheet of S, using fair values, is therefore as follows:

	S
Intangible assets (identified)	96
PPE	550
Net working capital	212
Net funds (net debt)	(98)
	760
Shares	469
Retained earnings	291
Total equity	760

As there has been a fair value uplift of 200 (760 – 560), a deferred tax liability arises in the consolidated accounts. Assuming S pays tax at 35%, a deferred tax liability of 70 (35% of 200) arises.

However, the reduction in the fair value of the identifiable net assets by the deferred tax liability of 70 increases the goodwill by the same amount which would be calculated as follows:

Goodwill calculation	
Fair value of the consideration	1,000
Fair value of 100% of net assets of S	(760)
Deferred tax	70
Goodwill	310

The group balance sheet immediately after the acquisition would be as follows:

	P	S	Adj	Group
Goodwill			310	310
Intangible assets (identified)		96		96
PPE	1,416	550		1,966
Investment in S	1,000		(1,000)	
Net working capital	888	212		1,100
Net debt	(661)	(98)		(759)
Deferred tax liability			(70)	(70)
Net assets	2,643	760	(760)	2,643
Shares	2,100	469	(469)	2,100
Retained earnings	543	291	(291)	543
Total equity	2,643	760	(760)	2,643

Tick-sheet: M&A Accounting

Acquisition accounting

- Must control the entity.
- Include 100% of fair value of identifiable assets and liabilities of subsidiary in group balance sheet.
- Where less than 100%, NCI is part of equity.
- Choice of goodwill calculation – fair value or net assets approach for NCI.
- Include 100% of the subsidiary's income and expenses in the group income statement on a line-by-line basis.
- The net income has to be split between that attributable to the NCI and that attributable to the equity holders of the parent.

Transaction costs

- M&A fees are immediately written off to retained earnings.
- Equity issue fees reduce equity.
- Under IFRS debt issue fees reduce the debt figure in the balance sheet but under US GAAP are shown as a deferred asset.

Equity accounting for associates/affiliates

- Must have the power to exert significant influence over the entity, but not control.
- Investment in associate is shown in one line on the balance sheet – one-line consolidation (the equity method).
- Initially investment in associate shown at cost, thereafter the investment increases or decreases to reflect the investor's share of the increase or decrease in the net assets of the associate.
- The income statement brings in, in one line, the investor's share of the profit after tax of the associate – note this is a post-interest and tax figure but is often shown around the EBIT level within the income statement.

Joint ventures

- A joint venture is a contractual arrangement whereby two or more parties undertake an economic activity that is subject to joint control.
- With a joint venture, no one party has control, but decisions require the consent of all parties.
- Under IFRS there are two allowable methods of accounting for joint ventures:
  - Equity method
  - Proportional consolidation

Proportional consolidation

- Bring in, line-by-line, the venturer's share of the assets and liabilities into the group balance sheet.
- Bring in, line-by-line, the venturer's share of the income and expenses into the group income statement.

Deferred tax

- A fair value exercise is carried out on acquisition. If this increases net assets, this is an acknowledgement that additional future economic benefits will flow to the enterprise. Therefore provision should be made for the additional tax payable in the future – a deferred tax liability. Conversely, if net assets have fallen, a deferred tax asset should be recognized.
- A deferred tax liability arising from the fair value exercise increases goodwill, and a deferred tax asset reduces goodwill.

Introduction

Ratios are financial analytical tools which, when applied to financial statements and similar data, help to assess a company's past performance, position and trends so that we can better forecast the future and make relevant financial decisions. Identifying the key metrics and understanding how they have been derived, i.e. the accounting, is essential to getting the most out of ratio analysis.

This chapter is, therefore, a link between the accounting sessions and the valuation, financing and modeling techniques which are based on the forecasts derived from historic accounting numbers.

The list of ratios can never be exhaustive and so we will run through only the key ratios. The definitions, possible variations, applications and interpretations will be explored for each.

Relative analysis

Interpreting financial metrics can be useful, however it should be done in a relative way. A profit of $100m is meaningless in its own right. We will interpret it in different ways if we know the prior year equivalent was $70m or $170m.

The same profit of $100m has different meanings if we know that the sales for the corresponding period were $800m or $200m (12.5% vs. 50% margin). However, ratio analysis is also best done in a relative way – comparing with the company's own past performance and/or relative to its peers.

- Understanding why the margin has grown from 11-12.5% over the year will help forecast future performance.
- Understanding why the 12.5% margin is less than the average for its peers (and how this relative change compares with its peers over the same period) will help forecast future performance and assist in understanding how the company should be valued.

This analysis is best attempted when industry and other economic data (tax rates, inflation, commodity prices, etc.) are understood.

Forecasting

If we can find a relationship between different financial metrics, i.e. there is a trend to the ratios, we can use the result to help drive the forecasts for the business. The better we are able to identify why a particular ratio moves in a particular way, the more valuable the forecasts that result.

Key Metrics

When extracting numbers from financials, a good analyst should be aware of the purpose of the analysis. This will steer the definition as to what is included and excluded from a metric. Typically the analysis is aimed at making the most credible forecasts (we are valuing/lending to a company based on what is likely to happen in the future). Consequently, when extracting numbers, the following should be considered. Is the number extracted:

1. Comparable with what has happened in previous periods, so that we have the most credible trend, e.g. are there one-off items which should be excluded?
2. Comparable with the definition of the other element of the ratio, e.g. if EBIT doesn't include profits from associates, then the investment in associates should be excluded from the definition of capital, in a return on capital calculation
3. Comparable with the same metric extracted for its peers, so that we are comparing like items, e.g. is net debt defined including all derivatives across the whole sector?
4. Indicative of what is likely to be ongoing performance, so that we can use it as the basis for forecasting, e.g. do we need to pro-forma acquisitions and disposals in any period?

In short, is the number to be extracted from the financials consistent and indicative of what is likely to happen in the future?

The following is a list of the key metrics (though, clearly, not exhaustive) used in analysis:

Income statement item	Typical adjustments	Typical analysis
Sales	Remove discontinued operations	Growth rates, margins
EBIT	Remove discontinued operations and exceptionals; should be net of JVs/associates	Growth rates, margins, interest cover, return on capital
D&A (for EBITDA) – typically found in notes	Only depreciation of tangibles and amortization of intangibles; ignore impairments	Growth rates, margins, interest cover, EBITDA – capex/interest, net debt/ EBITDA
Rental charge (for EBITDAR) – typically found in notes	Only on operating leases	Growth rates, margins, fixed charge cover
Interest charges	May want either gross income expense or net (of interest income); remove mark-to-market adjustments and impairments	Interest cover, fixed charge cover
Net income	Remove discontinued operations, exceptionals, all impairments and mark-to-market adjustments; all of these should be tax adjusted	EPS, growth rates, return on equity

Cash flow statement item	Typical adjustments	Typical analysis
Operating cash flow (OCF)	May be reported before or after tax and interest. In pure terms, should be pre-interest and tax.	Growth rate, margin, OCF/EBITDA, OCF/interest
Capex	May be gross capex or net (of disposals) capex. May include purchases (and disposals) of intangibles	Growth rate, Capex/depreciation, Net debt/EBITDA-capex, EBITDA-capex/interest
Dividends paid	Some Analysts use interim and proposed for the current year rather than the cash paid (which equates to last year's proposed and this year's interim).	Growth rate, payout ratio, dividend cover
Free cash flow	Many definitions depending on use. OCF less (possibly unlevered) tax and may be pre or post any of: gross capex, net capex, maintenance capex, interest, dividends paid.	Growth rate and others depending on definition

Balance sheet

The key metrics derived from the balance sheet are debt, net debt and equity. These are used in capital structure examination and returns analysis.

Balance sheet item	Typical adjustments	Part of net debt?	Part of capital employed?
Investments in JVs & associates	May include other investments which do not contribute to EBIT	No	Subtract
Cash and equivalents	May include (some) short-term investments	Yes	Subtract
Debt	Only borrowings - current and non-current (including finance/capital leases)	Yes	Add
Derivative assets and liabilities	Should only include those relating to financing, e.g. interest rate swaps, rather than operating	May form part of net debt	Add if included as part of net debt
Pensions	Should be net pension deficit (plan assets less obligations) less deferred tax asset thereon	Included in some definitions	Add
Preferred stock	Make sure not already included in debt or equity	Only if have debt characteristics	Add
Non-controlling interests (NCI)	May also be known as minority interests	No	Add
Equity	Include shares plus reserves – ensure other components aren't double counted, e.g. preference stock, NCI	No	Add
Operating leases (not on-BS)	Will need to look in notes to find numbers; capitalize to PV of minimum lease commitments or multiply rental charge by appropriate capitalization multiple	Included for sectors where buying vs. leasing varies across sector	Unlikely

Working capital

Additionally, the elements of working capital are useful in identifying the efficiency with which the company operates such as receivables days, supplier payment period and working capital turnover. Consequently, the components of working capital should be the resources used in the operating cycle of the business. Typically these will be inventories plus operating receivables less operating payables.

Profitability Ratios

The profit motive is behind most economic activity and so it is here that the analysis often begins.

The performance of the business is generally represented by the income statement. The following set of accounts will be used to illustrate the calculation and the analysis of the ratios.

Annual Report and Accounts

Group income statement

For the year ended 31 December			CHF million
Sales and other operating revenues	**6,187**	5,837	6,414
Purchases	**2,697**	2,899	2,544
Production and manufacturing expenses	**1,328**	1,303	1,370
Gross operating income	**2,162**	1,635	2,500
Selling, distribution and administration expenses	**1,252**	1,211	1,634
Depreciation, depletion and amortization	**94**	93	96
Impairment and losses on sale of businesses and fixed assets	--	67	21
Earnings (losses) from jointly controlled entities – after interest and tax	**5**	2	(3)
Earnings (losses) from associates – after interest and tax	**2**	1	(1)
Gains on sale of businesses and fixed assets	**21**	12	5
Profit before interest and taxation	**844**	279	750
Interest and other income	**3**	21	--
Finance costs	**152**	84	49
Net finance expense (income) relating to pensions and other post-retirement benefits	**(31)**	70	22
Profit before taxation	**726**	146	679
Taxation	**199**	58	198
Profit for the year	**527**	88	481
Attributable to			
Group shareholders	**517**	84	473
Minority interest	**10**	4	8
	527	88	481
Earnings per share – CHF			
Basic	**0.36**	0.06	0.33

Growth rates, e.g. sales	**Current year**	**Previous year**
$\text{Annual growth rate} = \frac{\text{Sales}_2}{\text{Sales}_1} - 1$	$\frac{6,187}{5,837} - 1 = 6.0\%$	$\frac{5,837}{6,414} - 1 = (9.0\%)$
$\text{Compound annual growth rate (CAGR)} = \left(\frac{\text{Sales}_n}{\text{Sales}_1}\right)^{\left(1/(n-1)\right)} - 1$		$\left(\frac{6,187}{6,414}\right)^{\left(1/(3-1)\right)} - 1 = (1.8\%)$

Possible variations

- Has relevance for most lines in the financials – income, costs, profits, cash flows, assets and liabilities
- Ensure the correct number of years of growth are used in CAGRs i.e. number of years of data minus 1

Interpretation and application

- Widely used to identify trends to assist in forecasting future performance
- The period for the CAGR should be that which is most relevant – a ten year CAGR is not relevant if the business significantly restructured three years ago, in which case the last three years (or maybe two) are most indicative of what is likely to happen in the future
- Identifying the reasons for the growth or decline are essential:
  - Sales growth arises from selling more products and/or increasing prices – is this due to a changing product mix, geographic focus, inflation environment, competitive environment, business acquisitions or discontinuance, etc.?
  - Looking at segmental information may give more clarity
  - Profit growth is explained by sales growth combined with the movement on costs. To isolate cost behavior we need to look at growth rates on individual cost lines and/or margins
  - In the current example, the previous year was a period in which sales suffered and so the current growth rate may not be most indicative of future growth. The negative CAGR suggests that trading hasn't returned to pre-slump levels. In this case it would be helpful to see segmental information, and have further historic data in order to understand the reasons for the results in the previous year

Margins, e.g. EBIT	**Current year**	**Previous year**
$\text{EBIT margin} = \frac{\text{EBIT}}{\text{Sales}} \times 100$	$\frac{(2{,}162 - 1{,}252 - 94)}{6{,}187} \times 100 = 13.2\%$	
		$\frac{331}{5{,}837} \times 100 = 5.7\%$

Possible variations

- A margin is (mostly) a profit figure divided by the sales
- The profit figure should always be normalized to be comparable – i.e. prior to any exceptional items
- Typical profit margins can be based on gross profit, EBITDAR, EBITDA, EBIT, PBT, Net income
- All pre-tax margins should exclude profits from associates/JVs, not only for consistency with all other uses of these profit metrics (ROC, EV multiples, etc), but also because sales do not include any results from associates/JVs and so any margin would be inconsistent
- Cash flow margins can be calculated, such as operating cash flow to sales, to help analyze the efficiency with which cash is created from sales
- Cost margins can be analyzed (e.g. staff costs/sales, rent/sales), to look at the development of these costs as activity (measured by sales) varies

Interpretation and application

- An EBIT margin compares the level of profit after all (normalized) operating costs generated from a unit of sales ($13.2 profit per $100 sales). If the movement on sales is explained by sales growth rates, then the EBIT margin can be used to explain how the operating costs have varied (reducing from $94.3 to $86.8 per $100 sales)
- An EBIT margin can be used to explain the movement in all operating costs. If more granularity is required in specific costs, then comparing different margins can be used. For example:
    - EBIT margin with EBITDA margin – the difference between EBIT and EBITDA is depreciation and amortization and so comparing the two margins can be used to analyze the movements in depreciation and amortization
    - EBITDA margin with EBITDAR margin – the difference between EBITDA and EBITDAR is operating lease rentals and so comparing the two margins can be used to analyze the movements in rentals
    - EBITDAR margin with gross profit margin (GPM) – the difference between EBITDAR and gross profit is other selling, general and administrative costs and so comparing the two margins can be used to analyze the movements in these
    - Analyzing the movements in the GPM will help to explain how the cost of goods sold structure has changed over time
    - In the current example, the company is making more profit per unit of sale than in the previous year (and so the unit costs must be less). Using the margin from the third historic year of 12.0% as the comparator for the most recent year, may be more meaningful as there were clearly trading difficulties arising in the previous year. Despite sales declining over the three years (though recovering from the previous year), margins have improved.

Returns ratios

Given enough resources, most businesses could generate a profit. The efficiency with which they do this is measured using returns ratios.

In order to do this, we need to understand the resources available to the business and so the capital structure derived from the balance sheet should be extracted. Based on the following balance sheet (and related net debt note), the capital structure could be:

Capital structure	**Current year**	**Previous year**	**Average**
Financial debt			
Short term	198	230	
Long term	798	783	
Gross debt	996	1,013	1,005
Related financial derivatives*			
Short term*	19	34	
Long term*	12	20	
Debt including derivatives	1,027	1,067	1,047
Cash and cash equivalents	(279)	(138)	
Related financial derivatives*	(24)	(30)	
Reported net debt	724	899	812
Pensions**	210	284	
Net debt incl. pre-tax pension deficit	**934**	**1,183**	**1,059**
Shareholders' equity	**1,687**	**1,334**	**1,511**
Non-controlling interests	112	113	
Investments in JVs	(32)	(29)	
Investments in associates	(45)	(45)	
Total capital employed	**2,656**	**2,556**	**2,606**

* assuming all derivatives are financial rather than operating
** assuming no tax adjustment

Annual Report and Accounts

Group balance sheet

At 31 December	CHF million	
Non-current assets		
Property, plant and equipment	**1,519**	1,408
Goodwill	**382**	371
Intangible assets	**132**	90
Investments in jointly controlled entities	**32**	29
Investments in associates	**45**	45
	2,110	1,943
Current assets		
Inventories	**544**	553
Trade and other receivables	**252**	352
Other current assets	**96**	101
Derivative financial instruments	**24**	30
Cash and cash equivalents	**279**	138
	1,195	1,174
Total assets	**3,305**	3,117
Current liabilities		
Trade and other payables	**177**	253
Derivative financial instruments	**19**	34
Financial debt	**198**	230
Current tax payable	**39**	11
Provisions	**--**	3
	433	531
Non-current liabilities		
Other payables	**3**	9
Derivative financial instruments	**12**	20
Financial debt	**798**	783
Deferred tax liabilities	**32**	22
Provisions	**18**	21
Defined benefit pension plan and other post-retirement benefit plan deficits	**210**	284
	1,073	1,139
Total liabilities	**1,506**	1,670
Net assets	**1,799**	1,447
Equity		
Share capital	**1,321**	1,317
Reserves	**366**	17
Shareholders' equity	**1,687**	1,334
Minority interest	**112**	113
Total equity	**1,799**	1,447

Group net debt

At 31 December	CHF million	
Financial debt		
Short term debt	**217**	264
Long term debt	**810**	803
Cash and cash equivalents	**303**	168
Total net debt	**724**	899

Ratios

Previous year	Current year	
Return on equity $= \frac{\text{Net income}}{\text{Equity}} \times 100$	$\frac{502}{1,687} \times 100 = 29.8\%$	
		$\frac{143}{1,334} \times 100 = 10.7\%$

Where net income has been calculated as:

Reported profit after tax and NCI	517	84	473
Less: gains on disposals*	(15)	(8)	(4)
Add: impairments*	--	67	21
Underlying net income	**502**	**143**	**490**

* assuming gains are taxable at the fiscal rate (30%) and impairments are not tax deductible

Possible variations

- Must be consistent between numerator and denominator
- As it is a measure of the return for the shareholders, the denominator should only include the equity holders capital (not preferred shareholders, nor NCI)
- The level of profit which is available to these shareholders is the residual after all other capital providers have been allocated their share. Hence the profit after preferred dividends and NCI
- The equity figure may be that at the end of the year (most freely available); at the start of the year (the amount available to generate the profits for the year); average in the year (the amount which has been generally available to generate the results)
- Could use market value measure of equity as the denominator, i.e. the market capitalization. This version measures the return on investing in the shares of the company at the current price. This can also be calculated as EPS / current share price

Interpretation and application

- ROE is typically an accounting measure of the annual rate of return (measured in profit terms) on the shareholders' investment (measured as their historic investment and that amount of the profit which they have allowed the company to retain). The higher the figure the more efficiently the shareholders' investment is being used to generate profits for them
- A ROE of 2% is bad – investors could get a higher rate of return investing in other companies or other asset classes, such as fixed income securities.
  A ROE of 29.8%, therefore, appears good. However, the absolute result has limited meaning. Manufacturers, hotel groups, construction companies, etc, are asset intensive and so require significant investment. They will have relatively low ROEs. By comparison, recruitment agencies may have little requirement for investment, and so capital, and may have very large ROEs
- The ROE should be compared across a group of peers
- The ROE should be compared year on year within the same company to analyze its development and trends over time
- If the ROE is to be measured in market value terms, using market capitalization as the denominator, then the result can be compared against the company's cost of equity to understand whether the company is creating shareholder value – giving a return greater than the cost of capital
- In the current example, despite the equity invested having risen by 26%, the ROE has grown enormously since the previous year. This is due to the low base profits from the previous year and the significant enhancement in margins explained above

Return on capital	**Current year**	**Previous year**
Return on capital employed (ROCE) = $\frac{\text{EBIT}}{\text{Capital}} \times 100$	$\frac{816}{2,656} \times 100 = 30.7\%$	$\frac{331}{2,556} \times 100 = 12.9\%$
Return on invested capital (ROIC) = $\frac{\text{EBIT} * (1 - t)}{\text{Capital}} \times 100$	$\frac{816 \times (1 - 30\%)}{2,656} \times 100 = 21.5\%$	$\frac{331 \times (1 - 30\%)}{2,556} \times 100 = 9.1\%$

Where: t is the tax rate – either fiscal or effective (as long as either is consistently applied)

Possible variations

- Must be consistent between numerator and denominator
- As it is a measure of the return for all the capital providers, the denominator should include all capital which has financed the operations – debt and equity
- The level of profit which is available to capital providers must be before making any allocations to them and so must be pre-interest. EBIT is a level of economic return available to all capital providers
- 100% of the EBIT of all subsidiaries (even those owned less than 100%) are included in EBIT. The NCIs are financing the group EBIT and so should be included in the definition of capital
- The profits from JVs and associates are not included in EBIT (to be consistent with every other use of EBIT) yet some of the capital raised by the business has been used to finance these investments.
  As EBIT excludes the profits from these investments, the amount invested should be removed from the capital
- The EBIT is not available to all the capital providers (in most jurisdictions) due to tax. Some definitions, therefore, tax the EBIT. An effective tax rate or fiscal tax rate should be applied consistently
- As with ROE, the capital figure may be that at the end of the year, at the start of the year or average in the year
- Could use market value measures of capital as the denominator, i.e. the enterprise value
- Simpler versions of ROC use a less rigorous definition of capital as total assets less current liabilities
- Other variants include return on assets (ROA= EBIT / Assets)

Interpretation and application

- ROC is typically an accounting measure of the annual rate of return (measured in profit terms) on the capital providers' investment (measured as their historic investment – and for shareholders, the amount of profit which they have allowed the company to retain). The higher the figure, the more efficiently the capital is being used to generate profits
- As with ROEs, a return of 10% has limited meaning due to different sectors having different investment requirements. The ROC should be compared across a group of peers
- The ROC should be compared year on year within the same company to analyze its development and trends over time
- If the ROC is to be measured in market value terms, using EV as the denominator, then the result can be compared against the company's WACC to understand whether the company is creating value – giving a return greater than the cost of capital. As the WACC is a post-tax measure, the numerator is best expressed in post-tax terms for consistency
- In the current example, the capital has remained relatively stable between the 2 years and so the growth in the ROC is explained by changes in the EBIT (as explained under sales growth and margin expansion above)
- The calculation can be disaggregated:

  $$\text{ROCE} = \frac{\text{EBIT}}{\text{Capital}} = \frac{\text{EBIT}}{\text{Sales}} \times \frac{\text{Sales}}{\text{Capital}}$$

- By comparing over time the EBIT margin and the levels of sales (activity) derived from the capital base of the company, we can see that the level of activity has increased only slightly (from $2.28 to $2.33 of sales per $1 of capital invested), whilst the EBIT margin has grown significantly. It is therefore the margin enhancement which primarily explains the ROC growth

Leverage ratios

Financial risk can be assessed using leverage ratios. As a result, these ratios are often used as covenants in loan documents. Additionally, these ratios can be used to assess the flexibility the company may have in raising new finance and what credit rating is relevant given their levels of debt.

	Current year	Previous year
Net debt / EBITDA $= \frac{\text{Net debt}}{\text{EBITDA}}$	$\frac{724}{910} = 0.8\text{x}$	$\frac{899}{424} = 2.1\text{x}$

Possible variations

- The numerator can vary in the same way that there are different definitions of net debt – whether or not to include:
  - Financial derivatives
  - Pensions (and whether pre or post-tax)
  - Capitalized operating leases (if included, the denominator should be EBITDAR)
- In addition, some definitions use gross debt before subtracting cash
- If EBITDA is not deemed to be a proxy for cash flow, then other variants may be used for the denominator, such as:
  - EBIT (where D&A is deemed to approximate to the true economic cost of maintaining the asset base)
  - EBITDA – Capex
  - Operating cash flow

Interpretation and application

- The assumption behind this ratio is that the EBITDA is a proxy for cash flow generated by the business and is therefore the cash flow available to support the company's debt. The lower the figure, the less time it would take to pay back the debt out of cash flow
- As capex can be a necessary cost of running the business then EBIT or EBITDA – Capex are used as better determinants of the cash flow available to service debt
- Where working capital movements are significant, then operating cash flows are used as the denominator
- Each version of the ratio should only be compared against those of the same definition
- In general terms, companies with figures greater than 3.5x would likely be non-investment grade. This is a rule of thumb and will significantly vary across sectors and geographic coverage
- In the current example, the previous year was a period in which trading suffered, leading to a significantly high 2.1x ratio. Borrowing had taken place when conditions were difficult and so the leverage ratios suffered in the slump. If there wasn't significant slack in the financial covenants, the company could have defaulted on the terms of their loans. Debt levels have been reduced over the last year as results have improved resulting in a less risky leverage ratio.

	Current year	Previous year
Net debt / capital = $\frac{\text{Net debt}}{\text{capital}}$	$\frac{724}{2,656} = 27.3\%$	
		$\frac{899}{2,556} = 35.2\%$

Possible variations

- The numerator can vary in the same way that there are different definitions of net debt – whether or not to include:
  - Financial derivatives
  - Pensions (and whether pre-or post-tax)
  - Capitalized operating leases
  - Cash as a deduction (i.e. net debt)
- In which case, the denominator should also include all these elements.
- The denominator must include all elements of financing – equity, debt, NCI less the amount of financing which has been invested in JVs and associates (as the ratio is aimed at measuring the proportion of the financing of the enterprise's operations that is debt financed).
- Other variants include (net) debt/equity (stated as a multiple).

Interpretation and application

- The ratio measures the proportion of the financing for the enterprise's operations which comes from debt. The higher the figure the riskier the leverage position. Low figures show a company with limited ability or desire for debt
- In the current example, the company has 27% of its financing from debt which has reduced over the year from 35%. The total capital has remained relatively stable and so the de-leverage has arisen from a reduction in the net debt – most of which is explained by the increase in cash
- If cash were to be eliminated from both the numerator and denominator, the ratio has gone from 39% to 35% over the period
- The increasing cash position gives the business increased flexibility for the future, although some Analysts may regard the build-up of cash as inefficient. Given the company's problems in the previous year, a store of cash may be necessary in order to placate lenders

Debt capacity ratios

Financial risk can be assessed using leverage ratios, as we have seen. The capacity of the company to service this debt is measured using coverage ratios which are also often used as covenants in loan documents.

	Current year	Previous year
$\text{Interest cover} = \dfrac{\text{EBITDA}}{\text{Net interest expense}}$	$\dfrac{910}{152-31-3} = 7.7\text{x}$	$\dfrac{424}{84+70-21} = 3.2\text{x}$

Possible variations

- As the numerator is deemed to be a proxy for cash flow, the definitions can vary significantly:
  - EBITDA
  - EBIT (where depreciation is deemed to be an economic cost of running the business)
  - EBITDA – Capex (where capex captures the significant cash flow arising from maintaining and growing the business)
  - Operating cash flow (but must be a pre-interest cash flow)
  - Operating cash flow less capex
- The numerator may also be adjusted to include investment income
- The denominator may be
  - Net interest expense
  - Gross interest expense
  - Cash interest paid (for cash based ratios and where there are significant discounted debt instruments such that the income statement interest charge does not reflect the cash payments)
- The exclusions from the denominator, to get a fairer reflection of the cost of servicing the debt, may include:
  - Fair value adjustments on financial instruments
  - The finance charge/income on pensions
  - The effects of capitalized interest

Interpretation and application

- This set of ratios is aimed at measuring the cash flow available to service debt against the annual service cost. Consequently, the numerator, the EBITDA in this case, is a proxy for cash flow generated by the business and is therefore deemed to be the cash flow available to service the company's debt. The interest should be a measure of the annual cost of servicing the debt, from either an income statement or cash flow perspective.
- The higher the multiple, the more cash flow is available for debt service and, hence, the more capacity the company has for further borrowing.
- In its simplest form, (EBITDA / net interest expense), clearly not all the cash flow (deemed to be EBITDA) is available for debt service (deemed to be net interest expense). Most businesses will have working capital requirements; have tax and capex payments to make; whilst also receiving investment income. Hence, there are weaknesses in using EBITDA as the numerator.
- The net interest charge in the income statement may be affected by many accruals based accounting policies, such as accounting for:
  - Capitalization of interest
  - Pensions
  - Discounted debt and finance fees
  - Leases
  - Fair values on financial instruments

- In addition, interest income has been netted off in the headline figure for net interest expense. Consequently, the denominator may not capture the true cost of the annual service charge
- As with most ratios, the definitions are rarely going to be a catch-all. However, it is the relative (to peers, to other years) interpretation using the same definition which is of most value
- It is most instructive to look over the past three years in the current example. The EBITDA fell by more than 50% between the first two years before recovering in the last. At the same time the net interest expense increased and then decreased. Consequently, it appears that the prior year was a very poor year but that the debt capacity of the company has improved markedly in the most recent year. However, if we strip out the effects of pensions and interest income, the EBITDA/interest expense has improved only marginally from 5.0x to 6.0x in the last two years, suggesting that the cost of debt finance has increased significantly for the company over this time (given the slight reduction in overall debt)

	Current year	Previous year
Fixed charge cover $= \frac{\text{EBITDAR}}{\text{Interest expense} + \text{rent}}$	$\frac{910 + 113}{152 + 113} = 3.9\text{x}$	
		$\frac{424 + 109}{84 + 109} = 2.8\text{x}$

Where: the rental charge (R) is the operating lease charge for the year, found in the notes as 113 and 109 respectively for the two years

Possible variations

- The same issues arise as to the appropriateness of EBITDAR as a proxy for the cash flow available for paying fixed charges. Consequently, deducting capex (and other operating cash flows) may be relevant. The numerator may also be adjusted to include investment income – which is available to pay fixed charges
- The same denominator variants arise as for other coverage ratios for the interest element, i.e. net interest vs. gross, expense vs. cash paid; together with the same possible exclusions such as fair value adjustments on financial instruments, pensions, etc.
- The rental charge may be:
  - Gross rental charge
  - Net amount (net of rental income)
  - Including or excluding the rents on equipment (so that rent on property is all that remains)

Interpretation and application

- A variant of the interest cover ratio is a fixed charge cover where we examine how easily the company can service its annual contractual obligations – interest and rent. This is, therefore, a more prudent measure of debt capacity
- The higher the multiple, the more cash flow is available for contractual obligations and, hence, the more capacity the company has for further borrowing
- In sectors where leasing is important to some members of the peer group, this ratio is most likely to give a picture of the relative financing capacity across the sector
- In the current example, the EBITDA has recovered in the last year, whilst at the same time the rental charges have remained fairly constant. This should lead to significant improvements in the ratio. However, the increase has been moderated by the sharp increase in the interest expense, as identified in the interest coverage analysis, and so the enhancement in financing capacity is less marked than would be expected by the improvement in operating

Working capital efficiency ratios

Companies can generate cash flow from operating performance. Much of this performance is measured by profitability ratios. However, the ability of a company to control its working capital can create value within a business. Ratios which analyze the changes in working capital can be used to indicate how this vital resource is being managed.

	Current year	Previous year
$\text{Inventory days} = \dfrac{\text{Inventory}}{\text{Costs of goods sold}} \text{x365}$	$\dfrac{544}{2{,}697 + 1{,}328} \text{x365} = 49\text{days}$	$\dfrac{553}{2{,}899 + 1{,}303} \text{x365} = 48\text{days}$
$\text{Receivable days} = \dfrac{\text{Receivables}}{\text{Sales}} \text{x365}$	$\dfrac{252}{6{,}187} \text{x365} = 15\text{days}$	$\dfrac{352}{5{,}837} \text{x365} = 22\text{days}$
$\text{Payable days} = \dfrac{\text{Payables}}{\text{Costs of goods sold}} \text{x365}$	$\dfrac{177}{2{,}697 + 1{,}328} \text{x365} = 16\text{days}$	$\dfrac{253}{2{,}899 + 1{,}303} \text{x365} = 22\text{days}$
Working capital cycle = Inventory days + Receivable days – Payable days	= 48days	= 48days

Possible variations

- The numerator should only be those balance sheets items that relate to working capital. For example, payables should merely be short-term liabilities owing to suppliers
- The numerator can be either the year end figure (to show the current position) or an average of the start and end of year (to tie in with the denominator which has been extracted over that same 12 month period)
- For inventory and payables, the cost of purchases can be used as the denominator, rather than the full costs included in cost of goods sold
- The denominator in all cases is net of sales taxes (such as VAT). However, both receivables and payables include sales taxes and so the output may be misleading

Interpretation and application

- Working capital is the funds used by the business in its operations. In general, a business will buy items of inventory, add value to them, sell them, receive the cash from selling them and at some stage in this process, pay cash over to suppliers for the items purchased. This is termed the working capital cycle.
- In some situations, suppliers or customers may have power over the company and so management's ability to influence payment terms may be compromised. The working capital ratios aim to highlight the ability of management to control the working capital of the company.
- The smaller the amount of funds tied up in working capital, the more efficient the organization. If inventories are held for a short time and customers pay quickly (as measured by inventory days and receivable days respectively), then funds are flowing around the business quickly. In contrast, if the company pays its suppliers slowly, the cash is available to the company for longer. This could be considered as a free (mostly) source of finance

- In the current example, the overall working capital remains unchanged. This is despite the strengthening of the time given to customers to pay (reduced by 7 days to 15 days over the year). Is this because the client mix is changing from credit to cash customers, or is it a policy of reducing the payment terms? What will be the effect on customers and their willingness to buy under new terms, etc.? At the same time there has been a matching weakening (shortening) in the payment days to suppliers. Similar questions should be asked as to why this has happened and what will be the effects in the future on purchasing behavior

Other working capital ratios are:

$$\text{Current ratio} = \frac{\text{Current assets}}{\text{Current liabilities}}$$

$$\text{Current ratio} = \frac{\text{Inventory + Receivables}}{\text{Payables}}$$

$$\text{Quick ration} = \frac{\text{Current assets - Inventory}}{\text{Current liabilities}}$$

$$\text{EBITDA efficiency} = \frac{\text{Operating cash flow}}{\text{EBITDA}}$$

Investment ratios

Is a company investing or divesting? Ideas as to the stage of development a business is in can be derived from analysis of the investment ratios. Analysis of how much investment is being made may also help to explain why the performance and leverage ratios are changing.

	Current year	Previous year
$\text{Capex / depreciation} = \dfrac{\text{Capex}}{\text{Depreciation}}$	$\dfrac{247}{94} = 2.6\text{x}$	$\dfrac{175}{93} = 1.9\text{x}$

Where: the capex (including acquisition of intangibles) has been found on the cash flow statements

Possible variations

- The denominator, depreciation, may vary in definition depending on the levels of disclosure available.
  It could be
  - Depreciation of only owned (not leased) assets (most consistent with pure capex)
  - Depreciation of all PPE
  - Depreciation and amortization (where either no separation is given or intangibles are an important asset to the business)
  - Depreciation including impairments (where no separate breakdown of impairments is given)
- The numerator must be consistent with this. For example, if amortization is included, then the acquisition cost of the intangibles must also be included
- Disposal proceeds can be eliminated from capex to derive net capex
- Capex growth, Capex/sales, capex/sales growth are all relative measures of investment. There is likely to be a time-lag before the resultant sales are received and so the ratio may be capex/next year's sales, for example

Interpretation and application

- There should be a relationship between the amount spent on buying assets (capex) and the measure of their wearing out (depreciation). Additionally, for many businesses it is necessary for there to be capex (build more factories) in order for the company to grow (produce more products). Consequently, there should be a relationship between capex and sales, albeit that this will likely be time-lagged
- If the capex/depreciation resulted in a multiple of 1.0x, then there is parity between the amount spent and the amount worn out, i.e. the company is replacing assets as they wear out (ignoring inflation and assuming depreciation rates are appropriate). A figure of greater than 1.0x suggests investment in the business, whilst a figure below suggests the business is not replacing worn out assets.
  An understanding of why a company is or is not investing should be sought so that we are better able to forecast the effects of this in the future
- When forecasting, it is likely that the capex/depreciation ratio will tend towards parity. As the business matures, it should have increasing amounts of replacement capex relative to expansion capex
- In the current example, the levels of capex have increased between the two years. Is this because capex was reduced in the downturn of the previous year, and/or is it the result of a new expansive phase by the company?
- When comparing this with the fixed charge cover, we can see that there have been few new operating leases taken on in the year. We should also look in the notes to the financials to discover the values of new finance (or capital) leases taken on in order to get the full picture as to the amount of growth in the asset base between the two years

Investor ratios

An investor is likely to be interested in all the ratios: how is the company performing, is it efficient, are there risks in its capital structure, etc. In addition, these investor ratios look at the levels of returns they can expect from their investment and whether this is affordable.

	Current year	Previous year
$\text{Dividend payout} = \frac{\text{Dividends}}{\text{Earnings}} \times 100\%$	$\frac{168}{517 - 21*(1-30\%)} = 33.4\%$	$\frac{88}{84 + 67 - 12*(1-30\%)} = 61.7\%$

Where: the dividends paid have been found on the cash flow statements, the reported net income has been adjusted for the impairment and gains on disposal, assuming that the tax rate is 30%, gains are taxable but impairments are not tax deductible

Possible variations

- Both parts of the equation could be either in gross terms or in per share terms
- The dividend can be either the dividend paid in the year or the amount relating to the period (i.e. any quarterly or interim dividends plus the final proposed dividend)
- The earnings focuses on the profits after all other costs have been excluded (after tax, prefs and NCI, but before exceptional items) available to equity shareholders. The same definition as for the numerator in earnings per share (EPS) – another key investor ratio. For EPS, use:
    - Weighted average equity shares (rather than year end or most up-to-date)
    - Either basic or diluted number of shares
- If the calculation is done using per share data, there may be slightly different results as the number of shares for EPS and DPS are likely to be different
- Inverting the equation gives the dividend cover – the amount of times the payout is covered by the profits

Interpretation and application

- The earnings are the profits that are available for the equity shareholders of the company. The dividends are what have been paid out to them. The dividend payout calculates what proportion of the shareholders' profits for the year is paid out. A large figure suggests the company is paying out significant amounts to their shareholders and therefore retaining small amounts for re-investment.
- In the early years of a company, there is often a need to invest in order to grow. This limits the flexibility of the management to pay a dividend, and the shareholders are generally supportive of this strategy as the investments made by the company should be giving returns higher than the cost of capital. As a company matures, there will be reduced opportunities available to invest funds in order to make high returns. In these situations, excess funds should be returned to shareholders either by share buybacks or dividends. Consequently, higher payout ratios will be expected in mature companies
- In the current example, the 61.7% dividend payout of the prior year is significant. This could be explained by:
    - The business has limited investment opportunities and so maintains a high dividend
    - A one-off special dividend
    - The need to maintain the total dividend payment despite profits falling
- It is unlikely to be the first of these given the reduction to 33.4% in the current year (unless the current year, itself, is a one-off). Given the analysis from the other ratios, the need to maintain a dividend despite profits falling is most likely to be the reasoning behind the large dividend payout in the previous year, with its return to more sustainable levels in the current year
- Once the share price is introduced, then significantly more investor ratios and multiples can be created. These are covered in the valuation sections

Introduction

An excellent working knowledge of the numbers contained within the financials is essential for Analysts to be in a position to value companies.

Why is valuation important?

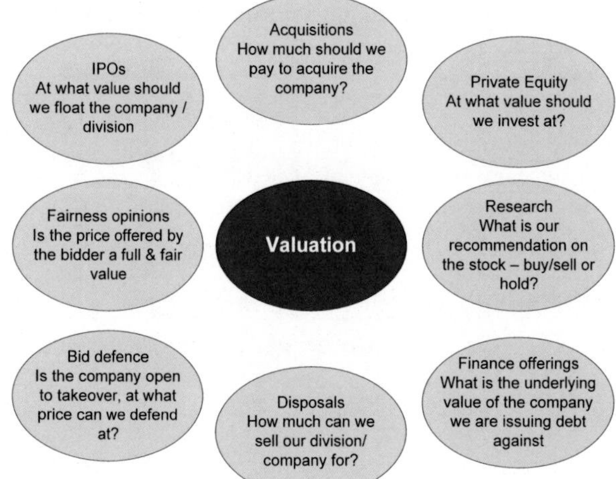

Valuation is based around a number of traditional valuation methodologies that are often supplemented with more contemporary ideas. The two traditional methodologies are:

- Comps
  - Comparable company analysis ('trading comps' or just 'comps')
  - Comparable transactions analysis ('precedent or transaction comps')
- Discounted cash flow valuation

Although valuation requires a thorough understanding of these methodologies, this on its own is not sufficient. Analysts must remember that crunching numbers through models does not give the answer. A valuation is a mixture of soft and hard skills and issues such as:

- Buyer motivations
- Seller motivations
- Potential legal issues
- Tax considerations
- Competitive pressures
- Potential economies of scale
- Market sentiment
- M&A strategic rationale
- Use of excess funding
- Ability to finance the deal

An Analyst's valuation work is normally presented in a valuation summary or 'valuation football pitch'. An example of a valuation summary is included below. The purpose of the summary is to visually disclose the range of valuations produced by the various valuation methodologies.

The valuation summary is a key component of a pitch book:

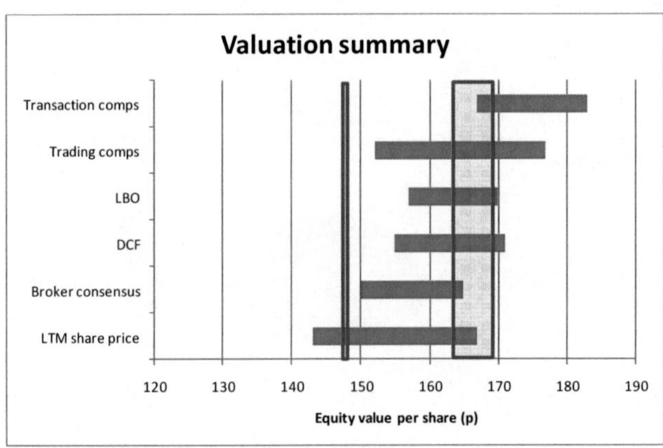

What is a Pitch Book?

The form and content of a pitch book will vary from bank to bank, even from team to team. However, there are two general types of pitch book:

General pitch book
Bankers use the general pitch book to guide their introductions and presentations during sales calls. These pitch books contain general information and include a wide variety of selling points bankers make to potential clients. The general pitch book will include an overview of the bank and detail its specific capabilities regarding finance, sales and trading (but, generally, **no content** on the bank's research franchise is permitted).
It does not differ much from deal to deal.

Deal-specific pitch book
Highly customized and usually requires at least one Analyst or Associate all-nighter to put together. (Although MDs, VPs, Associates and Analysts all work closely together to create the book.) Includes:

- Strategic rationale for the deal
- Valuation summary
- Valuations and financial modeling results
- Comparable company – transactions and industry analysis
- EPS accretion/dilution analysis
- The performance of other IPOs or similar offerings managed by the bank
- The bank's expertise as an underwriter in the industry, including its ranking in the 'league tables'

What Makes a Good Valuation Summary?

A good valuation summary will be the cornerstone of the pitch book. It will add credibility to the whole presentation if the valuations are sufficiently robust to hold up to close scrutiny.

A good summary will include:

- Current or pre-announcement equity price
- Key valuation bandings for:
  - DCF (possibly under different scenarios)
  - Trading comps
  - Precedent comps
  - Implied private equity valuations
- An estimated valuation range
- Broker consensus benchmark valuations
- LTM ('last 12 months') share price range

A poor summary can destabilize the entire pitch.

Common issues to be aware of:

- Valuation ranges are too tight – this suggests precision where there should be flexibility. It can suggest a possible failure to appreciate the sensitivities embedded in the valuation.
- Valuation ranges are too wide – this can suggest a lack of accuracy in the valuation. A very wide valuation range can suggest a lack of confidence in the valuation. Given the comments above, this seems like a no-win situation.
- The ultimate valuation range suggested by the summary is not supported by the valuation techniques used.
- The ultimate valuation range is too wide.
- The suggested valuation premiums cannot be justified. Relying on synergies and control premiums really will not carry much weight in isolation. Synergies must be justifiable and the drivers of the premiums must be fully understood and disclosed.
- Transaction comps are not consistent with the current market.
  This is especially an issue if the market has recently corrected and the comparable transaction are not that recent.
- Denominations are missing.
- There are no currencies mentioned.
- The x-axis not correctly labeled. The client needs to know what level of valuation is being discussed – equity value, equity value per share or enterprise value.

Valuation methodologies: an overview

Before embarking on a detailed examination, it is worth taking a high level view of each method.

The various valuation methodologies approach valuation from different perspectives. Some techniques are market-driven and so will reflect the current state of the market. Others are based on an academic approach and value the entity within a more theoretical environment.

A relative (or comparable) valuation values an entity with reference to the market. The relative valuation can be in relation to current trading (trading comps) or with reference to previous deals (transaction comps).

A transaction comp should produce a value higher than a trading comp. This is simply due to the transaction comp using an offer price to calculate its value rather than a current market price (as for trading comps). A transaction comp should capture the transaction control premium in its valuation.

The control premium is the premium over the pre-announcement price that is paid in order to secure control of the entity. Historically control premiums have been in the range 30-50% above the pre-announcement share price.

Relative valuations are very popular with research, investment bankers and private equity. The concept is easy to understand, clients are receptive to the idea and the technique is an effective communicator of a valuation concept.

Discounted cash flow (DCF) valuation is an example of an absolute valuation. The entity is valued (in theory) without (relative) reference to the market. DCF does require a greater level of technical understanding in order to appreciate the subtleties of the valuation drivers. The basis of DCF valuation is that the fair value of the entity is the present value of the cash flows it is capable of generating. It provides an excellent sense check on the relative valuation techniques. When performed well, DCF is a valuation approach that provides sufficient information for an in-depth justification of the drivers of value.

Valuation in context

Valuation must also be considered within the context of the deal.

Buy and sell-side transactions

Analysts may be advising a client on a purchase of an entity (buy-side advisory) or on a disposal (sell-side advisory). The side of the deal the Analyst is advising on will have a bearing on the valuation from a negotiation perspective. The valuation work will provide a benchmark for discussions. However, negotiation will determine the price paid for an acquisition, rather than the numbers generated by the analysis.

If advising on the buy-side the Analyst will be hoping to secure the most favorable transaction price for the client. If the Analyst is advising on a disposal, the client will want to maximize the value of the disposal.

Typical buy-side activities:

- Strategies for the acquisition
- Target searches
- Pitch book preparation
- Valuation – indicative offers
- Merger modeling for a public market transaction

- Advisory regarding financing possibilities and consequences
- Assisting with the legal documentation and the due diligence process
- Assessment of synergies
- Assistance regarding liaising with external parties
- Preparing the contracts and negotiation terms

Typical sell-side activities:

- Grooming the entity for sale
- Initial research and screening
- Preparation of the teaser – an anonymous presentation of the company profile.
- Pitch book preparation
- Putting together the information package or information memorandum
- Valuation work in respect of indicative offers
- Defense tactics if hostile public market approach
- Assisting with the legal documentation and the due diligence process
- Preparing the approach buyers list
- Assisting with data room (information disclosure) issues
- Assisting with management presentations
- Preparing the contracts and negotiation terms

Buy and sell-side advisors will often try to justify very different valuations. Naturally they should be trying to create the most value for their clients. However, this can create a significant stumbling block in terms of trying to complete a deal. It is a particular issue when the merger and acquisition (M&A) market is depressed and the sellers are clinging on to the higher historic values that were seen during the boom times and the buyers are reluctant to part with the funding in the face of a downturn.

There are a number of deal structures that can be used to bridge this expectations gap:

Earn-outs

An earn-out splits the purchase price into fixed and variable elements. The fixed element is an upfront payment paid on the completion of the deal. The variable element is paid during the post-acquisition period and is normally based on post-acquisition performance. This structure hedges the risk that the buyer might over-pay for the investment. It acts as an incentive for the acquired human capital to stay with the business and realize the additional value.

Vendor financing

Vendor financing has many different forms. In its most basic form, it is an agreement to defer part of the purchase price to a later date. The deferral can take the form of simple loans – vendor loan notes. These notes will normally rank below senior creditors. However, they can be sweetened by offering an equity upside. For instance, the loan notes could be structured to be convertible into equity, thus providing the seller with an equity upside, whilst maintaining the protection of the loan note.

Retaining a minority stake

This can simply involve the seller retaining a residual stake in the entity they have just sold. This allows the seller to benefit from any equity upside post-acquisition.

Escrow accounts

An escrow account ring fences part of the acquisition proceeds in a separate bank account. Escrow accounts are useful when the valuations are agreed but there is uncertainty about certain future risks. The holdback into escrow allows the deal to complete and provides some protection to the buyer.

Flip protection

Flip protection is usually related to forced sales. Often in forced sales the price agreed is lower than the seller would have agreed to under normal circumstances. Flip protection is an agreement with the buyer that states that if the target is resold within a pre-defined period, the gain is shared between the two parties.

Private vs. public transactions

In the context of M&A, the terms 'private' and 'public' usually refer to whether or not the target company's shares are publicly quoted on a stock exchange. The public/private distinction is an important distinction from a valuation perspective.

Generally a public market transaction will have more publicly available information. This access to information will make the valuation process easier relative to a private company valuation.

A private company valuation introduces its own unique problems, such as:

- Limited publicly available information
- A lack of broker or equity research coverage
- The need to discount the valuation due to liquidity issues
- A lack of comparable companies and/or transactions

Types of transactions work:

- Private sell-side: more work in preparatory and early marketing phases, e.g. preparing Information Memorandum, contacting buyers, preparing the data room
- Private buy-side: more work in marketing and closing phases, e.g. assessing information, preparing bids, liaising with financiers
- Public sell-side: drafting response statement(s); formal recommendation/valuation work may be required (e.g. fairness opinion)
- Public buy-side: may make offer on buyer's behalf; help draft offer document; formal confirmations (e.g. cash funding) may be required

There are also specific regulatory requirements and procedural considerations for public takeovers.

Enterprise and equity value

Enterprise value (EV) is a key concept in valuation. Although ultimately an equity value is required, many valuations are performed at the enterprise level and the equity value is then derived from this value.

EV is the theoretical full take-out value for an entity. If an entity is taken over, the acquirer would take control of the equity and assume the debt liabilities. The acquirer would also take control of any cash on the target's balance sheet.

EV is a capital structure neutral metric as it includes all claims on the entity. This is useful as it improves comparability with entities with different capital structures.

EV is also referred to as:

- Total enterprise value (TEV)
- Firm value (FV) (often with US banks and clients)
- Entity value
- Gross or total capitalization
- Leverage market capitalization

The basic definition of EV is built up from a market capitalization calculation. The calculation will then include all other claims on the business.

Typical additional components of EV are:

- Net debt
- Non-controlling interest

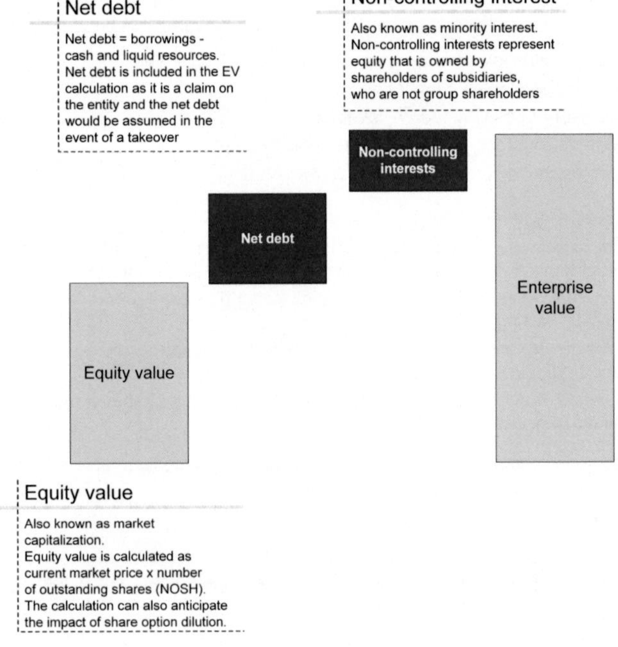

EV definitions will vary depending on the context they are applied to. For instance, an EV trading comp may also need to reflect additional components such as:

- Joint ventures and associates
- Present value of operating lease commitments
- Pension deficits
- Cash working capital adjustments

Financial modeling

Comps and DCF methods will produce valuations based on a number of underlying assumptions. Small changes in these assumptions often have a very large impact on the overall valuation result. There is little credibility turning up to a client and stating that the valuation is $7.91. Clients know valuations are subjective. A sensible valuation range must be presented – clients will be much more receptive to a valuation range of $7.85-7.95.

This valuation range is not however a pie-in-the-sky spread around a pin-point valuation output. The spread is determined with reference to sensitivity analysis. This is where financial modeling skills come in. A financial model allows Analysts to:

- Flex assumptions easily
- Run sensitivity analysis on key variables
- Run different scenarios for forecasts (base, upside and downside cases)

Sensitivity analysis in a financial model is typically run using data tables. The illustration below is a data table extracted from a Fitch Learning financial model. The data table runs the model a number of times, but substitutes different values into the model for key variables. In this case, the model has been run 25 times using different combinations of the variables EBITDA exit multiple and WACC. The data table is testing share price sensitivities.

Share price sensitivity					
WACC					EBITDA multiple
	6.6x	7.1x	7.6x	8.1x	8.6x
5.12%	14.23	14.79	15.36	15.92	16.49
5.62%	13.70	14.24	14.78	15.32	15.86
6.12%	13.20	13.71	14.23	14.74	15.25
6.62%	12.72	13.21	13.70	14.19	14.68
7.12%	12.26	12.73	13.20	13.67	14.13

In this case, given the sensitivity analysis, the valuation range could be defined as between 13.21-15.32.

Dealing with uncertainty

Clearly valuation has to deal with an uncertain world. We are inherently attempting to value the future performance of an entity in today's term, so that it can be bought today.

This uncertainty is dealt with in different ways:

- Some Analysts will build bigger models, with more detailed assumptions, as a way of dealing with the uncertainty. However, this method cannot eliminate uncertainty and often it results in big, cumbersome models that turn into 'black box' calculators where the drivers of value are lost in the detail.

- A very sensible way to deal with uncertainty is to use a valuation range. These ranges are determined with reference to sensitivity analysis within the models as well as the exercise of judgment and experience.
- The more 'quant' orientated Analysts may embark on probabilistic models to quantify the uncertainty.

However, uncertainty is often dealt with by relying on other brokers' or consensus estimates. If the valuation is wrong, the blame is passed onto the broker. If it turns out to be right, the credit is taken by the Analyst.

Tick Sheet – Valuation Methodologies

The traditional valuation methodologies are:

- Comps
  - Comparable company analysis ('trading comps' or just 'comps')
  - Comparable transactions analysis ('precedent or transaction comps')
- Discounted cash flow valuation

A good valuation summary will include:

- Current or pre-announcement equity prices
- Valuation bandings for different valuation approaches:
  - DCF (possibly under different scenarios)
  - Trading comps
  - Precedent comps
  - Implied private equity valuations
- An estimated valuation range
- Broker consensus benchmark valuations
- LTM ('last 12 months') share prices

EV is the theoretical full take-out value for an entity.

If an entity is taken over, the acquirer would take control of the equity and assume the debt liabilities.

The acquirer would also take control of any of the cash on the target's balance sheet.

Introduction

Trading comparables is a relative valuation technique that uses public company information to infer a valuation on a target company. The valuation works on the premise that similar or comparable companies tend to be valued on a similar or comparable basis on the public markets.

The method is often used for:

- Buy-side M&A
- Sell-side M&A
- Fairness opinions
- Initial public offering (IPO) valuations
- Share repurchases
- Follow on financing
- LBO valuations

The method is very popular with investment bankers and research Analysts. Clients are also very receptive to the valuation technique as the concept is very digestible and is not steeped in technical jargon.

However, there are some issues that Analysts should be aware of:

- The quality of the analysis is dependent on the quality of the comparable inputs. The process is inherently flawed as no two companies are truly comparable.
- Trading comps is often heavily reliant on accounting information. As the initial chapters of this manual have highlighted, accounting numbers are prone to manipulation and are often inconsistently applied within the peer group, as well as internationally.
- Trading comps will normally use forecast information to perform the valuation. This invariably means relying on equity research. This presents no problems if all the comparable companies are covered – however, equity research houses do not cover all companies. Trading comps can therefore become an increasingly spurious exercise if equity research is unavailable.
- Loss making companies often don't lend themselves well to trading comps valuation due to the common reliance on the earning metrics.
- The valuation does not include a control premium. This is not a flaw as such, just a characteristic of the valuation.

Trading comps – a four-step structured approach

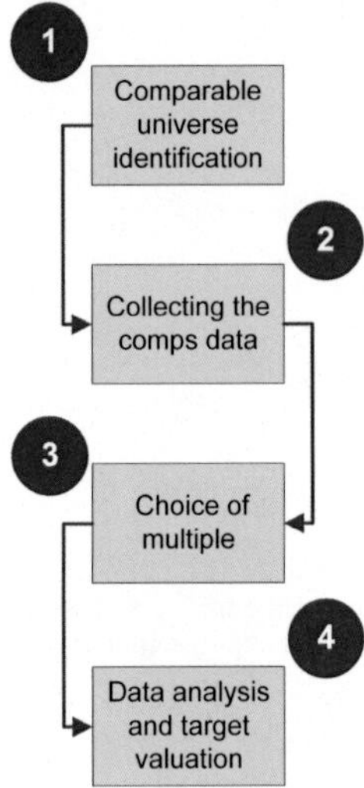

Comps process overview

The trading comps process can be structured into four steps. Cadbury plc will be used as a case study comparable company. The four-step process will be applied to Cadbury's numbers in order to calculate a comparable multiple.

The trading comps process essentially collects information in relation to a number of comparable companies (the comparable universe). The majority of this information will be financial in nature. However, narrative information will also be collected in order to develop a more rounded picture of the market the comparables operate in.

The process makes use of valuation multiples. A valuation multiple is simply an expression of a company's market value in relation to key statistics. The statistics are assumed to be drivers of the company's value. There must be a logical relationship between the statistic and the market value. The most common statistics used are earnings metrics.

There are two basic types of multiple:

- Enterprise value multiples
- Equity value multiples

Enterprise value multiples capture the full value of the claims of the capital providers on the company. The relative metric (the denominator of the multiple) must also therefore relate to the enterprise. For instance, if the metric is an earnings metric, then the earnings metric must be an enterprise value level metric. That is, both debt and equity capital providers have a claim on the earnings metric. Enterprise level metrics are revenue, EBIT or EBITDA for example.

Equity multiples capture the equity investors' claim on the company. The metric must again be consistent with the equity claim. The relevant earnings metric is normally net income, as this is claimed or owned by equity capital providers.

The financial information is then used to calculate valuation multiples such as:

- EV/Revenue
- EV/EBIT
- EV/EBITDA
- P/E

These multiples provide a basis for comparison of the companies in the comparable universe. Companies will trade on different multiples. There will always be reasons for differences in the trading multiples. It is the Analyst's job to make sure that the differences in trading multiple levels are understood and are justifiable.

A trading comps model will also calculate a plethora of financial ratios that will be used to support the multiple justifications.

At this stage, Analysts will have a number of important decisions to make:

- Which comparable companies should be relied on for the target valuation?
- What type of multiple is most appropriate to value the target?
- How does the target company fit into the comparable universe?
- Is the target a company that should be valued at a premium or a discount to the comparable universe?
- What multiple range should be applied to the target?

Once these very important questions have been addressed, the Analyst will have an appropriate range of multiples with which to value the target. The multiple range is then applied to the financials of the target to arrive at a valuation. The valuation is driven off the decisions and analysis derived from the comparable universe.

What are the key drivers of a multiple?

There are generally three key drivers of a multiple:

- The quality of earnings or cash conversion
- The risk profile of the earnings
- Growth rates

These drivers are fundamental to understanding what lies behind a multiple and why some companies trade with multiples that are at a premium or a discount to the rest of their comparable universe.

The three drivers are derived from a simplified DCF valuation model. Whilst the following equations are not essential front of head knowledge, they do assist in understanding how and why multiples behave in a particular way.

The ideas behind the drivers are based on the premise that the enterprise value is the present value of the cash flows that belong to debt and equity capital providers. This cash flow is better known as free cash flow to the enterprise or free cash flow to the firm (FCFF).

This is the basic principle of a DCF valuation. If we assume for illustration purposes, that future free cash flows will grow at a constant rate (g) in perpetuity, then the EV is as follows:

$$\frac{FCF}{(WACC - g)}$$

Therefore EV is the discounted stream of cash flows that are claimed (or owned) by debt and equity holders.

Growth (g) is driven by the rate of reinvestment of earnings (b) and the return on capital generated on the reinvestment (r).

Where:

FCF = Net operating profit less adjusted taxes: (NOPAT) x (1 - the reinvestment rate (b))

g = Growth rate (growth is driven by the rate of reinvested earnings (b) and the return on invested capital (r): g = r x b

WACC = Weighted average cost of capital

This idea can now be converted into a multiple by dividing both sides of the equation by EBITDA:

$$\frac{EV}{EBITDA} = \frac{FCF \div EBITDA}{(WACC - g)}$$

With this equation the drivers of the multiple can be conceptually extracted:

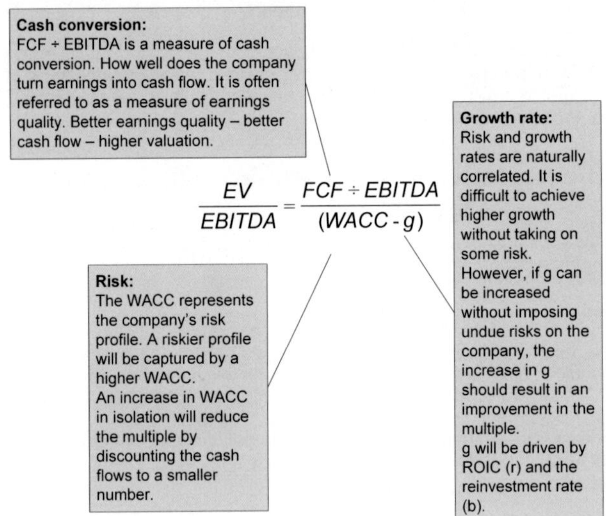

The drivers can be further broken down by examining the components of each variable. Thus when explaining the behavior of a multiple, an Analyst should be prepared to consider the drivers below. The examination can focus on earnings margin development, working capital management, capex spend in relation to D&A, risk-free rates, etc. Any one of these variables could explain a multiple's behavior in relation to its peers.

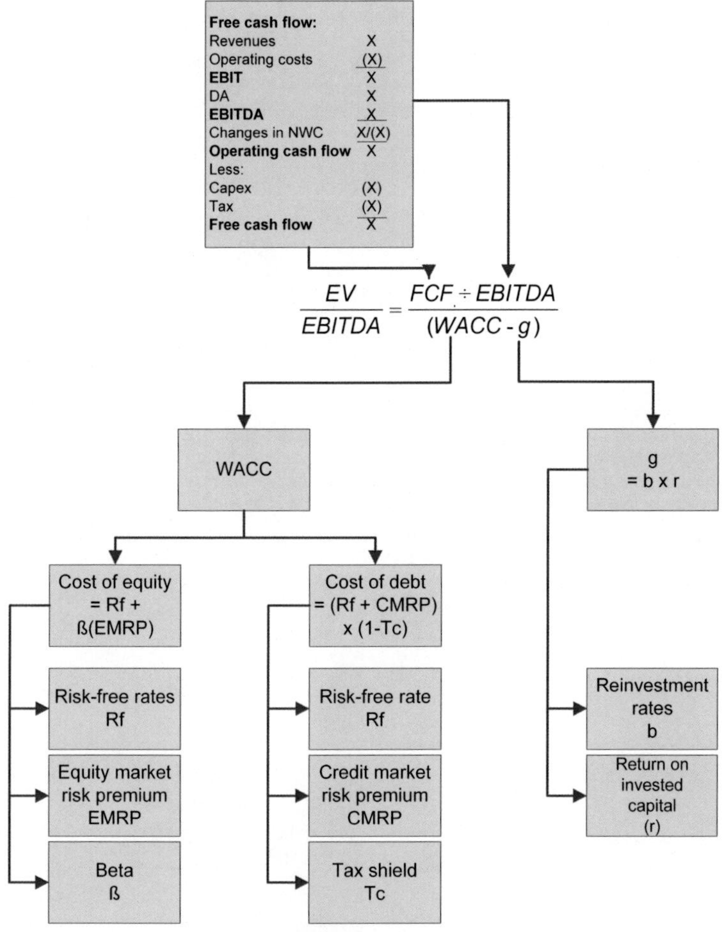

It is a simple model based on simplistic assumptions, however the purpose is to encourage the development of a thought process that examines as many variables as possible – rather than just stating a multiple is high because the market has strong expectations. That is far too thin an explanation when considering issues on a professional level.

Step 1: Comparable universe identification

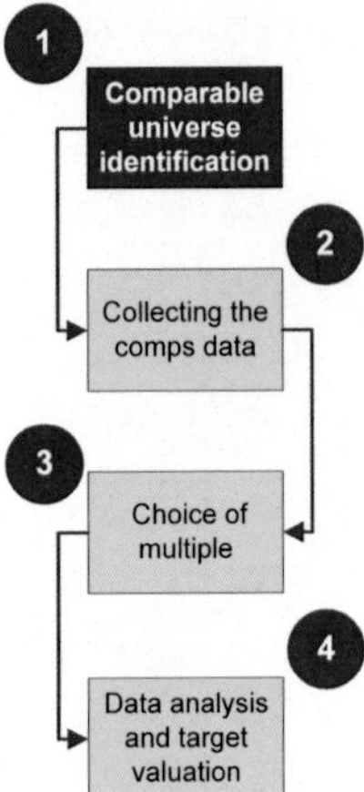

The choice of the comparable universe is the bedrock decision for trading comps. Get the comparable universe wrong and the valuation will be wrong. The key idea to think about when selecting the comparable universe is that the selection is attempting to replicate the characteristics of the target company through a portfolio of companies. The portfolio – the comparable universe – will be used to construct a comparable multiple for valuation purposes. That multiple needs to reflect the cash, risk and growth characteristics that are indicative of the target company.

The comparable universe choice will consider:

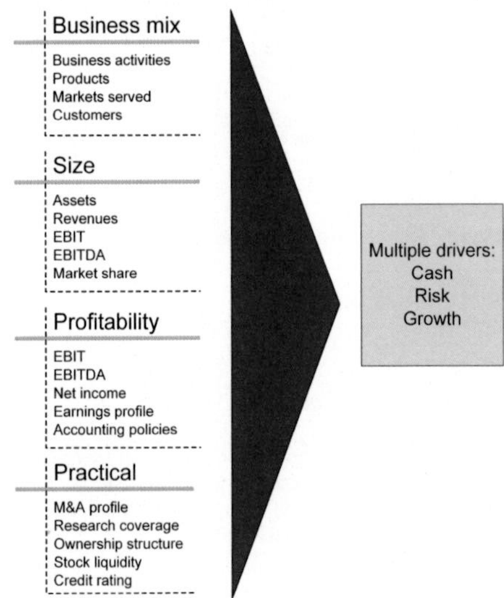

When constructing the comparable universe, it is the quality of the comparable that counts, not the quantity of companies included in the universe. A comparable universe of 20 companies is likely to have a significant amount of statistical noise. Often the comparable universe is made up of 7-9 high quality comparables.

Assistance in Choosing the Comparable Universe

Get the comparable universe wrong and your trading comp valuation will be wrong. Make sure you investigate your comparable universe thoroughly and use all the resources that are available to you:

- Talk to the right people – deal and industry teams
- Review previous presentations
- Recent prospectuses
- Company websites often include competitor references
- Equity and credit research reports sometimes include comparable universes to support their comps work
- Standard Industry code (SIC) run
- Bloomberg descriptions
- Bloomberg relative value function (RV)
- FACTSET and Bloomberg comps functions
- Competition section in 10K / Prospectus
- Other sources: Hoover's in-depth records

Be careful with the data sources' comparable search functions. These comp search functions are basic search algorithms. The search functions will not analyze the comparable universe in any great detail. They tend to be purely sector driven functions.

Pitch book Comparable Universe Summary

A comparable universe summary is often included in pitch books. The summary below uses moon phases or 'pies' to illustrate comparability. The diagram can prove to be an excellent visual communicator to support a comparable universe decision. The shading on the moon phase illustrates the degree of comparability – the redder the moon, the better the comparability.

Comparable universe assessment

	Size	Markets	Margin	Growth rates
Company A	●	●	◕	◕
Company B	◕	◑	●	○
Company C	◕	◔	●	●
Company D	○	●	○	◔

Step 2: Collecting the comps data

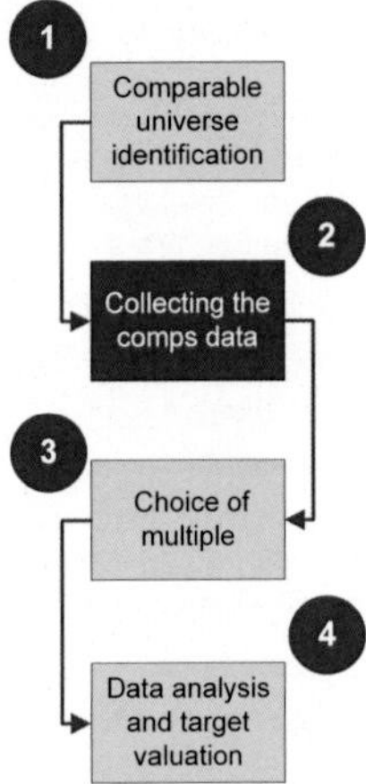

With the comparable universe now selected, sufficient information must now be collected to allow the calculation and justification of the comparable multiples.

Cadbury plc will be our comparable case study company. At this stage, most Analysts will not be making any choices about which type (EV/EBITDA, EV/EBIT or P/E) of multiple to calculate. This type of decision-making is best done when all of the comparable information has been collected.

For the purposes of this illustration however, we will collect sufficient data for an EV comparable multiple. Collecting data for an EV comp should provide sufficient information to calculate an equity level multiple too.

Enterprise value

EV has been discussed a number of times in this manual. EV is the cost of buying the right to the whole of an enterprise's core cash flow. It is the full takeout value of the firm in an M&A situation.

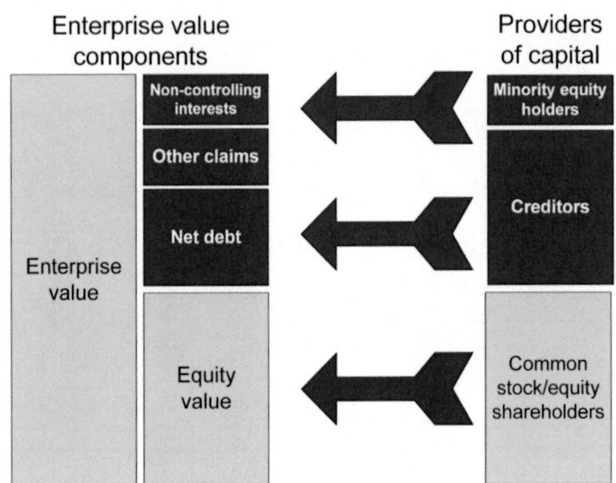

Enterprise value can be thought of as having three components:

- Total EV – the value of all of the entity's activities. This includes associates, joint ventures, investments and non-core assets
- Operating EV – the value of all operating activities (excludes non-operating assets, usually investments, and sometimes associates and joint ventures)
- Core EV – focuses on the core operations of the entity

Most valuation multiples will focus on a core EV, as we will examine later.

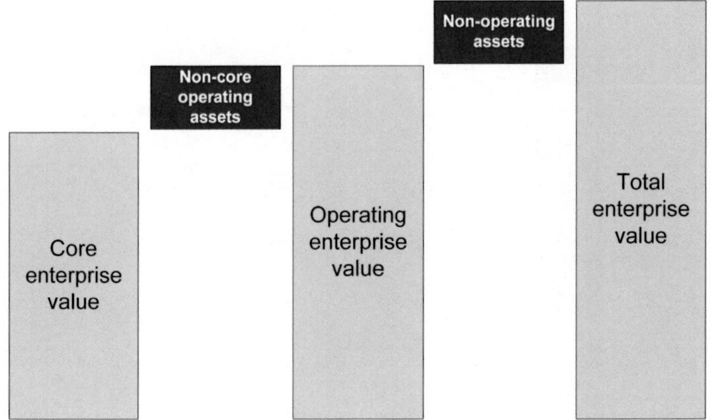

- Log onto ThomsonONE.com
- Go to Company Views on the left-side menu → Fundamentals → Comparable Analysis (you can also access this by looking at the Key Competitors section on the Company Overview page)
- Comparables criteria can be refined by clicking on the down arrow at the top of the page

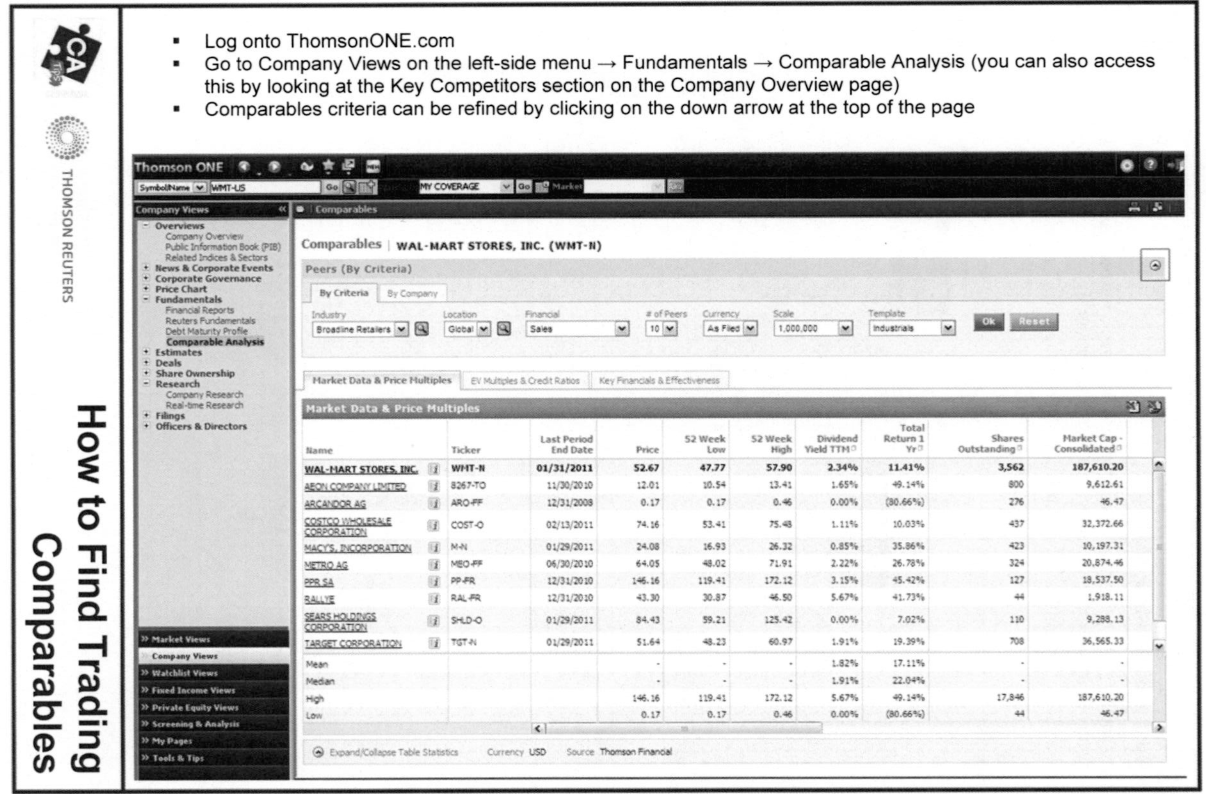

Name	Ticker	Last Period End Date	Price	52 Week Low	52 Week High	Dividend Yield TTM	Total Return 1 Yr	Shares Outstanding	Market Cap - Consolidated
WAL-MART STORES, INC.	WMT-N	01/31/2011	52.67	47.77	57.90	2.34%	11.41%	3,562	187,610.20
AEON COMPANY LIMITED	8267-TO	11/30/2010	12.01	10.54	13.41	1.65%	49.14%	800	9,612.61
ARCANDOR AG	ARO-FF	12/31/2008	0.17	0.17	0.46	0.00%	(80.66%)	276	46.47
COSTCO WHOLESALE CORPORATION	COST-O	02/13/2011	74.16	53.41	75.48	1.11%	10.03%	437	32,372.66
MACY'S, INCORPORATION	M-N	01/29/2011	24.08	16.93	26.32	0.85%	35.86%	423	10,197.31
METRO AG	MEO-FF	06/30/2010	64.05	48.02	71.91	2.22%	26.78%	324	20,874.46
PPR SA	PP-FR	12/31/2010	146.16	119.41	172.12	3.15%	45.42%	127	18,537.50
RALLYE	RAL-FR	12/31/2010	43.30	30.87	46.50	5.67%	41.73%	44	1,918.11
SEARS HOLDINGS CORPORATION	SHLD-O	01/29/2011	84.43	59.21	125.42	0.00%	7.02%	110	9,288.13
TARGET CORPORATION	TGT-N	01/29/2011	51.64	48.23	60.97	1.91%	19.39%	708	36,565.33
Mean			-	-	-	1.82%	17.11%	-	-
Median			-	-	-	1.91%	22.04%	-	-
High			146.16	119.41	172.12	5.67%	49.14%	17,846	187,610.20
Low			0.17	0.17	0.46	0.00%	(80.66%)	44	46.47

THOMSON REUTERS

How to Find Trading Comparables

Source: Thomson Reuters

Calculating EV – Equity value component

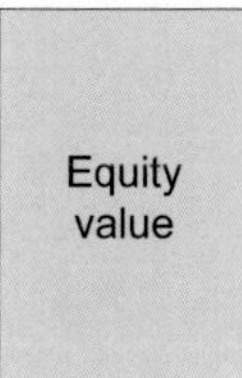

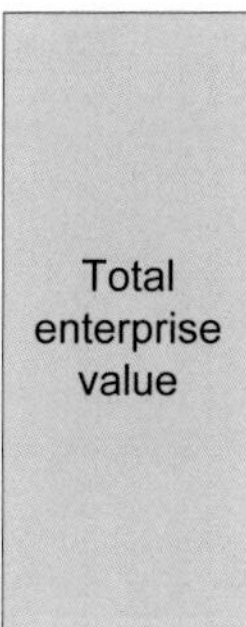

Equity value is also called market capitalization or market cap. The mathematics of the calculation is relatively straightforward, although the practicalities can be more involved.

Market capitalization = Current share price x Number of shares outstanding (NOSH)

The current share price can be picked up from:

- The Financial press – The Financial Times, Wall Street Journal, etc.
- Data service providers – Thomson One, FACTSET, CAPIQ
- Company websites

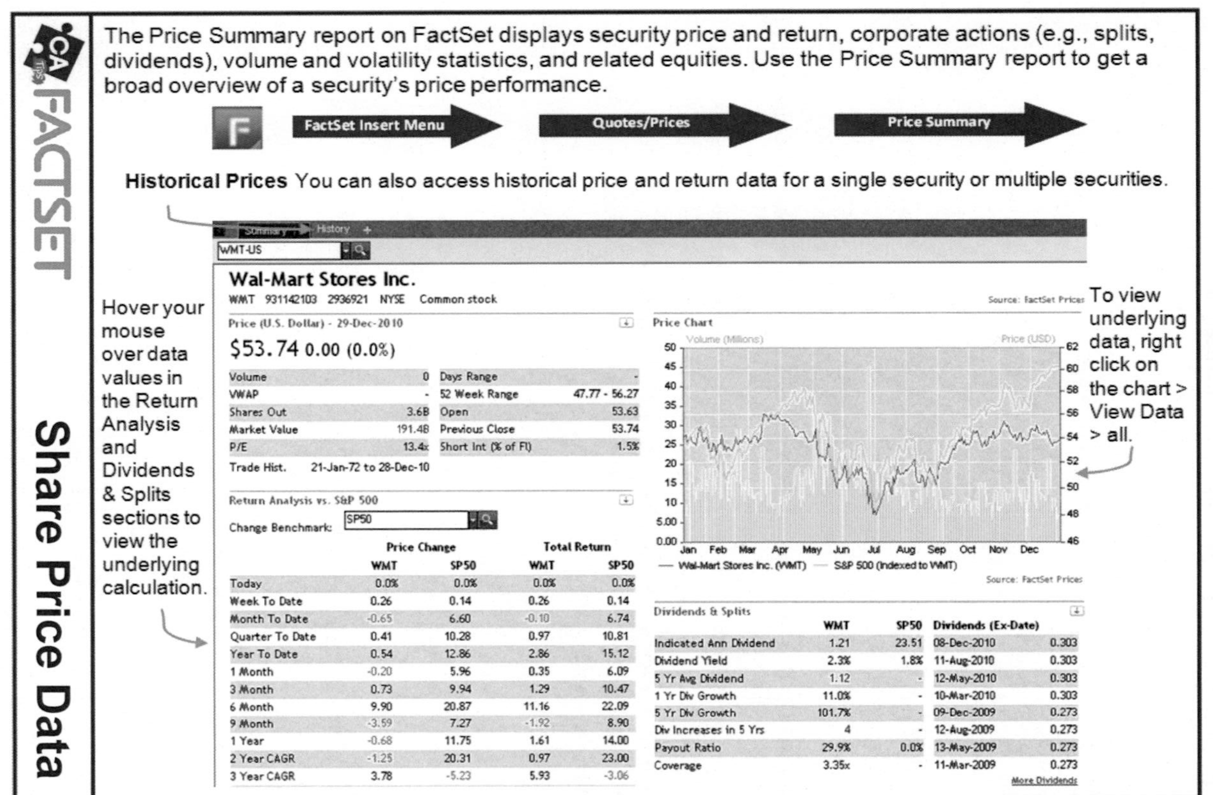

Volume	0	Days Range	-
VWAP	-	52 Week Range	47.77 - 56.27
Shares Out	3.6B	Open	53.63
Market Value	191.4B	Previous Close	53.74
P/E	13.4x	Short Int (% of FI)	1.5%

	Price Change		Total Return	
	WMT	SP50	WMT	SP50
Today	0.0%	0.0%	0.0%	0.0%
Week To Date	0.26	0.14	0.26	0.14
Month To Date	-0.65	6.60	-0.10	6.74
Quarter To Date	0.41	10.28	0.97	10.81
Year To Date	0.54	12.86	2.86	15.12
1 Month	-0.20	5.96	0.35	6.09
3 Month	0.73	9.94	1.29	10.47
6 Month	9.90	20.87	11.16	22.09
9 Month	-3.59	7.27	-1.92	8.90
1 Year	-0.68	11.75	1.61	14.00
2 Year CAGR	-1.25	20.31	0.97	23.00
3 Year CAGR	3.78	-5.23	5.93	-3.06

	WMT	SP50	Dividends (Ex-Date)	
Indicated Ann Dividend	1.21	23.51	08-Dec-2010	0.303
Dividend Yield	2.3%	1.8%	11-Aug-2010	0.303
5 Yr Avg Dividend	1.12	-	12-May-2010	0.303
1 Yr Div Growth	11.0%	-	10-Mar-2010	0.303
5 Yr Div Growth	101.7%	-	09-Dec-2009	0.273
Div Increases in 5 Yrs	4	-	12-Aug-2009	0.273
Payout Ratio	29.9%	0.0%	13-May-2009	0.273
Coverage	3.35x	-	11-Mar-2009	0.273

Source: FactSet

Using the FACTSET =FDS Code Builder

The Documentation CA Tip above notes the use of =FDS coding as a source of share price information. =FDS codes allow FACTSET data to be incorporated into Excel financial models. This allows up-to-date information to be streamed into the workbook.

The coding syntax is straightforward:

=FDS("Ticker","ITEM(SDATE,EDATE,FRQ)")

ITEM – indicates the FACTSET data item

SDATE – start date

EDATE – end date

FRQ - frequency

The syntax is very useful to know for regular coding. However, the FACTSET Excel add-in includes the =FDS code builder. The code builder has similar functionality to the Excel function wizard.

=FDS code builder set up:

- Step 1 – Go to the FACTSET Excel link menu and Lookup > FQL Formula Lookup
- Step 2 – Choose library
- Step 3 – Choose a category, then browse for a formula or search using keywords
- Step 4 – Highlight a formula, then click Select
- Step 5 – Specify the dates and optional arguments
- Step 6 – Click OK to bring the formula into the spreadsheet
- Step 7 – Modify the formula to =FDS syntax
- Step 8 – Select the FACTSET Excel link then select =FDS Codes > Recalc All

Share Price Denominations

Sometimes companies will use a different currency in their financials to the currency their stock trades in. The share price will therefore need to be translated into the base currency of the financials.

Analysts must translate the share price using the latest available spot exchange rate. If the spread on the exchange rate is reasonably narrow, the mid-price exchange rate is acceptable.

The difficulty with the basic market capitalization calculation is the number of shares (NOSH). The NOSH will be published in the latest set of financials. However, this is unlikely to be sufficiently up to date for valuation purposes. Companies can take a number of weeks to report financials, so even at best, the reported NOSH will be out of date.

There are two options available to the Analyst:

- Rely on a data provider for a NOSH number. Care must be taken here – data providers may not have the most up-to-date information in their databases. It is a useful exercise to cross-check the data provider's NOSH against another source. This NOSH method is acceptable in many circumstances. However, if the NOSH has been subject to recent changes and the comp is being used for a live deal or for numbers that will be subject to client review, reliance on a data provider may not be acceptable.
- A more precise NOSH number can be derived by rolling forward the NOSH from the latest reported financials. The NOSH is rolled forward using stock exchange announcement for any equity issues or buy backs. These roll forwards are normally reserved for deal comps or instances where there is a lack of trust in the data service numbers.

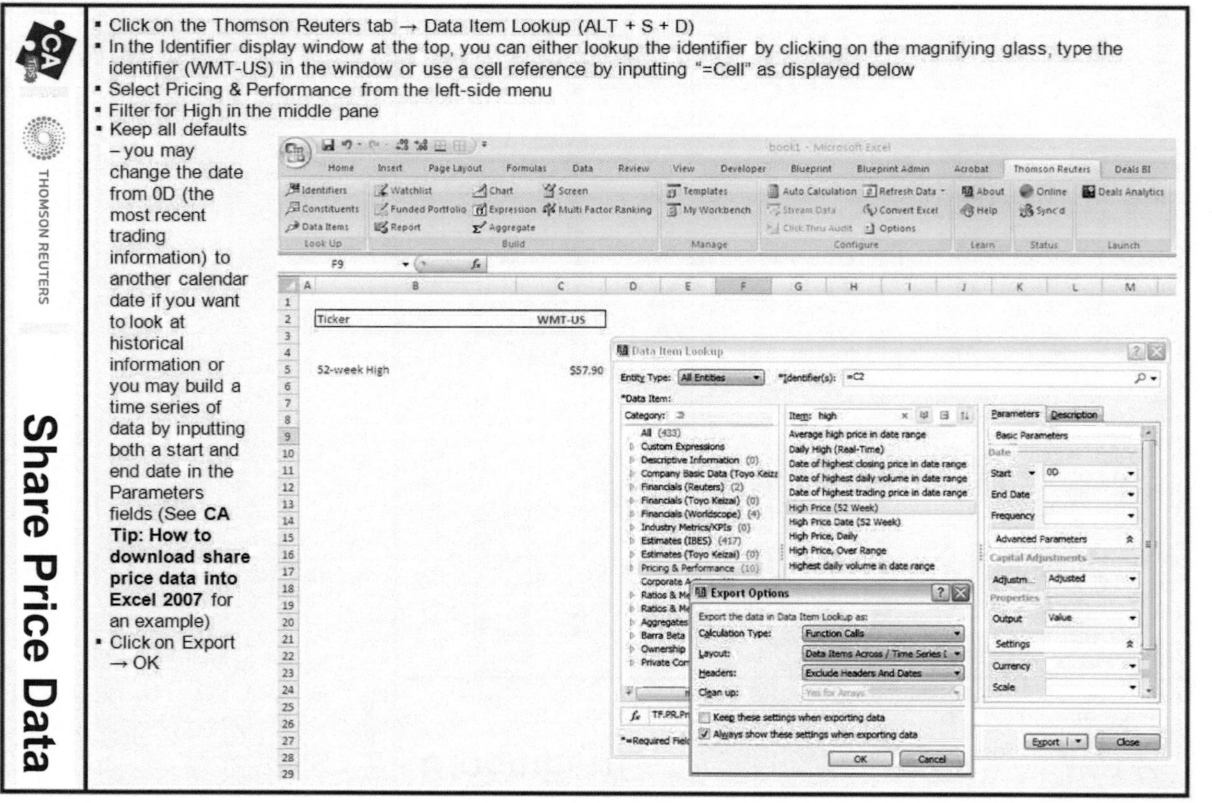

Source: Thomson Reuters

Getting NOSH on Bloomberg

Bloomberg

Key pricing and NOSH information can be accessed through the Bloomberg company description screen.

Key strokes:

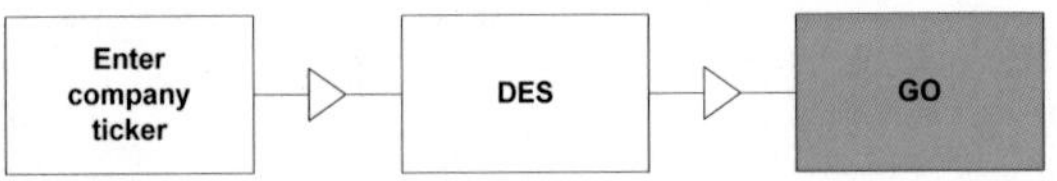

CBRY LN GBp Acquired by KFT US on 03/08/2010 EquityDES
Click here to see details

DESCRIPTION Page 1/11

CBRY LN CADBURY PLC Food-Misc/Diversified
98) Generate Report

Cadbury PLC manufactures and sells beverages and confectionery products. The Company sells chocolates, candy, soft drinks and other beverages through wholesale and retail outlets internationally.

STOCK DATA			GBp
1)GPO	Price	3/ 5	863
	52Wk High	3/ 5/2010	869
	52Wk Low	4/24/2009	478.47
	YTD change		75.02
	YTD % Change		9.52%
	Round Lot		1
2)FA	Shares Out	2/26/2010	1391.483M
	Market Cap		GBP 12008.49M
	Float		1385.42M
3)TRA	1 Yr Total Return		
	BETA vs. UKX		.78
4)OMON	Options Available		

DIVIDENDS	Semi-Annual			GBp
5)DVD	12 Mth Yld - Net			1.95%
	Dividend Growth	5YR		-2.42%
	Ex-Date	Type		Amt
	2/ 5/10	Spec. Cash		10.00
EARNINGS				GBP
6)ERN	Ann Date	3/10/10 (Est)		
	Trailing 12mo EPS			.197
7)EE	Est EPS	12/2009		.364
	P/E	43.81	LT Growth	12.73
	Est P/E	23.71	Est PEG	1.86

Source: Bloomberg

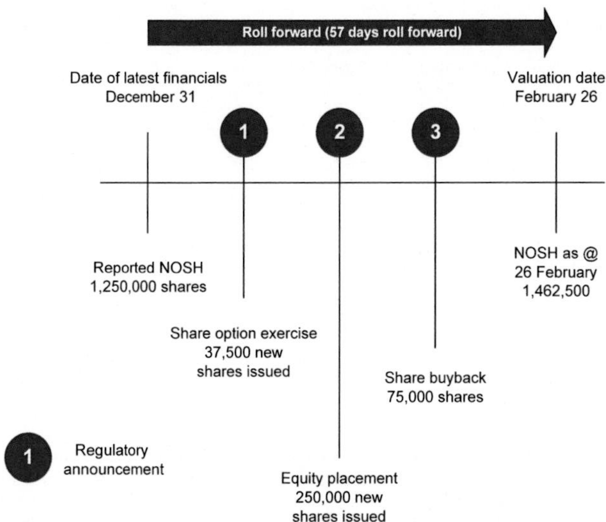

An additional difficulty with the NOSH calculation is the sheer amount of terminology that surrounds the number. In a set of financials, there are a number of NOSH variants such as:

- Authorized – the number of shares the company is legally allowed to issue
- Issued – the number of shares issued by the company (includes treasury shares)
- Outstanding – the number of shares issued – net of treasury shares
- Weighted average – this is a NOSH number used purely for EPS calculations

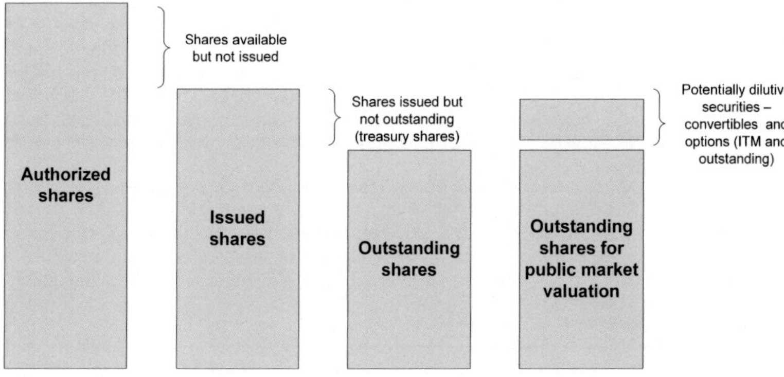

Analysts need to initially focus on the outstanding number of shares for the basic market cap calculation.

Cadbury comp

The Cadbury basic market capitalization calculation:

Cadbury plc		
Currency	£	
Current share price	5.58	
52 week high	5.62	
52 week low	4.78	
NOSH (m)	1,361	
		£m
Current share price	5.58	
NOSH (m)	1,361	
Market capitalization		7,594

It is a useful idea to present 52 week share price highs and lows as a benchmarking exercise. The share price dates would also be noted in practice. Market capitalization is the major component of EV. It is therefore very useful to get a feel for the EV number in relation to the market cap trading performance. The dates will give a feel for market sentiment. In this example we can see that Cadbury is trading very near its 52 week high and hence the market cap will be near its maximum.

Dual Class Shares

Some companies have more than one class of equity that will feed into the market capitalization calculation. We are not talking here about an entity having common and preferred shares, which are two different types of security.

Different classes of share are created when companies wish to issue a certain class of share to a particular group of investors. These shares are commonly called Class A and Class B shares. There is normally a voting distinction between the classes. For instance, sometimes the Class B shares may have inflated voting rights, e.g. 10 votes for every share held. Hence key investors are provided with greater control over the company's actions.

Many companies list dual class shares. Ford Inc has two classes of share. The B shares are family held and allow the family to control 40% of the vote whilst holding only 4% of the equity. Berkshire Hathaway, Warren Buffet's investment company, has two classes of shares. The B shares in Berkshire have 1/30th of the equity interest of an A share and 1/200th of the voting power.

American Depository Receipt (ADR)

An ADR is a certificate that provides US investors with ownership of shares in non-US companies. ADRs trade in the US equity markets. ADRs are issued by US depository banks. The major depository banks are:

- JP Morgan
- Citi
- Deutsche Bank
- Bank of New York Mellon

ADRs were first introduced by JP Morgan in 1927 on Selfridges equity.

The share ownership the ADR represents is usually expressed as an ADR ratio. That is, 1 ADR would represent x number of shares in the foreign entity. The price of an ADR normally tracks the underlying share in relation to the ADR ratio.

From a market capitalization calculation perspective, the Analyst risk here is double counting. ADRs are a representation of underlying NOSH. These shares are already issued and outstanding. They are held by the depositary banks. The banks are merely issuing a certificate on the underlying. Therefore it would be a double counting error to calculate the market capitalisation on NOSH and the ADR (in relation to the ADR ratio).

Documentation

Documenting your work is vital. Your superiors will review your work and will wish to know the source of your data and any relevant background detail. Good documentation will make the review more efficient and you will spend a lot less time justifying your work. Mistakes will be found and resolved quickly if the reviewer can see the background detail.

Excel makes documentation very straightforward through the use of comments. Insert a comment (Shift + F2) in your work and record:

- Your name (this should be set up on your profile)
- The source of the data
- Any cross referencing/checking
- Any adjustments made to the raw data
- Any thoughts relevant to the number
- Any issues that need further clarification

If in doubt – insert the comment:

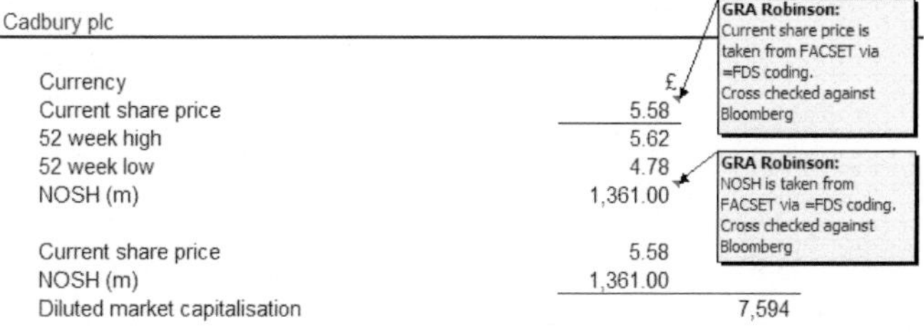

Cadbury plc		
Currency	£	
Current share price	5.58	
52 week high	5.62	
52 week low	4.78	
NOSH (m)	1,361.00	
Current share price	5.58	
NOSH (m)	1,361.00	
Diluted market capitalisation		7,594

=FDS coding (share prices and NOSH)

Information requirement	=FDS coding syntax
Closing share price	=FDS(A1,"P_PRICE(0)")
52 week high	=FDS(A1,"P_PRICE_HIGH_52W(0)")
52 week low	=FDS(A1,"P_PRICE_LOW_52W(0)")

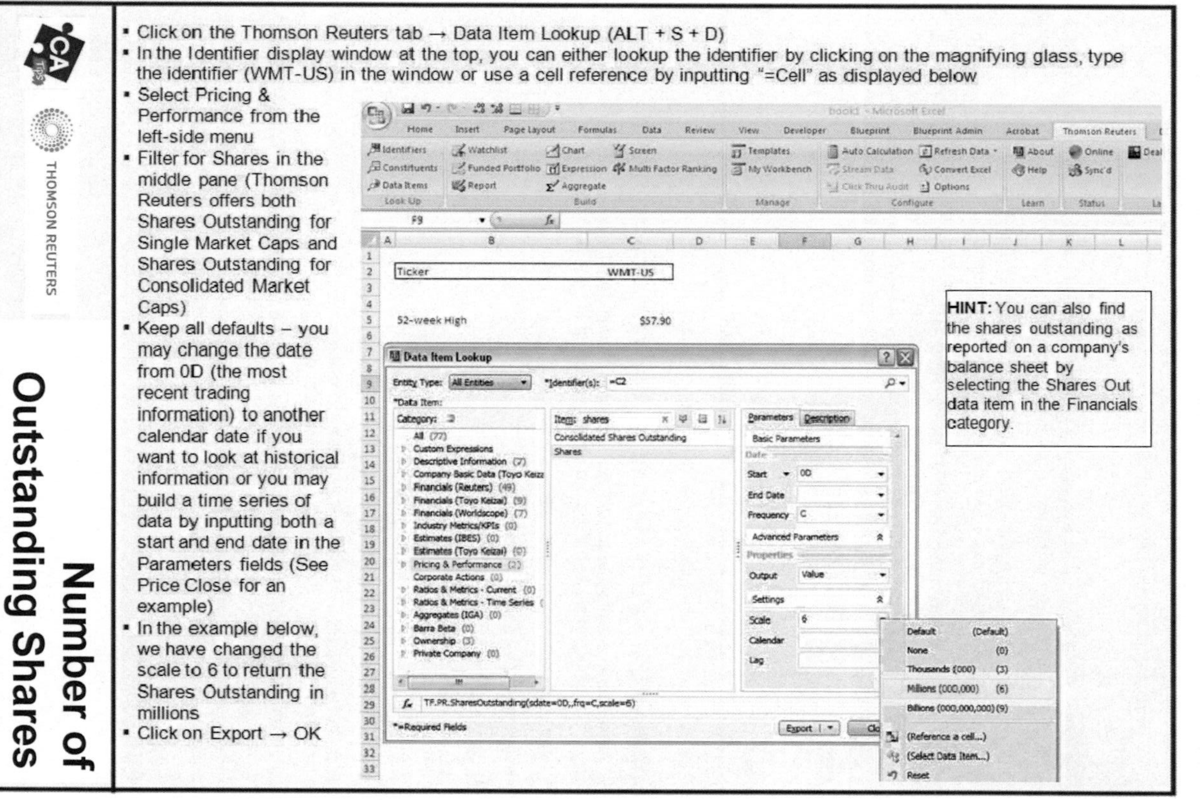

Source: Thomson Reuters

Fully Diluted Equity Value

It is sometimes relevant to adjust the market capitalization for the impact of dilutive securities.

In M&A situations, the value should be adjusted for the impact of all in-the-money securities, i.e. all outstanding options.

However in computing trading comp multiples, there is some debate as to whether one should adjust mutiples for the impact of all in-the-money securities or just those that are exercisable (e.g. some time expired requirement has been satisfied) and in-the-money at the date of the comps valuation.

Calculating EV – Fully diluted equity value component

A public market comp will often anticipate the impact of potentially dilutive securities on the market cap. These potentially dilutive securities are equity claims on the company.

Potentially dilutive security issues include:

- In-the-money (ITM) equity options
- ITM convertible debt
- ITM convertible preference shares

ITM equity options

The fully diluted equity value calculation anticipates the exercise of ITM equity options. ITM equity options have two impacts on the diluted equity value and therefore the EV:

- There is an increase in the NOSH which reflects the issue of new shares on the assumed exercise of the options.
- In order to exercise the options, the option holders will have to pay the exercise or strike price of the option. This is a cash inflow for the company. The increase in cash flow will reduce net debt.

The impact of ITM equity options can be calculated in two ways – using:

- The treasury method
- ITM buy-out cost method

The two methods will give the same answer. In the following illustration we will consider the impact of all in-the-money options (not just the exercisable ones).

Interpreting the Options Note

Many Analysts make significant mistakes with the options note. A lack of understanding or appreciation of the terminology is the main cause of error.

Key option terminology:

- Exercise or strike price – the price at which an option can be exercised
- WAEP – weighted average exercise price
- In-the-money – an option is in-the-money (ITM) if the exercise price is below the current market price
- Out-of-the-money – an option is out-of-the-money (OTM) if the exercise price is greater than the current market price
- Exercise or vesting period – is the period the option must be held before the option can be exercised
- Outstanding – an option is deemed outstanding if it has been issued
- Exercisable – an option is exercisable if held beyond the exercise or vesting period. The option is said to have vested.

Options in Cadbury Schweppes plc

The key number is the **outstanding** number of options. It is assumed that if the option is ITM it will vest on takeover and the option will become an equity claim irrespective of whether it is vested or exercisable

	Balance outstanding at the beginning of the year	Granted	Exercised	Cancelled	Balance outstanding at the end 01/05/2008	Exercise prices for options outstanding at 01/05/2008 in the range (in £ unless otherwise stated)	Weighted average exercise price of options outstanding at 01/05/2008 (in £ unless otherwise stated)	Weighted average contractual life in months of options outstanding at 01/05/2008	Exercisable at 01/05/2008	Weighted average exercise price of options currently exercisable at 01/05/2008 (in £ unless otherwise stated)
a	10,200,449	3,627[1]	1,924,791	354,571	7,924,714	3.15–4.69	4.03	35.09	102,505	3.59
c	26,174,016	–	1,759,474	25,002	24,389,540	3.31–4.83	4.24	46.22	24,389,540	4.24
d	8,979,975	–	344,239	33,778	8,601,958	4.40–5.70	4.82	79.45	8,521,708	4.81
e	22,076,797	–	1,819,344	273,511	19,983,942	4.40–5.72	4.83	22.56	19,472,192	4.81
f	368,726	–	15,011	19,430	334,285	2.74–3.78	2.98	16.31	–	–
	481,472	–	19,385	11,242	450,845	4.23–5.21	4.65	30.25	–	–
h	236,940	–	31,385	20,824	184,731	2.74–3.78	3.05	26.94	3,587	3.39
	139,390	–	8,771	2,538	128,081	4.23–5.22	4.62	44.62	–	–
j	579,275	–	224,037	18,477	336,761	3.02–4.48	4.12	19.42	35,499	3.56
	198,923	–	–	846	198,077	4.59–4.69	4.68	38.16	–	–
	166,376	–	244	132,020	34,112	$7.93	$7.93	13.97	–	–
l	1,536,822	–	197,868	132,084	1,206,870	$9.14	$9.14	6.48	–	–
	359,676	–	4,468	33,812	321,396	$9.67	$9.67	18.48	–	–
n	1,759,359	–	48,648	189,467	1,521,244	$9.14	$9.14	6.48	–	–
	452,300	–	1,152	66,328	384,820	$9.67	$9.67	18.48	–	–

The key column to pick up in an options note for the diluted equity value calculation in an M&A deal is the **outstanding** options column.

The treasury method

The treasury method works on the assumption that the proceeds from the share option exercise will be used to buy back shares in the market at full market value. Therefore the net dilution from the share option exercise is net of this buyback.

The following steps are required for the treasury method calculation. The numbers relate to Cadbury and the calculations are shown in the subsequent Excel spreadsheet extract.

1. Calculate the proceeds from the share option exercise (£280.07m).
2. This involves identifying the share options that are in-the-money (ITM).
3. Given the disclosures in the financials the ITM determination is normally calculated with reference to the weighted average exercise price (WAEP).
4. The proceeds = Number of options ITM x Exercise price
   These proceeds are used to buy back shares at full market value = Proceeds ÷ Current share price (50.19m shares).
5. Therefore the net dilution = Number of shares issued through option exercise - Buyback = 62.57m – 50.19m = 12.38m shares net dilution.

The dilution can be expressed in terms of the net impact on EV = 12.38m shares x Current share price = £69.05m. This net impact on EV comprises two forces:

- The impact on market capitalization of the new shares issued as a result of the share option exercise (Number of new shares issued x Current market price)
- The cash proceeds received as a result of the option exercise which will increase the cash number and reduce net debt (Number of new shares issued x Exercise price).

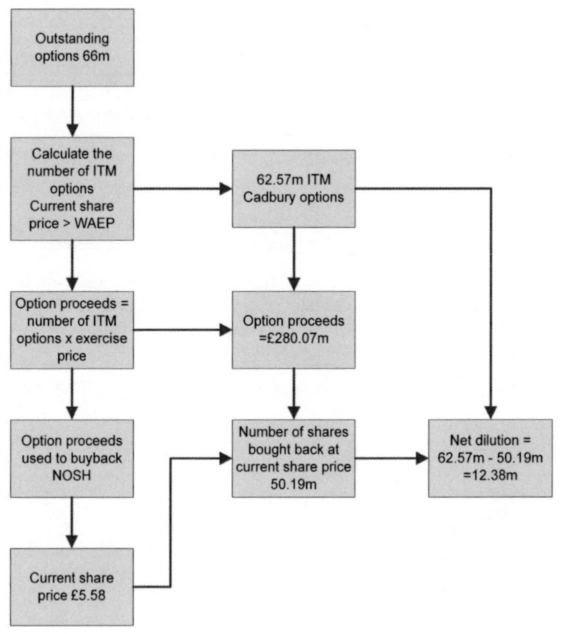

Treasury method	**Outstanding**	**WAEP**		**ITM?**	**No of ITM options**	**Proceeds**	
Current share price	5.58						
Share option scheme 1	7.92	4.03	2	Yes	7.92	31.94	1
Share option scheme 2	24.39	4.24		Yes	24.39	103.41	
Share option scheme 3	8.60	4.82	3	Yes	8.60	41.46	
Share option scheme 4	19.98	4.83		Yes	19.98	96.52	
Share option scheme 5	0.33	2.98		Yes	0.33	1.00	
Share option scheme 6	0.45	4.65		Yes	0.45	2.10	
Share option scheme 7	0.18	3.05		Yes	0.18	0.56	
Share option scheme 8	0.13	4.62		Yes	0.13	0.59	
Share option scheme 9	0.34	4.12		Yes	0.34	1.39	
Share option scheme 10	0.20	4.68		Yes	0.20	0.93	
Share option scheme 11	0.03	5.18		Yes	0.03	0.18	
Share option scheme 12	1.21	5.97		No	--	--	
Share option scheme 13	0.32	6.32		No	--	--	
Share option scheme 14	1.52	5.97		No	--	--	
Share option scheme 15	0.38	6.32		No	--	--	
Number of outstanding options	66.00						
Proceeds from option exercise						280.07	4
Current market price						5.58	
Number of share bought back at full price (proceeds ÷ current share price)						50.19	4
Number of ITM share options					62.57		
Net dilution of option exercise						12.38	5
Net Impact (net dilution x current share price)						69.05	
Increase in market capitalisation					349.12		
Cash proceeds from option exercise					(280.07)		
Net impact						69.05	

The net buy-out method

The net buy-out method calculates the option dilution impact by calculating what it would cost the company to buy out the existing options. The method is based on the costs that would be triggered if a company was bought out. Standard change of control clauses generally require outstanding options (whether or not they have vested) to be bought out by the acquirer. The option holder is offered an amount of cash (in this hypothetical buy out, the offer is the current share price) in exchange for the options. The amount is settled net, so the buy-out cost is the net buy-out = Current share price - Exercise or strike price.

Buy out cost = Number of ITM options x (Current share price - Exercise or strike price)

Using Cadbury as the example again, we can see that the net buy out cost method produces the same result as the treasury method. The net dilution impact on EV of £69.05m can be split into the impact on market capitalization (£349.12m) and cash proceeds from the option exercise (280.07m).

Net buy-out method	Outstanding	WAEP	ITM?	No of ITM options	Net Buy out cost
Current share price	5.58				
Share option scheme 1	7.92	4.03	Yes	7.92	12.28
Share option scheme 2	24.39	4.24	Yes	24.39	32.68
Share option scheme 3	8.60	4.82	Yes	8.60	6.54
Share option scheme 4	19.98	4.83	Yes	19.98	14.99
Share option scheme 5	0.33	2.98	Yes	0.33	0.87
Share option scheme 6	0.45	4.65	Yes	0.45	0.42
Share option scheme 7	0.18	3.05	Yes	0.18	0.47
Share option scheme 8	0.13	4.62	Yes	0.13	0.12
Share option scheme 9	0.34	4.12	Yes	0.34	0.49
Share option scheme 10	0.20	4.68	Yes	0.20	0.18
Share option scheme 11	0.03	5.18	Yes	0.03	0.01
Share option scheme 12	1.21	5.97	No	--	--
Share option scheme 13	0.32	6.32	No	--	--
Share option scheme 14	1.52	5.97	No	--	--
Share option scheme 15	0.38	6.32	No	--	--
Number of outstanding options	66.00				
Number of ITM share options				62.57	
Net buy-out cost					69.05
Increase in market capitalisation					349.12
Cash proceeds from option exercise					(280.07)
Net impact					69.05

Analysts must be able to present the option dilution numbers using both methods.

Convertible securities

Fully diluted EV calculations must also capture potentially dilutive securities such as convertible debt and convertible preference shares.

ITM convertible securities are securities whose conversion price (exercise or strike price) is less than the current market price. ITM convertible instruments will add to the equity value by increasing the NOSH. (NOSH: Calculated by dividing the face value of the instrument by the conversion price.)

It should be noted that if the convertible security is ITM, the income statement must be adjusted post-tax. There will be a notional increase in net income for the post-tax coupon or dividend.

OTM instruments will remain in net debt.

Cadbury comp

The Cadbury diluted market capitalization calculation:

Cadbury plc		
Currency	£	
Current share price	5.58	
52 week high	5.62	
52 week low	4.78	
NOSH (m)	1,361	
		£m
Current share price	5.58	
NOSH (m)	1,361	
ITM convertible debt	--	
Net diluted NOSH (m) - treasury method	**12.38**	
Diluted market capitalization		**7,663**

The diluted market capitalization has increased by £69m – the net dilutive impact calculated using the treasury method.

Calculating EV – Net debt component

Net debt is included in the EV calculation as it represents the debt providers' claims on the value of the firm. Typically the basic net debt calculation captures the on-balance sheet debt claims on the entity.

Basic net debt is defined as:

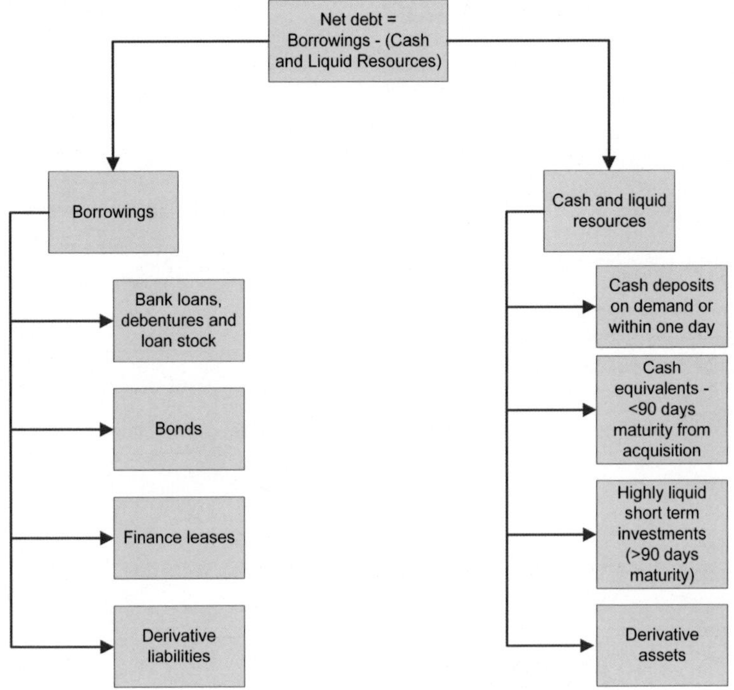

Cadbury comp

The Cadbury comp below includes the net debt numbers. The share option impact has been presented in two ways:

Net presentation – the dilution is included in the net diluted NOSH number. This method follows the treasury method calculation. Gross presentation – the dilution is included as an increase in new NOSH as a result of the share option exercise in the market capitalization calculation. The cash proceeds are then brought in as part of the net debt cash line. Some Analysts may include the cash proceeds outside the net debt line.

Cadbury plc		
Currency	£	
Current share price	5.58	
52 week high	5.62	
52 week low	4.78	
NOSH (m)	1,361	
		£m
Current share price	5.58	
NOSH (m)	1,361	
ITM convertible debt	--	
Net diluted NOSH (m) - treasury method	**12.38**	
Diluted market capitalization		**7,663**
Borrowings < 1 year	1,189	
Borrowings > 1 year	1,194	
OTM convertible debt	--	
OTM convertible preferred stock	--	
Cash and cash equivalents	(251)	
Short-term investments	(247)	
		1,885
EV		**9,548**

Alternative presentation of option dilution		
Current share price	5.58	
NOSH (m)	1,361	
New shares issued under option	**63**	
		7,944
Borrowings < 1 year	1,189	
Borrowings > 1 year	1,194	
Cash and cash equivalents	(251)	
Cash proceeds from option exercise	**(280)**	
Short-term investments	(247)	
		1,605
EV		**9,548**

Ultimately the presentation is discretionary as the bottom line EV impact is the same whatever presentation format is followed.

Why is it 'Net' Debt?

Cash can be considered unemployed capital or non-operating capital. It should therefore be excluded from the EV calculation as there is no corresponding income return included in the denominator of an EV multiple.

This argument however can be flawed. In some industries such as retail, cash might be considered an operating asset. It is then part of the working capital used to run operations and generate value. Not all cash is working capital though. If Analysts are pursuing this argument they will have to identify what element of cash is working capital and what element is 'excess'. Only excess cash should be netted off against the debt number.

Calculating EV – Other claim components

EV must include **all** claims on the entity, not just the market capitalization and net debt. This might include claims that are not recognized on the balance sheet or claims relating to items that should be treated as debt, even if they are not accounted for debt – such as:

- Pension deficits
- Operating lease commitments
- Preferred stock holdings

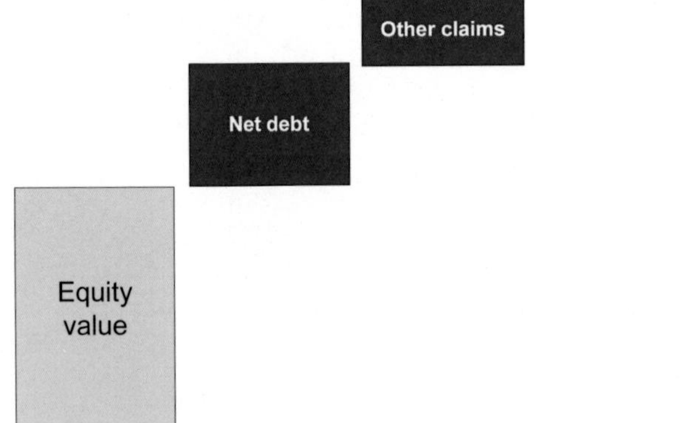

The adjustments in relation to operating lease commitments and pension deficit issues were covered earlier. Even though neither number is treated as a debt instrument, both are in substance debt-like claims on the entity and should be treated as claims in the EV calculation.

Pension Surplus

If an entity is fortunate enough to run a funded defined benefit scheme that has a pension surplus (assets > benefit obligation), the EV calculation does not adjust for the surplus. That is, the surplus is not a deduction against EV and is not treated as a liquid resource.

The asset surplus is ring fenced from the entity and cannot be used to satisfy any non-pension claims against the entity. If the entity has a pension surplus, the impact on EV is Nil.

Cadbury comp

The Cadbury comp has now been adjusted for the debt-like claims on EV. The detail behind some of these adjustments were covered in other sections.

Cadbury plc

Currency	£	
Current share price	5.58	
52 week high	5.62	
52 week low	4.78	
NOSH (m)	1,361	
		£m
Current share price	5.58	
NOSH (m)	1,361	
ITM convertible debt	--	
Net diluted NOSH (m) - treasury method	12.38	
Diluted market capitalization		7,663
Borrowings < 1 year	1,189	
Borrowings > 1 year	1,194	
OTM convertible debt	--	
OTM convertible preferred stock	--	
Cash and cash equivalents	(251)	
Short-term investments	(247)	
Net debt		1,885
Pension deficit - funded schemes		**144**
Pension deficit - unfunded schemes		**15**
Non-controlling interest (book value) – see below		12
Investment in associates (book value) – see later in this section		(28)
EV		**9,691**
PV of the operating lease commitments		**270**
EV (lease adjusted)		**9,961**

Calculating EV – Non-controlling interests (minority interest)

Non-controlling interests (NCI) are external equity interests in the subsidiaries of a group of entities. They represent an equity claim on the group outside the market capitalization of the group shareholders.

The reason for including NCI in the EV calculation is that the earnings metric used in the denominator of the EV multiple (e.g. EBITDA) will include 100% of the EBITDA of these subsidiaries which have external equity interests. So the NCI has a claim on some of the EBITDA.

NCI numbers are disclosed on the balance sheet, usually as a component of equity at book value. Ideally a market value should be included in the EV calculation. However, the NCI is normally immaterial to the overall EV calculation and the extra work that would be needed in order to derive a market value cannot be justified.

However, if the NCI is significant, a market value should be calculated. If the subsidiary which has the NCI is listed, the market value calculation is a straightforward NCI percentage of its market capitalization.

Problems do arise if the NCI is significant and the subsidiary is unlisted. Analysts will then have to value the NCI equity claim. This requires a full valuation (DCF and/or comps) exercise on the subsidiary.

Cadbury comp

Cadbury does not own 100% of all its subsidiaries. This is picked up by reviewing the equity components on the balance sheet. The extract below shows that Cadbury has a small NCI or minority interest. It is unlikely that this NCI will be material to the overall comp and therefore the book value has been included in the EV calculation.

	Equity	
28	Share capital	136
28	Share premium account	38
28	Other reserves	850
28	Retained earnings	2,498
28	**Equity attributable to equity holders of the parent**	3,522
29	**Minority interests**	12
	Total equity	3,534

Source: Cadbury annual report

Calculating EV – Joint ventures, associates and other non-operating investments

JVs and associates/affiliates for the most part are accounted for using the equity method. The equity method accounts for earnings generated by these entities by bringing into the income statement the group's share of post-tax earnings. This line item is normally disclosed below the EBIT line in the income statement. The investment in JVs and associates is a non-current asset line included on the balance sheet at book value.

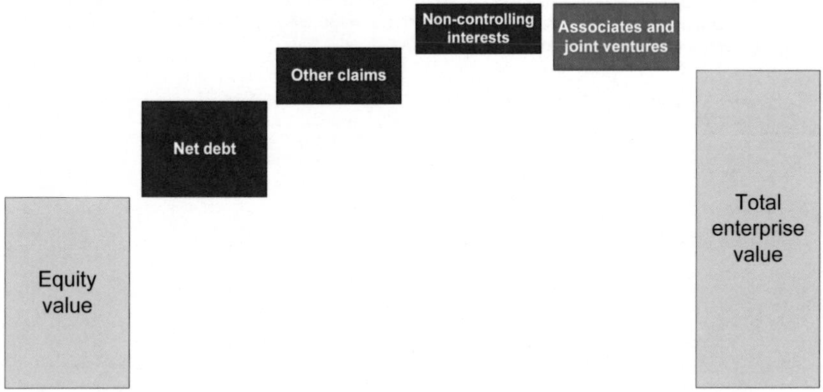

The market value of joint ventures and associates should be reflected/captured in the market capitalization calculation. However, most Analysts will wish to strip out this value from the EV calculation.

The value of JVs and associates are stripped out of the EV calculation because they create an inconsistency between the denominator and the numerator in the multiple. The inconsistency arises due to accounting mechanics.

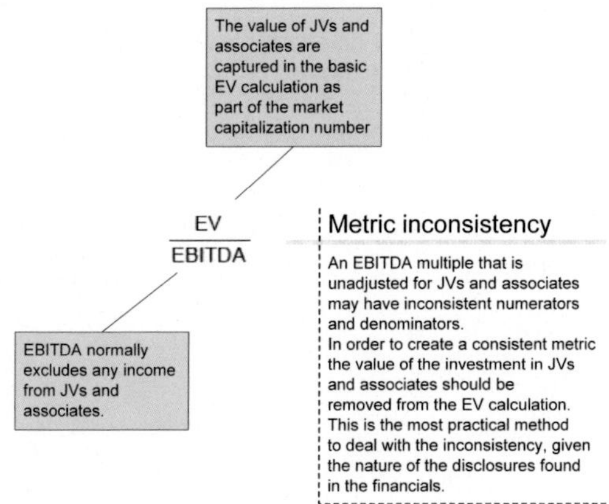

Ideally the JV and associate numbers should be adjusted in the EV calculation at market value. If the JV or associates are listed, this is just a matter of bringing in the group share of the market capitalization of the JV or associate. However, if the investments are unlisted and only if the size of the investments warrant the additional work (DCF and/or comps), a market value adjustment should be made.

Cadbury comp

Cadbury has investments in associates. These investments are relatively small. A book value of £28m for the associates is unlikely to be material to the overall EV calculation. As a result it is likely that a book value will be used in the EV calculation.

	Assets	
	Non-current assets	
14	Goodwill	2,288
15	Acquisition intangibles	1,598
15	Software intangibles	87
16	Property, plant and equipment	1,761
17	Investment in associates	28

Source: Cadbury annual report

Proportional Consolidation

Proportional consolidation is currently permitted under IFRS (See M&A transaction accounting section). The method is sometimes used to account for investments in JVs and is a method that is seen in continental Europe. The results and balance sheet line items of the JV are included line by line in the group financials. Therefore, the multiple inconsistency issues mentioned above are not relevant. The value of the JV would be included in the EV (through the market capitalization calculation) and the EBITDA numbers.

Some Analysts may still attempt to remove these values (disclosure permitting) in order to present a clean, core EV multiple. The quality of disclosure can often frustrate this process.

Cadbury comp (full pro-forma)

The EV calculation below includes all of the adjustments discussed in the notes above. A nil balance means that the line item is not relevant to Cadbury but it is an adjustment that can be relevant for some companies.

Cadbury plc

Currency	£	
Current share price	5.58	
52 week high	5.62	
52 week low	4.78	
NOSH (m)	1,361	
		£m
Current share price	5.58	
NOSH (m)	1,361	
ITM convertible debt	--	
Net diluted NOSH (m) - treasury method	12.38	
Diluted market capitalization		7,663
Borrowings < 1 year	1,189	
Borrowings > 1 year	1,194	
OTM convertible debt	--	
OTM convertible preferred stock	--	
Cash and cash equivalents	(251)	
Short-term investments	(247)	
Net debt		1,885
Pension deficit - funded schemes		144
Pension deficit - unfunded schemes		15
Non-controlling interest (book value)		12
Investment in associates (book value)		(28)
EV		**9,691**
PV of the operating lease commitments		270
EV (lease adjusted)		**9,961**

Post-balance Sheet Date Review

A significant part of the investigation required to construct the EV number is driven from the financials. However, Analysts must make sure they are aware of post-balance sheet date events. The financials at the best of times are out of date. The EV numbers must be the most up-to-date numbers, reflecting all new news.

The metric

The most common denominators used in multiples are earnings metrics such as:

- Revenues
- EBITDA
- EBIT(A)

Some sector teams will use sector specific denominators. Sector specific multiples are discussed later in the notes.

The key principle behind the multiple denominators is that it should be a driver of the numerator (EV or equity value).

Revenue

Revenue has been pushed as a metric of choice because it is generally comparable across different accounting frameworks. This argument can be flawed for several reasons:

- Revenue recognition is a weak area of accounting. Entities have enough latitude with the presentation of their revenues for comparability issues to arise. Admittedly the influence of accounting is less problematic at the revenue level than it is to earnings metrics further down the income statement.
- The main criticism of the revenue number is that it presents an incomplete picture of the business, its operations and its cost structure. Hence, it is not necessarily reflective of the ability to generate cash flow. If two companies have different cost structures, then multiples based on revenues will be meaningless.

Revenue is claimed by debt and equity providers of capital. Therefore it should only be applied to EV level multiples. However, it is a metric of last resort. It came to prominence during the late 90s technology bubble as it was used to value loss-making companies. With no earnings to value, revenue was one of the few viable alternatives.

EBITDA

EBITDA has become the metric of choice for a number of Analysts. It goes some way to address the problems associated with inconsistent accounting policies. It does ignore the D&A which is a constant source of inconsistency. It is a cleaner earnings metric than EBIT. However, Analysts must be aware that it is not a perfect metric.

EBITDA:

- Still ignores changes in working capital
- Is only a rough proxy for cash flow
- Is still subject to revenue and operating cost recognition issues
- Ignores the costs of capital expenditure and tax, both of which are key drivers of value
- Creates a comparability issue if leasing is prevalent in the sector. EBITDA ignores all the income statement charges relevant to finance (capital) leases, but is after operating lease charges

The EBITDA can be modified to address some of these issues. Some Analysts have used operating free cash flow as a modified EBITDA metric:

EBITDA	X
Changes in net working capital	X/(X)
Maintenance capex	(X)
Operating free cash flow	X

Maintenance capex is the capital expenditure required to maintain the current earnings ability and competitive position of the entity. Operating free cash flow benefits from being a cleaner metric.

EBIT

EBIT is also used as a numerator in valuation metrics. It does suffer from the inconsistency issues that arise from the reliance on D&A numbers. However as it is after D&A, it is probably a more useful metric for capital intensive industries

If an adjustment for the operating lease commitments has been made to EV, the EBIT metric must also be adjusted. The adjustment treats the operating lease commitments as a debt-like item and accounts for the lease as if it were a finance (capital) lease. Therefore the operating lease charge is converted to a depreciation and interest charge.

The EBIT metric must therefore be adjusted and a notional interest charge added back to the metric. Likewise if a pension deficit is included in the EV calculation, the EBIT metric must be reviewed to ensure that the current service charge is the only deduction.

EBITDAR

If an operating lease conversion adjustment is included in the EV calculation, the most appropriate denominator is the EBITDAR metric. This is calculated by adding back the full operating lease charge (i.e. the rental) to EBITDA. This metric provides a level playing field as it ignores all charges in relation to leasing.

Which period's metric

The choice of metric type (Revenue, EBIT or EBITDA for instance) is not the only decision to be made about the metric. Analysts will also have to decide what period should be used for the metric. The metric could be based on any of the following earnings metrics:

- Historical
- Last 12 months (LTM)
- Current
- Forecast

Whatever metric is chosen, it is normally applied to a snapshot EV at the valuation date.

Historical

Historical earnings act mainly as a benchmark against the more forward looking metrics. Public companies do not trade (nor are they valued) on historical numbers.

LTM (last 12 months)

LTM numbers are used to reflect the most recent publicly available information. Debt and equity capital markets will factor this information into the pricing of market capitalization and debt. It is therefore important that the metrics capture the most up-to-date information.

A LTM number is constructed using annual and interim financials. Most European listed companies are required to publish financials twice a year. In the US, the Securities Exchange Commission requires listed companies to report quarterly. The filing is called a 10Q.

As a result of the frequency of US filings, the US LTM numbers have greater scope to be up-to-date.

The construction of a LTM earnings metric (assuming US quarterly reporting) is illustrated below:

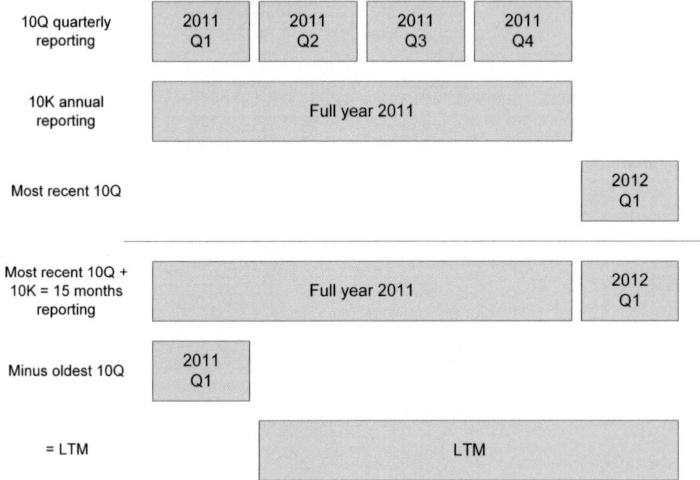

Whilst benchmarking the company's performance through the use of historical data is a useful exercise, most public companies tend to be valued or trade on forward or forecast results.

This information can be found in:

- Research reports
- I/B/E/S (consensus research estimates)
- FactSet estimates (consensus research estimates)
- CAPIQ (consensus research estimates)

Broker or Consensus Numbers?

Broker research is more reliable than consensus estimates as a primary source of information. Consensus estimates are an average of submitted research. A consensus service is an excellent tool to benchmark a particular broker's estimate against a wider population. It is also a useful source of quick and dirty forecast numbers. However, consensus estimates will hide outliers behind the average number. Furthermore, no narrative supporting the forecast consensus numbers will be provided.

Individual broker research is written by experts who follow the company on a day-to-day basis. The research report will provide a detailed narrative supporting the forecast numbers. A good research broker should provide reliable information.

However, reliance on a single broker can be problematic. Analysts will not then have an appreciation of the sentiment behind the forecasts in relation to the wider broker population. Is their choice of broker particularly bullish?

For this reason it is probably a good idea to review a selection of broker research to ensure there is some consistency in outlook.

Alternatively benchmark the particular broker forecasts against consensus estimates.

The most widely used consensus estimate is I/B/E/S (Institutional Brokers Estimation Service) owned by Thomson Reuters. It is a database of research estimates that date back as far as 1976 for US data and 1987 for international data.

Common sources of consensus estimates are:

- I/B/E/S
- First call
- CAPIQ
- Thomson One
- Bloomberg

FactSet Estimates (1)

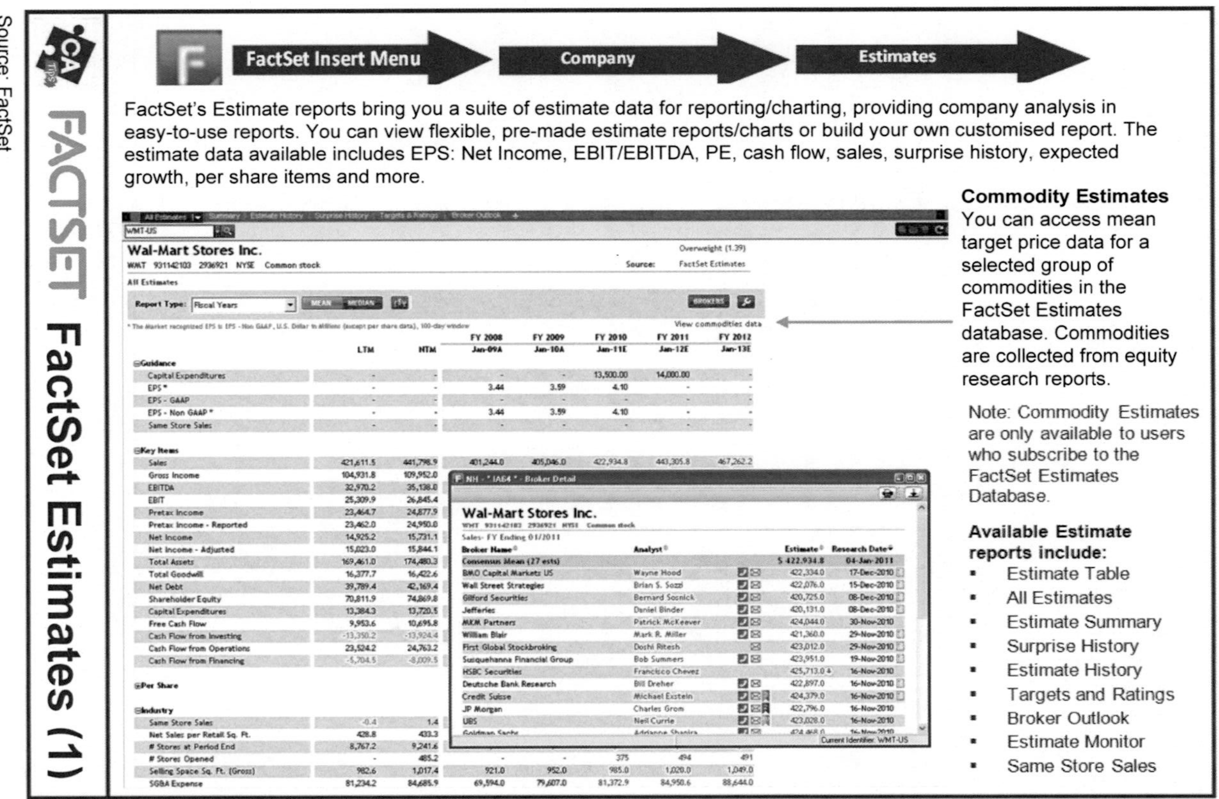

FactSet's Estimate reports bring you a suite of estimate data for reporting/charting, providing company analysis in easy-to-use reports. You can view flexible, pre-made estimate reports/charts or build your own customised report. The estimate data available includes EPS: Net Income, EBIT/EBITDA, PE, cash flow, sales, surprise history, expected growth, per share items and more.

Commodity Estimates

You can access mean target price data for a selected group of commodities in the FactSet Estimates database. Commodities are collected from equity research reports.

Note: Commodity Estimates are only available to users who subscribe to the FactSet Estimates Database.

Available Estimate reports include:

- Estimate Table
- All Estimates
- Estimate Summary
- Surprise History
- Estimate History
- Targets and Ratings
- Broker Outlook
- Estimate Monitor
- Same Store Sales

Source: FactSet

FactSet Estimates (2)

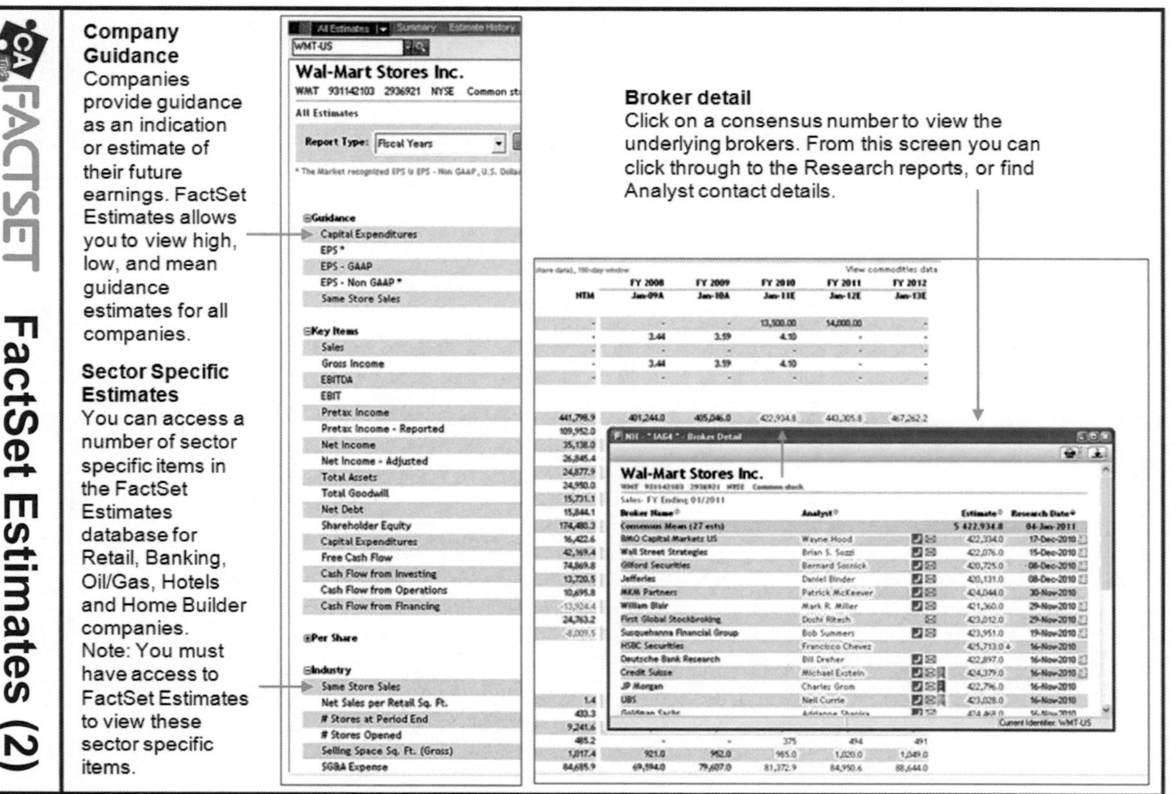

Company Guidance
Companies provide guidance as an indication or estimate of their future earnings. FactSet Estimates allows you to view high, low, and mean guidance estimates for all companies.

Sector Specific Estimates
You can access a number of sector specific items in the FactSet Estimates database for Retail, Banking, Oil/Gas, Hotels and Home Builder companies. Note: You must have access to FactSet Estimates to view these sector specific items.

Broker detail
Click on a consensus number to view the underlying brokers. From this screen you can click through to the Research reports, or find Analyst contact details.

Source: FactSet

How to Import Consensus Estimates

THOMSON REUTERS

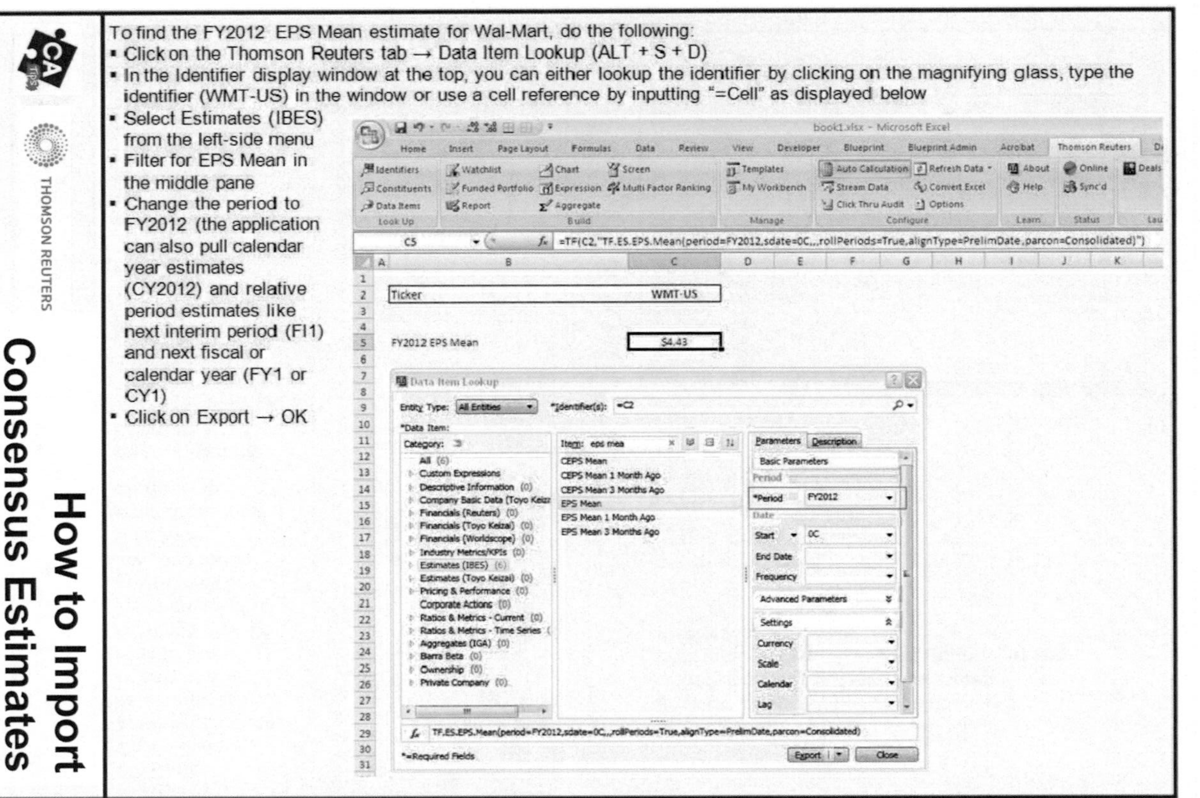

To find the FY2012 EPS Mean estimate for Wal-Mart, do the following:

- Click on the Thomson Reuters tab → Data Item Lookup (ALT + S + D)
- In the Identifier display window at the top, you can either lookup the identifier by clicking on the magnifying glass, type the identifier (WMT-US) in the window or use a cell reference by inputting "=Cell" as displayed below
- Select Estimates (IBES) from the left-side menu
- Filter for EPS Mean in the middle pane
- Change the period to FY2012 (the application can also pull calendar year estimates (CY2012) and relative period estimates like next interim period (FI1) and next fiscal or calendar year (FY1 or CY1)
- Click on Export → OK

Source: Thomson Reuters

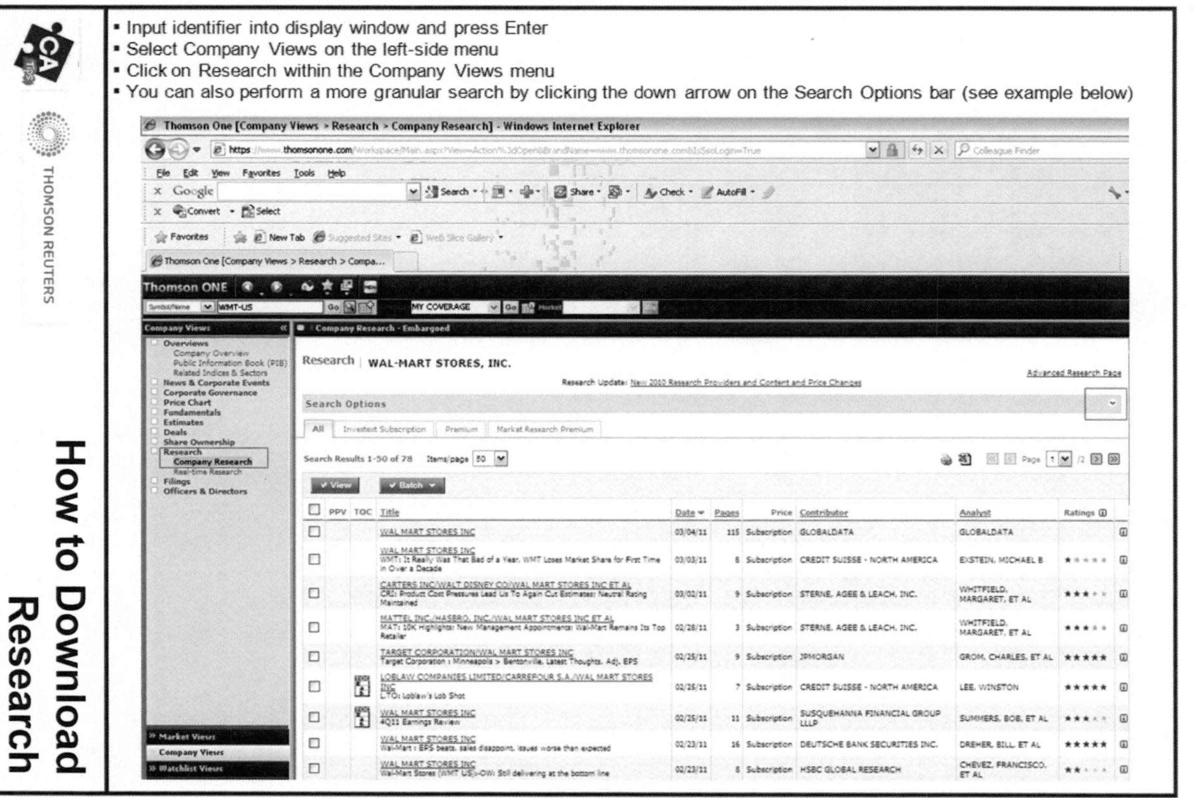

Source: Thomson Reuters

Current

A current earnings metric is actually a forecast number. It is often assumed incorrectly to be a historic number.

Many brokers will refer to this as a forecast year.

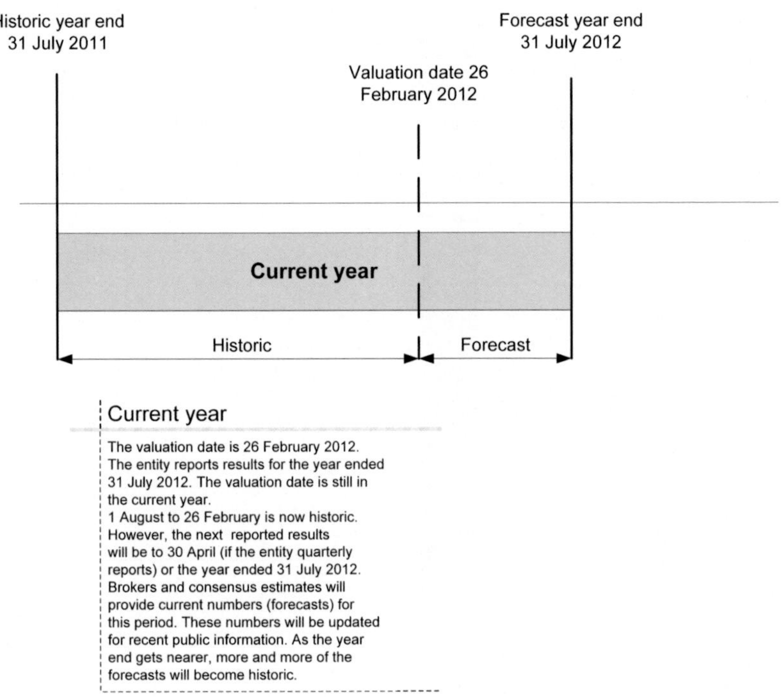

Current year

The valuation date is 26 February 2012. The entity reports results for the year ended 31 July 2012. The valuation date is still in the current year.
1 August to 26 February is now historic. However, the next reported results will be to 30 April (if the entity quarterly reports) or the year ended 31 July 2012. Brokers and consensus estimates will provide current numbers (forecasts) for this period. These numbers will be updated for recent public information. As the year end gets nearer, more and more of the forecasts will become historic.

Forecast

Some research brokers do not use the 'current' terminology. They will consider all numbers that are forward looking as forecast numbers.

The forecast numbers will be provided either by research brokers or consensus estimates.
If Analysts are relying on broker estimates, they must get an understanding of the metric definitions the broker is using in their forecasts. Brokers for the most part do not explicitly state their definitions or what adjustments they have made. Metric definitions also vary between brokers.

Reconciling and Understanding the Broker Definitions

Blind reliance on broker forecasts is unwise. Analysts should attempt to reconcile the historic broker metrics in order to get an understanding of the forecast metric definitions.

In the example below, Cadbury reported an EBIT of £388m. However, the broker is using an EBIT of £634m. This is a significant difference that must be understood before relying on the forecast numbers.

Income statement

£m	FY07A	FY08A	FY09F	FY10F	FY11F
Revenue	4699	5384	5893	6201	6547
Cost of sales	-2504	-2870	-3074	-3074	-3182
Operating costs	-1450	-1636	-1847	-2060	-2194
EBITDA	**745.0**	**878.0**	**971.5**	**1067.3**	**1171.5**
DDA & Impairment (ex gw)	-272.0	-240.0	-200.0	-207.0	-217.0
EBITA (1)	**473.0**	**638.0**	**771.5**	**860.3**	**954.5**
Goodwill (amort/impaired)	-18.0	-4.0	-4.0	-4.0	-4.0
EBIT	455.0	634.0	767.5	856.3	950.5

Source: RBS equity research

Reported EBIT	388	Per income statement
Restructuring costs	194	Note 4
Non-trading cost	(1)	Note 4
Non-recurring trading costs	57	Note 3
EBIT normalised (EBITA)	638	
DA	240	Note 34 - excl. gw impairment
EBITDA normalised	878	

The reconciling items can normally be found by reviewing the notes to the financials. Obvious hiding places of these adjustments are:

- The EBIT note (note 3&4 in Cadbury's financials)
- Reconciliation of EBIT to operating cash flow (note 34)
- The face of the income statement

Now that the metric can be reconciled, we can see that the broker has stripped out non-recurring items from the EBIT definition. These historics will have been used by the broker as a platform for the forecasts. Therefore as the historics are free from non-recurring items, we can be confident that non-recurring noise has not been embedded in the forecast metrics.

Which Forecast Period to use for Multiples?

Valuation is a forward-looking exercise. Companies trade on forward looking numbers. The issue often arises concerning which set of forecast numbers to use – the current forecast numbers or the following year?

The current year forecast numbers will tend to be more credible as they are focusing on the near term forecast horizon. However, the decision is subjective and dependent on the valuation date. Considering the February 26, valuation date example above, the current period 'forecast' is actually mainly historic (August 1 to February 26).

In this case, it may be acceptable for an Analyst to rely on the 2013 forecast numbers as these are more forward-looking than the partly historic 2012 current forecast numbers.

Normalizing the metric

All the financial metrics used in comparable company analysis must be adjusted for non-recurring items to ensure the highest quality of comparability.

The usual suspects are:

- Asset write downs
- Impairments
- Restructuring costs
- Reorganization costs
- Inventory write-offs
- Profits and losses on disposals of PPE
- Litigation expenses

Adjustments to the earnings metrics may also have a tax line impact. Any adjustment to an EBIT, EBITDA and EBITDAR metric will be made pre-tax. However, the tax line will have to be adjusted for the tax impact if post-tax metrics are required.

The illustration below shows the post-tax treatment for a restructuring charge adjustment:

	Total £m
Continuing operations	
Revenue	5,384
Trading costs	(4,803)
Restructuring costs	(194)
Non-trading items	1
Profit from operations	388
Share of result in associates	10
Profit before financing and taxation	398
Investment revenue	52
Finance costs	(50)
Profit before taxation	400
Taxation	(30)
Profit for the period from continuing operations	370

EBIT	388
Restructuring costs	194
EBIT normalised	582
Share of associate	10
Investment revenue	52
Finance cost	(50)
Profti before tax	594
Tax	(84)
Net income normalised	510
Restructuring costs (post tax)	(140)
Net income as reported	370

GRA Robinson: The most significant component of these restructuring costs is typically redundancy payments. These were considered non-recurring

GRA Robinson: The tax line is adjusted for the normalisation of the restructuring cost. The statutory corporate tax rate is assumed to be 28%. = 30 + (194 x 28%) = £84m

GRA Robinson: The redundancy costs are brought back into the income statement post tax to reconcile the net income line

Source: Cadbury annual report

Finding Company News for Normalization Purposes

Bloomberg

Information for normalization adjustments can be found in:

- Company filings
- Research reports
- Prospectuses
- Press releases
- Proxy statement (US SEC filing)
- Bloomberg corporate actions calendar - Key strokes: Ticker CACS <GO>

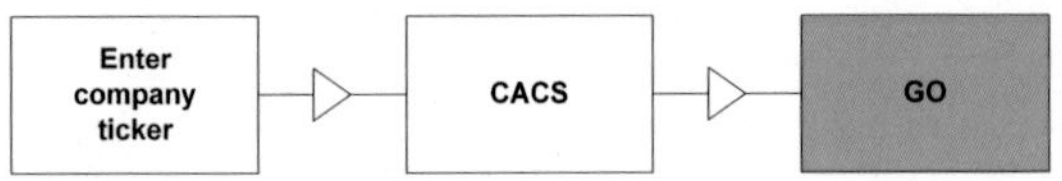

Picking a Relevant Broker Report

Broker research is available through:

Bloomberg

- Bloomberg – key stroke Ticker <BRC> <GO>

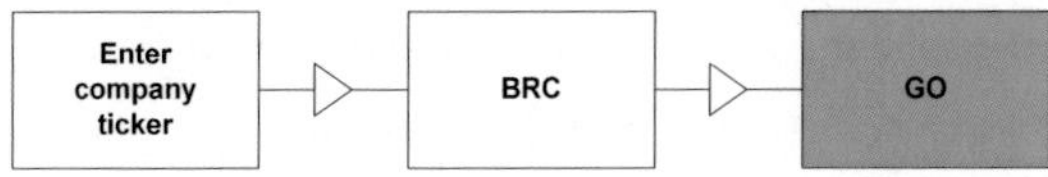

- Thomson One
- FactSet
- Internal library services

A research search using an information provider will produce an extensive list of research notes. Many of these notes will be one page flash notes that contain new flash information.

Finding data for a comp requires detailed forecast information.

The service providers will not provide access to all available research on a particular company. If a particular research piece is required, a charge may be levied. Research can be expensive. It is important that you are confident you are buying relevant and useful research.

The reason for using broker research is to ascertain the market's current perception of the future. The choice of the broker research is therefore dependent on:

- Dates – research brokers will produce in-depth research reports prior to and after regulatory filing dates.
- Events – research notes are often event driven. Major events such as M&A deals may trigger a detailed report.
- Number of pages – research reports of 3-7 pages generally don't contain the requisite level of detailed financial information. Often 3-4 pages of these reports will be disclaimers. A lengthy report is likely to contain financial forecast information.
- Broker credibility – brokers are ranked each year. Some brokers are better than others. Know your ranked brokers and use them where possible.
- Know who the corporate broker is. A corporate broker's forecasts may not coincide with the market's consensus.

Calendarization (annualization)

Companies within the comparable universe are unlikely to have the same financial period ends. Analysts will often apply the technique of calendarizing the earnings metrics. Calendarization will time apportion the earnings metrics to a common year period. The technique aims to produce comparable time period data that smoothes out seasonal and cyclical differences.

The period end to calendarize to is the Analyst's choice – calendarization can be to:

- The target company's period end
- A standard year end
- The acquirer's year end if in a M&A situation

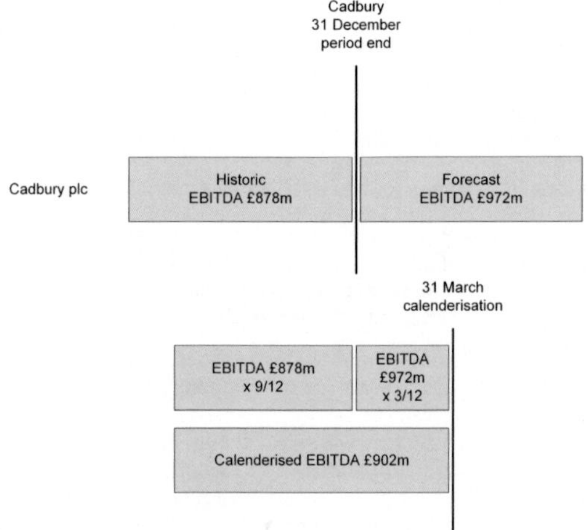

Additional financial data

A trading comps database must also collect additional data that might not be used directly in the multiple calculation. This data is used to assess comparability and to understand the drivers of the multiples.

This information is essential in order to understand why multiples may trade above or below the comparable universe average. The comps database should collect any information that supports a justification of a multiple using the following as benchmarks:

- Cash
- Risk
- Growth

Examples of relevant additional financial data:

- Metric growth rates
- Earnings margins
- Credit ratios and statistics such as interest cover, leverage multiples
- Payout ratios
- Costs of capital
- Market capitalization
- Market share data

Step 3: Choice of multiple

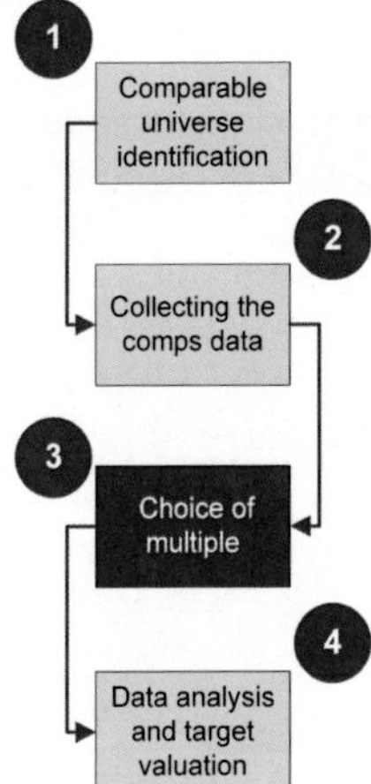

Analysts have a number of vital choices at step 3 in the comps process:

- What level of multiple (EV or equity value) should be applied in the valuation?
- If using an EV multiple – which earnings metric is most appropriate?

Equity or Enterprise Level Multiples

EV and equity value multiples are used extensively through the industry. Some sectors will be more reliant on EV multiples, whilst others prefer the equity level. Both multiples have their merits. The table below summarizes the relative merits of the different multiple levels:

EV multiples	Equity multiples
Rely on denominators that are less prone to accounting issues	More relevant to equity valuation
Are capital structure neutral	Are more familiar to investors
Are comprehensive. They capture the full claim on the enterprise.	Arguably involve less subjectivity than EV multiples, especially in terms of assessing off balance sheet claims
Make it easier to capture off-balance sheet and debt-like claims.	Are much more prone to accounting issues
Have a wide spectrum of applicable multiples	
Are technically harder to communicate to clients	
Have an increased reliance on market values	
Require additional technical work to derive an equity value from an enterprise value	

Trading Comparables

The following section will review the relative merits of the most common multiple forms.

EV – Revenue multiples

What are the positives?	What are the problems?
Although a relatively crude measure, it is the least prone metric to accounting manipulation and distortion.	Seasonality can cause comparability issues.
Very useful when there are significant accounting differences between the comparables.	Ignores the cost structure of the business. Sales multiples cannot be used to directly derive margin information.
Can be used to value loss making, start up and development stage companies.	Revenues do not necessarily translate into cash flow.
Can be used when comparables have similar margins.	Revenue recognition issues can create accounting comparability issues.

EV – EBITDA multiples

What are the positives?	What are the problems?
EBITDA is closer to a cash flow measure as it ignores D&A.	It ignores depreciation, interest and tax. These are real costs of doing business and are drivers of value.
It captures the impact of the company's cost structure.	Cannot be used if EBITDA is negative.
Most companies will generate positive EBITDA, therefore providing a wider universe to select comparables from than if a metric further down the income statement was used.	Leasing can distort the use of the metric – better to rely on EBITDAR in this case.
EBITDA multiples are most useful if the comparable universe has a similar level of capital intensity.	Affected by accounting policy issues such as revenue and cost recognition, leasing, possible proportional consolidation issues.

EV – EBITDAR multiples

What are the positives?	What are the problems?
Ignores the income/expenses in relation to leasing. Provides a level playing field for comparables where lease accounting is inconsistently applied.	
EBITDAR is closer to a cash flow measure as it ignores D&A.	It ignores depreciation, interest and tax. These are real costs of doing business and are drivers of value.
It captures the impact of the company's cost structure.	Cannot be used if EBITDAR is negative.
Most companies will generate positive EBITDAR, therefore providing a wider universe to select comparables from.	
EBITDAR multiples are most useful if the comparable universe has a similar level of capital intensity.	Affected by accounting policy issues such as revenue and cost recognition, possible proportional consolidation issues.

EV – EBIT multiples

What are the positives?	What are the problems?
It captures the impact of the company's cost structure.	D&A policies may create comparability issues.
Useful for capital intensive companies as the metric captures the D&A charges.	Leasing can distort the use of the metric – better to rely on EBITDAR.
Useful for comparable universes with comparable D&A policies.	Affected by accounting policy issues such as revenue and cost recognition, leasing, possible proportional consolidation issues.

EV – NOPLAT multiples

What are the positives?	What are the problems?
NOPLAT (net operating profit after adjusted taxes) is a pre-interest but post-tax operating metric.	NOPLAT introduces additional metric subjectivity into the calculation.
NOPLAT multiples are often thought of as de-geared price earnings multiples.	

Trading Comparables

EV – operating FCF multiples

What are the positives?	What are the problems?
Operating FCF is EBITDA minus maintenance capex and net working capital changes. The metric uses cash flow rather than a proxy to on such as EBITDA. Less susceptible to accounting manipulation than any of the earnings metrics.	Cannot be used if cash flow is negative. Narrows the comparable universe population.

PE multiples

What are the positives?	What are the problems?
Widely understood and established with clients. Makes the multiple an easy communicator of ideas.	Equity level earnings are very prone to accounting distortion.
The calculation is quick and easy.	Cannot be used if earnings are negative. Requires high earnings visibility.
Less subjective than EV multiples.	Capital structure dependant. The above make comparability increasingly difficult.

Price to book multiples

What are the positives?	What are the problems?
A useful measure where tangible assets are the value drivers of the entity.	Unreliable if assets are recognized at book value.
Used mainly in financial institution groups. Financial institutions have large asset bases that are used to produce fractional margins on large numbers. Significant elements of their asset bases are valued at fair value on the balance sheet thus making the multiple more reliable.	Book values may not be comparable due to accounting policy issues. It is not a reliable measure unless the majority of the balance sheet is valued at fair value.

Sector Specific Multiples

Earlier in this chapter we talked about the construction of a multiple. The numerator is the value (whether it is equity or EV) and the denominator is a value driver. Often the value driver is an earnings metric. EBIT, EBITDA and EBITDAR are well used earnings based value drivers. However a number of industries will have their own specific multiples. The numerator often remains EV or equity value. It is the value driver that tends to be the sector specific element.

For instance:

Sector	Sector multiples
Financial institutions	P / Book value P/ Embedded value P/ Assets under management
Metals and mining	P/ NPV EV / Reserves EV per production tonne
Media	EV / Subscribers EV / Total screens EV / Broadcast cash flows EV / (EBITDA-Capex)
Real estate	P/ Net asset value EV / Funds from operations EV / Funds available for distribution

Full Cadbury comp

Cadbury plc

Currency	£	
Current share price	5.58	
52 week high	5.62	
52 week low	4.78	
NOSH (m)	1,361	
		£m
Current share price	5.58	
NOSH (m)	1,361	
ITM convertible debt	--	
Net diluted NOSH (m) - treasury method	12.38	
Diluted market capitalization		7,663
Borrowings < 1 year	1,189	
Borrowings > 1 year	1,194	
OTM convertible debt	--	
OTM convertible preferred stock	--	
Cash and cash equivalents	(251)	
Short-term investments	(247)	
Net debt		1,885
Pension deficit - funded schemes		144
Pension deficit - unfunded schemes		15
Non-controlling interest (book value)		12
Investment in associates (book value)		(28)
EV		**9,691**
PV of the operating lease commitments		270
EV (lease adjusted)		**9,961**

	Historic	Current	Forecast	CAGR
Revenue	5,384	6,048	6,365	8.73%
EBIT	638	817	911	19.49%
EBITDA	878	1,017	1,117	12.79%
EBITDAR	928	1,067	1,167	12.14%
EBIT margins	11.85%	13.51%	14.31%	
EBITDA margins	16.31%	16.82%	17.55%	
EBITDAR margins	17.24%	17.64%	18.33%	
Revenue growth rates		12.33%	5.24%	
EBIT growth rates		28.06%	11.51%	
EBITDA growth rates		15.83%	9.83%	
EBITDAR growth rates		14.98%	9.37%	
EV multiples:				
EV / Revenue	1.80x	1.60x	1.52x	
EV / EBIT	15.2x	11.9x	10.6x	
EV / EBITDA	11.0x	9.5x	8.7x	
EV / EBITDAR	10.7x	9.3x	8.5x	

Multiples Presentation

Revenue multiples are typically presented to 2 decimal places in a comps sheet. The remaining multiples are usually presented to 1 decimal place. This is because revenue multiples can be quite small and so warrant the additional disclosure of 2 decimal places.

The EV / EBITDAR multiples must be calculated using an operating lease adjusted EV in order to be consistent with the EBITDAR denominator.

CAGR Calculations

CAGR is a compound annual growth rate. It is an average compounded growth rate over a number of periods. The equation is:

$$CAGR = \left(\frac{\text{Ending value}}{\text{Beginning value}}\right)^{\left(\frac{1}{\text{\# of years}}\right)} - 1$$

It is a very common comp output as it can help to justify why a particular company within the comp has a higher or lower multiple.

Step 4: Target valuation

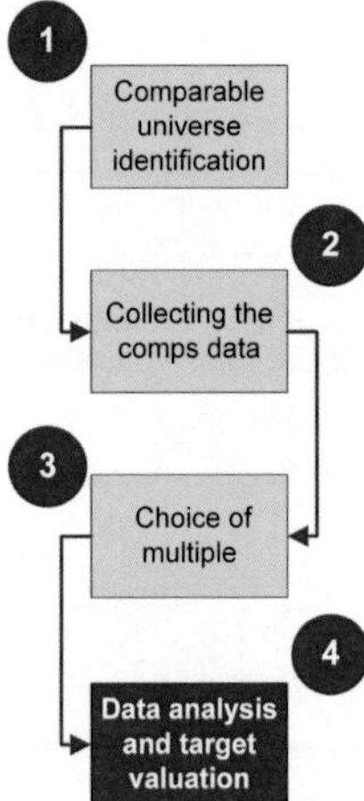

Step 4 requires the identification of a suitable comparable multiple in order to value the target. All of the comparable information has been collected and stored in the comps sheets (see the full Cadbury comp detail above – there will be a comps sheet like this for each comparable company). The data is now collected and disclosed in a comps output sheet as illustrated below.

The form and content of the comps output sheet will vary from team to team, but should include as a minimum:

- EV and equity values for all comparables (in both local and base currencies)
- All key multiples (historic and forecast)
- Key operating and credit metrics
- Dispersion measures for key numbers (mean, median, highs and lows)

Below is an example of an abbreviated comps output sheet for food producers.

Food producers
in USDm unless stated otherw

Company name	Country	EV local currency	EV base currency	EBITDA growth - next 2 yrs	EBITDA margin (Current)	EV/ EBITDA (Current)	EV/ EBITDA (Forecast)
Cadbury plc	UK	9,691	15,797	8.73%	16.82%	9.5x	8.7x
Sara Lee Corp	US	9,670	9,670	16.40%	13.30%	15.4x	13.4x
HJ Heinz	US	14,640	14,640	5.20%	17.40%	13.2x	12.7x
Campbell Soup	US	11,510	11,510	5.90%	19.10%	11.9x	10.2x
Maximum		14,640	15,797	16.4%	19.1%	15.4x	13.4x
Minimum		9,670	9,670	5.2%	13.3%	9.5x	8.7x
Mean		11,378	12,904	9.1%	16.7%	12.5x	11.2x
Median		10,601	13,075	7.3%	17.1%	12.6x	11.5x
Hershey Inc	US	12,227	12,227	3.07%	19.82%	11.3x	11.0x

Analyzing the Dispersion Metrics

Every comp output sheet will include dispersion metrics such as:

- Mean
- Median
- High
- Low

These metrics are often neglected when analyzing the comps output sheet.

The metrics provide a snapshot overview of the distribution of the comps work across the comparable universe. The analysis of the mean and median statistics provides information about the skewness of the comps universe and how the target company may fit into the overall universe.

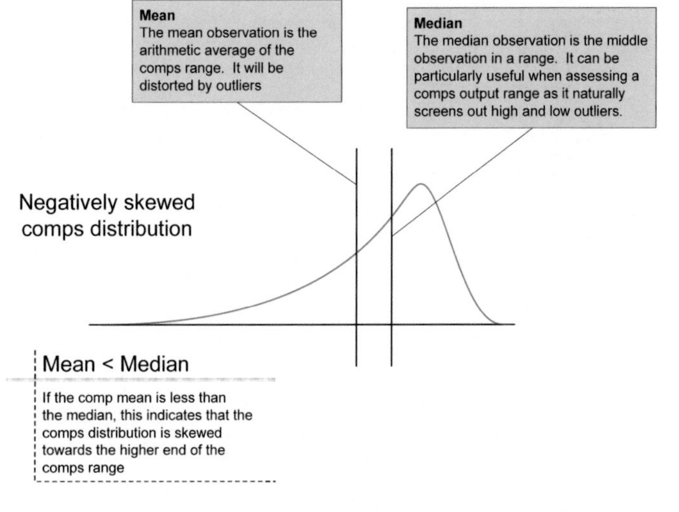

Comps Output Sheet – Local and Base Currencies

Different reporting currencies can create a few issues when presenting the comps output sheet.

Differences in currency presentation are irrelevant for multiples, margins and growth rates, as they are relative measures. However, currencies are an issue when presenting absolute monetary numbers such as:

- EV
- Market capitalization

A comps output sheet usually discloses this information in the local currency. The local currency information is then translated into a base currency. The base currency is usually the currency of the target company, in an M&A situation.

Snapshot metrics such as EV and market capitalization must be translated as at the valuation date spot rate. Income statement data, if presented, should be translated at the average exchange rate for the period. Balance sheet data, if presented, should be translated using the balance sheet date closing rate.

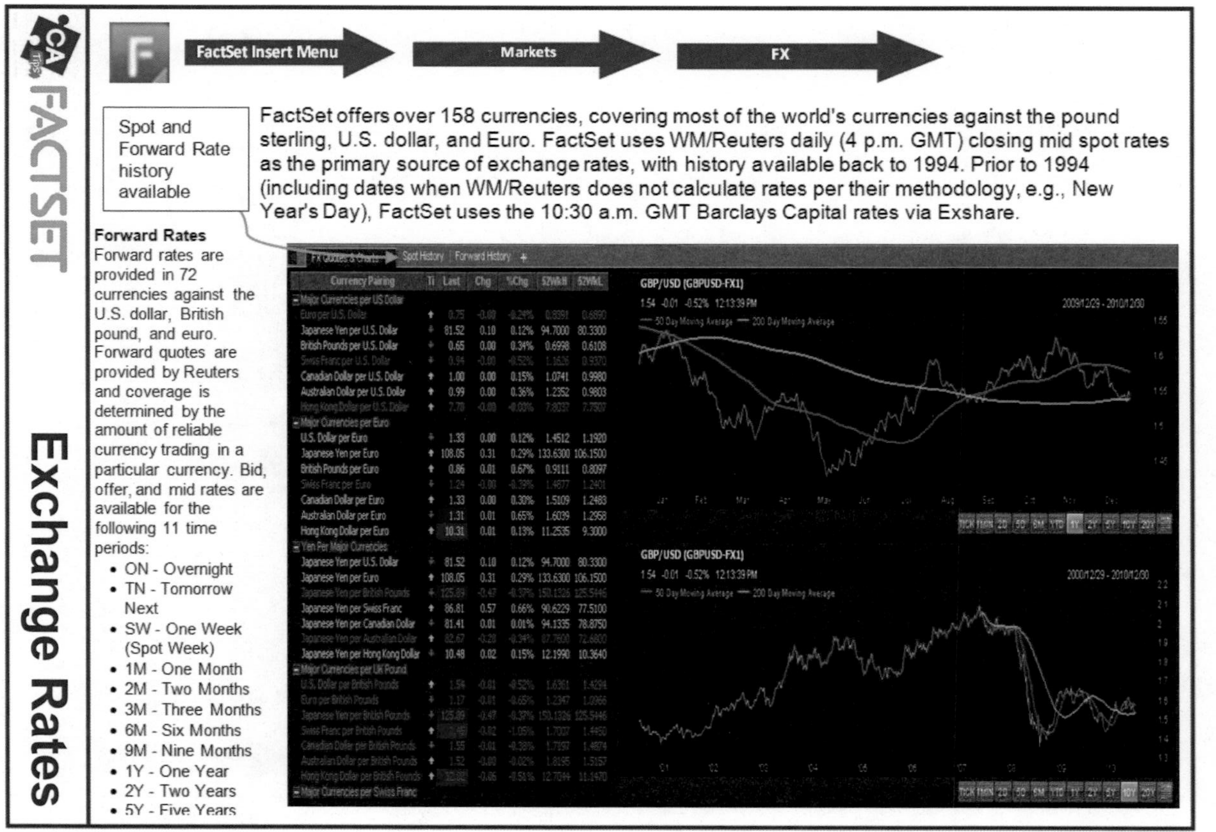

Source: FactSet

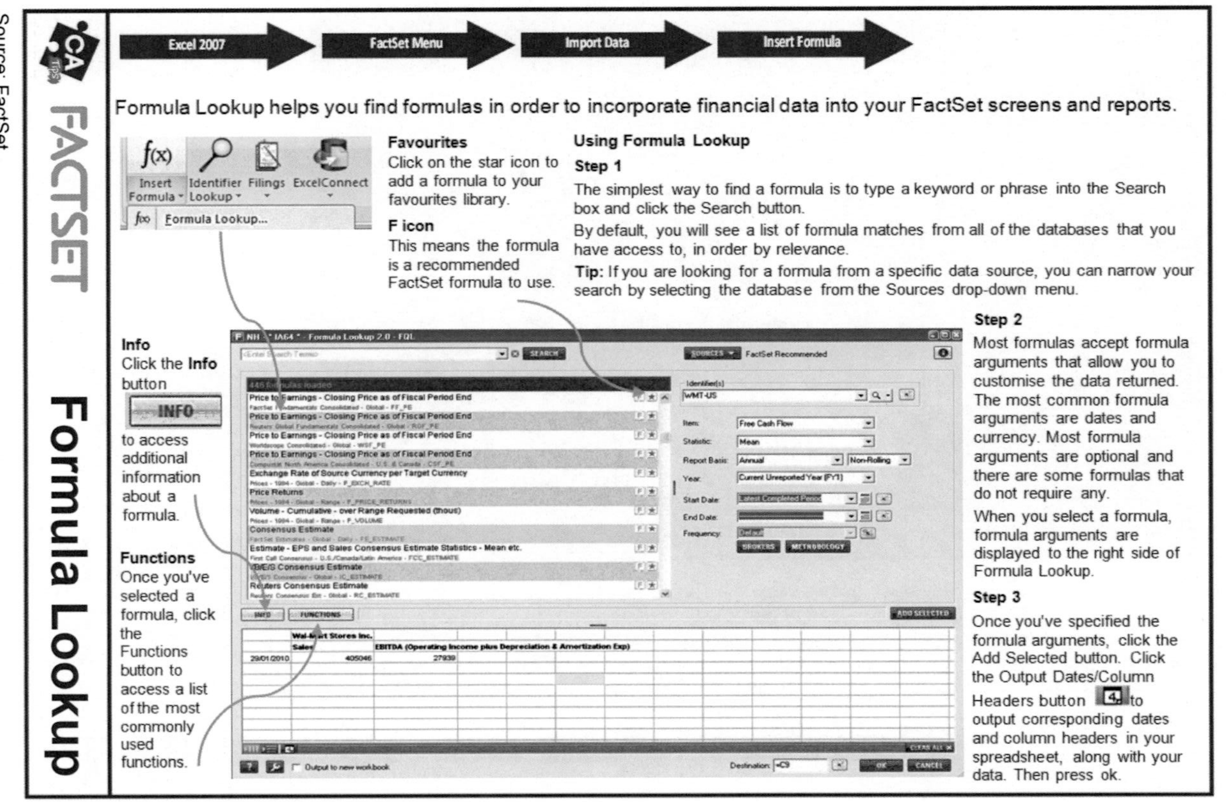

Source: FactSet

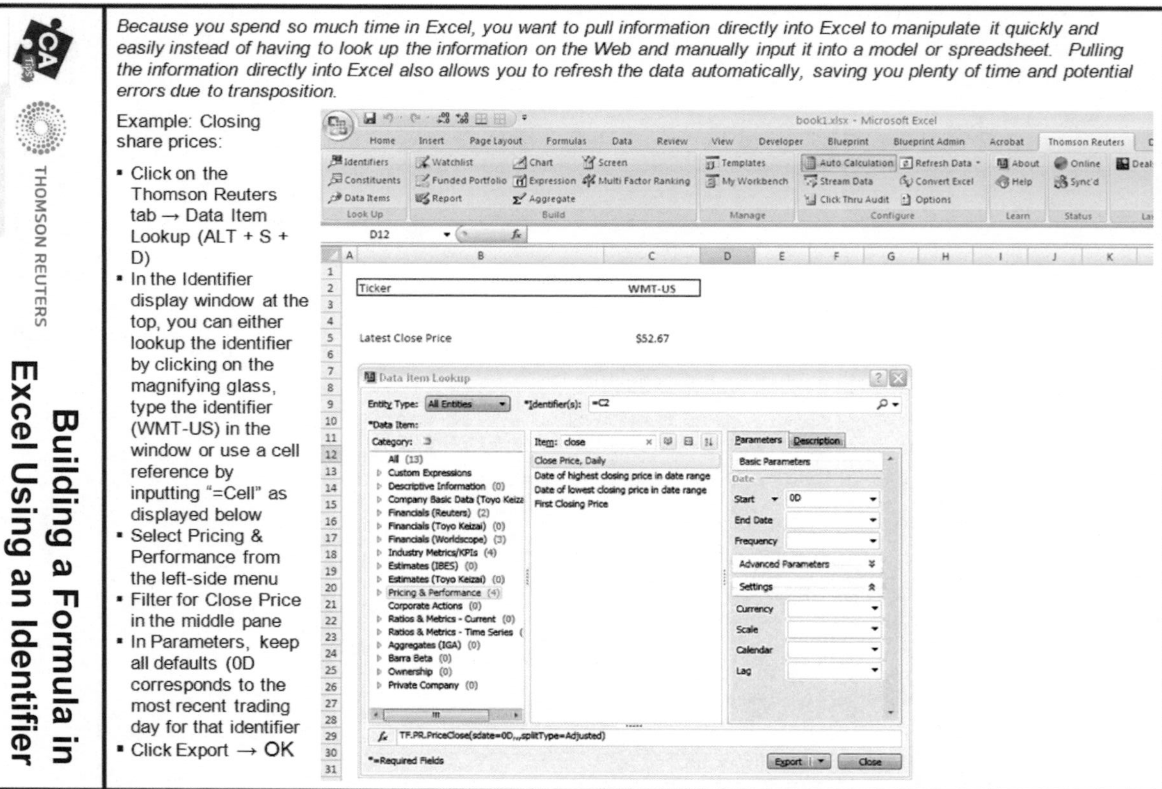

THOMSON REUTERS

Building a Formula in Excel Using an Identifier

Because you spend so much time in Excel, you want to pull information directly into Excel to manipulate it quickly and easily instead of having to look up the information on the Web and manually input it into a model or spreadsheet. Pulling the information directly into Excel also allows you to refresh the data automatically, saving you plenty of time and potential errors due to transposition.

Example: Closing share prices:

- Click on the Thomson Reuters tab → Data Item Lookup (ALT + S + D)
- In the Identifier display window at the top, you can either lookup the identifier by clicking on the magnifying glass, type the identifier (WMT-US) in the window or use a cell reference by inputting "=Cell" as displayed below
- Select Pricing & Performance from the left-side menu
- Filter for Close Price in the middle pane
- In Parameters, keep all defaults (0D corresponds to the most recent trading day for that identifier
- Click Export → OK

Source: Thomson Reuters

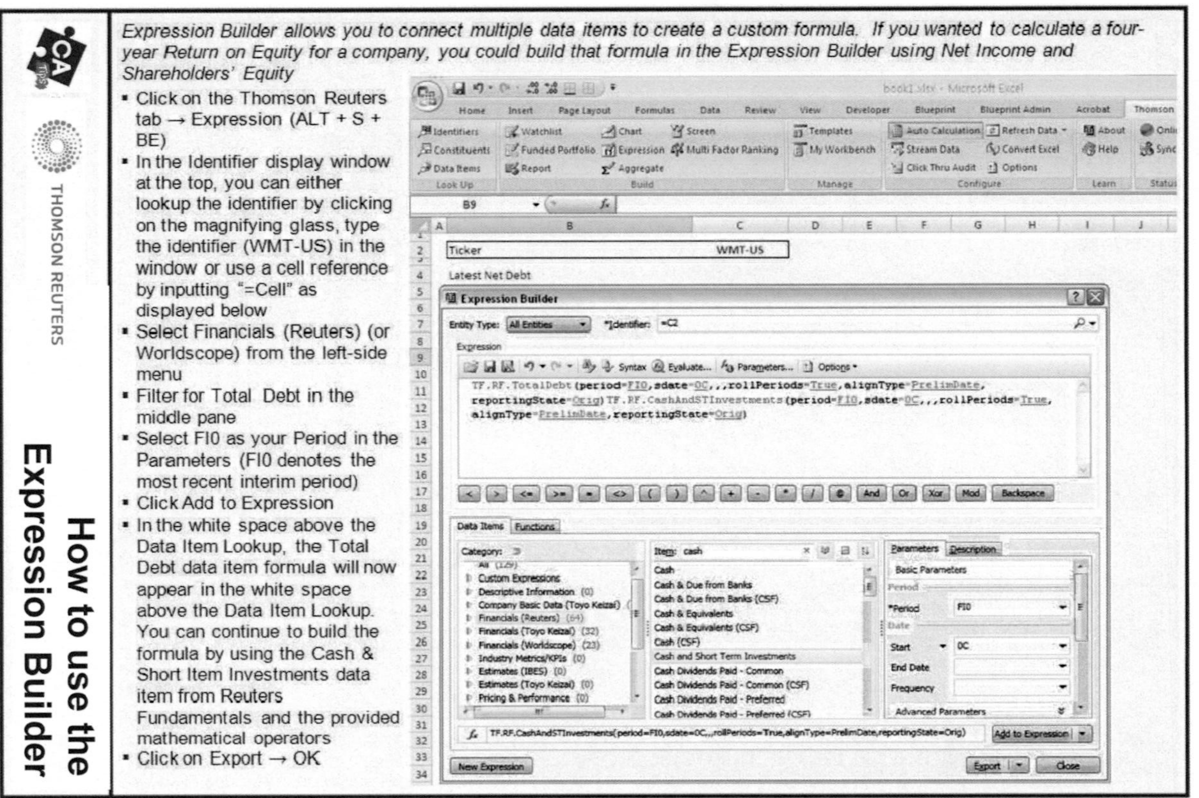

Source: Thomson Reuters

=FDS coding

FACTSET

Information requirement	=FDS coding syntax
Company ticker	=FDS(A1,"FG_COMPANY_NAME")
Closing share price	=FDS(A1,"P_PRICE(0)")
52 week high	=FDS(A1,"P_PRICE_HIGH_52W(0)")
52 week low	=FDS(A1,"P_PRICE_LOW_52W(0)")
NOSH	=FDS(A1,"FF_COM_SHS_OUT(ANN,0,,,RF)")
Exchange rates	=FDS(A1,"P_EXCH_RATE(EUR,USD,0)")

Why do Multiples Trade at a Discount/Premium?

The comps output sheet will illustrate that multiples will trade at a discount or premium to the mean of the universe. Analysts must understand why these multiples trade away from the central tendency of the comparable universe.

Possible explanations could be:

- Different margins
- Different growth rates
- Different earnings quality (cash generation ability and working capital management)

- Relative competitive positions
- Market risks
- Differences in country market sentiments
- Differences in corporate governance
- Management credibility

- Relative 52 week high and low position
- Bid speculation
- Market mis-pricing
- Earnings volatility
- Index rally
- Index tracking demand
- Degree of free float
- Ownership restrictions for foreign investors
- Accounting differences (GAAP)

- Over leverage
- Potential contingent liabilities
- Recent positive/negative news flow

Comp Sheet Review (Sanity and Presentation Checks)

The comps output sheet is a key pitch book presentation sheet and will come under close scrutiny from your associates, VPs and above. Clients will also focus on this part of the pitch book. Therefore it must be thoroughly reviewed prior to presentation.

Key review points:

- Stand back and review the big picture numbers – do they make sense?
- Understand the outliers in the comps sheet – why are they trading at a premium or discount?
- What is the forward multiple behaviour?
- What are the key multiples that drive the comparable multiple choice?
- Presentation – font size and style consistency/decimal places/alignment
- Check foreign exchange translation
- Benchmark numbers against implied DCF multiples
- Use most recent financial numbers
- Make sure all classes of shares captured
- Review the post-balance sheet period for announcements
- Review the post-balance sheet period for stock splits, consolidations, equity issues, convertible security conversions, acquisition and divestures
- Footnote and comment on all adjustments or queries
- Don't submit numbers you don't fully understand
- Check and check again

Assessing the target

The comps output sheet is used to review the comparable universe and to assess how the target company fits into the universe. The fit of the target company will then be used to select a suitable comparable metric in order to work out an implied valuation of the target based on the comparable universe.

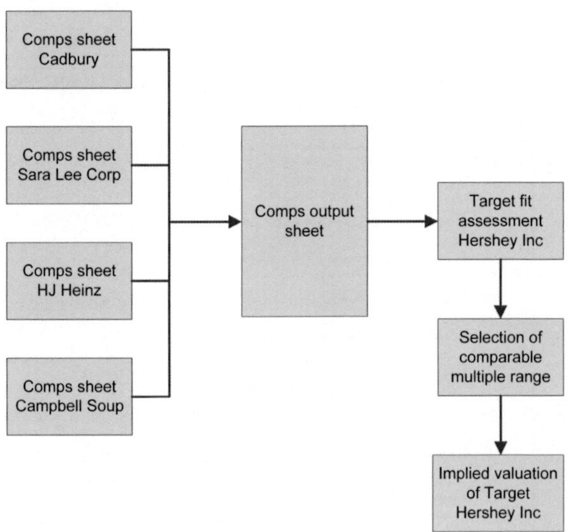

The fit assessment for Hershey's is completed by reviewing the comparable metrics and operating statistics included in the comps output sheet. A comparable multiple will be chosen on the basis of this assessment.

Food producers

in USDm unless stated otherw

Company name	Country	EV local currency	EV base currency	EBITDA growth - next 2 yrs	EBITDA margin (Current)	EV/ EBITDA (Current)	EV/ EBITDA (Forecast)
Cadbury plc	UK	9,691	15,797	8.73%	16.82%	9.5x	8.7x
Sara Lee Corp	US	9,670	9,670	16.40%	13.30%	15.4x	13.4x
HJ Heinz	US	14,640	14,640	5.20%	17.40%	13.2x	12.7x
Campbell Soup	US	11,510	11,510	5.90%	19.10%	11.9x	10.2x
Maximum		14,640	15,797	16.4%	19.1%	15.4x	13.4x
Minimum		9,670	9,670	5.2%	13.3%	9.5x	8.7x
Mean		11,378	12,904	9.1%	16.7%	12.5x	11.2x
Median		10,601	13,075	7.3%	17.1%	12.6x	11.5x
Hershey Inc	US	12,227	12,227	3.07%	19.82%	11.3x	11.0x

Using the comps sheet above the following observations could be made:

- Hershey's 3.07% EBITDA growth rate and margin of 19.82% is most closely aligned with Campbell Soup
- Hershey has a similar sized EV to Campbell Soup
- Both companies use US GAAP and so the accounting should be similar
- Hershey does not have the EBITDA growth rates of the comparables that are trading on the higher multiples. Hershey has the lowest growth rates in relation to the comparable universe

This could suggest that Campbell Soup's current EV/EBITDA of 11.9x may be a useful multiple as a benchmark. Hershey does not have as strong EBITDA growth rates as Campbell Soup (5.90%). Growth rates are a strong driver of a multiple, therefore it might be sensible to discount the comparable multiple below the 11.9x Campbell Soup multiple to take the lower Hershey growth rate into account.

The comparable multiple decision is judgmental and can have a significant impact on the implied EV and equity values.

Rather than rely on a single pinpoint EV/EBITDA multiple to value Hershey, a range of multiples should be chosen and a valuation range produced. This can be very effectively presented using Excel's data table sensitivity (see CA Tip – Valuation ranges and sensitivity capture below.)

The illustration below shows how Hershey is valued using a comparable EV/EBITDA multiple. An EV/EBITDA comparable valuation will produce an implied EV for Hershey. This implied EV will have to be disaggregated to an implied equity value in order to produce a per share result.

Equity value breakdown

EV multiples will produce an implied EV valuation of the target. Whilst this is useful information to have from an M&A perspective, in the sense it provides an idea of the financing requirement (a 100% acquirer will have to buy out the whole of the equity and will possibly have or wish to refinance the existing debt claims), an equity value per share will be required for the equity investors.

Therefore the implied EV will have to be disaggregated to an equity value.

The breakdown essentially strips out all non-equity claims from the implied EV number. Thus the standard disaggregating components are:

- Net debt
- Other claims (pension deficits and operating lease commitments if relevant)
- Non-controlling interests
- Associates and joint ventures

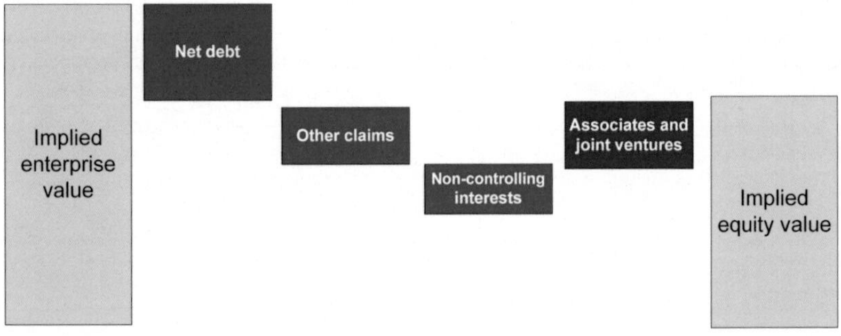

Pension deficits and operating lease commitments will only be disaggregated if they are included in the comparable EV calculations.

Fair values should be used when the items are material to the equity value disaggregation.

The market value of JVs (unless proportionally consolidated) and associates will need to be added into the implied equity value as they were stripped out of the comparable multiple numbers previously. If the JVs and associates are immaterial to the overall implied equity value, book values may well suffice.

The implied equity value will then be divided by the NOSH.

A diluted NOSH calculation can be performed applying the treasury method to the outstanding equity options in the target company.

Hershey Inc

Currency		$
Current share price		41.57
52 week high		42.25
52 week low		30.27
Exchange rate USD:GBP		1.53
Comparable EV/EBITDA 2010 (say)		10.0x
EBITDA 2010		1,082
Implied EV		**10,820**
Borrowings < 1 year	502	
Borrowings > 1 year	1,506	
Cash and cash equivalents	(37)	
Net debt		(1,970)
Pension deficit - funded schemes		(41)
Non-controlling interest (book value)		(32)
Investment in associates (book value)		--
Implied equity value		8,777
Class A common stock	299	
Class B common stock	61	
Treasury stock	(133)	
Option dilution	14	
NOSH		241
Implied equity value per share		36.39

Earnings metrics:	**Historic**	**Current**	**Forecast**	**CAGR**
Revenue	5,299	5,459	5,596	2.76%
EBIT	861	900	929	3.87%
EBITDA	1,044	1,082	1,109	3.07%
EBITDAR	1,094	1,132	1,159	2.93%
EBIT margins	16.25%	16.49%	16.60%	
EBITDA margins	19.70%	19.82%	19.82%	
EBITDAR margins	20.65%	20.74%	20.71%	
Revenue growth rates		3.02%	2.51%	
EBIT growth rates		4.53%	3.22%	
EBITDA growth rates		3.64%	2.50%	
EBITDAR growth rates		3.47%	2.39%	
Source: RBS research				
Implied EV multiples:				
EV / Revenue	2.04x	1.98x	1.93x	
EV / EBIT	12.6x	12.0x	11.6x	
EV / EBITDA	10.4x	10.0x	9.8x	
EV / EBITDAR	9.9x	9.6x	9.3x	

Valuation Ranges and Sensitivity Capture

Valuation number crunching is technical. The implied valuation is ultimately judgemental. There are a number of key variables that are applied to produce an implied comparable valuation. Choices with regard to the:

- Comparable valuation multiple
- Particular broker and its forecasts

...are two key sensitive and judgemental variables used in a comparable valuation.

It is key therefore that Analysts produce a valuation range in order to capture the impact of these sensitivities.

Excel's data table functionality (featured in *Complete Investment Banker: Part II*) provides a simple and very effective sensitivity tool. A well-built comps sheet can be set up to iterate a number of possible valuation outcomes in relation to key variables.

The table below is an extract from the Hershey comparable valuation model used throughout this chapter. A data table has been setup to value Hershey using different comparable EV/EBITDA multiples (9.8x to 10.2x) and EBITDA forecasts ($977m to $1,193m).

Implied equity value per share sensivity

EBITDA 2010	EV/EBITDA				
	9.8x	9.9x	10.0x	10.1x	10.2x
977	31.20	31.61	32.01	32.42	32.82
1,028	33.29	33.72	34.14	34.57	35.00
1,082	35.49	35.94	36.39	36.83	37.28
1,136	37.69	38.16	38.63	39.10	39.57
1,193	39.99	40.49	40.98	41.48	41.97

Even with a relatively tight range of variables, it is clear that the different comparable multiples and forecasts have a marked impact on the equity value per share output.

A valuation range of $33.72 to $39.10 per share might now be justifiably supported with reference to the variable sensitivity. The width of the valuation range must be considered carefully and must be in line with how the deal is being communicated to the client.

- A range that is too tight may infer science and precision that cannot be guaranteed
- A wide range may suggest a lack of conviction
- Buy-side ranges may sink to the lower end of a valuation range
- Sell-side ranges may float to the upper end of a valuation range
- The range may be further tailored in relation to other valuation techniques once a valuation summary ('football pitch') is put together
- The $33.72 to $39.10 per share range appears to be an acceptable range

Hershey is trading in this example at $41.57 with a 52-week high of $42.25. Given the trading comps is suggesting a valuation range of $33.27-$39.10, it would seem that the current trading price is overvaluing the company in relation to its peers.

What is the Analyst's Role?

An early responsibility for an Analyst will be the maintenance of a comps model.

This will involve:

- Keeping the model up-to-date (share price, NOSH and exchange rate data)
- Updating the model for new earnings announcements
- Knowing the background stories for the comparable companies
- Watching news flow on the comparable companies and analyzing the impact on the comps
- Updating the model for new research numbers
- Adding new comparable companies
- Comps output pitch book preparation
- Profile preparation using key comps data

Tick Sheet – Trading Comps

Trading comps – a four-step structured approach

- Comparable universe identification
- Collecting the comps data
- Choice of multiple
- Data analysis and target valuation

Equity and EV level multiples

- EV is the cost of buying the right to the whole of an enterprise's core cash flow.
- It is the full takeout value of the firm in an M&A situation.

There are generally three key drivers of a multiple:

1. The quality of earnings or cash conversion
2. The risk profile of the entity
3. Growth rates

Key comp skills:

- Getting an up-to-date NOSH
- FactSet = FDS coding
- Dealing with dual stock classes
- Documentation of your work
- Deriving fully diluted equity values using the treasury or buy-out method
- Net debt calculations
- Pension deficit and operating lease commitment adjustments
- NCI adjustments
- JV and asociates consistency of adjustments
- Using and reconciling broker research
- Knowing when to use consensus estimates
- Annualization
- Historic / LTM / Current / Forecast – establishing the numbers
- Choice of multiple – know the relative strengths and weaknesses of each multiple
- Comps output sheet preparation, analysis and review
- Assessing the target and fit with the comparables
- Equity value breakdown

Introduction

Transaction comps is a relative valuation technique that uses public transaction information to infer a valuation on a target company. The valuation works on the premise that valuations of similar or comparable transactions tend to be on a relatively consistent basis on the public markets.

The broad approach is similar to trading comps, however the valuation is based on looking at what happened in previous transactions. In practice, it is very difficult to find previous transactions that are similar to the transaction being considered.

This valuation method has one key advantage over trading comps and DCF valuations – it captures the control premium in the valuation.

The control premium is the additional amount paid in order to gain control of an entity. In other words, it is the extra amount that has to be paid to encourage the previous owners to sell their equity stakes. This additional amount would also reflect the willingness of the acquirer to get the benefit of synergies and strategic fit of the target.

The control premium is sometimes known as a 'market clearing price'. The size of the control premium is sector and deal specific. A rough benchmark control premium would be between 20-30% on the pre-announcement price.

Other names for transactions comps are:

- Pre-deals
- Precedent comps
- Co-Co transactions

Transaction comps add an element of reality to the valuation process as they use transactions that actually happened. The information is normally highly transparent and in the public domain – although in reality it can be a difficult task tracking down sufficiently reliable information.

A transaction comps database can also be used to demonstrate M&A trends and activity within a sector such as:

- Consolidation trends
- Foreign investment
- Private equity investment
- Divestiture strategies
- Investor appetite
- Frequency of types of transaction

Transaction comps are especially useful when analyzing change of control transactions.

Premium paid analysis, a by-product of transaction comps, is discussed later.

However, there are some flaws with transaction comps that Analysts should be aware of:

- The method assumes that a fair price was paid for a transaction.
- Transaction comps only works well when the comparable universe is relatively recent.
- The valuation can be significantly affected by the business cycle.

- The quality of the analysis is dependent on the quality of the comparable data available. The process is inherently flawed as no two transactions are truly comparable.
- The population of available and relevant transactions is usually relatively small.
- Transaction comps is often heavily reliant on accounting information. As the initial chapters of this manual highlighted, accounting numbers are prone to manipulation and are often inconsistently applied both within the local peer group and internationally.
- Loss making companies often don't lend themselves well to transaction comps valuation due to the common reliance on the earnings metrics.

Note: Some of the technical number crunching associated with transaction comps is very similar to trading comps. Where this is the case, there will be a cross reference to the material in the Trading *Comps* chapter rather than duplicating material.

Transaction comps – a four-step structured approach

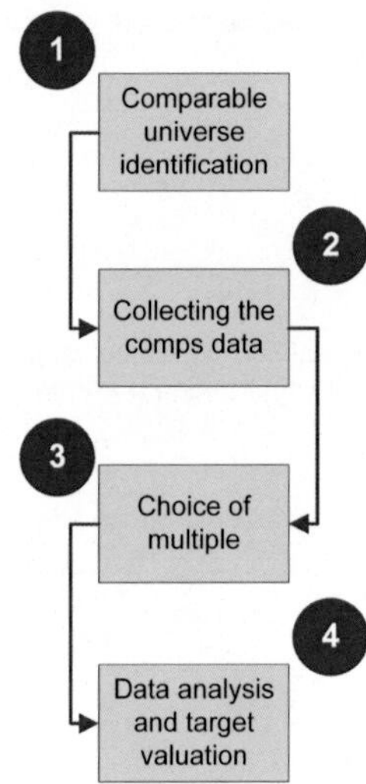

Comps process overview

The transaction comps process is structured in much the same way as trading comps. The process will be illustrated with the Kraft/Cadbury transaction.

The key steps are:

- A comparable transactions universe will be identified
- Deal information will be collected
- Transaction multiples will be calculated for this information
- These multiples will then be applied to a target company

We will use Hershey Inc as our target company again.

The same types of key questions as for trading comps will need to be answered:

- Which comparable transactions should be relied on for the target valuation?
- What type of multiple is most appropriate to value the target?
- How does the target company fit into the comparable transaction universe?
- Should the target company be valued at a premium or discount to the comparable transaction universe?
- What multiple range should be applied to the target?

Step 1: Comparable transaction universe identification

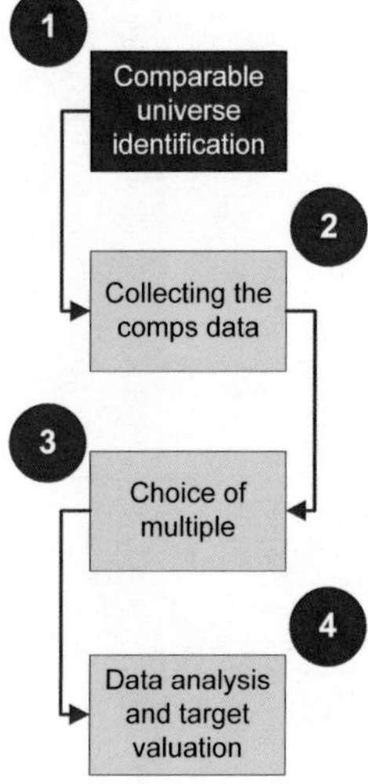

Transaction Comps

Transactions comps rely on the quality of the transactions universe in the same way as trading comps. A poorly constructed transactions universe will result in a poor valuation. The construction of the transactions comparable universe however follows a different approach to trading comps.

The transactions universe must be populated with similar transactions. Even though the population of transactions is large (SDC Platinum – one of the main M&A databases has 250,000+ transactions), transactions can vary so much in nature that it needs to be appreciated that any comparable database created will not be perfect.

Comparable universe criteria will consider:

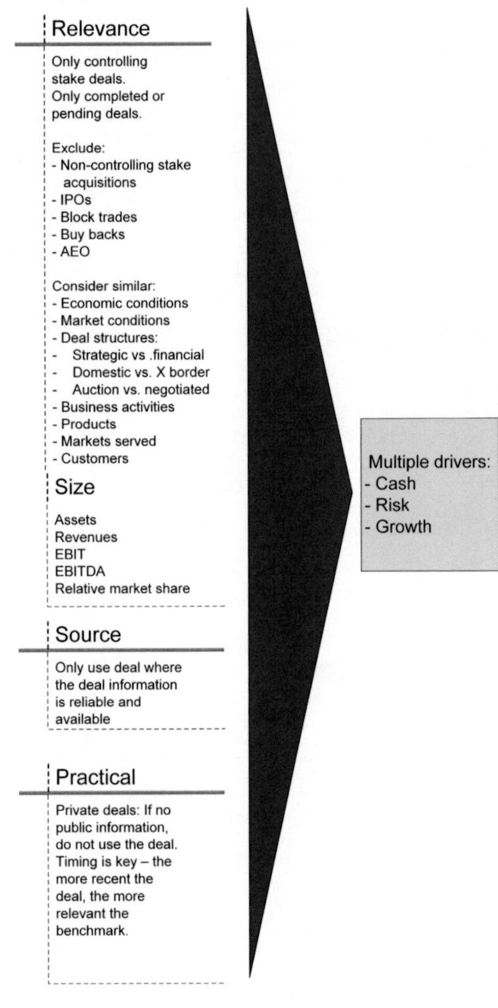

Finding Comparable Transaction Source Data

Analysts have to follow a pragmatic approach to sourcing comparable transaction data. There are a number of different sources, none of which tends to provide the level of information required to put a comprehensive transaction comp valuation together. Whilst the data service providers will produce lists of potentially comparable transactions, Analysts cannot rely on the numbers disclosed by the providers. Analysts must always seek source documentary evidence of the numbers in relation to the deal.

Potential M&A database sources for transaction listings:

- Thomson Financial
- SDC Platinum
- M&A monitor
- MergerMarket.com
- FACTSET MergerStat
- Bloomberg <Equity> MA - Advanced search
- Factiva news runs
- Press releases
- Previous pitch books
- Industry teams
- Client discussions
- Existing transaction comps databases
- Company filings – 8K filings (significant events)
- Company filings – 10K filings (significant transaction during the year)
- Equity research reports
- Prospectuses

Landmark Transaction Comps

Certain landmark M&A transactions need to be included in the universe. Failure to do so will prompt obvious but embarrassing questions – also landmark transactions that have been advised on by your institution are often included to demonstrate experience within the sector, if the comp is being used to pitch to clients. The transaction still needs to be comparable.

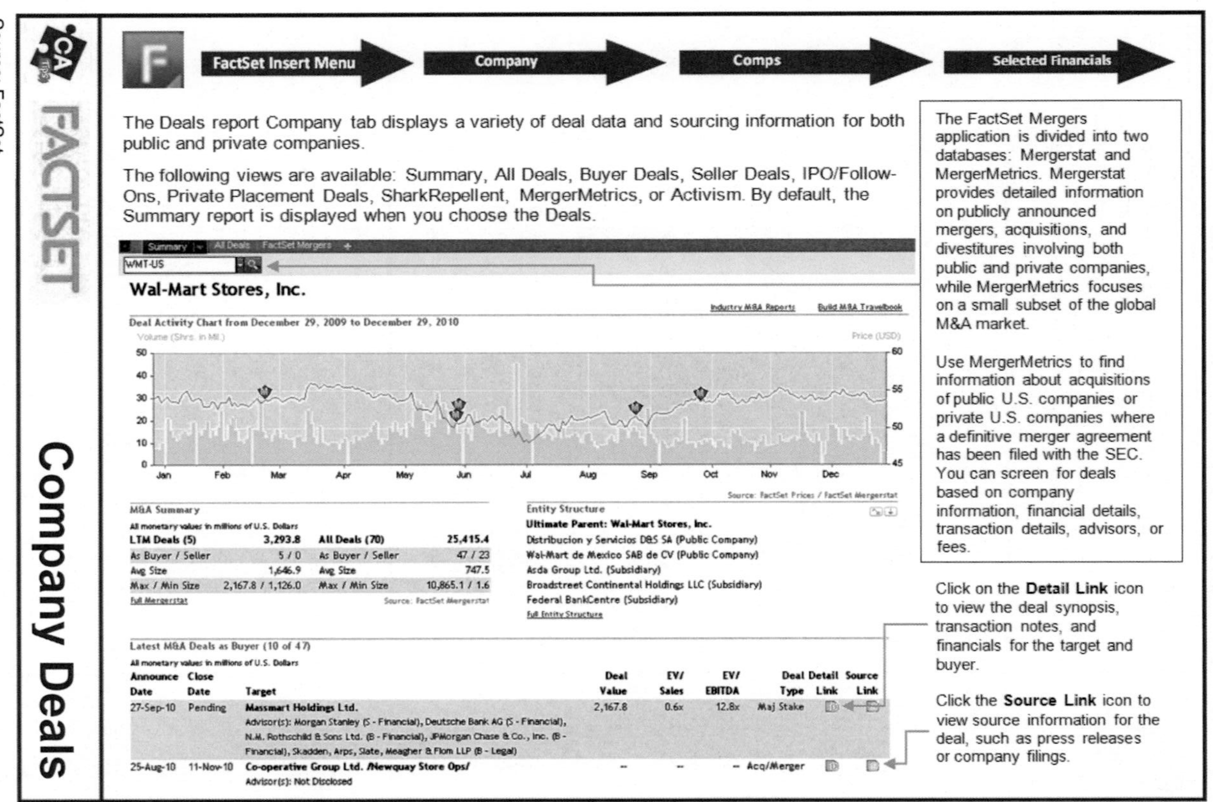

Source: FactSet

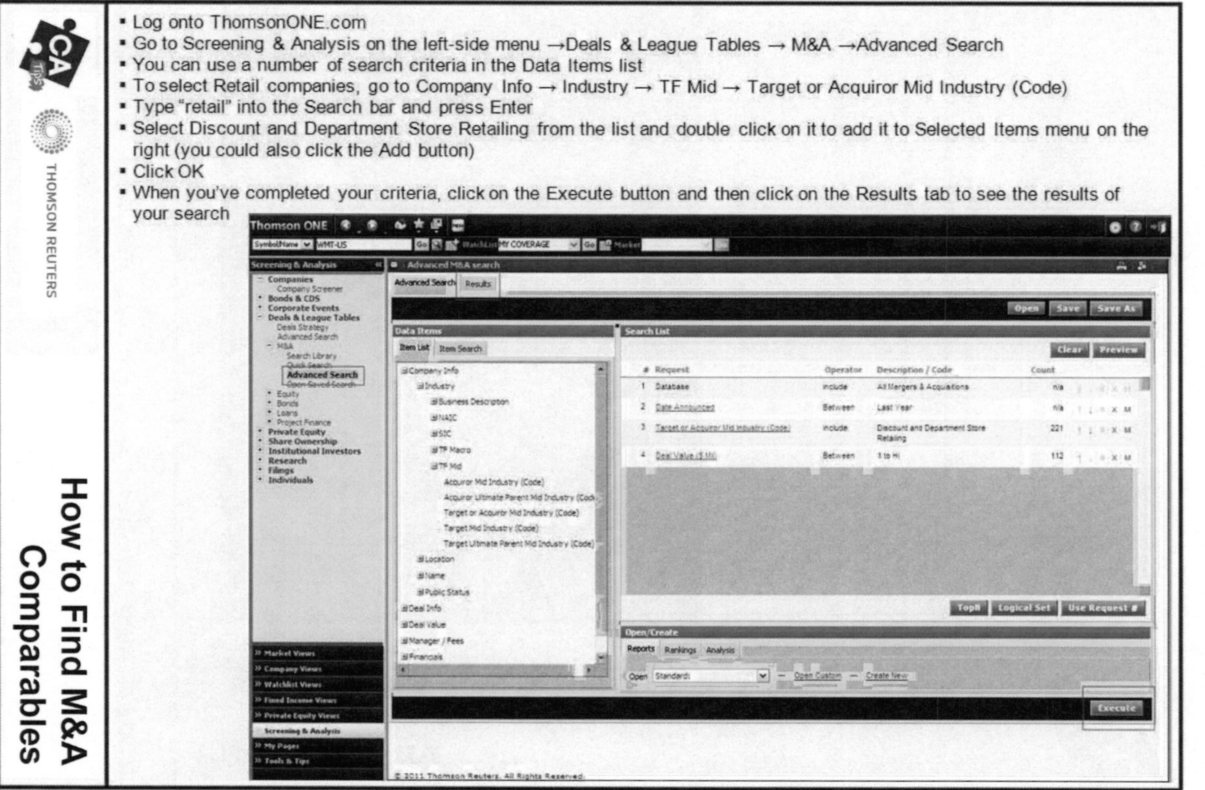

Source: Thomson Reuters

Using the Bloomberg MA Search Functionality

Bloomberg includes a strong M&A search function. **Bloomberg**

Key stroke:

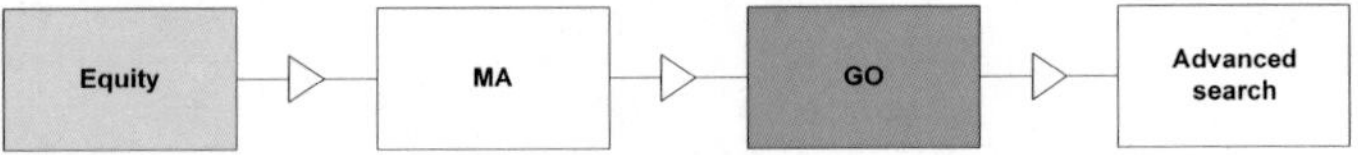

The search set up is not dissimilar to SDC Platinum (See following CA Tip). The Bloomberg screenshot below illustrates the various search criteria available to Analysts. The key when using these databases is to use these criteria precisely. A failure to do this will result in a M&A deal search that produces a list that runs into hundreds of transactions.

Narrow your search definitions (this applies to all M&A databases) to a:

- Narrow range of recent dates
- Pick narrow industry codes
- Narrow the deal size to be in line with the target deal

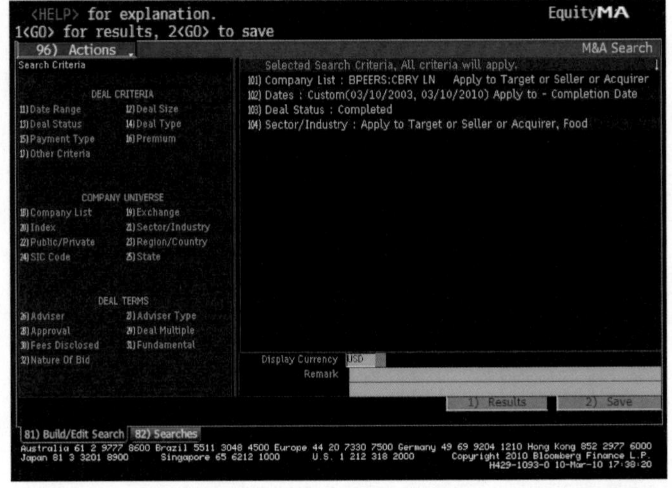

Source: Bloomberg

Using the SDC Platinum Database

SDC platinum is an M&A database used by a number of investment banks. It holds a database of 116,100+ US and 147,000+ international transactions. The database has historic transaction data from 1979 to present (US transactions) and 1985 to present (internationally). The information is sourced from over 200 news sources, SEC filings and their international counterparts, trade publications, wires and proprietary surveys of investment banks, law firms and other advisors.

SDC M&A search:

- Open up SDC and log in and click on the Mergers and Acquisitions tab.
- Select US Targets and click on OK.
- Type in date range 1/1/2006 to 06/31/2010.

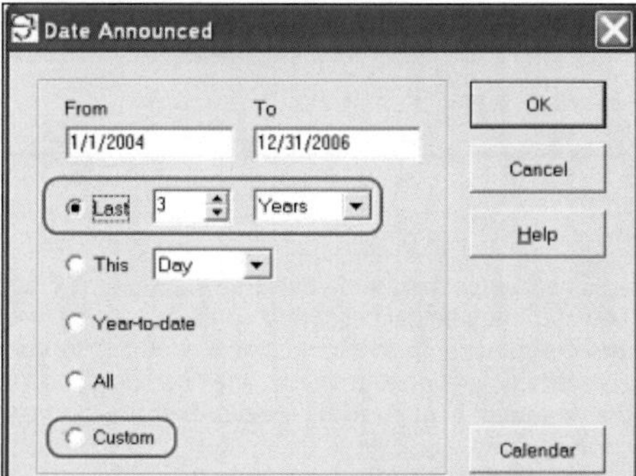

Search fields are categorized into tabs:

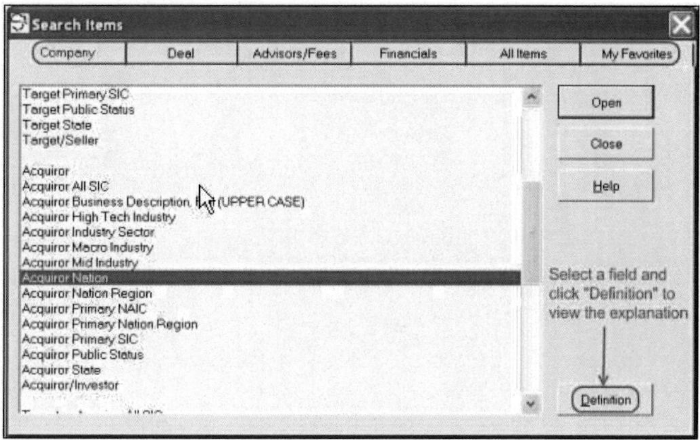

Using SDC (cont.)

Three types of report are available on SDC Platinum:

- New Custom
- SDC Standard
- Tear Sheet

A new custom report allows Analysts to create their own report format and content. A tear sheet is a ready-made deal summary.

Search results can be exported as a txt file or as an Excel file. After creating your report, click Save on the Report Output for Request screen.

Choose your location in the Save in box and click save.

Pitch Book Comparable Universe Summary

A transaction comparable universe summary is often included in pitch books. The summary below uses moon phases or 'pies' to illustrate comparability. The diagram can prove to be an excellent visual communicator to support a comparable universe decision. The shading on the moon phase illustrates the degree of comparability – the redder the moon, the better the comparability.

Comparable universe assessment

	Transaction relevance	Transaction size	Information quality	Buyer type	Deal structure
Company A	●	●	◕	◕	●
Company B	◕	◑	●	○	◑
Company C	◕	◔	●	●	◔
Company D	○	●	○	◔	●

Step 2: Collecting the comps data

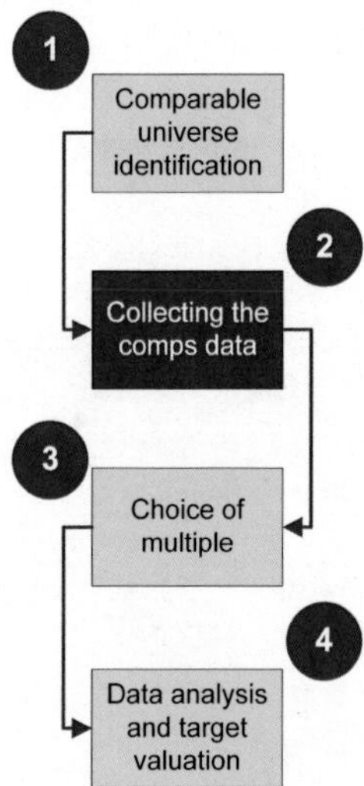

Once the comparable transaction universe has been identified, the data can be collected on a spreadsheet. The M&A databases may provide transaction information, however Analysts will rarely rely on this information for comps purposes. The transaction information must be verified with reference to the original source documentation.

Finding reliable source documentation is the most difficult part of transaction comps. Analysts must be pragmatic in their approach and be prepared to investigate a wide and varied source list. It is better to eliminate a comparable transaction than include it without cross-checking it against a reliable data source.

Transaction Comps

The Bloomberg deal sheet (a click through from the Bloomberg M&A database search) is a good starting point for the transaction comps process. The deal sheet includes some very useful deal data. However, Analysts must not rely on this information – why?

- There is no background data for the multiples
- Analysts may calculate the multiples differently
- The source data must be reviewed to ensure transaction comp data integrity
- The premiums need to be verified
- Sometimes the data provider data is not correct

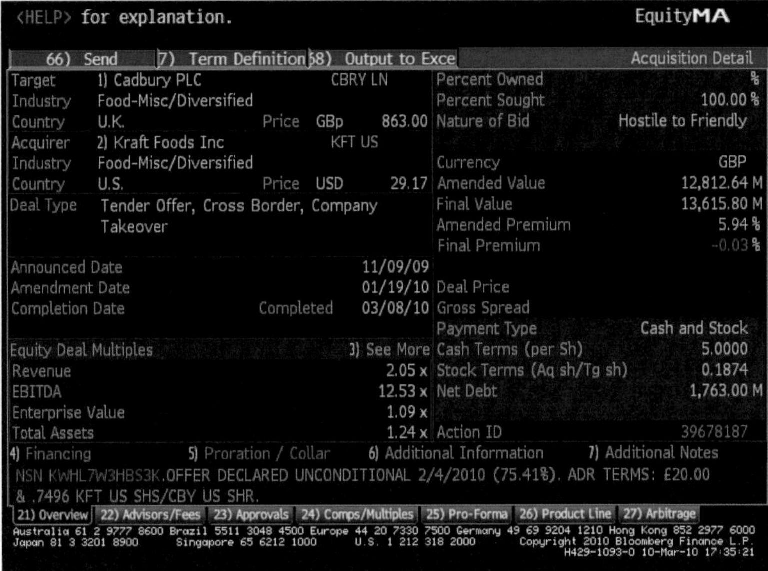

Source: Bloomberg

Cross-checking Comparable Transaction Source Data

The M&A transaction lists produced by the M&A databases should be treated as lists of potential transactions. Any data that is provided by these databases must be cross-checked against original source documentation.

Transaction source documents:

- Perfect information (PI)
- Thomson Financial
- SDC Platinum
- M&A monitor
- MergerMarket.com
- FACTSET MergerStat
- EDGAR online
- Hoovers.com
- SEC website
- Company filings – 8K filings (significant events)
- Company filings – 10K filings (significant transactions during the year)
- Prospectus
- Schedule 14D-1 and 14D-9 – offers to purchase – US only tender offers
- Merger proxies – US only notice of special shareholder meetings
- S4 registration statements – US only – equity issues in relation to transactions
- Proxy statement – US only
- Search engines
- Factiva news runs

As with trading comps, most transaction multiples tend to be at the EV level. The major difference is the source of the equity valuation that feeds into the EV calculation – trading comps derive the equity valuation from current share prices, whereas transaction comps will derive the equity value from the transaction equity value. In other words, rather than using current share prices, the equity value calculation uses the offer price for the deal.

This deal information must be sourced from the original source documents. Analysts should be searching for offer documents. These are the most reliable source of information – but they can be hard to find at times.

The extract below is taken from the Kraft offer document for Cadbury.

The Final Offer

Kraft Foods offers to acquire the entire issued and to be issued share capital of Cadbury on the terms and conditions set out within this document and, in the case of Cadbury Shares held in certificated form, the Acceptance Forms. Under the terms of the Final Offer, Cadbury Shareholders will be entitled to receive:

for each Cadbury Share	**500 pence in cash**
	and
	0.1874 New Kraft Foods Shares

representing, in aggregate, 840 pence per Cadbury Share (based on the closing share price of US$29.58 per Kraft Foods Share on 15 January 2010, the last trading day prior to the date of this document, and an exchange rate of US$1.63 to £1.00 as at 18 January 2010).

In addition, the Cadbury Board has advised Kraft Foods that it will be declaring a dividend of 10 pence per Cadbury Share by way of a Special Dividend. This will, in effect, enable Cadbury Shareholders to receive 10 pence out of the planned final dividend of 12.3 pence per share previously announced by Cadbury, subject to board and shareholder approval, which would otherwise not become payable. †

Assuming the vesting and exercise of all share options and awards under the Cadbury Share Schemes:

- the Final Offer values the entire issued and to be issued share capital of Cadbury at approximately £11.9 billion; and
- 265 million New Kraft Foods Shares will be issued (assuming full acceptance of the Final Offer), representing approximately 18% of the existing share capital and 15% of the enlarged share capital of Kraft Foods.

Source: Kraft Offer document for Cadbury plc

A typical offer document comprises:

- Letter from the acquirer's Board
- Recommendation
- Acceptance procedures
- Offer conditions
- Financial information

The key offer information is normally included in the letter from the acquirer's Board of Directors. The extract above was taken from the Kraft board letter.

This extract provides source documentation that can be used to calculate the offer value that will feed into the transaction EV calculation.

Cadbury transaction comp			Source
	USD	£	
Cash value (500p per share)		5.00	Offer document
Kraft share price (1 day before final offer) US$	29.58		Offer document
Exchange rate	1.63		Offer document
Equity value (0.1874 Kraft shares per share)		3.40	Offer document
Equity transaction value per Cadbury share		**8.40**	Offer document
Cadbury NOSH (fully diluted) pre-announcement		1,414	Offer document
Equity transaction value		**11,879**	

The Cadbury deal was a mixture of cash and equity. Therefore the transaction equity value was calculated with reference to a cash value and the value of the Kraft share-for-share exchange ratio (0.1874 Kraft shares valued at $29.58 for every Cadbury share – an exchange rate of $1.63:£1.00 gave an equity value for the share-for-share exchange of £3.40). The transaction equity value was £8.40 per share.

Share-for-Share Offer Valuation

Share-for-share exchanges are normally expressed as an exchange ratio. The acquirer will offer x number of shares for every one share in the target. The Kraft offer for Cadbury was part cash/part equity. The offer was 0.1874 Kraft shares for every Cadbury share. This exchange ratio is needed to calculate the value of the consideration for the Cadbury equity.

The calculation of Cadbury's EV and equity value should be completed in the base currency (GBP) and if necessary for presentation purposes converted. Balance sheet information will be converted at the spot rate. Income statement metrics will be translated at the average exchange rate for the relevant period.

A	Kraft exchange ratio	0.187
B	Kraft share price (pre-announcement - final offer 15/01/2010)	29.58
	Value of Kraft offer (US$) (A x B)	**5.54**
	Exchange rate at 18/01/2010	1.63
	Value of Kraft offer (GBP)	**3.40**

The total transaction equity value is then calculated using a diluted NOSH. The diluted NOSH has been calculated using the treasury method as discussed previously.

This equity value per Cadbury share will be used in the premium paid analysis (see later notes in this chapter) to calculate the premiums in relation to pre-announcement share prices.

Once the Analyst arrives at the transaction equity value, the EV calculation reverts back to a standard comps calculation. The latest available financials will be used to calculate EV. Market values will be used if material and available for the standard EV components:

- Net debt
- Non-controlling interest
- Pension deficits (if relevant)
- Operating lease commitments (if relevant and using an EV/EBITDAR multiple)
- JVs and associates

Transaction Comps

Cadbury transaction comp			Source
		£	
Cash value (500p per share)		5.00	Offer document
Kraft share price (1 day before final offer)			
US$	29.58		Offer document
Equity value (0.1874 Kraft shares per share)		3.40	Offer document
Equity transaction value per Cadbury share		**8.40**	Offer document
Cadbury NOSH (fully diluted)		1,414	Offer document
Equity transaction value (£m)		**11,879**	
	£m	**£m**	
Borrowings < 1 year	1,189		Latest financials
Borrowings > 1 year	1,194		Latest financials
OTM convertible debt	--		Latest financials
OTM convertible preferred stock	--		Latest financials
Cash and cash equivalents	(251)		Latest financials
Short term investments	(247)		Latest financials
Net debt		1,885	
Pension deficit – funded schemes		144	Latest financials
Pension deficit – unfunded schemes		15	Latest financials
Non-controlling interest (book value)		12	Latest financials
Investment in associates (book value)		(28)	Latest financials
EV		**13,907**	
PV of the operating lease commitments		270	Latest financials
EV (lease adjusted – only to be used with EBITDAR)		**14,177**	

Deferred Consideration

Deferred consideration is a common component of deal structures. The deferred consideration is normally a deferred payout that is linked to underlying performance targets or perhaps linked to the retention of key human capital. If recent transaction comps are included in the comparable universe, deferred consideration may still be outstanding. Analysts should assess the probability of the payout being satisfied and determine whether it should be included in the transaction EV calculations. The assessment will be conducted with reference to research, post-acquisition performance in relation to targets and the terms of the deferred consideration offer.

Grossing up a Partial Acquisition

As mentioned earlier, Analysts must ensure that the transactions in the comp are controlling stake acquisitions – that is a control premium is included in the offer value.

Controlling partial stake acquisitions can be included in the comparable transactions universe, however the equity stake purchased must be grossed up to reflect a 100% acquisition, as the transaction equity value will be used to calculate an EV that will reflect 100% of the claims on the entity.
A 75% equity transaction value cannot be added to 100% of net debt, non-controlling interests etc.

Cadbury transaction comp			Source
		£	
Cash value (500p per share)		5.00	Offer doc
Kraft share price (1 day before final offer) US$	29.58		Offer doc
Equity value (0.1874 Kraft shares per share)		3.40	Offer doc
Equity transaction value per Cadbury share		**8.40**	Offer doc
Cadbury NOSH (fully diluted)		1,414	Offer doc
Equity transaction value (£m)		**11,879**	
Percentage acquired		75.00%	
Grossed up equity transaction value (£m)		**15,839**	

Metrics

Transaction comps metrics are normally based on LTM (pre-announcement numbers). Even though at the time of the transaction forward multiples would have been used – now that the transaction has taken place, the LTM metrics attempt to reflect what the buyer actually bought. So transaction comp metrics are generally backward-looking (typically looking at the last twelve months of financial information available prior to the announcement date).

These metrics must be normalized for non-recurring and non-core line items as for trading comps. Typical LTM metrics are:

- Revenue
- EBIT
- EBITDA
- EBITDAR (if leasing is an issue)
- Net income (for equity level multiples)

Using Brokers' Research

Forward transaction multiples

Transaction comps can utilize forecast information for multiple construction. This is usually a sector specific issue. Certain industries such as technology and bio-tech tend to focus more on projected numbers for transaction comps purposes, however, care must be taken to use research that was issued pre-announcement. This ensures that the forecast information is clean of acquisition expectations and influence.

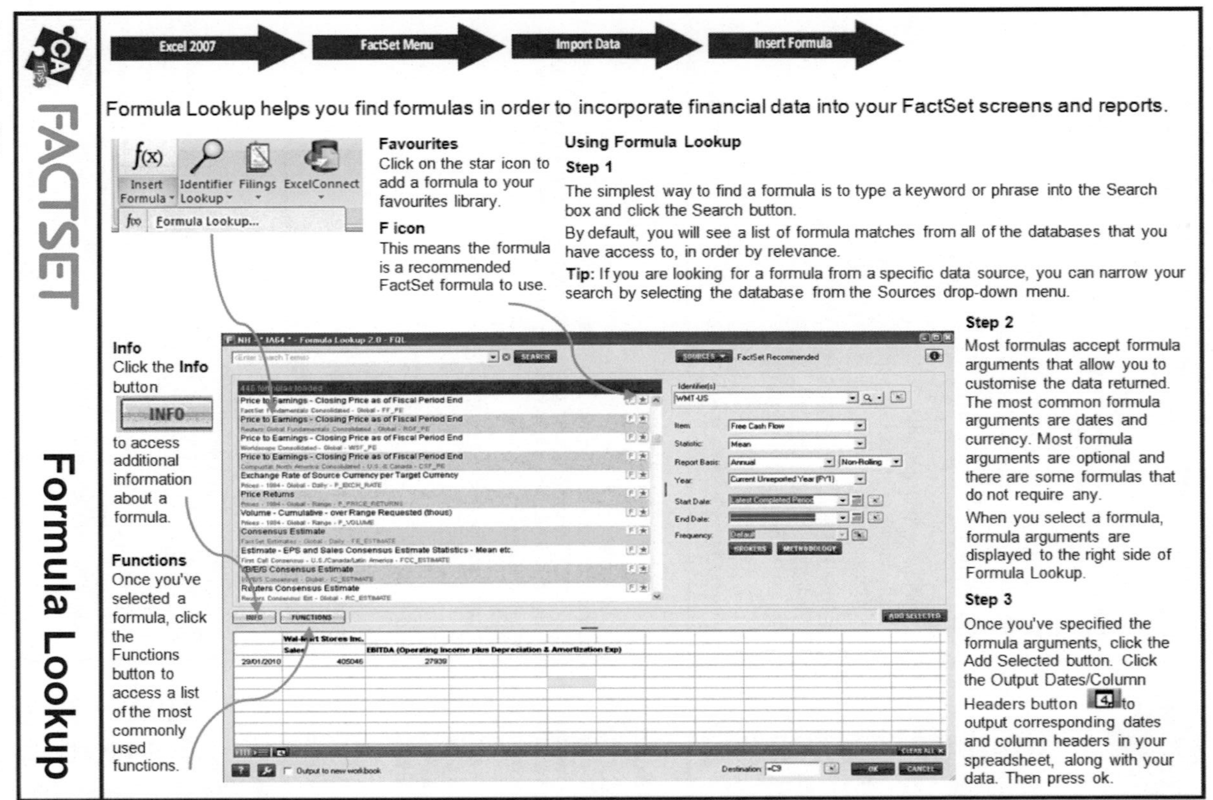

Source: FactSet

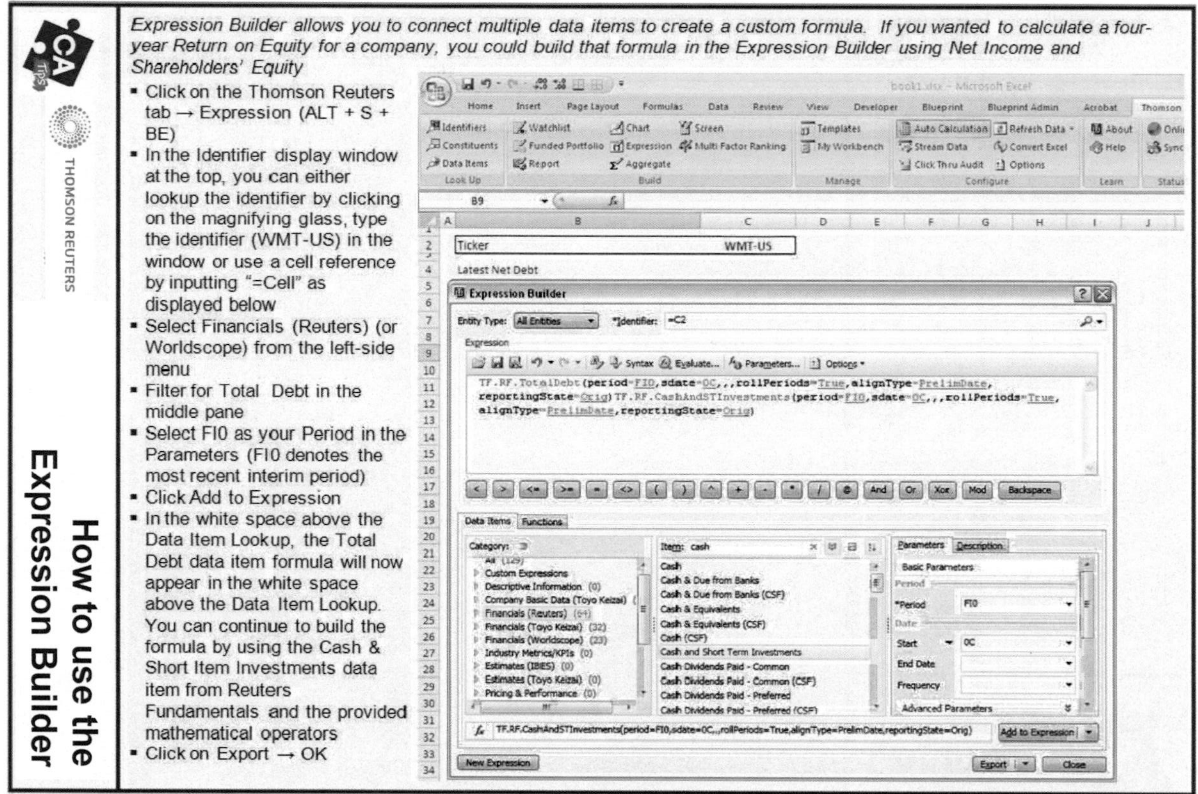

How to use the Expression Builder

THOMSON REUTERS

Expression Builder allows you to connect multiple data items to create a custom formula. If you wanted to calculate a four-year Return on Equity for a company, you could build that formula in the Expression Builder using Net Income and Shareholders' Equity

- Click on the Thomson Reuters tab → Expression (ALT + S + BE)
- In the Identifier display window at the top, you can either lookup the identifier by clicking on the magnifying glass, type the identifier (WMT-US) in the window or use a cell reference by inputting "=Cell" as displayed below
- Select Financials (Reuters) (or Worldscope) from the left-side menu
- Filter for Total Debt in the middle pane
- Select FI0 as your Period in the Parameters (FI0 denotes the most recent interim period)
- Click Add to Expression
- In the white space above the Data Item Lookup, the Total Debt data item formula will now appear in the white space above the Data Item Lookup. You can continue to build the formula by using the Cash & Short Item Investments data item from Reuters Fundamentals and the provided mathematical operators
- Click on Export → OK

Source: Thomson Reuters

=FDS Coding

Information requirement	=FDS coding syntax
Company ticker	=FDS(A1,"FG_COMPANY_NAME")
Closing share price	=FDS(A1,"P_PRICE(0)")
52 week high	=FDS(A1,"P_PRICE_HIGH_52W(0)")
52 week low	=FDS(A1,"P_PRICE_LOW_52W(0)")
NOSH	=FDS(A1,"FF_COM_SHS_OUT(ANN,0,,,RF)")
Exchange rates	=FDS(A1,"P_EXCH_RATE(EUR,USD,0)")

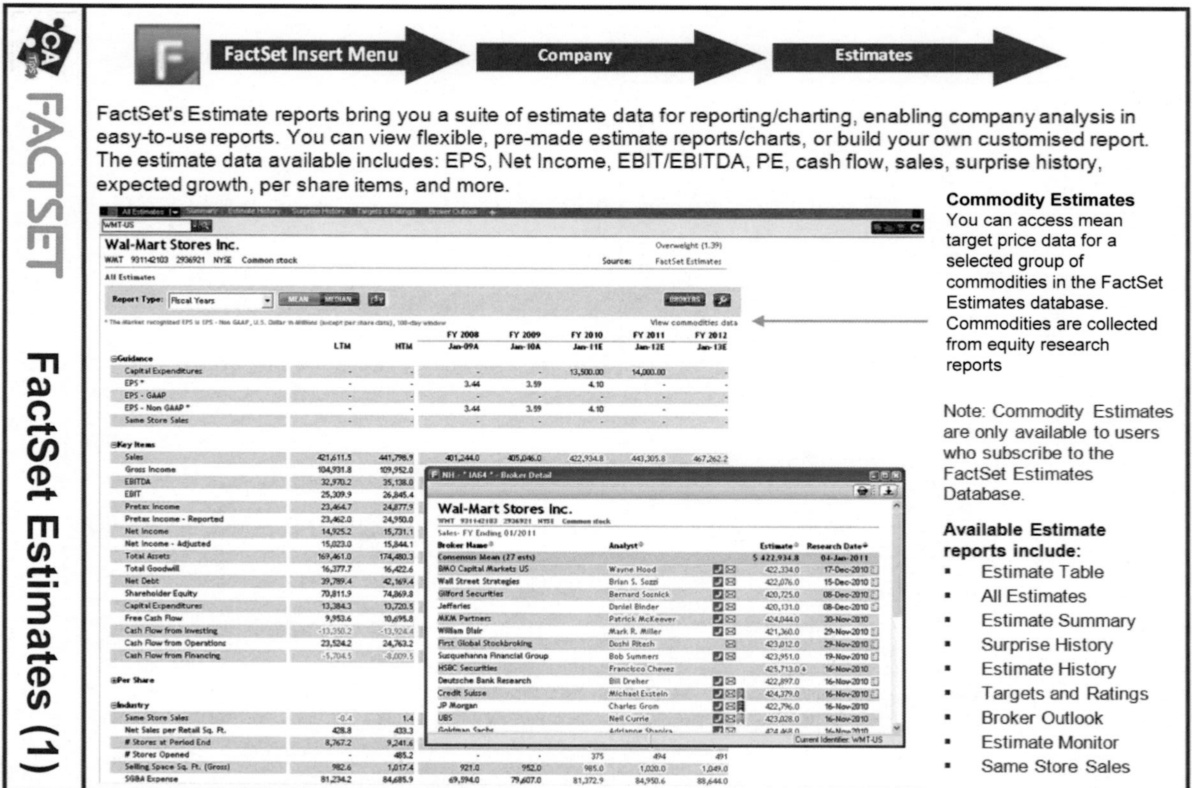

Source: FactSet

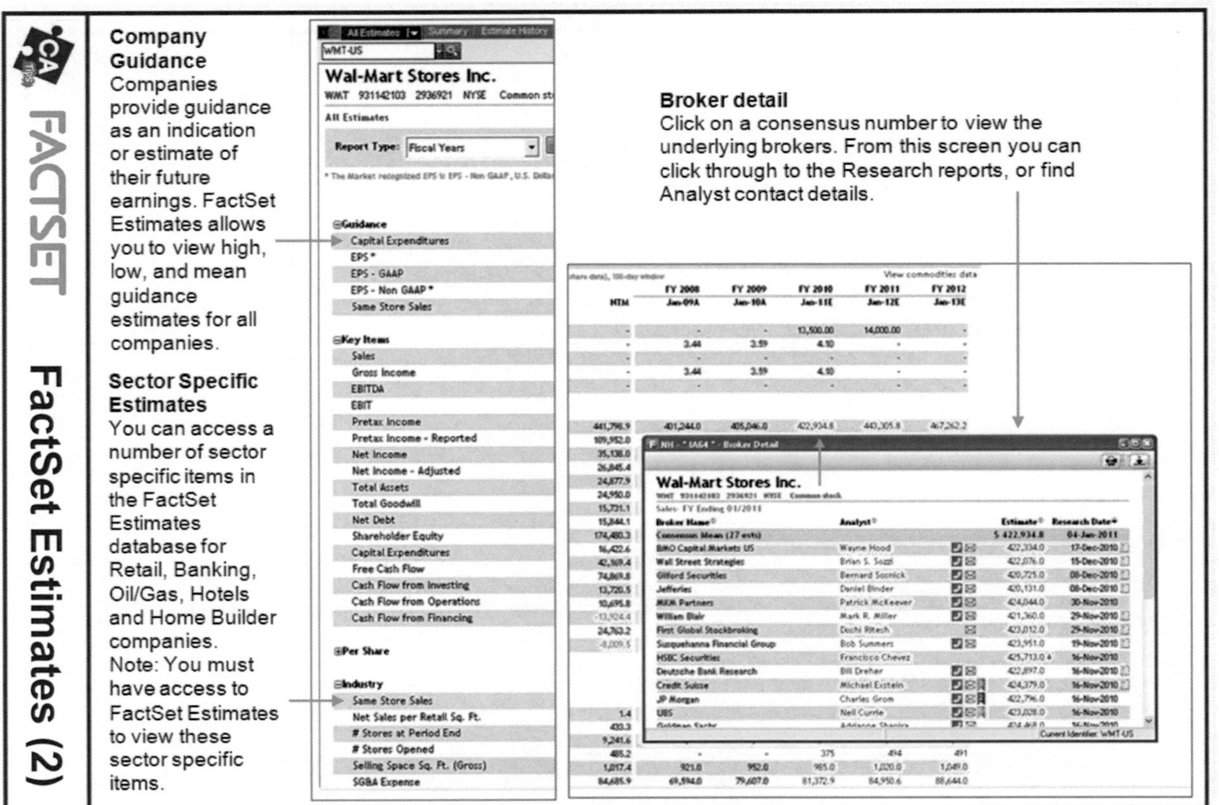

Source: FactSet

How to Import Consensus Estimates

THOMSON REUTERS

To find the FY2012 EPS Mean estimate for Wal-Mart, do the following:

- Click on the Thomson Reuters tab → Data Item Lookup (ALT + S + D)
- In the Identifier display window at the top, you can either lookup the identifier by clicking on the magnifying glass, type the identifier (WMT-US) in the window or use a cell reference by inputting "=Cell" as displayed below
- Select Estimates (IBES) from the left-side menu
- Filter for EPS Mean in the middle pane
- Change the period to FY2012 (the application can also pull calendar year estimates (CY2012) and relative period estimates like next interim period (FI1) and next fiscal or calendar year (FY1 or CY1)
- Click on Export → OK

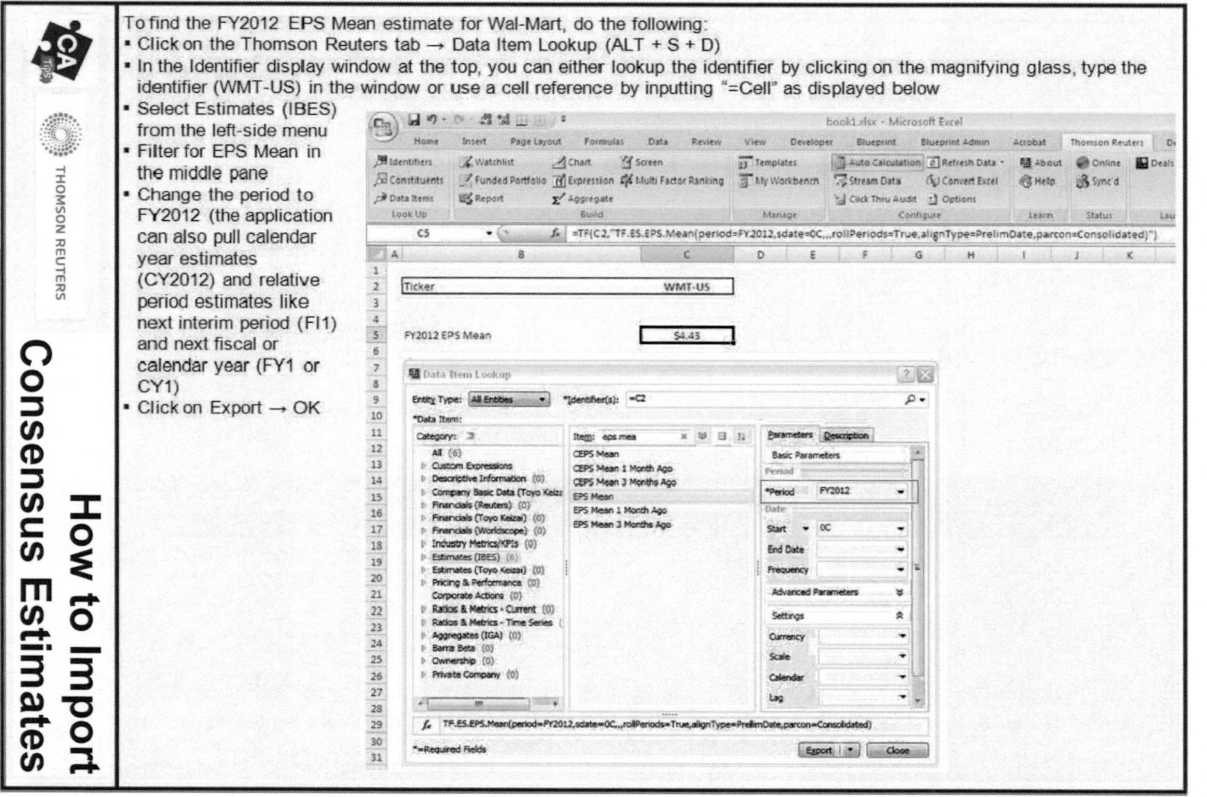

Source: Thomson Reuters

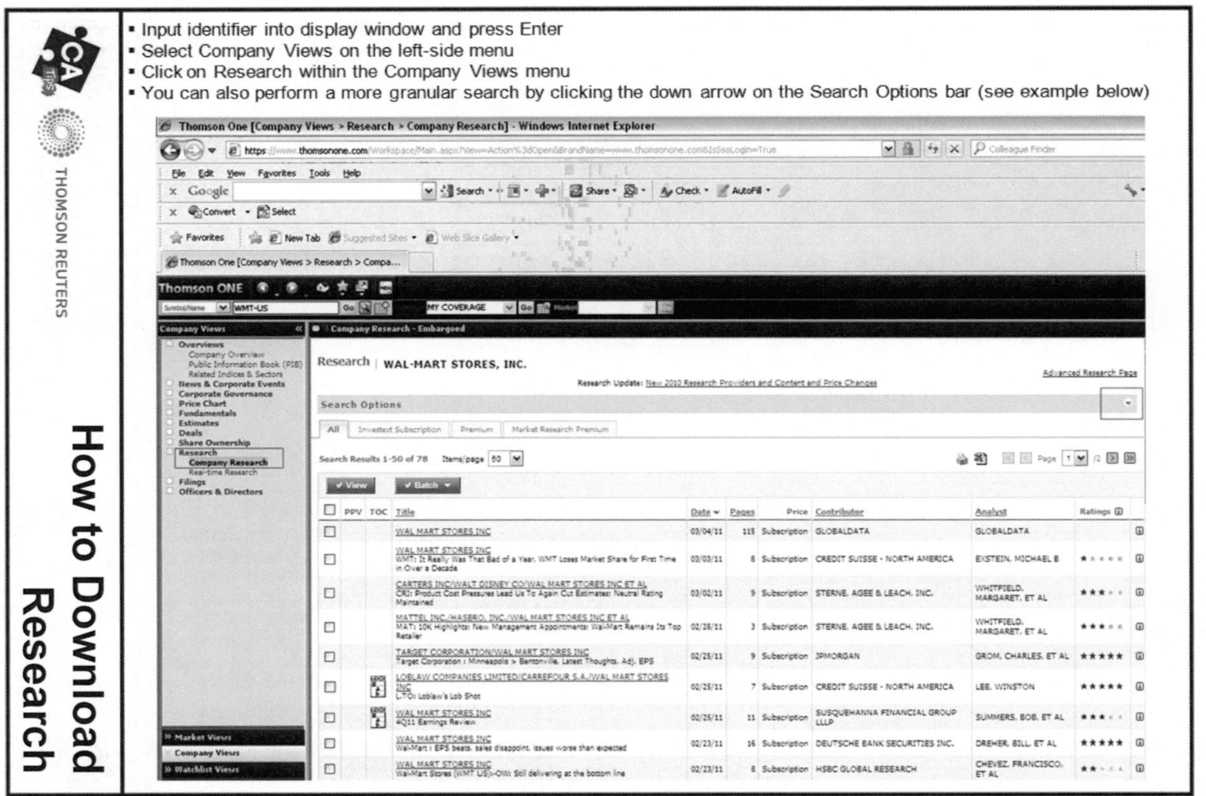

Source: Thomson Reuters

Step 3: Choice of multiple

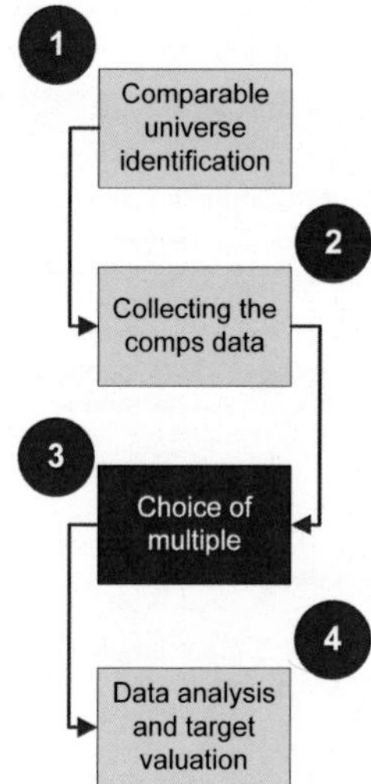

Analysts have a number of vital choices at step three in the comps process:

- What level of multiple (EV or equity value) should be applied in the valuation?
- If using an EV multiple – which earnings metric is most appropriate?

The issues surrounding the choice of multiple are examined extensively in the Trading Comps chapter and are equally applicable to transaction comps.

Sector specific multiples are also used for transaction comps where applicable.

Equity or Enterprise Level Multiples

EV and equity value multiples are used extensively through the industry. Some sectors will be more reliant on the EV, whilst others prefer the equity level multiple. Both multiples have their merits. The table below summarizes the relative merits and demerits of each type of multiple:

EV multiples	Equity multiples
Rely on denominators that are less prone to accounting issues	More relevant to equity valuation
Are capital structure neutral	Are more familiar to investors
Are comprehensive. They capture the full claims on the enterprise	Arguably involve less subjectivity than EV multiples, especially in terms of assessing off balance sheet claims
Make it easier to capture off-balance sheet and debt-like claims	Are much more prone to accounting issues
Have a wide spectrum of applicable multiples	
Are technically harder to communicate to clients	
Have an increased reliance on market values	
Require additional technical work to derive an equity value	

Full Cadbury transaction comp

Kraft – Cadbury transaction comp				Source
Acquirer	Kraft Inc			
Target	Cadbury plc			
Announcement date	07 Sep 09			
Announcement date (final offer)	19 Jan 10			
		£	%	
Pre-announcement price – 1 day – 04 Sep 09		5.68	47.90%	
Pre-announcement price – 1 week – 28 Aug 09		5.81	44.59%	
Pre-announcement price – 1 month – 07 Aug 09		5.83	44.10%	
			£	
Cash value (500p per share)			5.00	Offer document
Kraft share price (1 day before final offer) US$		29.58		Offer document
Equity value (0.1874 Kraft shares per share)			3.40	Offer document
Equity transaction value per Cadbury share			**8.40**	Offer document
Cadbury NOSH (fully diluted)			1,414	Offer document
Equity transaction value (£m)			**11,879**	
		£m	**£m**	
Borrowings < 1 year		1,189		Latest financials
Borrowings > 1 year		1,194		Latest financials
Cash and cash equivalents		(251)		Latest financials
Short term investments		(247)		Latest financials
Net debt			1,885	
Pension deficit – funded schemes			144	Latest financials
Pension deficit – unfunded schemes			15	Latest financials
Non-controlling interest (book value)			12	Latest financials
Investment in associates (book value)			(28)	Latest financials
EV			**13,907**	
PV of the operating lease commitments			270	Latest financials
EV (lease adjusted)			**14,177**	
Earnings metrics:	**LTM**			
Revenue	5,384			Pre-announcement
EBIT	638			Pre-announcement
EBITDA	878			Pre-announcement
EBITDAR	928			Pre-announcement
EBIT margins	11.85%			
EBITDA margins	16.31%			
Revenue growth rates				
EBIT growth rates				
EBITDA growth rates				
EV transaction multiples:				
EV / Revenue	2.58x			
EV / EBIT	21.8x			
EV / EBITDA	15.8x			
EV / EBITDAR	15.3x			

Multiples Presentation

Revenue multiples are typically presented to two decimal places in a comps sheet. The remaining multiples are normally presented to one decimal place. This is because revenue multiples can be quite small and so warrant the additional disclosure of two decimal places.

The EV / EBITDAR multiple must be calculated using an operating lease adjusted EV in order to be consistent with the EBITDAR in the denominator.

Step 4: Target valuation

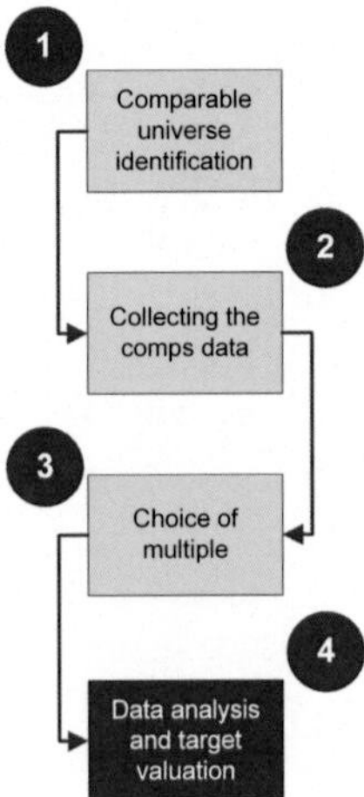

Step 4 requires the identification of a suitable comparable transaction multiple in order to value the target. All of the comparable information has been collected and it is stored in the comps sheets (See the full Kraft-Cadbury comp detail above – there will be a comps sheet like this for each comparable transaction). The data is now collected and disclosed in a comps output sheet – see below.

The form and content of the comps output sheet will vary from team to team but should include:

- EV and equity values for all comparables
- All key multiples
- Transaction background information
- Deal structures and offers
- Dispersion measures for key numbers (mean, median, highs and lows)

Additional Key Data for the Transaction Comp Output Sheet

The construction and use of a transaction comp sheet is not just a number crunching exercise. Analysts must know the transactions in the universe. The transaction comps sheet will be used to collect data to support the background data for the deal.

Key data	Information detail
The announcement date	The announcement date is the date that the deal was announced to the public. This date is the reference point for premium paid analysis. Premiums will be calculated with reference to share prices in the period prior to the announcement date and the deal completion date. Premiums are normally calculated with reference to one day, one week and one month prior to the announcement date.
Target	Note the full legal name of the target. This information will be found on the face of the 10K or in the financials. If the target is a division or a subsidiary of a parent company, note the parent company and list the businesses of the target.
Acquirer	List the legal name – from the financials. Describe the motivations of the acquirer – strategic buy/financial sponsor and brief M&A rationale.
Business description	Useful background information. Extract from the financials or the Bloomberg description (DES) page.
Transaction status	Note whether the deal is completed or pending. Deal data for pending deals will be subject to change up to the point of completion. Terminated deals are normally excluded from the comps process as the control premiums and the multiples were not realised. This information can be taken from the M&A database. It is always useful to cross-check against news runs.
Prices	If a cash offer – state the offer price per share. If a share offer – state the exchange ratio and value the equity offer. This is the exchange ratio x one day pre-announcement share price. If a mixed offer – state the offer price and exchange ratios. All of this information must be taken from original source documentation.

Transaction Comps

Below is an example of an abbreviated comps output sheet for food producer transactions:

Food producers

in USDm unless stated otherwise

		Transaction values					Transaction multiples		Pre-announcement equity prices			
Acquiror	Target	EV	Eq. value	EBITDA growth - next 2 yrs	EBITDA margin (LTM)	EV/ Revenue (LTM)	EV/ EBITDA (LTM)	Price / Earnings (LTM)	1-day	1-week	1-month	Announce ment date
Kraft (US)	Cadbury (UK)	22,669	18,135	8.73%	16.31%	1.10x	15.8x	23.2x	5.68	5.81	5.83	Sep 09
Mars (US)	WM Wrigley (US)	22,637	17,204	7.78%	17.45%	1.21x	17.5x	24.5x	55.05	54.64	50.94	Apr 08
Koninklijke (NA)	Giant Sweets (US)	2,795	2,180	6.30%	12.34%	0.65x	10.9x	19.2x	36.14	35.34	33.45	Jul 07
Albertson (US)	Juicy Choc (UK)	12,447	10,829	3.56%	9.56%	0.46x	7.1x	15.6x	21.41	21.23	20.89	
Maximum		22,669	18,135	8.73%	17.45%	1.21x	17.5x	24.5x	55.05	54.64	50.94	
Minimum		2,795	2,180	3.56%	9.56%	0.46x	7.1x	15.6x	5.68	5.81	5.83	
Mean		15,137	12,087	6.59%	13.91%	0.86x	12.8x	20.6x	29.57	29.26	27.78	
Median		17,542	14,017	7.04%	14.32%	0.88x	13.3x	21.2x	28.78	28.29	27.17	

							Pre-announcement premiums		
Acquiror	Target	Nature of bid	Deal status	Deal type	Deal structure	% acquired	1-day	1-week	1-month
Kraft (US)	Cadbury (UK)	Friendly	Completed	Takeover	Cash/Equity	100.00%	47.90%	44.59%	44.10%
Mars (US)	WM Wrigley (US)	Friendly	Completed	Takeover	Cash	100.00%	21.96%	22.54%	27.79%
Koninklijke (NA)	Giant Sweets (US)	Friendly	Completed	Takeover	Cash	100.00%	16.92%	18.76%	23.10%
Albertson (US)	Juicy Choc (UK)	Friendly	Completed	Takeover	Equity	100.00%	34.23%	34.78%	35.82%
Maximum							47.90%	44.59%	44.10%
Minimum							16.92%	18.76%	23.10%
Mean							30.25%	30.17%	32.70%
Median							28.09%	28.66%	31.81%

Hershey Inc	US	12,227	10,515	3.07%	19.82%

Analyzing the Dispersion Metrics

Every transaction comps output sheet will include dispersion metrics such as:

- Mean
- Median
- High
- Low

These metrics are often neglected when analyzing the transaction comps output sheet.

The metrics provide a snap shot overview of the distribution of the transaction comps work across the comparable universe. The analysis of the mean and median statistics provides information about the skewness of the comps universe and how the target deal may fit into the overall universe.

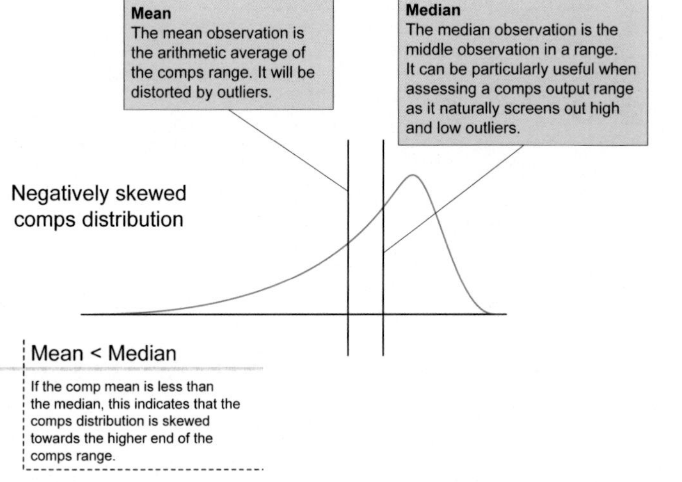

Mean < Median

If the comp mean is less than the median, this indicates that the comps distribution is skewed towards the higher end of the comps range.

Transaction Comps Output Sheet

Local and base currencies

Comparable reporting currencies can create a few issues when presenting the transaction comps output sheet.

Differences in currency presentation are irrelevant for multiples, margins and growth rates, as they are relative measures. However, currencies are an issue when presenting absolute monetary numbers such as:

- Transaction EV
- Transaction equity values

A transaction comps output sheet usually discloses this information in the local currency. The local currency information is then translated into a base currency. The base currency is usually the currency of the target transaction.

Snapshot metrics such as transaction EV and equity values must be translated at the pre-announcement spot rate. Income statement data, if presented, should be translated at the average exchange rate for the period of the metric. Balance sheet data, if presented, should be translated using the balance sheet date closing rate.

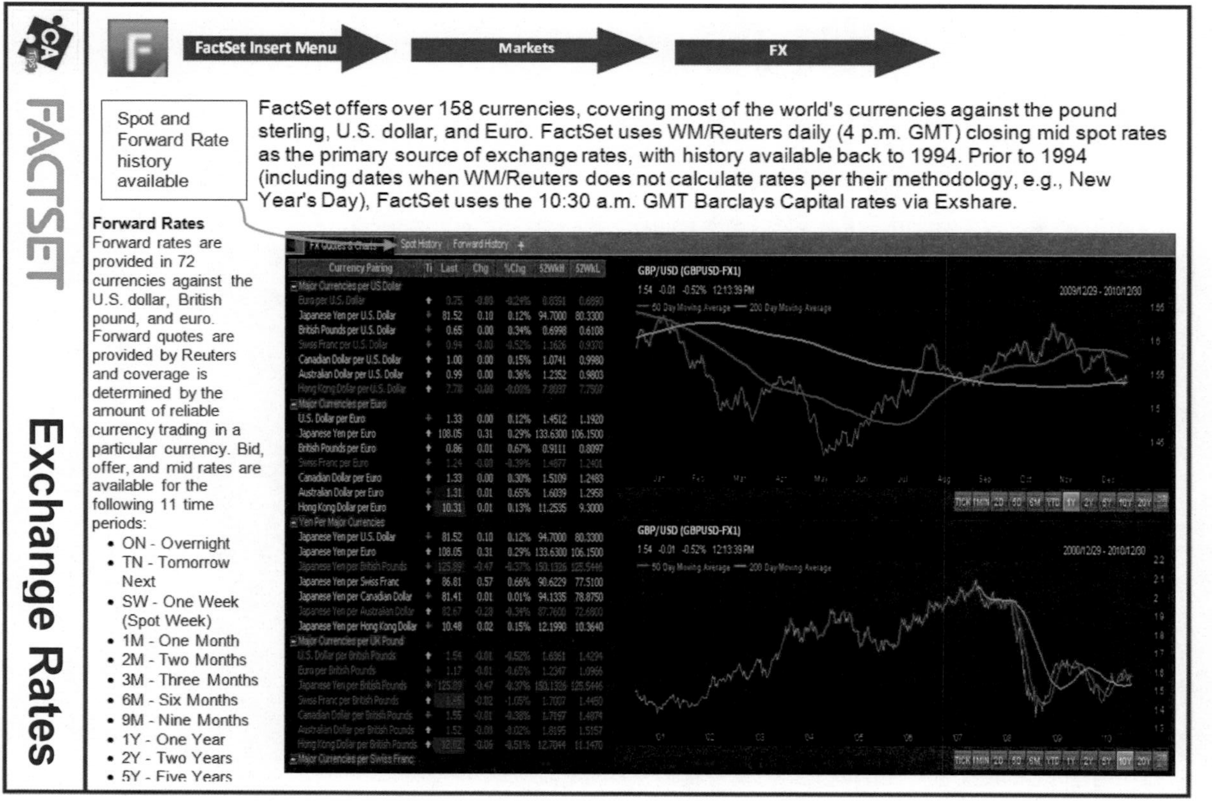

Source: FactSet

Transaction Comps

The choice of the comparable transaction multiple used to value the target company requires a similar thought process to trading comps.

The target in this example will continue to be Hershey Inc. In order to select a comparable transaction multiple, Hershey must be placed into the comparable universe in order to identify the most appropriate comparable multiples to be used.

The choice of an appropriate comparable transaction multiple will consider:

- Growth rates in earnings metrics
- Margins
- Similar type of transaction (size/deal structure/nature of the bid/offer premiums)

Considering Hershey Inc and the transaction comps sheet above, the Hershey transaction is similar to Juicy Choc in terms of size and growth rates. However, Juicy Choc (bought at 7.1x EBITDA) has a much lower EBITDA margin. Hershey has a stronger margin than Wrigley's (bought at 17.5x EBITDA). These two transactions provide a marker for the Hershey choice of multiple. The universe mean EV/EBITDA is 12.8x with a 13.3x median. Hershey's margins are above the mean and median for the comparable universe.

Despite this information, the choice of multiple is still a subjective decision. However, a transaction EV/EBITDA multiple could be justified in the region of 13-14x EBITDA on the strong EBITDA margins and weaker than average growth rates.

Equity value breakdown

EV multiples will produce an implied EV valuation of the target. Whilst this is useful information to have from an M&A perspective, in the sense it provides an idea of the financing requirement (a 100% acquirer will have to buy out the whole of the equity and will possibly have or wish to refinance the existing debt claims), an equity value per share will be required for the equity investors.

Therefore the implied EV will have to be disaggregated to an equity value.

The breakdown essentially strips out all non-equity claims from the implied EV number. Thus the standard disaggregating components are:

- Net debt
- Other claims (pension deficits and operating lease commitments if relevant)
- Non-controlling interests
- Associates and joint ventures

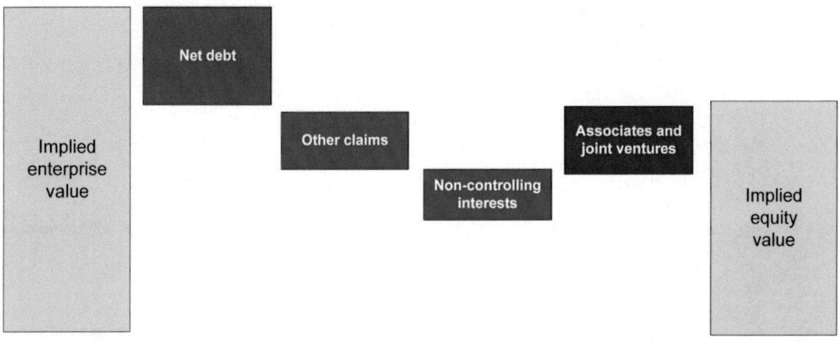

Pension deficits and operating lease commitments will only be disaggregated if they are included in the comparable EV calculations.

Fair values should be used when the items are material to the equity value disaggregation.

The market value of JVs (unless proportionally consolidated) and associates will need to be added into the implied equity value as they were stripped out of the comparable multiple numbers previously. If the JVs and associates are immaterial to the overall implied equity value, a book value will probably suffice.

The implied equity value will then be divided by NOSH, most probably a diluted figure.

A diluted NOSH calculation can be performed by applying the treasury method to the outstanding equity options in the target company.

Hershey Inc

Currency		$
Current share price		41.57
52 week high		42.25
52 week low		30.27
Exchange rate USD:GBP		1.53
Comparable transaction EV/EBITDA		14.0x
EBITDA LTM		1,082
Implied EV		**15,148**
Borrowings < 1 year	502	
Borrowings > 1 year	1,506	
Cash and cash equivalents	(37)	
Net debt		(1,970)
Pension deficit - funded schemes		(41)
Non-controlling interest (book value)		(32)
Investment in associates (book value)		--
Implied equity value		13,105
Class A common stock	299	
Class B common stock	61	
Treasury stock	(133)	
Option dilution	14	
NOSH		241
Implied equity value per share		54.33

Earnings metrics:	**LTM**
Revenue	5,459
EBIT	900
EBITDA	1,082
EBITDAR	1,132
EBIT margins	16.49%
EBITDA margins	19.82%
EBITDAR margins	20.74%
Revenue growth rates	3.02%
EBIT growth rates	4.53%
EBITDA growth rates	3.64%
EBITDAR growth rates	3.47%
Source: RBS research	
Implied EV multiples:	
EV / Revenue	2.77x
EV / EBIT	16.8x
EV / EBITDA	14.0x
EV / EBITDAR	13.4x

Valuation Ranges and Sensitivity Capture

Valuation number crunching is technical. The implied valuation is ultimately judgemental. There are a number of key variables that are applied to produce an implied transaction comparable valuation.

Choices with regard to the:

- Comparable valuation multiple
- Broker and its forecasts

...are two key sensitive and judgemental variables used in a comparable valuation.

It is key therefore that Analysts produce a valuation range in order to capture the impact of these sensitivities.

Excel's data table functionality (See the Financial Modeling part of the manual) provides a simple and very effective sensitivity tool. A well-built comps sheet can be set up to iterate a number of possible valuation outcomes in relation to key variables.

The table below is an extract from the Hershey comparable valuation model used throughout this chapter. A data table has been set up to value Hershey using different comparable EV/EBITDA (13.8x to 14.2x) multiples and EBITDA LTMs ($977m to $1,193m).

Implied equity value per share sensivity

EBITDA LTM				EV/EBITDA	
	13.8x	13.9x	14.0x	14.1x	14.2x
977	47.40	47.80	48.21	48.61	49.02
1,028	50.34	50.76	51.19	51.61	52.04
1,082	53.43	53.88	54.33	54.78	55.23
1,136	56.53	57.00	57.47	57.94	58.41
1,193	59.78	60.27	60.77	61.26	61.75

Even with a relatively tight range of variables, it is clear that the different comparable multiples and forecasts have a marked impact on the equity value per share output.

A valuation range of $50.76 to $57.94 per share might now be justifiably supported with reference to the variable sensitivity. The width of the valuation range must be considered carefully and must be in line with how the deal is being communicated to the client.

- A range that is too tight may infer science and precision that cannot be guaranteed
- A wide range may suggest a lack of conviction
- Buy-side ranges may sink to the lower end of a valuation range
- Sell-side ranges may float to the upper end of a valuation range
- The range may be further tailored in relation to other valuation techniques once a valuation summary ('football pitch') is put together

The $50.76 to $57.94 per share range appears to be an acceptable range variance.

Premium paid analysis

Premium paid analysis can be used to generate a potential offer price from a target's 'clean' share price. Firstly, the comparable universe is analyzed to determine the most appropriate premium to apply.

Key factors to be considered when determining the most appropriate premium are:

- The nature of the transaction
- The state of the market
- The size of the transaction
- The intended deal structure

Once a comparable premium is identified it is applied to a clean target share price, in order to produce an indicative takeover valuation. This valuation will implicitly include a control premium.

The idea of the 'clean' price is to use an 'unaffected share price', i.e. prior to announcement of possible sale or before the 'evaluating strategic alternatives' press release.

Premium pricing points are typically:

- One day pre-announcement
- One week pre-announcement
- One month pre-announcement

These time frames are used to analyze if, or how information has leaked into the market in relation to the deal and how the market prices reacted.

The premium (looking at comparable transactions) is calculated as follows:

$$\text{Premium (\%)} = (\text{Offer price} / \text{Pre-announcement price}) - 1$$

The illustration below shows how the Cadbury share price reacted after the deal went public in September 2009. Calculating a deal premium on a post-announcement share price is not particularly relevant as the bid will be priced to an extent into the share price.

The offer price for the premium calculation will use the prevailing share price information as at the offer date.

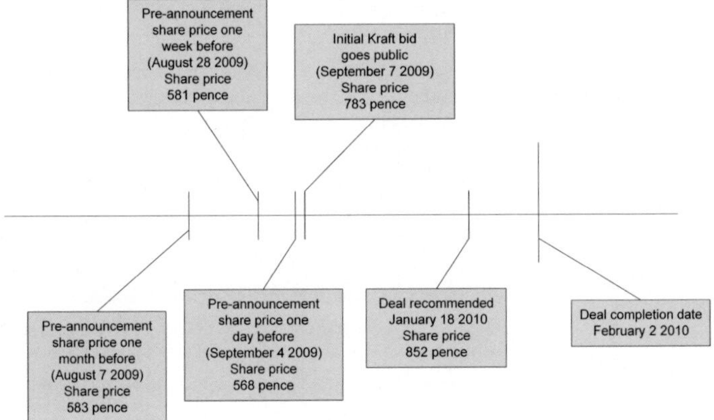

Food producers					
in USDm unless stated otherwise					
		Pre-announcement equity prices			
Acquiror	Target	1-day	1-week	1-month	Announcement date
Kraft (US)	Cadbury (UK)	5.68	5.81	5.83	Sep 09
Mars (US)	WM Wrigley (US)	55.05	54.64	50.94	Apr 08
Koninklijke (NA)	Giant Sweets (US)	36.14	35.34	33.45	Jul 07
Albertson (US)	Juicy Choc (UK)	21.41	21.23	20.89	
Maximum		55.05	54.64	50.94	
Minimum		5.68	5.81	5.83	
Mean		29.57	29.26	27.78	
Median		28.78	28.29	27.17	

		Pre-announcement premiums		
Acquiror	Target	1-day	1-week	1-month
Kraft (US)	Cadbury (UK)	47.90%	44.59%	44.10%
Mars (US)	WM Wrigley (US)	21.96%	22.54%	27.79%
Koninklijke (NA)	Giant Sweets (US)	16.92%	18.76%	23.10%
Albertson (US)	Juicy Choc (UK)	34.23%	34.78%	35.82%
Maximum		47.90%	44.59%	44.10%
Minimum		16.92%	18.76%	23.10%
Mean		30.25%	30.17%	32.70%
Median		28.09%	28.66%	31.81%

Analyzing the information above for the food producers' transactions, we can see that the premiums on average are in the region of 30%. The premiums are relatively stable over the one month pre-announcement period. This suggests that deal news has not leaked to any great extent onto the market pre-announcement.

If we used this information to value Hershey on a premium paid basis, we would apply a 30% premium to the current share price (if we considered this a clean price) of $41.57.

Hershey Inc	
Currency	$
Current share price	41.57
52 week high	42.25
52 week low	30.27
Exchange rate USD: GBP	1.53
Current share price	41.57
Premium paid	30.00%
Implied equity price based on 30.00% premium paid	**54.04**

The sensitivity analysis on the premium paid below suggests an implied equity valuation range of $51.96 to $56.12.

Implied equity value per share sensitivity					
					Premium paid
	25.0%	27.5%	30.0%	32.5%	35.0%
54.04	51.96	53.00	54.04	55.08	56.12

Using Bloomberg to Get Share Price Data

Bloomberg

Analysts should know how to access share price data from Bloomberg. This data is often used in pitch books and company profiles.

Key stroke:

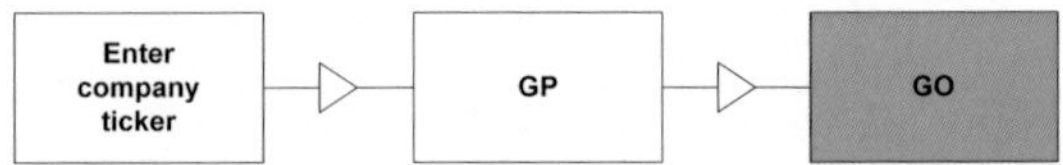

This Bloomberg screen allows the Analyst to alter the share price graph data sets:

- Share price ranges
- Frequency of observations
- Moving averages
- Trading volume graphs

Source: Bloomberg

Annotating Bloomberg Share Price Graphs

Bloomberg

Key stroke:

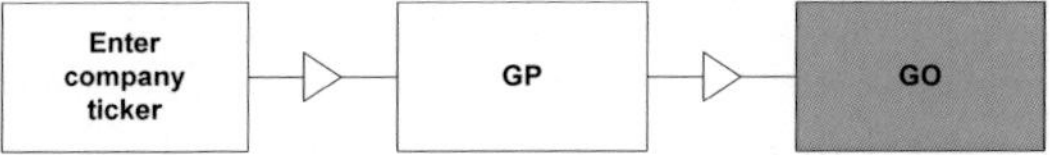

This Bloomberg screen allows the Analyst to annotate the share price graphs (see sub-menu below):

- Annotation for news events
- Trend lines
- Support levels

Source: Bloomberg

Share price data can be imported directly into Excel. Bloomberg offer an add-on Excel menu. The menu (see below) is a menu-driven import wizard. This is a useful function for pitch book presentations and company profiles as the graphs can be built in accordance with the IBD presentation protocols, rather than relying on Bloomberg screen dumps. A Bloomberg screen dump in an IBD pitch book will look unprofessional.

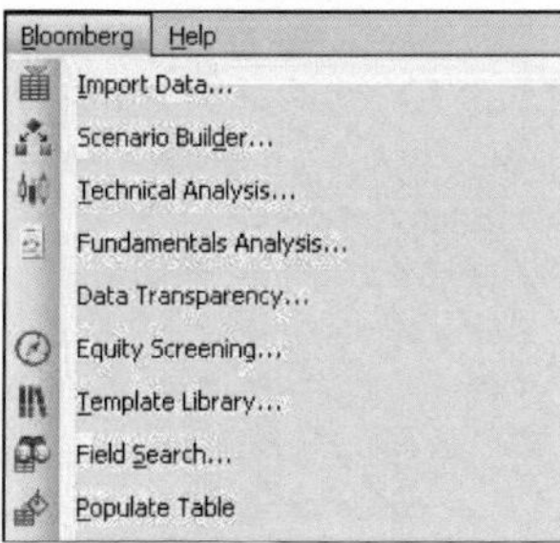

What is the Analyst's Role?

An early responsibility for an Analyst will be the maintenance of a transaction comps model. This will involve:

- Keeping the model up-to-date (share price, NOSH and exchange rate data)
- Updating the model for new deal announcements
- Knowing the background stories for the comparable transactions
- Watching deal flow and analyzing the impact on the comps
- Adding new comparable transactions
- Comps output pitch book preparation

Tick Sheet – Transaction Comps

Transaction comps – a four step structured approach:

- Comparable universe identification
- Collecting the comps data
- Choice of multiple
- Data analysis and target valuation

Transaction comps are used to analyze trends:

- Consolidation trends
- Foreign investment
- Private equity investment
- Divestiture strategies
- Investor appetite assessment
- Frequency of types of transaction
- Premiums paid

Equity and EV level multiples.

EV is the cost of buying the right to the enterprise's core cash flow. It is the full takeout value of the firm in an M&A situation.

Key comp skills/issues:

- Getting an up-to-date NOSH
- FACTSET = FDS coding
- Documenting your work
- Fully diluted equity values using the treasury or buy-out method
- Net debt calculation
- Pension deficit and operating lease commitment adjustments
- NCI adjustments
- JV and associates implications
- Comp output sheet preparation, analysis and review
- Assessing the target and comparable fit
- Equity value breakdown
- Equity value sensitivities

Introduction

The discounted cash flow valuation (DCF) technique estimates the standalone intrinsic value of an entity as the sum of the present values of the expected future cash flows. It is a going concern valuation as it is based on the entity's ability to generate cash flows into the future.

The method is often used for:

- Buy-side M&A
- Sell-side M&A
- Fairness opinions
- Initial public offering (IPO) valuations
- Share repurchases
- Follow on financing
- LBO valuation sense check

DCF valuation is a fundamental valuation tool, however its relevance depends on specific circumstances and deal dynamics. It is especially relevant if there is a lack of comparable companies or transactions for relative valuation purposes. DCF valuations can also act as a benchmarking tool against other forms of valuation.

As the technique focuses on cash flow, there is less scope for accounting manipulation or inconsistency to impact the valuation. However, the technique is highly sensitive to a number of key variables such as cash flow drivers, discount rates and terminal value calculations. As a result of such sensitivities, DCF valuations are usually associated with extensive sensitivity and scenario analysis.

DCF valuation is very popular with investment bankers and research Analysts. The method forces Analysts to be forward looking and to examine in more detail, the drivers of value and the entity's strategic and competitive positions. Arguably DCF makes Analysts think more about drivers of value, relative to comparable techniques.

As the theory behind DCF valuation is not complicated, it is relatively straightforward to put a DCF valuation model together. However, DCF valuations presented by Analysts can be very poor and lack professional substance. The Analyst must focus on developing a consistent valuation story ensuring the theoretical valuation assumptions are consistent with the drivers of value within the business.

For example, if the DCF valuation is forecasting improving profit margins, these must be justified. It is not just a case of stating that the company is increasing prices and reducing costs. The Analyst needs to support the assumption of improving margins with a background story, for example:

- Does the company have the competitive position to price set in the market?
- What competitive edge allows them to do this?
- What are the barriers to entry?
- Can these barriers to entry prevent new entrants eroding the margin development?
- What capital expenditure requirements will be necessary to develop and sustain a product in the market, whilst improving the margins?
- How will this capital expenditure be financed?

The assumptions must then be benchmarked against peers, broker research and industry reports. Is the valuation consistent with trading comps etc.?

DCF is not an end in itself but primarily a discussion and negotiation tool. The negotiation must be built on a solid foundation, with all drivers supported by a strong story. Failure to do this will place Analysts in a weak negotiating position.

Summary

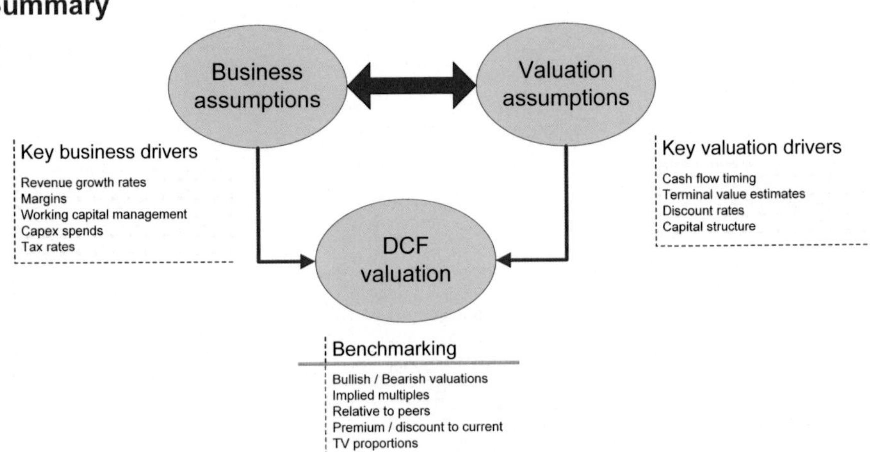

DCF valuation – a six-step structured approach

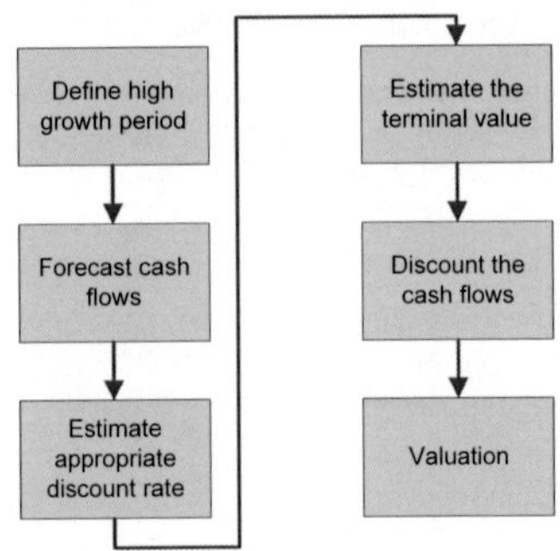

The DCF valuation process has been broken down into a six step approach. These steps provide a structure to completing the valuation and should ensure that the key decisions are considered at the right time during the valuation process.

As with the trading and transaction comps chapters, the target case study company will be Hershey Inc. The process will be applied to Hershey, in order to illustrate the process of putting a robust DCF valuation together.

Step 1: Define the high growth period

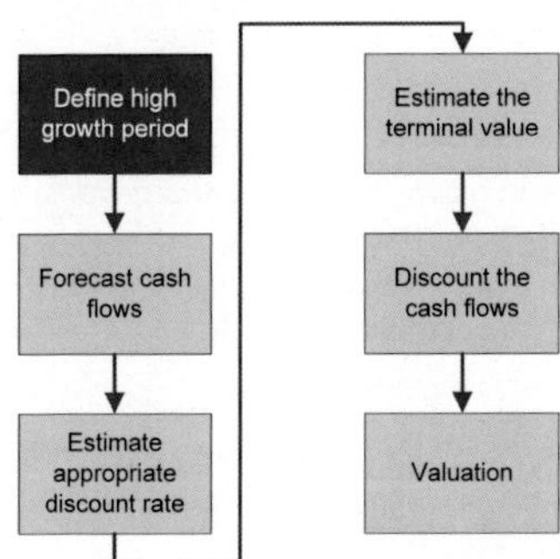

The foundation of a DCF is that the value of a company is the present value of a stream of cash flows generated by the company. The issue of 'how long should the cash flow forecasting period be' must be addressed before we can start answering other key questions like:

- What is the definition of this cash flow?
- What discount factor should be applied in order to discount these cash flows?

Hershey Inc was founded in 1894 by Milton S Hershey and is one of the oldest chocolate companies in the US. Attempting to estimate how long this company will continue to generate cash flows for is almost impossible. Will the firm continue for another 15, 20 or 50 years? Arguably the decision as to whether a cash flow stream will continue for 40 or 50 years is almost pointless, as the impact of discounting on a cash flow stream so far in the future makes the difference largely immaterial.

To deal with this most DCF models assume a two stage growth profile:

- A high growth (visible) period followed by
- A constant growth (or terminal value) period

High growth period

The high growth period is the time that the target company is expected to have a competitive advantage and is growing at a rate that exceeds that of its peers. The length of this high growth period is one of the key assumptions in a DCF valuation.

This high growth period should be driven by fundamentals.

High growth firms would be expected to:

- Reinvest earnings
- Have a higher risk
- Invest in capex
- Generate a strong return on capital

Forecast cash flows are estimated in detail for the high growth period. This forecasting is reviewed as part of Step 2. Towards the latter part of the high growth period, the company will start to mature and growth will start to slow down. This reflects the fact that high growth is not sustainable into perpetuity.

Firms cannot keep growing at rates greater than the rest of the economy because:

- Markets are competitive – high growth will attract new entrants and the excess returns will be shared across a wide spectrum of market agents.
- Barriers to entry erode – what are the barriers to entry now? How long can they be maintained? How strong will they remain?
- Technological advances create new markets.

The longer the high growth period, the more detailed forecasting will be required. Therefore longer high growth periods will introduce additional forecasting risk into the valuation.

The Length of the High Growth Period

The length of the high growth period is often driven by convention. Most DCF models Analysts come across will be two stage models with five or ten year high growth periods. Some industry teams such as utilities and infrastructure will run DCF valuations with high growth periods as long as 20 to 25 years.

There is no requirement for Analysts to be constrained to conventional five or ten year high growth period two stage DCF models. Often forcing a company's cash flow and competitive profile into an artificially constrained high growth period will lead to valuation consistency issues. These inconsistencies are often reflected in inappropriate terminal values.

The length of the high growth period should be assessed with reference to the sustainability of competitive advantage.

An assessment of competitive advantage can be completed with reference to such tools as:

- Porter's five forces competitive analysis
- SWOT analysis
- PEST analysis
- Product life cycle analysis
- BCG matrix analysis

These tools will provide information supporting the source and possible sustainability of the competitive advantage.

Terminal period

The high growth period will be followed by a period of constant growth known as the terminal value period. The terminal value period is where the company has matured and is typified by a constant rate of cash flow growth or decline.

For now, the value of the terminal period will be estimated on the basis of a constant rate of cash flow growth. However as we will see later, there are a number of terminal value estimation options (covered in step 4):

A typical two-stage DCF valuation model

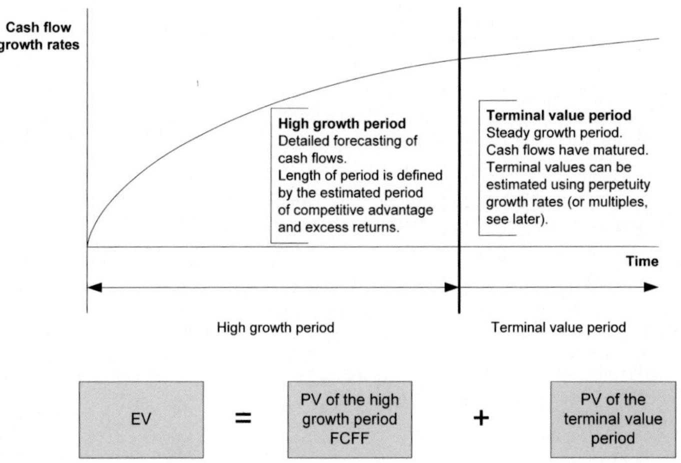

EV = PV of the high growth period FCFF + PV of the terminal value period

Step 2: Forecast cash flows

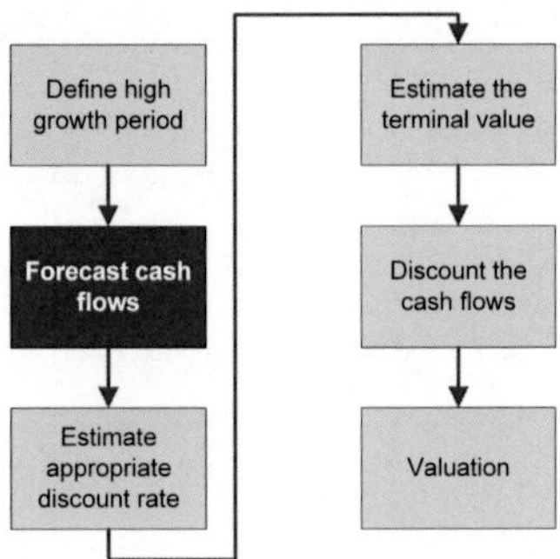

DCF valuations are based on cash flow forecasting. One of the reasons why accounting is such a key skill for Analysts is the need to be able to derive and analyze cash flows for valuation purposes.

The DCF technique is based on value being driven by the present value of the company's cash flow stream. The cash flow definition depends on what level of valuation is being sought. Just like trading and transaction comps, a DCF valuation can be performed at the equity or enterprise value level.

Enterprise value level DCF valuations are the most common so this chapter will focus on DCF at the enterprise value level. However, reference will be made to equity level valuations later on.

Just as a recap: EV is the cost of buying the right to an enterprise's core cash flows. It is the full takeout value of the firm in an M&A situation.

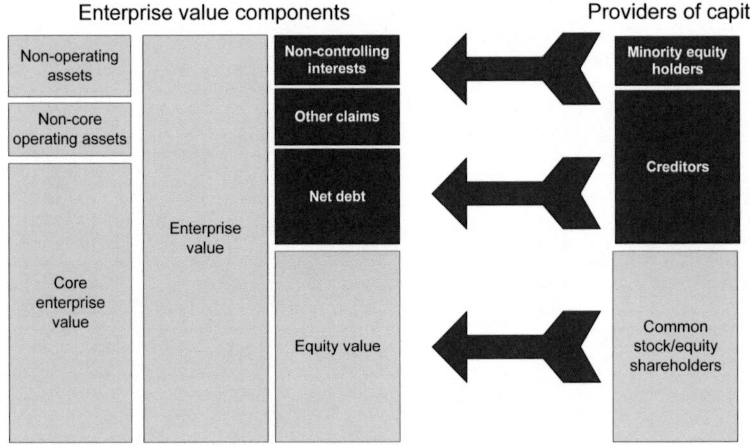

If an EV level DCF valuation is being performed, the cash flows being discounted must be those that belong to both the debt and equity providers of capital. This cash flow is known as free cash flow to firm (FCFF).

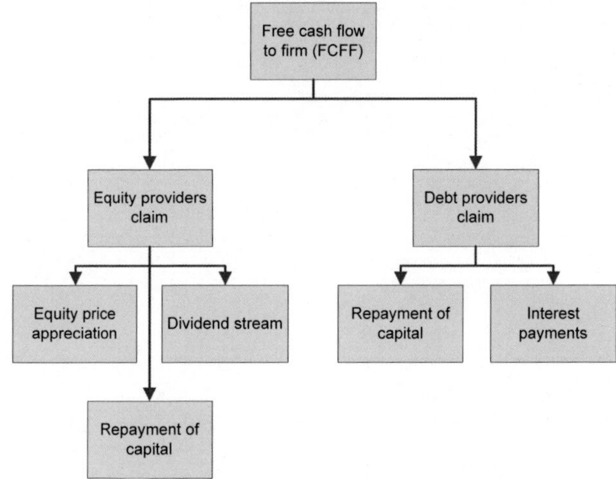

An alternative way of approaching the FCFF definition is to think of it as the cash flow pool owned by the providers of capital. Out of this pool, dividend and interest payments will be made and capital can be repaid. Any remaining cash flow is reinvested within the company. Cash flow reinvestment should generate a return that can drive future FCFF growth and consequently the equity price.

Therefore, the FCFF cash flow definition is a cash flow before:

- Any distributions to the providers of capital in the form of dividends or interest
- Any contributions from the providers
- Any returns of capital to the providers

Irrespective of whether the DCF is an equity or enterprise level valuation, the initial cash flow derivation is the same. Most FCFF derivations start from the revenue line followed by associated operating costs. This level of detail is very useful as it provides detailed information about the drivers of cash flow.

There are five key drivers of FCFF:

- Revenue growth rates
- EBITDA margins
- Changes in net working capital
- Capex (capital expenditure)
- Cash taxes on operations

Discounted Cash Flow Valuation

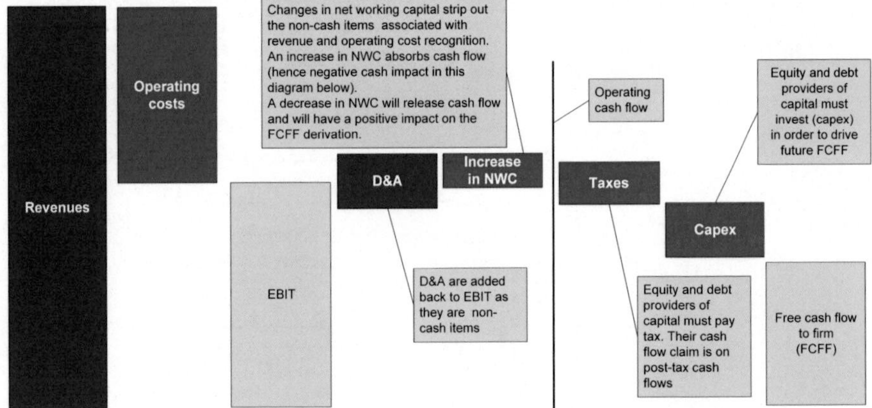

The support for this derivation is covered in the accounting chapters.

There is no standard FCFF presentation, however the most common forms are presented below:

Standard accounting derivation of FCFF

Revenues	4,947
Operating costs	(4,489)
EBIT	458
D & A	311
EBITDA	769
Decrease/(increase) in working capital	117
Capex (net)	(190)
Tax on operations	(170)
FCFF	**526**

NOPAT derivation of FCFF

Revenues	4,947
Operating costs	(4,489)
EBIT	458
Tax on operations	(170)
NOPAT (EBIT x (1-Tc))	288
D & A	311
Decrease/(increase) in working capital	117
Capex (net)	(190)
FCFF	**526**

Where:

NOPAT (NOPLAT) = Net operating profit after taxes

Tc = Effective tax rate on EBIT

Ultimately the only difference between the presentations is the location of the taxes line item disclosure.

FCFF derivation from net income

Some Analysts will derive FCFF from net income.

The typical net income FCFF derivation would be:

Net income	497
DA	311
Other non-cash items	(209)
Decrease/(increase) in working capital	117
Capex (net)	(190)
FCFF	**526**

Whatever the starting point, the FCFF estimation should result in the same output.

However, this method does not offer the driver transparency of a FCFF derivation working from the revenue line. It is not possible from this information to understand the drivers of the net income growth, such as revenue growth rates and margin development.

Tax on Operations

The inclusion of an incorrect tax number in the FCFF derivation is one of the most common errors found in DCF valuation work. The tax number used for FCFF purposes is not the tax number found in the financials.

Remember that we are deriving a FCFF. This is a cash flow that is claimed by both debt and equity providers of capital. Therefore it must be before any distributions to these providers and therefore is capital structure neutral. Any tax line in the financials will include the benefit of the interest tax shield. Therefore the interest tax shield must be excluded from the tax estimates so that only the unlevered tax is used in the FCFF forecasts.

There are a number of acceptable methods to strip out the impact of the interest tax shield from the FCFF forecasts. Two of the most common forms are outlined below:

Method 1 – EBIT is taxed using an unlevered tax rate

Method 1 forecasts EBIT and an unlevered tax rate in detail each year. The taxed EBIT (EBIT x (1 - unlevered tax rate)) or NOPAT (Net operating profit after taxes) is then adjusted for working capital changes and capex to arrive at FCFF.

Method 2 – Interest tax shield is calculated using a levered tax rate and removed from the tax line

Method 2 forecasts interest and a levered tax rate in detail each year. The interest tax shield is then calculated as Interest x Tax rate. This tax shield is then stripped out of the tax line per the accounts to give the unlevered tax figure for DCF FCFF purposes. This method requires detailed tax, debt and interest forecasting. It is usually associated with 3-statement DCF FCFF models.

Marginal vs. Effective Tax Rates

The tax rate can be either the marginal or effective tax rate. This terminology can cause a significant amount of confusion for Analysts.

The effective tax rate is an average tax rate based on accounting earnings metrics.

The marginal tax rate (often referred to as the statutory or fiscal tax rate) is the prevailing corporate rate of tax that applies to the last currency unit of taxable income. It is the legally imposed rate of tax.

The marginal tax rate varies from country to country. The marginal rate of tax is normally included in the financials (10K or annual report).

Federal statutory income tax rate	35.0%
Increase (reduction) resulting from:	
State income taxes, net of Federal income tax benefits	2.2
Qualified production income deduction	(1.7)
Business realignment initiatives	.7
Other, net	.5
Effective income tax rate	36.7%

Source: Hershey Inc 10K

When forecasting, there is a choice between using the effective and the marginal tax rate. It is far more reliable to use the marginal tax rate since the effective tax rate is really a reflection of the difference between the accounting and the tax rules. The CA Tip – Net operating losses illustrates tax forecasting using the marginal tax rate.

If a company is investing heavily in new capex, the effective tax rate will often fall below the marginal rate as the benefits of the capex expansion generate tax relief in the form of accelerated taxable allowances. However, as the company matures, the capex investment will normalize. As a result the effective tax rate will tend towards the marginal rate of tax.

The marginal rate is very useful when trying to strip out the impact of something (e.g. interest or losses) from the tax figure published.

Net Operating Losses (NOLs)

Taxes are not calculated on accounting profit, they are based on taxable income. Tax legislation varies from country to country. However, it is a relatively standard piece of tax legislation to allow companies who make taxable losses, to carry these losses forward and set them against future earnings.

The period over which the tax losses can be carried forward varies according to the tax legislation of the particular country. UK companies, for instance, can carry forward their losses into perpetuity. In the US, the carry forward is limited in most cases to 20 years. In Italy, the carry forward is only five years.

Tax losses can create a cash flow benefit for the company in the future and therefore have a value. The use of the effective tax rate works well for profitable companies paying taxes in full on taxable income but can be misleading when it has been substantially affected by items such as losses. If companies are utilizing previous losses to set against current and future profits, the effective tax rate will be lower whilst losses are being utilized and a tax loss memorandum should be modelled for greater forecast accuracy.

The tax calculation below is relatively standard. The tax is estimated using EBITDA as a proxy for taxable profit before depreciation and interest. Interest and tax allowable depreciation (capital allowances in the UK or Modified accelerated cost recovery (MACRS) in the US) are deductible against EBIITDA in most jurisdictions.

In this example, the company is generating taxable losses for the first two periods. These losses are accumulated in the tax loss memorandum (incurred line) and carried forward until the company becomes profitable. Once profitable, the carried forward tax losses are set against the taxable income from period 3 onwards (used line in the tax loss memorandum).

Tax calculation						
EBITDA	300	435	609	853	1,194	1,671
Less:						
Deductible interest	(75)	(83)	(91)	(100)	(110)	(121)
Tax allowable depreciation	(450)	(473)	(496)	(521)	(547)	(574)
Taxable income	(225)	(120)	22	232	537	976
Loss memorandum:						
Losses start	--	225	345	323	91	--
Incurred	225	120	--	--	--	--
Used	--	--	22	232	91	--
Losses end	225	345	323	91	--	--
Income subject to tax	--	--	--	--	446	976
Marginal tax rate	30.00%	30.00%	30.00%	30.00%	30.00%	30.00%
Cash taxes paid	--	--	--	--	134	293

The tax losses from the first two periods are sufficient to fully offset the taxable income from periods 3 and 4. Taxable income from period 5 is partially offset.

As a result of the tax legislation supporting this example, the company does not start paying tax until period 5, even though it was tax profitable from period 3.

This level of tax modeling is essential if a company has tax losses, however it will mean that the forecasts will have to model interest and therefore debt, as well as tax allowable depreciation. This adds further driver detail to the model and further forecasting risk.

Forecasting the FCFF drivers

FCFFs will be forecast for every period during the high growth period. As the high growth period comes to an end and competitive advantages are eroded, the FCFF profile will mature to a constant rate of growth, ready for the terminal value estimations.

As mentioned earlier, there are five key drivers of FCFF:

- Revenue growth rates
- EBITDA margins
- Changes in net working capital
- Capex (capital expenditure)
- Cash taxes on operations

Forecasting these drivers requires detailed knowledge of the company being valued. This knowledge can be accumulated from a number of areas:

- The financials
- Broker research
- Strategic assessment tools such as:
  - Porter's five forces competitive analysis
  - SWOT analysis
  - PEST analysis
  - Product life cycle analysis
  - BCG matrix analysis

The financials

The financials will provide historic information which is a useful starting point for the forecasts. However, if the historics are being used to derive forecast assumptions for FCFF, the historics must be normalized for non-recurring and non-core items.

Broker research

Broker research will provide the forecasts for the initial part of the high growth period (usually up to three years). Consensus broker estimates can also be used for FCFF forecasts.

Picking a Relevant Broker Report

Bloomberg

Broker research is available through:

- Bloomberg – key stroke Ticker <BRC> <GO>

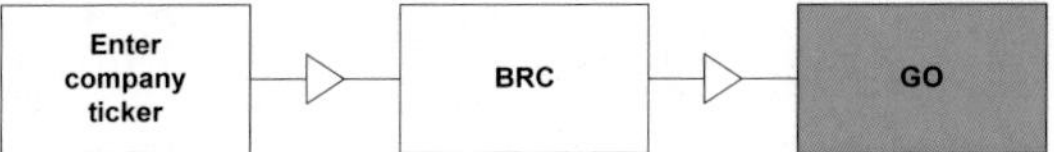

- Thomson One
- FACTSET
- Internal library services

A research search using an information provider will produce an extensive list of research notes. Many of these notes will be one page flash notes that contain new flash information.

DCF FCFF forecasting requires detailed forecast information.

The service providers will not provide access to all available research on a particular company. If a particular research piece is required, a charge may be levied. Research can be expensive. It is important that you are confident you are buying relevant and useful research.

The reason for using broker research is to ascertain the market's current perception of future expectations. The choice of the broker research is therefore dependent on:

- Dates – research brokers will produce in-depth research reports prior and after regulatory filing dates.
- Events – research notes are often event-driven. Major events such as M&A deals may trigger a detailed report.
- Numbers of pages – research reports of between 3-7 pages generally do not contain the requisite level of detailed financial information. Often 3-4 pages of these reports will be disclaimers. A lengthy report is likely to contain financial forecast information.
- Broker credibility – brokers are ranked each year. Some brokers are better than others. Know your ranked brokers and use them where possible.
- Know who the corporate broker is. A corporate broker's forecasts may not coincide with the market's consensus.

Broker or Consensus Numbers?

Broker research is more reliable than consensus estimates.

Individual broker research is written by experts who follow the company on a day-to-day basis. The research report will provide a detailed narrative supporting the forecast numbers. A good research broker should provide reliable information.

Consensus estimates are an average of the research submitted by individual brokers. Consensus estimates will hide outliers behind the average number. Also it is just a number, no narrative supporting the forecast consensus numbers will be provided. The most widely used consensus estimate is I/B/E/S (Institutional Brokers Estimation Service) owned by Thomson Reuters. It is a database of research estimates that date back as far as 1976 for US data and 1987 for international data.

Common sources of consensus estimates:

- I/B/E/S
- First call
- CAPIQ
- Thomson One
- Bloomberg

Reliance on one broker can also be problematic. An Analyst will not have an appreciation of the sentiment behind the forecasts in relation to the wider broker population. If you do not know sentiment regarding forecasts in the wider community, the impact of reliance on a single broker won't be known.

This over-reliance is overcome by either:

- Selecting more than one reputable broker with which to base forecasts on
- Benchmarking the broker forecasts against consensus estimates.

The drivers

- Revenue growth
- EBITDA margin
- Changes in net working capital
- Capex
- Cash taxes on operations

The illustration below provides an outline of the types of drivers that can be used for the key FCFF lines and how they should ideally be driven as the company forecasts mature. These drivers can be sector and industry specific. The drivers outlined below are generic for illustration purposes.

	Metric	Driver options	Maturity profile
	Revenues	Revenue growth rates – top line / divisional / geographic area / SBU	Long-term revenue growth rate
-	Operating costs	% of revenues	In line with long-term margins
=	EBIT		
+	D&A (other non-cash items)	Capex / Depn multiples	Multiples trend towards 1
=	EBITDA	Can be margin driven	Long-term sustainable margin
+/-	Changes in NWC	% change in revenues / Inventory days / Days receivable / Days payable	Stable NWC – in line with revenue and cost driver maturity
=	Operating cash flow		
-	Cash taxes on operations	Effective tax rate on EBIT / Detailed tax forecasting	Trend towards marginal tax rates
-	Capex (net)	% of sales/ Detailed capex forecasting	Sustainable capex % (sector specific)
=	Free cash flow to firm		

The focus of maturing the FCFF profile is to ensure that there is a smooth transition in the FCFF growth profile between the end of the high growth period and the terminal value period. Failure to smooth the profile can lead to terminal value estimation problems.

High Growth Period Disconnects on Terminal Period Transition

A common flaw in DCF valuation work is the failure to mature the FCFF profile as it approaches the end of the high growth period. Terminal value estimations make use of the high growth period forecasts. If the forecasts are too bullish, the terminal values will be overstated. The DCF can then look inconsistent, over-valued and starts to lose credibility.

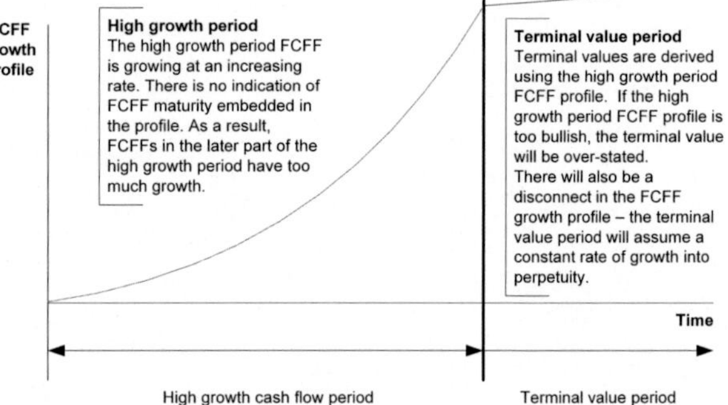

An inability to appropriately mature the FCFF within the defined high growth period is normally an indication that the high growth period is not long enough. Extend the high growth period if the FCFF profile cannot be matured within the timeframe.

A more appropriate FCFF profile:

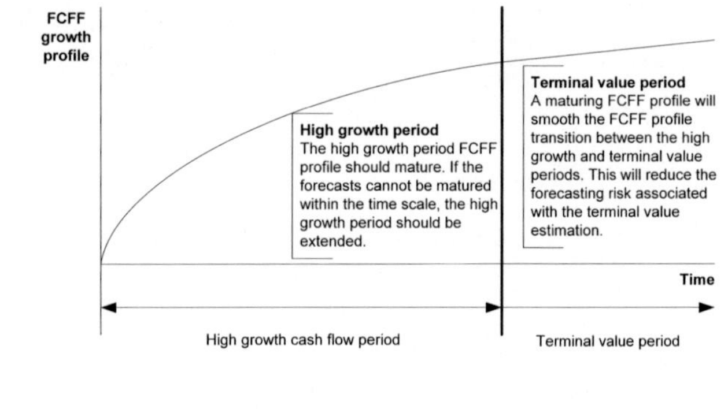

Hershey FCFF drivers and high growth period forecasts (2010-2019)

The extract below illustrates the forecast FCFF for Hershey Inc.

The FCFF forecasts were derived from three sources:

1. Historic 07-09 numbers. This information was sourced from Hershey's 10K filing. The historic information has been normalized in order to present a consistent set of information from which to forecast.
2. Forecast 10-11 numbers. This information was sourced from a research broker. The numbers were reconciled so that the broker adjustments were understood. The research numbers were also benchmarked against other brokers and consensus estimates (see CA Tip Broker or consensus numbers? – above)
3. Forecast 12-19 numbers. The use of historic and broker information provides a five year platform with which the Analyst can now forecast the remainder of the high growth period FCFF profile. (The in-house inputs are denoted by the blue font and yellow background). The FCFF growth by 2019 has matured to 2.68%. Capex ($166m) is slightly in excess of depreciation ($158m), thus suggesting capex is mainly maintenance expenditure. This level of capex should be sufficient to maintain a revenue growth rate of 2.00% (2019 growth rate assumption below). The EBITDA margins, effective tax rates and working capital have stabilized. All of which is indicative of a mature FCFF profile.

Forecast drivers	31 Dec 07	31 Dec 08	31 Dec 09	31 Dec 10	31 Dec 11	31 Dec 12	31 Dec 13	31 Dec 14	31 Dec 15	31 Dec 16	31 Dec 17	31 Dec 18	31 Dec 19
Revenues growth		3.78%	3.21%	3.02%	2.49%	3.20%	3.00%	3.00%	3.00%	2.65%	2.50%	2.30%	2.00%
EBITDA margin	15.54%	16.34%	19.70%	19.82%	19.82%	19.80%	19.80%	19.80%	19.80%	19.80%	19.80%	19.80%	19.80%
Capex/Sales	3.84%	5.12%	3.30%	3.21%	3.49%	3.20%	3.00%	2.98%	2.80%	2.70%	2.60%	2.40%	2.40%
Capex/Depn	0.61x	1.06x	0.96x	0.96x	1.08x	1.05x	1.05x	1.05x	1.05x	1.05x	1.05x	1.05x	1.05x
Decr/(incr) in w'cap/ ∆ in sales		(71.12%)	(54.55%)	20.63%	(70.59%)	(30.00%)	(24.00%)	(20.00%)	(18.00%)	(16.00%)	(14.00%)	(12.00%)	(10.00%)
Tax/EBIT (unlevered tax rate)	37.17%	36.78%	35.41%	34.90%	34.97%	35.00%	35.00%	35.00%	35.00%	35.00%	35.00%	35.00%	35.00%

Broker/In-house forecasts	31 Dec 07	31 Dec 08	31 Dec 09	31 Dec 10	31 Dec 11	31 Dec 12	31 Dec 13	31 Dec 14	31 Dec 15	31 Dec 16	31 Dec 17	31 Dec 18	31 Dec 19
Revenues	4,947	5,134	5,299	5,459	5,595	5,774	5,947	6,126	6,309	6,477	6,639	6,791	6,927
EBIT	458	590	861	900	929	967	1,008	1,039	1,081	1,116	1,150	1,189	1,213
D&A	311	249	183	182	180	176	170	174	168	167	164	155	158
EBITDA	769	839	1,044	1,082	1,109	1,143	1,178	1,213	1,249	1,282	1,314	1,345	1,372
EBIT	458	590	861	900	929	967	1,008	1,039	1,081	1,116	1,150	1,189	1,213
Tax (excl interest tax shield)	170	217	305	314	325	339	353	364	378	391	403	416	425
Cash flow													
Capex	190	263	175	175	195	185	178	183	177	175	173	163	166
Decr/(incr) in w'cap	117	(133)	(90)	33	(96)	(54)	(42)	(36)	(33)	(27)	(23)	(18)	(14)
FCFF	526	226	474	626	493	566	605	631	661	690	717	747	767

Free cash flow to equity (FCFE)

The analysis so far has focused on FCFF. A FCFF DCF will produce an EV valuation. The EV can be broken down to equity value very easily, as was demonstrated in the comps chapters.

Some sector teams may however use the free cash flow to equity model (FCFE). FCFE does not represent a huge departure from the traditional dividend discount models. One way to think of FCFE is that it is the potential dividend stream to equity holders or it is the cash flow that belongs to equity providers of capital.

The derivation of FCFE is illustrated below. It is just an extension of the FCFF definition taking into consideration distributions to and net contributions from debt capital providers:

Revenues	4,947
Operating costs	(4,489)
EBIT	458
DA	311
EBITDA	769
Decrease/(increase) in working capital	117
Capex (net)	(190)
Tax on operations	(170)
FCFF	526
Interest tax shield	41
Interest paid	(118)
Net debt issued	45
Preferred dividends	(14)
FCFE	480

FCFF and FCFE models should produce the same valuations in theory.

The FCFF models are preferred as they are easier to apply in practice. FCFE models require the forecasting of interest and therefore debt line items. These can be subjective line items to forecast and add further risk to the model.

Step 3: Estimate appropriate discount rate

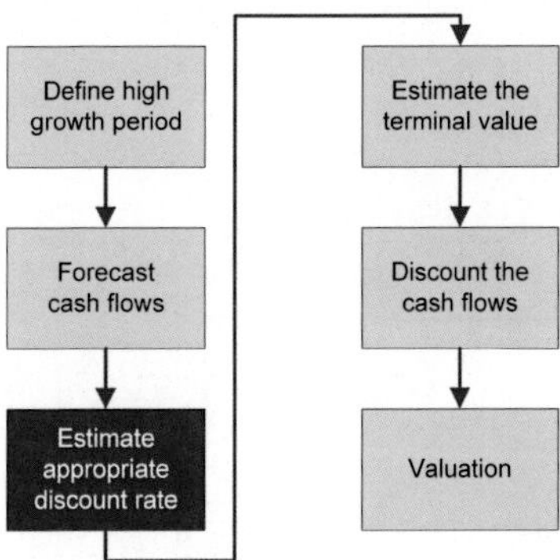

DCF valuation is built on a foundation of present values and discounting. Picking an appropriate discount rate is therefore a fundamental decision.

There are a number of key issues that must be addressed:

1. The discount rate must be consistent with the cash flow being discounted.
2. The discount rate must be justifiable – it is one of the most sensitive inputs in the DCF valuation.

Focusing on FCFF DCF valuations:

- FCFF is a cash flow that belongs to or is claimed by debt and equity providers of capital:

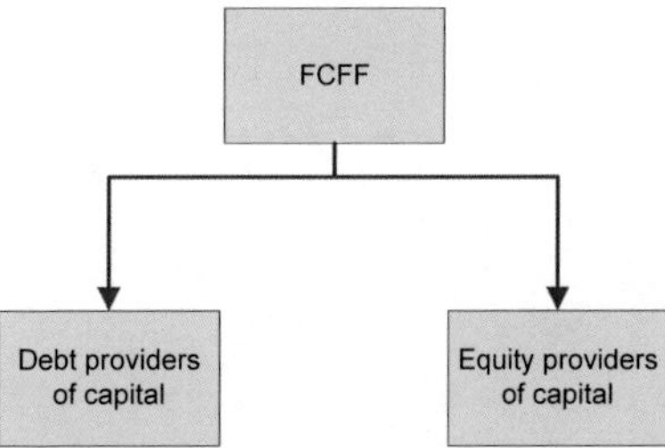

The present value of this cash flow stream must therefore be discounted by applying a cost of capital to the cash flows that reflects the costs of both capital providers.

An equity cost of capital and a debt cost of capital must be estimated. These costs of capital are then averaged in proportion to the market values of the long-term target capital structure. This average is called a weighted average cost of capital (WACC). This WACC is then used to discount the future cash flows of the company back to present value. The act of discounting the future cash flows risk adjusts the cash flows in present value terms.

A similar logic is used for discounting FCFE back to its present value. The FCFE is a cash flow that belongs to or is claimed only by equity capital providers. Therefore the present value is calculated by discounting the FCFE by the cost of equity capital only.

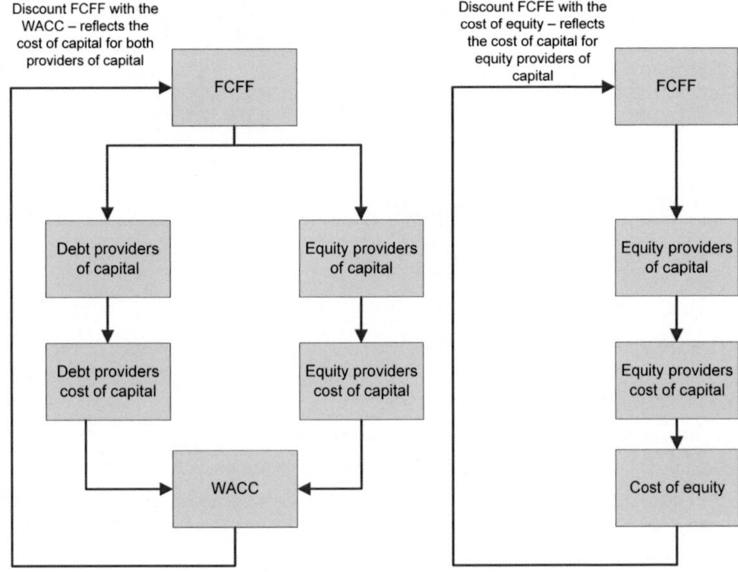

The key issue at this stage is to ensure that the right cash flows (FCFF vs. FCFE) are discounted with an appropriate and consistent cost of capital.

In summary:

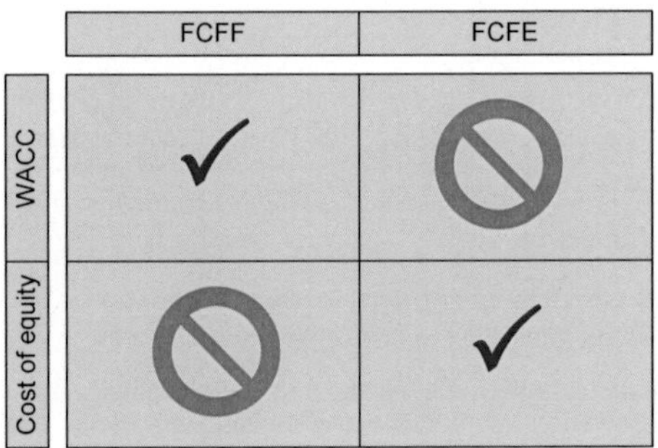

Cost of capital

The cost of capital demanded by the capital providers compensates them for the risks they adopt when investing. The higher the risk, the higher the return capital providers will demand. The higher returns are reflected in a higher cost of capital.

Equity capital providers will demand higher returns relative to debt providers.

This is because equity:

- Returns (dividends) are not fixed or guaranteed
- Ranks lower than debt on liquidation
- Has the last claim on the assets

Debt capital providers on the other hand have a fixed return and rank higher than equity providers in terms of distributions and liquidation. Debt capital providers can also have their investment secured on the assets on the company. In most tax jurisdictions, the interest paid to debt capital providers is tax deductible. This reduces the net cost of debt capital from the company's perspective.

The cost of capital for any capital provider is based on the same fundamentals:

The Marginal Investor

Bloomberg

The cost of capital estimated for use in a DCF valuation should reflect that of the marginal provider of capital. However, it must be clarified that it is the marginal investor of the company being valued. The Bloomberg HDS screen provides an excellent source of shareholder information. Analyzing this information will provide an insight to the geographic location of the majority of the investors. This can be used as a proxy for the marginal investor.

Bloomberg key stroke:

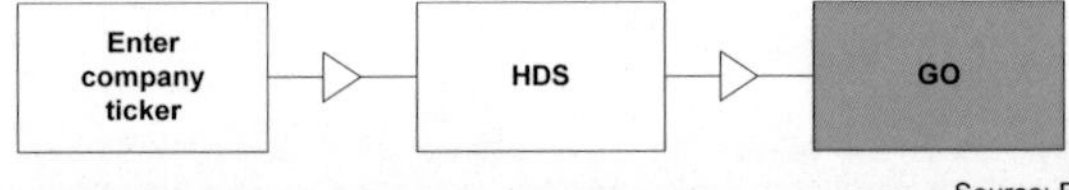

Source: Bloomberg

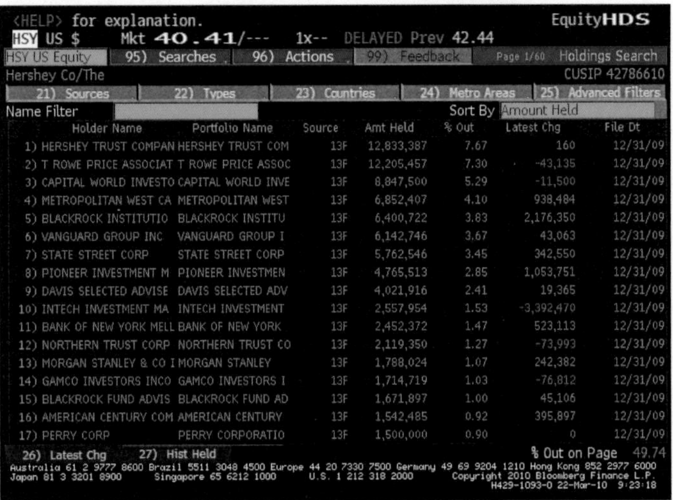

<HELP> for explanation. EquityHDS

HSY US $ Mkt 40.41/--- 1x-- DELAYED Prev 42.44

HSY US Equity | 95) Searches | 96) Actions | 99) Feedback | Page 1/60 Holdings Search

Hershey Co/The CUSIP 42786610

21) Sources | 22) Types | 23) Countries | 24) Metro Areas | 25) Advanced Filters

Name Filter Sort By Amount Held

Holder Name	Portfolio Name	Source	Amt Held	% Out	Latest Chg	File Dt
1) HERSHEY TRUST COMPAN	HERSHEY TRUST COM	13F	12,833,387	7.67	160	12/31/09
2) T ROWE PRICE ASSOCIAT	T ROWE PRICE ASSOC	13F	12,205,457	7.30	-43,135	12/31/09
3) CAPITAL WORLD INVESTO	CAPITAL WORLD INVE	13F	8,847,500	5.29	-11,500	12/31/09
4) METROPOLITAN WEST CA	METROPOLITAN WEST	13F	6,852,407	4.10	938,484	12/31/09
5) BLACKROCK INSTITUTIO	BLACKROCK INSTITU	13F	6,400,722	3.83	2,176,350	12/31/09
6) VANGUARD GROUP INC	VANGUARD GROUP I	13F	6,142,746	3.67	43,063	12/31/09
7) STATE STREET CORP	STATE STREET CORP	13F	5,762,546	3.45	342,550	12/31/09
8) PIONEER INVESTMENT M	PIONEER INVESTMEN	13F	4,765,513	2.85	1,053,751	12/31/09
9) DAVIS SELECTED ADVISE	DAVIS SELECTED ADV	13F	4,021,916	2.41	19,365	12/31/09
10) INTECH INVESTMENT MA	INTECH INVESTMENT	13F	2,557,954	1.53	-3,392,470	12/31/09
11) BANK OF NEW YORK MELL	BANK OF NEW YORK	13F	2,452,372	1.47	523,113	12/31/09
12) NORTHERN TRUST CORP	NORTHERN TRUST CO	13F	2,119,350	1.27	-73,993	12/31/09
13) MORGAN STANLEY & CO I	MORGAN STANLEY	13F	1,788,024	1.07	242,382	12/31/09
14) GAMCO INVESTORS INCO	GAMCO INVESTORS I	13F	1,714,719	1.03	-76,812	12/31/09
15) BLACKROCK FUND ADVIS	BLACKROCK FUND AD	13F	1,671,897	1.00	45,106	12/31/09
16) AMERICAN CENTURY COM	AMERICAN CENTURY	13F	1,542,485	0.92	395,897	12/31/09
17) PERRY CORP	PERRY CORPORATIO	13F	1,500,000	0.90	0	12/31/09

26) Latest Chg 27) Hist Held % Out on Page 49.74

Australia 61 2 9777 8600 Brazil 5511 3048 4500 Europe 44 20 7330 7500 Germany 49 69 9204 1210 Hong Kong 852 2977 6000
Japan 81 3 3201 8900 Singapore 65 6212 1000 U.S. 1 212 318 2000 Copyright 2010 Bloomberg Finance L.P.
H429-1093-0 22-Mar-10 9:23:18

Some Analysts make the error of performing a DCF valuation on a target company using the cost of capital of the acquiring company. A DCF valuation is a standalone valuation and must reflect the cost of capital of the incumbent providers of capital. The DCF is totally independent of the influence and motivations of the acquiring company.

Risk-free rate

The risk-free rate is the return on a risk-free asset, where the actual return is equal to the expected return. For an asset to be considered risk-free it must have:

- No default risk
- No re-investment risk (i.e. no uncertainty about re-investment rates)

Therefore any investment (debt or equity provision to a company) will demand a premium over and above the risk-free return. In practice, the risk-free benchmark rate is usually taken to be a government bond. Most OECD government bonds are 'nearly' risk-free and act as an appropriate proxy for a risk-free rate.

Some government bonds are not appropriate proxies for risk-free rates, especially if there is any risk of default.

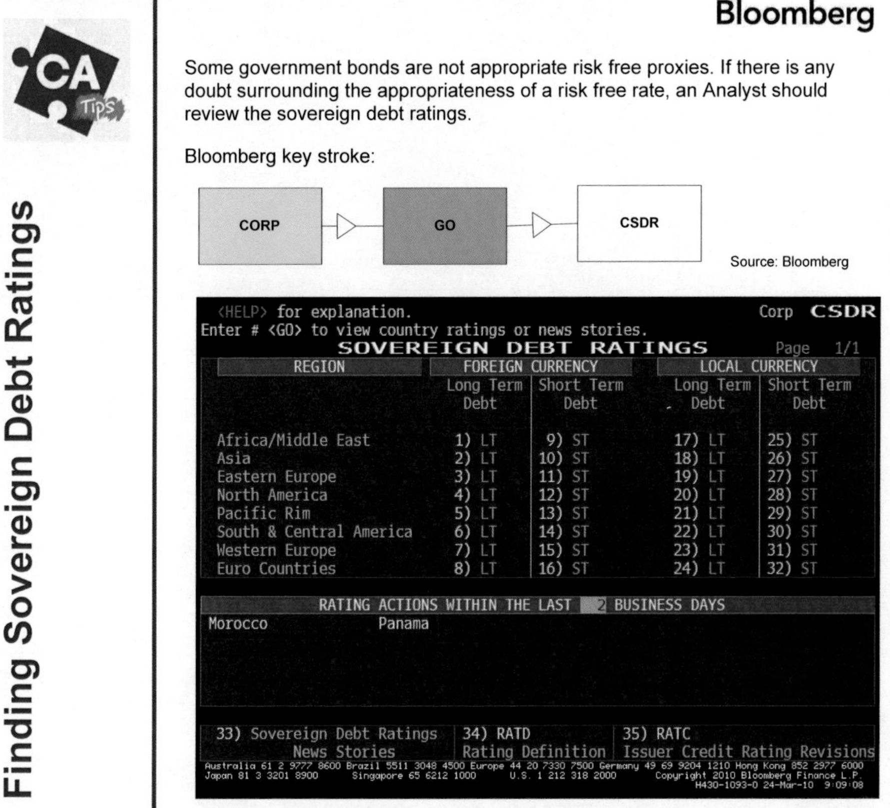

Some government bonds are not appropriate risk free proxies. If there is any doubt surrounding the appropriateness of a risk free rate, an Analyst should review the sovereign debt ratings.

Bloomberg key stroke:

Source: Bloomberg

Risk-free Rate Proxies

Bloomberg

Government bonds are issued with different maturities.

The key question is: What is the appropriate government bond maturity to use for a DCF valuation. The choice is an important one as the shape of a government bond yield curve can produce material differences in the risk-free rate.

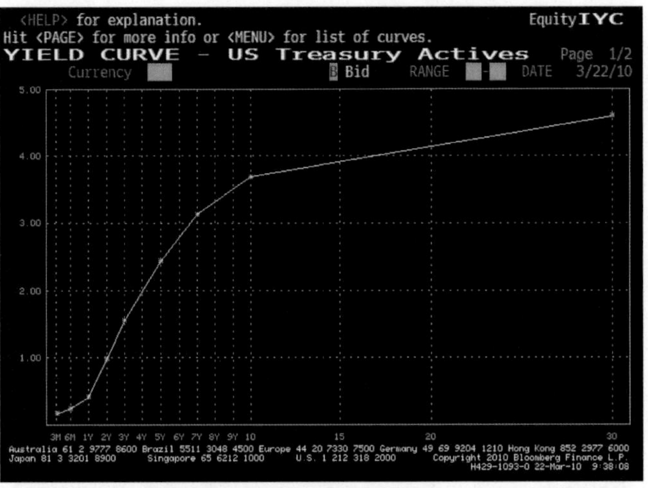

Source: Bloomberg

The US treasury yield curve example above illustrates how the choice of maturity (or the point on the yield curve) can give rise to materially different risk-free rates. (10 year at 3.6460% vs. 30 year at 4.5804%). Given that the risk-free rate is the benchmark for the cost of capital calculations, this type of difference will have a material impact on the WACC and subsequently the overall valuation.

The theory is that the risk-free rate and hence the choice of government bond maturity should reflect the length of the company's cash flow projections. A typical DCF has an investment horizon in excess of 30 years (taking into consideration the terminal value). Therefore the theory would suggest a 30 year government bond maturity would be an appropriate risk-free rate proxy.

In reality, most Analysts tend to use a 10 year government bond maturity for the risk-free rate. The 10 year market is more liquid than the 30 year market. As a result, any implied liquidity premiums will be smaller in the 10 year risk-free rate proxy.

It is generally assumed that domestic government bond rates are used as the risk-free proxy. For instance, US companies should use a US Treasury (for instance Hershey's risk-free rate would probably be based on a 10 year US Treasury). However, if multinational businesses fund their operations using global capital markets, a weighted average risk-free rate could be calculated.

Finding Risk-free Rates

Bloomberg

Typically, Analysts will use a 10 year government bond as a risk-free proxy and a benchmark for the cost of capital calculations. This information is relatively easy to find for mature markets.

The usual sources are:

- Front page of The Financial Times
- Wall Street Journal
- Bloomberg IYC screen

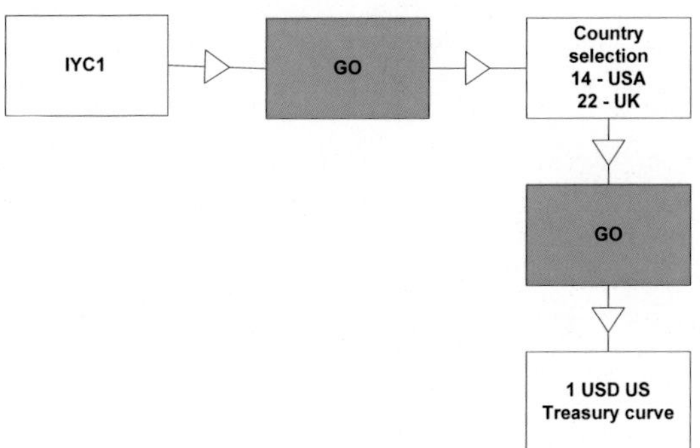

- Bloomberg BTMM page (Money Markets screen)

Key strokes:

- DCM Group
- Datastream

Building a Hershey WACC

The Hershey Inc WACC calculation will be built on a risk-free rate of 3.646%. This is the 10 year US Treasury rate taken from the Bloomberg IYC1 US Treasury screen in the last CA Tip. This rate will be the benchmark rate used to calculate Hershey's cost of equity and debt capital.

WACC calculation	
Risk-free rate	3.646%

Cost of debt (Kd)

The cost of debt is the return demanded by the debt providers of capital. It is calculated as a premium over and above the risk-free rate. Debt providers of capital face greater risk investing in corporates than in domestic government bonds (there are the odd exceptions to this statement!) and thus must be rewarded for this additional risk.

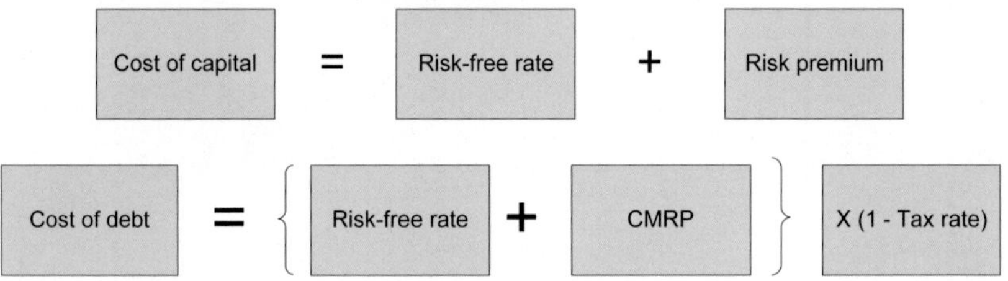

The additional premium included in the cost of debt calculation is known as the credit market risk premium or the credit spread. The higher the credit risk, the larger the credit market risk premium.

Interest paid is tax deductible for the company. Therefore the true cost of debt to the company is net of the interest tax shield.

Don't Double Count the Interest Tax Shield

The interest tax shield is included by convention in the cost of capital calculation. The tax shield can be dealt with in one of two ways:

- In the cost of debt calculation by expressing the cost of debt net of the tax shield
- In the WACC calculation directly

Most financial models tend to include the interest tax shield benefit in the cost of debt calculation, as this is the effective cost of debt capital to the company.

However, the tax shield benefit can only be included once in the DCF valuation. This is one of the reasons why the unlevered tax is included in the FCFF derivation as the tax shield is taken account of in the discounting.

Where to Find Credit Spreads

Public outstanding debt – find the current yields on traded debt:

- Bondware (www.bondware.com)
- Bondsonline (www.bondsonline.com)
- Bloomberg – key stroke:

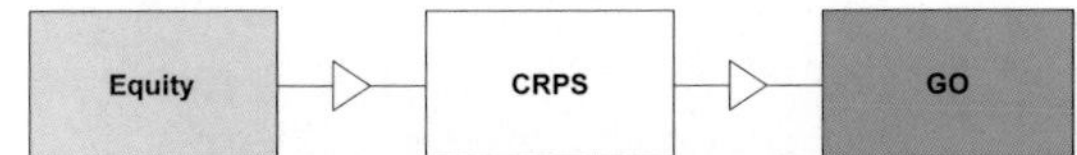

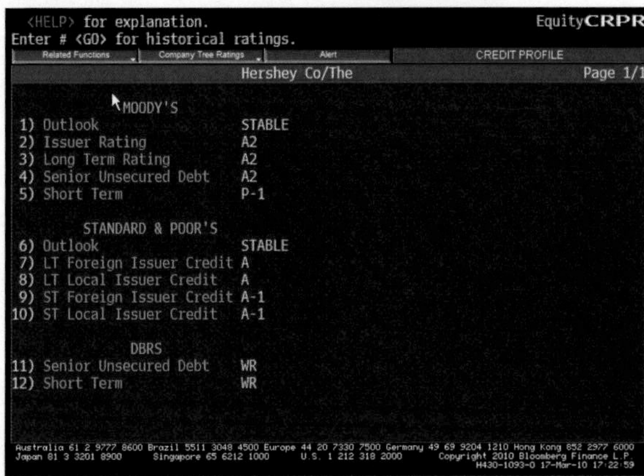

Source: Bloomberg

Credit spread:

- Check with the deal team leader
- Rating Advisory Team – check the credit rating and verify the current credit spread. If the company does not have a credit rating, review comparables and imply a credit rating and spread. If there are no suitable comparables, a synthetic credit rating can be estimated and credit spread implied. S&P's Corporate Rating Criteria provides guidance on their credit rating methodology.
- Talk to the Debt Capital Markets team
- Talk to the Leveraged Finance team if the credit rating is high yield
- Review financials for yields on recently issued bonds
- If no bonds have been issued – review recent bank borrowings
- Comparable company analysis – review comparable companies' recently issued public bonds
- Ask the client as appropriate

Building a Hershey WACC

Hershey Inc is a well-rated company with investment grade (A rated) issued bonds. The credit risk spread has been estimated at 96 basis points (or 0.96%). The US marginal income tax rate is 35%. The cost of debt, net of the interest tax shield, is 2.99%.

- The risk-free rate is a 10 year US Treasury rate taken from Bloomberg and cross-checked against the Wall Street Journal.
- The credit risk premium is based on the current spreads (at the time of writing) for US A rated bonds. The A rating was taken from the Bloomberg credit profile screen – see previous CA Tip.
- The income tax rate was cross-checked against the Hershey 10K.

WACC calculation - cost of debt	
Risk free rate	3.646%
CRP	0.96%
Tax rate (marginal)	35.00%
Cost of debt	2.99%

Cost of equity (Ke)

The cost of equity is the return demanded by the equity providers of capital. It is calculated as a premium over and above the risk-free rate. The equity providers of capital face greater risk investing in corporates than domestic government bonds and thus must be rewarded for this additional risk.

This additional premium for risk will be larger than that demanded by the debt providers of capital. The equity providers face greater risk than the debt providers due to the equity ranking on distributions and liquidation relative to debt providers.

Most Analysts will use the capital asset pricing model (CAPM) to estimate the cost of equity. CAPM has been the established cost of equity theory since the 1970s. Even though empirical studies have questioned its ability to estimate a reliable cost of equity, it is still the most common form of cost of equity estimation.

Alternative theories are available such as:

- Arbitrage pricing theory
- Multi-factor models

Both of the above theories are technically more advanced than CAPM. However, the difficulties associated with practical application and the communication of these theories to clients has led to reluctance to use these methods in practice.

CAPM

As with all costs of capital, the equity cost of capital is a risk-free rate plus a risk premium.

Assume for a moment that Hershey's equity shares are exactly as risky as the market. The cost of Hershey's equity would be the US ten year risk-free rate, plus a US equity market risk premium (EMRP).

What exactly is EMRP?

The EMRP can be estimated in practice in two ways:

- The historical EMRP
- The implied EMRP

The historical EMRP is the most common method of deriving an EMRP. In most cases, the EMRP is an average return of a stock index, over an extended period of time (Rm), over and above the average risk-free return (Rf) for the same period. The EMRP therefore is an average (Rm-Rf).

The historic EMRP estimation is dependent on:

- The time horizon of observation
- Whether the average is produced using an arithmetic or geometric mean

The historic EMRP is then used as a basis for a forward looking premium in the cost of equity calculation.

There are obvious dangers using the past as a predictor of the future. The approach also assumes that the risk aversion of the investors and the riskiness of the stock index has not changed over time.

The implied equity EMRP is a more theoretical approach that backs out the EMRP from current equity prices. The approach follows the theory that the value of a share (in a perfect world) equals the present value of the future cash flows. Treating all the variables as known and correct (i.e. future growth rates, risk-free rates etc.) the model derives what the EMRP must be to give the current equity stock price.

The model makes sense theoretically. However, it works on the assumption that the forecasting is correct and the market is currently placing a fair valuation on the equity under examination.

Where to Find EMRP?

Equity risk premiums can be sourced from:

- Ibbotson Associates (www.ibbotson.com)
- Research
- Sales and Trading
- Damodaran (www.stern.nyu.edu/~adamodar)

Most Analysts use an EMRP between 3-6% – depending on the stock index and the valuation being sought.

Some banks recommend the use of a macro-region EMRP due to companies accessing increasingly globalized capital markets.

Ibbotson measures the risk premium as the historical performance margin of stocks relative to Treasuries between 1926 and the present, using an arithmetic mean. This implicitly assumes that over a long period of history, we will see convergence to the right EMRP number.

Beta

Hershey, as a single stock, does not replicate the risk of the US equity market. It does not have the same risk as the market.

The beta variable in the cost of equity calculation adjusts the EMRP to reflect relative volatility of an individual stock.

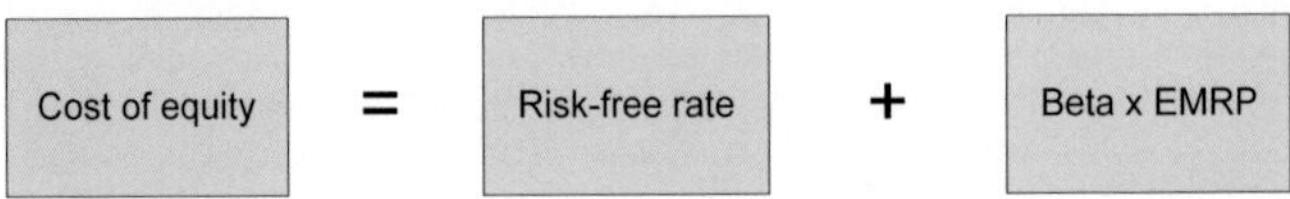

More formally, beta is described as the coefficient that measures the stock's volatility relative to a market index. It is often described as the covariance (co-variance is a measure of co-movement between two variables) of a stock in relation to an overall market index.

Historical betas

Betas are normally estimated by regressing historical individual stock returns against the market returns. The slope of the regression line is the beta of the stock.

	What this means?	Possible sectors
ß > 1.0	The stock is generally riskier than the market	Technology
ß = 1.0	The stock is generally as risky as the market	Retail
ß < 1.0	The stock is generally less risky than the market	Utility

Beta Ranges

Raw betas normally fall within the range 0.4-1.8. Beta results that fall outside this range should be:

- Re-examined,
- Regressed again with different parameters
- Compared to peers

Betas that approach close to zero suggest that the stock has little or no correlation with the market. A government security for instance may have a beta close to zero. It is possible to have beta less than zero. This suggests that the stock moves in the opposite direction to the market. Gold is often described as having a negative beta.

Bloomberg is a commonly used source for betas.

The Bloomberg key strokes are:

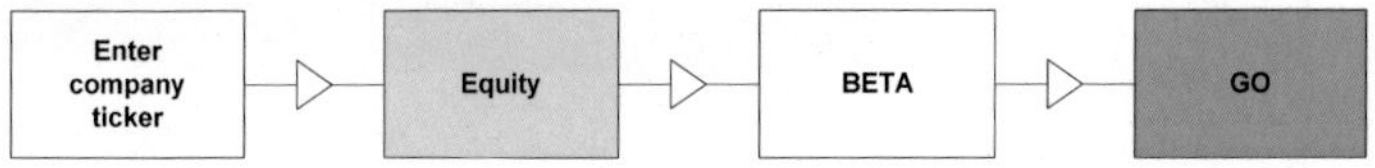

Bloomberg runs a historical regression in order to estimate the beta. However, the regression requires a number of parameters to be defined:

- The time horizon of observation
- The frequency of observation
- The market index

The Bloomberg screen below is a beta regression for Hershey Inc. The parameters were defined as:

- The time horizon of observation – two year range
- The frequency of observation – weekly observations
- The market index – S&P 500 index

These decisions are essential and can have a material impact on the regressed beta and subsequently on the overall valuation.

See CA Tip – Differences in beta parameters.

Beta Ranges (cont.)

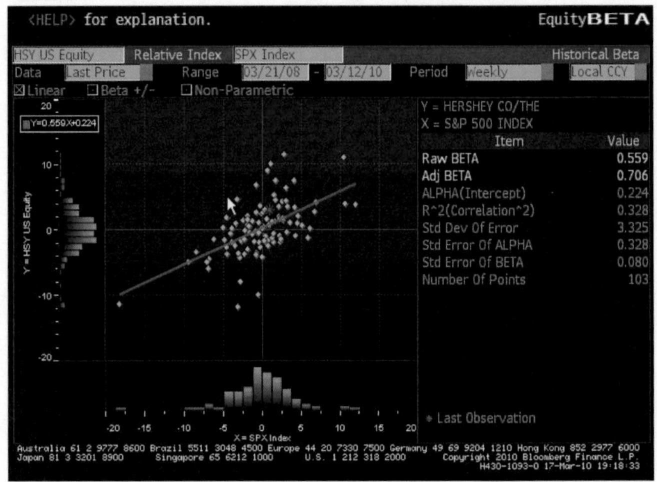

In this example, the raw beta (the slope of the regression line) is 0.559 (the adjusted beta is 0.706 and will be discussed later).

What does this actually mean? The 0.559 provides an empirical indication of the relationship between the stock and market returns. It suggests that Hershey is less risky relative to the market. Therefore the cost of capital demanded by the Hershey stockholders should be less that that demanded from the market as a whole (i.e. a lower risk premium that the EMRP).
The beta of 0.559 when multiplied by the EMRP, will factor down the overall risk premium. The beta effectively tailors the EMRP to the individual Hershey stock under examination.

Differences in Beta Parameters

The Bloomberg regression requires a number of parameters to be defined:

- The time horizon of observation
- The frequency of observation
- The market index

The beta parameter choices are key to generating a statistically relevant historical beta regression. There is often a temptation to extend the frequency of observations and the length of time horizons observed, in order to improve the statistical quality of the beta.

Including a longer time horizon as part of the regression choice can produce a beta that is increasingly irrelevant. Companies evolve and change over time, as do their risk profiles. Performing a ten year historical regression will provide more data points for the regression. However, these data points may be in relation to a very different company to the one that needs to be valued today.

Most beta providers allow daily, weekly, monthly and quarterly observations. Obviously the more frequent the observation, the more observations the regression will observe. The regression will need a critical mass of observations in order to produce a statistically reliable regression plot. However, the choice between using monthly data and weekly data involves a trade-off between any bias caused by infrequency of trading and the preference towards recent data.

The choice of which market to regress the individual stock against can have a material impact on the beta output. For instance, British Airways (now International Airlines Group) is a British incorporated company, but it is a multi-national business. Should the beta be regressed against a national index such as the FTSE 100 or would a global index like MSCI World be more suitable?

The beta parameter issues are highlighted with the Hershey betas below. Both betas were sourced from Bloomberg on the same day, but used different parameters for the regression:

Bloomberg two year weekly beta regressed against the S&P 500 index:

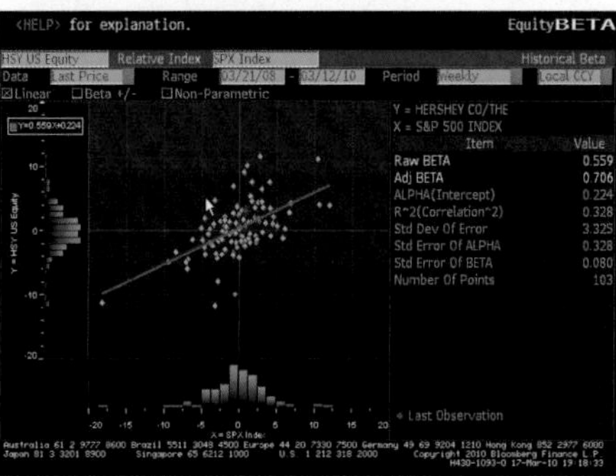

Differences (cont.)

Bloomberg five year monthly beta regressed against the S&P 500 index:

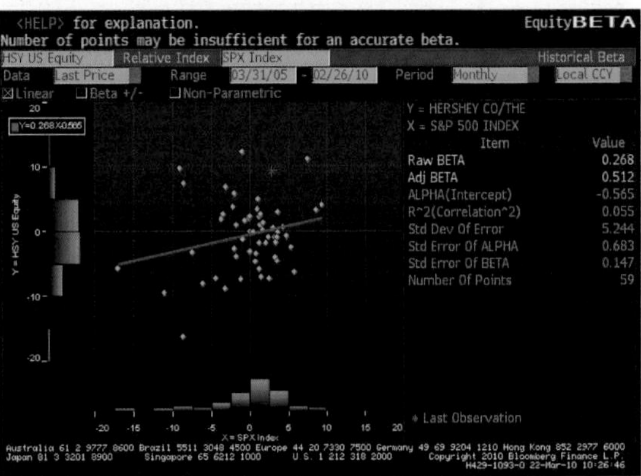

Alternative Beta Sources

Bloomberg is probably the most common source of regressed historical betas. However, there are a number of available alternatives:

- Barra (www.mscibarra.com) – Barra derives its betas using its own risk models. Their models produce a predicted beta that is a forecast of a stock's sensitivity to the market. The Barra beta is also known as the fundamental beta as it is derived from a range of 13 fundamental risk factors, such as size, yield, p/e ratios and industry risk exposure. Barra is often viewed as the best quality beta available, with Bloomberg as a strong and very accessible second choice.
- Datastream – current and historical betas (www.datastream.com)
- Capital IQ *(www.capitaliq.com/)*
- Morningstar *(www.morningstaronline.com)*
- Ibbotson (*www.ibbotson.com)*
- Value Line (www.valueline.com)
- S&P (www.standardandpoors.com)
- Risk measurement service (www.london.edu/index.html)
- AGSM (*www.agsm.edu.au)*
- Beta source (www.betasource.co.uk)
- Comparable betas – using comparable company betas to derive an appropriate beta
- Internal regressed betas – regress stock and market returns using Excel regression functionality

Bloomberg Data Interpretation

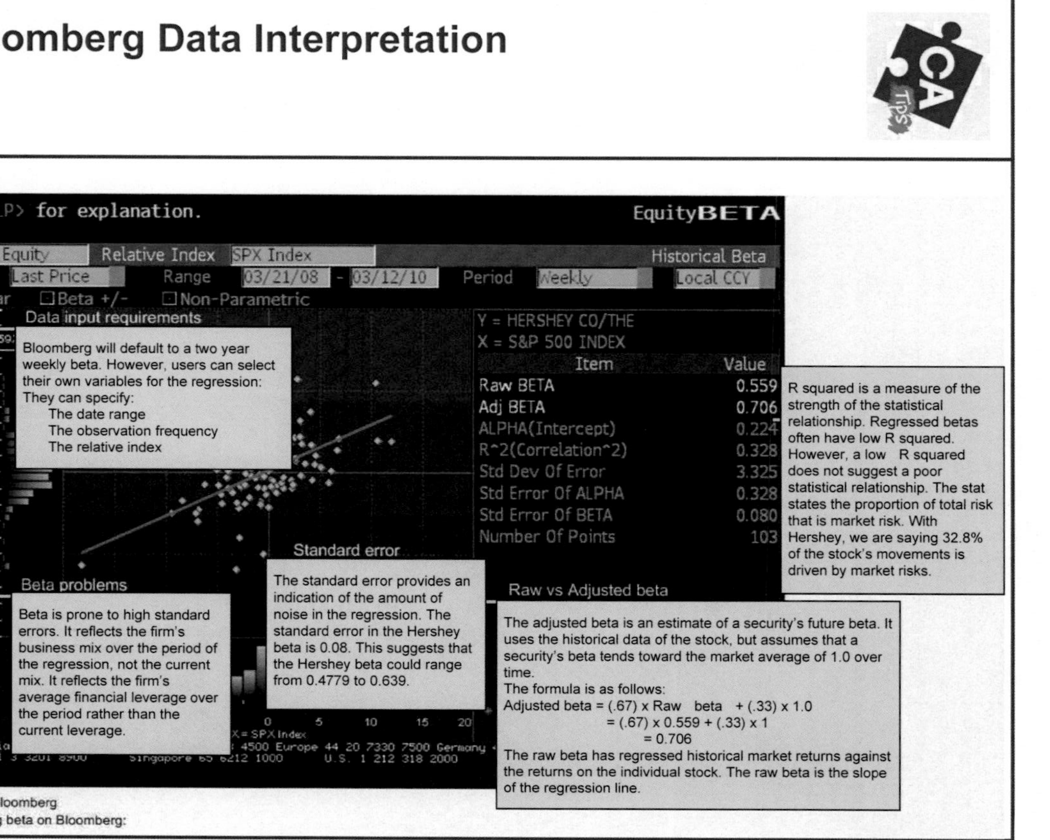

Source: Bloomberg

Accessing beta on Bloomberg:

The historical beta approach has a number of significant problems:

- It does not recognize that a company's operations change over time. A historical beta will only recognize the impact of a change in a company's risk profile slowly over time. For instance, RJR Nabisco divested its tobacco business in 1999. This immediately changed the risk profile of the group. A historical beta will only reflect this change as time progresses.
- A historical beta will be influenced by one-off events. The 1984 Union Carbide accident in India took place in the middle of a strong bull market. This negative company specific news had the effect of keeping the Union Carbide beta artificially low for most of the 1980s.
- The market index used to regress against the stock may be too narrowly defined and dominated by a few dominant stocks.
- The historical beta reflects the current financial risk only.

Overcoming historic beta issues

Adjusted betas

Historical betas are subject to the above criticisms. The bulk of these criticisms are a result of the historical nature of the beta estimation. A number of beta providers produce adjusted betas. The adjusted beta is an attempt to make a historical beta more forward looking.

It is generally accepted that estimated raw betas tend towards 1 over time. This phenomenon was first identified by Blume (1971) who found that adjusting estimated equity betas towards 1 improved their ability to forecast subsequent period stock returns.

One explanation is that the movement in estimated betas towards 1 over time reflects conscious decisions by management to keep the risk level of the firm around the average for the market. As firms grow, they take on more new investments. If managers consciously choose new projects to diversify, the aggregate firm's beta will tend towards 1.

See the above CA Tip – Bloomberg beta interpretation for an illustration of the adjusted beta calculation for Hershey Inc.

Re-leveraging beta to target

Regressed betas will reflect current leverage or financial risk. These betas are often referred to as levered or equity betas. If the current leverage is believed to be materially different to the target leverage, the beta can be adjusted or re-levered.

There are a number of different de-leveraging equations in the academic world. Most Analysts will use the method outlined below:

1. Obtain a regressed beta which will reflect current leverage. If the target leverage is materially different to the current leverage, the beta can be re-levered to the target leverage.
2. The levered beta is de-levered with a de-leveraging equation (see below). The levered beta is de-levered using the current D/E market value ratio and the prevailing marginal tax rate. The de-levered beta is also known as an asset beta. This beta reflects the risk profile of the company in the absence of leverage.
3. The unlevered beta is then re-levered using the target D/E ratio at market value using the re-leveraging equation below.
4. The re-levered beta is then substituted back into the existing CAPM equation in order to estimate the cost of equity.

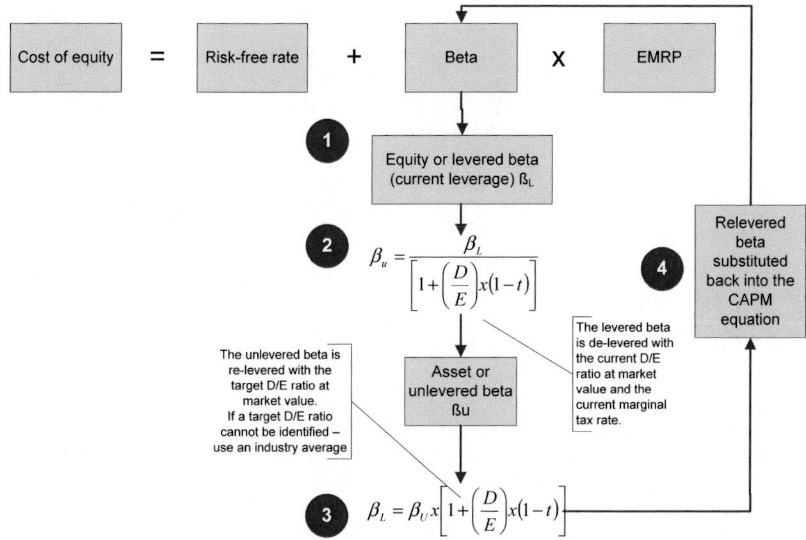

The re-levered beta improves on the standard regressed beta as it introduces a forward looking leverage into the beta. This is especially useful if the capital structure of the company is anticipated to change materially over the medium to long-term.

Comparable betas

A comparable beta is one that is derived from industry comparable companies, rather than regressing the historic returns of the stock against the market. Comparable betas are useful:

- If the company being valued has undergone significant operational changes that have materially altered its risk profile. These changes will not be captured by the regressed beta
- If the company being valued is unlisted or it is a division/subsidiary of a larger group
- If the company being valued does not have a service beta
- If the service beta is believed to be statistically unreliable

The estimation of a comparable beta follows a similar approach to the beta re-leveraging to target D/E.

1. A universe of comparable betas is identified. (Similar sector, size and systematic risk)
2. The comparable betas are de-levered using current D/E at market value ratios and the prevailing marginal tax rates relevant to each comparable company.
3. The now unlevered comparable betas are then re-levered using the target D/E ratio at market value for the target company. The mean/median of the re-levered comparable betas can be used. If there are significant outliers the median may be a better measure than using an average.
4. The re-levered beta is then substituted back into the existing CAPM equation in order to estimate the cost of equity.

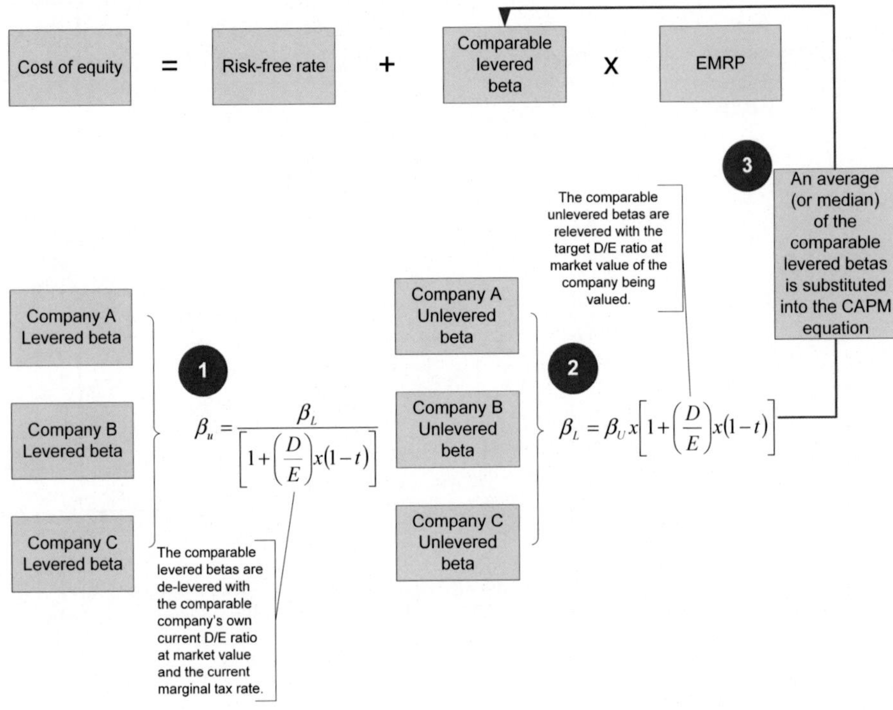
Cost of equity
=
Risk-free rate
+
Comparable levered beta
X
EMRP
3
An average (or median) of the comparable levered betas is substituted into the CAPM equation
The comparable unlevered betas are relevered with the target D/E ratio at market value of the company being valued.
Company A Levered beta
Company B Levered beta
Company C Levered beta
1
$\beta_u = \frac{\beta_L}{\left[1+\left(\frac{D}{E}\right)x(1-t)\right]}$
The comparable levered betas are de-levered with the comparable company's own current D/E ratio at market value and the current marginal tax rate.
Company A Unlevered beta
Company B Unlevered beta
Company C Unlevered beta
2
$\beta_L = \beta_U x\left[1+\left(\frac{D}{E}\right)x(1-t)\right]$

Small Cap Premiums

It has been argued in the past that CAPM is not a precise estimator of the cost of equity, especially when attempting to estimate small cap costs of equity. Because size is an important factor in determining risk, Analysts often include an additional small cap premium in the cost of equity estimation.

Ibbotson Associates provides the most popular source of small cap premiums as part of the benchmark publication Stocks, Bonds, Bills and Inflation (SBBI) yearbook. Ibbotson Associates measures the small stock premium using data going back to 1926. Other studies have examined the small stock premium over shorter time periods, but have arrived at similar results.

A recent edition of Ibbotson Associates' SBBI yearbook lists a size premium for small cap stocks of 3.47%. SBBI also shows that for very small companies, those falling in the tenth decile of the New York Stock Exchange, the size premium can approach 5.78%. A 350 basis point addition to the cost of equity will almost always have a material impact on the overall valuation derived from a DCF valuation.

The CAPM equation is therefore adjusted to:

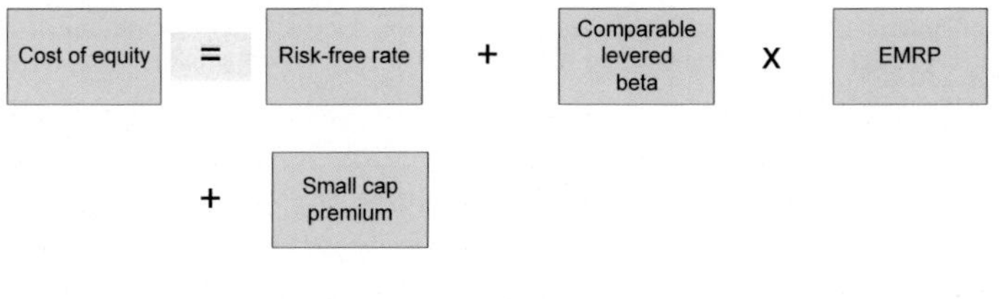

Building a Hershey WACC

The cost of equity is naturally higher than the cost of debt at 8.46% – this reflects the higher risk exposure of equity.

- The risk-free rate is a ten year US Treasury rate taken from Bloomberg and cross-checked against the Wall Street Journal. This is the same ten year US Treasury rate as the debt cost calculation.
- The beta was sourced from Bloomberg (two year weekly beta regressed against the S&P 500 market index)
- The EMRP of 6.82% was taken from the Bloomberg WACC screen and cross-checked against Value Line and CAPIQ for reasonableness.

WACC calculation - cost of equity	
Risk free rate	3.646%
Levered Bloomberg Adjusted Beta (2yr weekly)	0.706
EMRP	6.82%
Cost of equity	8.46%

The cost of equity calculation alters if the beta is sourced from comparables. The calculations below illustrate the comparable beta method in conjunction with the discussions above.

WACC calculation - cost of equity with comparable beta	
Risk free rate	3.646%
Comparable Beta	0.83
EMRP	6.82%
Cost of equity	9.31%

	Levered beta	Current D/E	Marginal tax rate	Unlevered beta	Target D/E	Target tax rate	Comparable beta
Company A	0.68	26.00%	30.00%	0.58	18.00%	35.00%	0.69
Company B	0.89	30.00%	28.00%	0.73	18.00%	35.00%	0.85
Company C	0.98	25.00%	32.00%	0.84	18.00%	35.00%	0.95
High	**0.98**			**0.84**			**0.95**
Mean	**0.85**			**0.71**			**0.83**
Median	**0.89**			**0.73**			**0.85**
Low	**0.68**			**0.58**			**0.69**

Weighted average cost of capital

The Weighted Average Cost of Capital (WACC) is the discount rate that will be applied to the forecast FCFF to produce an EV level DCF valuation.

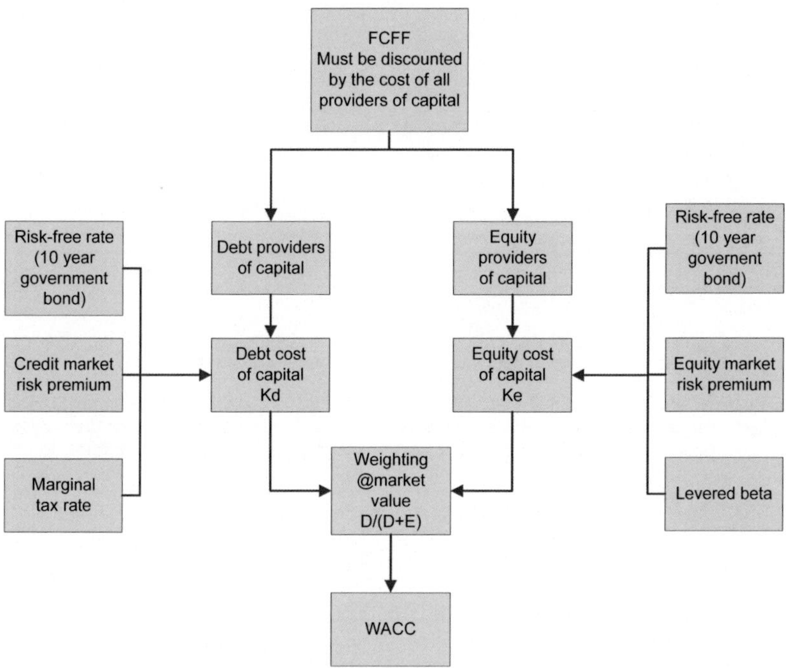

It reflects the opportunity cost to all capital providers weighted by their relative contributions to the total capital of the company.

However, the WACC itself should primarily reflect the company's business risk (i.e. expect to end up with very different WACCs if you are valuing a technology company and a utility operator.)

Technically the WACC weighting should not be based on the current weighting of the capital structure (the current D/(D+E) ratio).

The weighting is normally based on some measure of the:

- Target capital structure
- Long run capital structure
- Optimal capital structure

The capital structure weightings will be benchmarked against:

- Comparables (as a benchmark for long run capital structures)
- Current D/(D+E) market value ratios (the company's capital structure may be mature)

Capture all Forms of Capital

Analysts must watch out for all forms of capital (common, preferred, savings, tracker, mezzanine, bonds, debt, etc.) and make sure that they are included in the WACC calculation.

Building a Hershey WACC

Once the components of the WACC calculation are estimated – the cost of equity and debt – they are then weighted using an estimate of the target or long-term capital structure.

Hershey Inc is an established and mature business operating in a stable sector. Its credit rating and capital structure have been relatively stable for a number of years, therefore for the purposes of this WACC calculation, the current D/(D+E) at market value ratio was taken as a proxy for the target or long-term weighting.

The target D/(D+E) at market value ratio was assumed to be 16.28%.

Thus the WACC is estimated as:

WACC calculation	
Risk free rate	3.646%
CRP	0.96%
Tax rate (marginal)	35.00%
Cost of debt	2.99%
Levered Bloomberg Adjusted Beta (2yr weekly)	0.706
EMRP	6.82%
Cost of equity	8.46%
Target gearing (D/D+E)	16.28%
WACC	7.57%

The WACC was calculated as:

$$= Ke \text{ x } \frac{D}{D+E} + Kd \text{ x } \frac{E}{D+E}$$

Where:

D/(D+E)	= Target or long-term capital structure at market value
Ke	= Cost of equity
Kd	= Cost of debt

Step 4: Estimate the terminal value

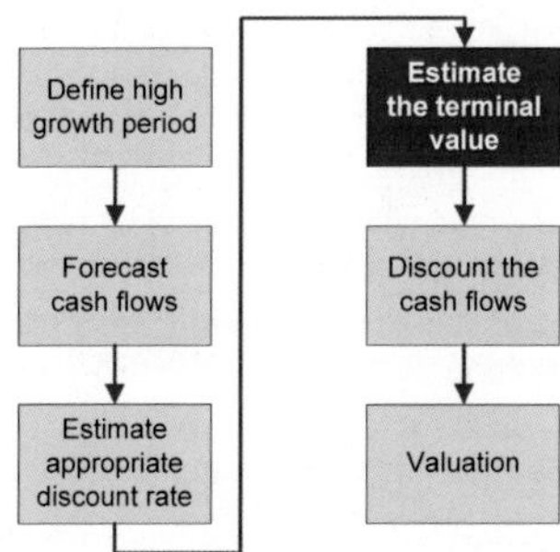

Once the FCF profile has matured the remaining EV will be captured by a terminal value calculation. There are three main terminal value calculation approaches used in DCF valuations:

- Cash flow growth perpetuity
- Reinvestment method
- Multiple approach

It is not necessary to favor one approach over another. Each approach is a useful benchmark against the alternatives. The terminal value calculation is not a precise science – sanity checking the terminal value estimation is the only possible way of providing some confidence in the numbers generated by the terminal value calculations.

This terminal value calculation will account in many cases for the majority of the valuation. However, it must be noted that terminal values are not calculations independent of the high growth period. They are in fact fully dependent on the high growth period. If the high growth period assumptions are inconsistent or in some way flawed, the terminal value will also be flawed. (This was illustrated in Step 2 in the CA Tip – High growth period disconnects on terminal period transition.)

Cash flow growth perpetuity

The cash flow growth perpetuity approach estimates the terminal value using the terminal FCFF (i.e. the last FCFF estimate of the high growth period). The calculation assumes that the terminal FCFF will subsequently grow at a constant rate into perpetuity.

The standard cash flow growth perpetuity terminal value calculation will discount the constant growth FCFF perpetuity back to a terminal year value. For instance, a ten year high growth period DCF will express the terminal value in time period 10 terms. The terminal value still needs to be discounted back to time period 0 in order to be included in the overall EV valuation.

The standard calculation for a ten year high growth period terminal value is:

$$TV_{t=10}^{t:11-\infty} = \frac{FCFF_{10}(1+g)}{WACC - g}$$

$FCFF_{10}$	=	Free cash flow to firm in the terminal year (time period 10)
g	=	FCFF perpetuity growth rate
$TV_{t=10}^{t:11-\infty}$	=	Terminal value expressed in time period 10 terms, capturing the terminal value of cash flows from time period 11 into perpetuity

The determination of the perpetuity growth rate is obviously critical to the overall terminal value calculation. The growth rate is estimated with reference to:

- Current growth rates. Past growth rates are not always a reliable indicator of future growth rates, however empirical studies have shown that there is a correlation between current and future growth rates. A firm growing currently at 30% per year probably has a higher and more sustainable growth rate than a company growing at 10%.
- Size of the firm. The size of a firm is often indicative of its relative success, however as firms become larger it becomes increasingly difficult to maintain such a high level of growth.
- GDP growth rates. Growth rates should be benchmarked against current GDP growth rates. A company cannot sustain growth into perpetuity at a rate greater than the rest of the economy as a whole.
- Mature comparable companies' growth rates assumptions.
- Gordon's growth model (see later.) Gordon's growth model states that growth is driven by the re-investment of earnings back into a business and the return generated on this re-investment. If a company does not re-invest earnings or does not generate sufficient returns on this reinvestment, it cannot theoretically support high levels of growth. The growth model is used mainly to justify a growth rate, rather than to estimate one.

Implied Terminal Multiples

The terminal value estimated using the cash flow growth perpetuity can be used to imply a terminal multiple. The implied multiple can then be used as a cross-check on the size of the perpetuity growth rate assumptions.

Terminal value calculated using a cash flow growth perpetuity

$$TV_{t=10}^{t:11-\infty} = \frac{FCFF_{10}(1+g)}{WACC-g}$$

Implied terminal multiple

$$= \frac{TV_{t=10}^{t:11-\infty}}{EBITDA_{10}}$$

The terminal value calculated using the cash flow growth perpetuity is divided by the terminal EBITDA.
This produces an implied terminal multiple that can be benchmarked against peers.

In the example below, the undiscounted terminal value of $14,045m has been calculated using the cash flow perpetuity method. The terminal multiple is implied by dividing the terminal value by the terminal EBITDA $1,372m. The implied terminal EV/EBITDA of 10.2x can then be benchmarked against peers and the implied multiples generated by the DCF itself. If the benchmark multiples were less than the implied terminal multiple, it may suggest that the terminal value is too bullish. At the very least, the benchmarking exercise may possibly suggest the need for further review of the terminal assumptions.

Terminal value - cash flow perpetuity	
Terminal FCFF	767
Perpetuity growth rate	2.00%
WACC	7.57%
Terminal value	14,045

Reinvestment

The reinvestment method is an extension of the cash flow growth perpetuity, but combines elements of Gordon's Growth Model into the calculation. The benefit of this method is that it creates a correlated driver between the assumed growth rate and the level of reinvestment required in order to sustain the growth rate assumption. If the growth rate assumptions are increased, the retention of NOPAT will also increase. In other words, it forces the Analyst to think about the fact that to have growth, there must be investment (as opposed to just appearing out of thin air).

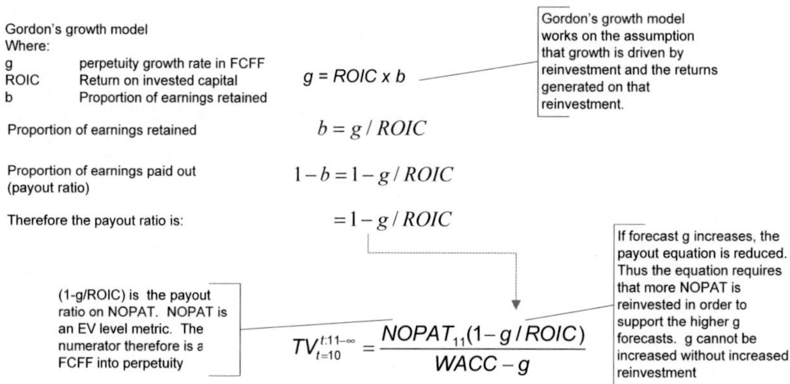

Multiple approach

The multiple approach estimates the terminal value on the basis that the target company will be valued at the end of the high growth period using public market valuations. The approach introduces relative valuation into the DCF valuation.

The terminal value is typically calculated by applying an appropriate range of comparable multiples (EV multiples if performing a FCFF valuation) to the target's terminal earnings metrics. The terminal value is normally based on a review of comparable trading multiples. However, in certain circumstances, transaction multiples can be used. This depends on the nature of the exit under consideration. These transaction multiples however will capture a control premium.

Getting comfort on the exit multiple assumptions can only come from benchmarking the multiples against other sources or by backing out the growth rate that is implied in the multiple and benchmarking it against the fundamentals of the business.

The example below is based on a Hershey DCF model. The terminal value is estimated using a terminal EV/EBITDA multiple of 10.0x. The multiple is applied to a terminal year EBITDA of $1,372m. This gives a terminal value of $13,720m expressed in terminal year terms (time 10 in this illustration).

The 10.0x EBITDA terminal multiple was based on a review of comparable multiples. Some Analysts will review comparable multiples and work on the assumption that there are no multiple arbitrages over the high growth period. That is they will use current multiples as a basis to determine the terminal multiple. This is generally a bullish assumption.

Many Analysts will adjust the terminal multiple downwards to reflect the realization and maturity of the growth profile over the high growth period.

Terminal value – exit multiple	
Terminal EBITDA	1,372
Terminal EV/EBITDA	10.0x
Implied terminal value	13,720

There are a number of dangers associated with the use of multiples to estimate a terminal value:

- The adjustment of comparable multiples to reflect the maturity in the growth profile needs to be embedded in the terminal multiple and can be somewhat arbitrary.
- The use of multiples in the terminal value calculation tends to distract the mind of the Analyst away from thinking about growth rates. It is easy to think a 10x EBITDA multiple is entirely appropriate without even contemplating the implied growth rate in the multiple. It is essential to back out the growth rate implicit in the terminal value so that it can be benchmarked against comparables as well as the growth assumption in the visible and terminal periods.

  See CA Tip – backing out g from the terminal multiple.

Benchmarking Terminal Multiples

The terminal value is an estimated value that can account for 60-80% of an EV. The main way Analysts will get comfort on the estimated terminal value will be through:

- Benchmarking the terminal multiple against comparables
- Reviewing the terminal multiple against the EV multiples implied by the overall DCF valuation
- Backing out the growth rate implied in the exit multiple

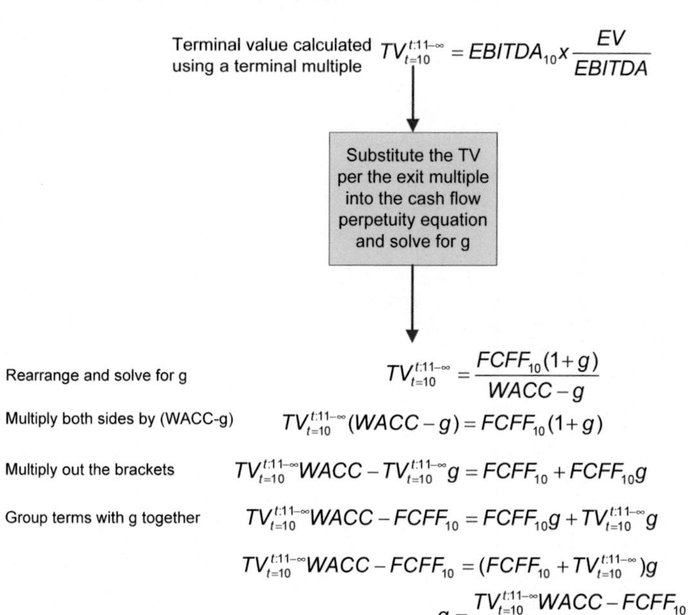

Backing Out g from the Terminal Multiple

Backing out the Hershey Inc growth rate from the 10x EBITDA terminal value multiple

Terminal value calculated using a terminal multiple $TV_{t=10}^{t11-\infty} = EBITDA_{10} x \frac{EV}{EBITDA}$

$$TV_{t=10}^{t11-\infty} = \$1{,}372m_{10} x 10.0$$

$$TV_{t=10}^{t11-\infty} = \$13{,}720m$$

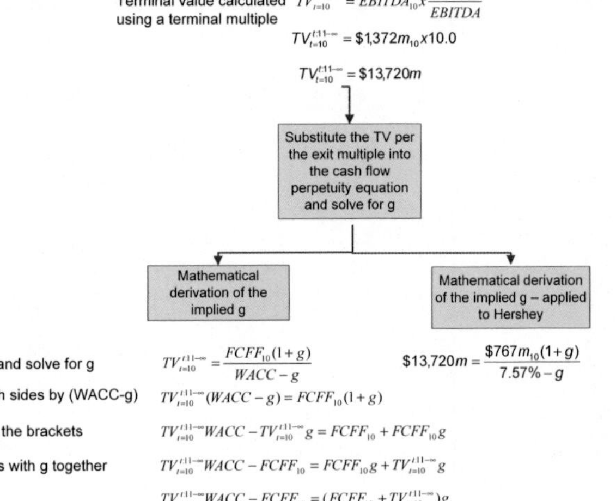

Rearrange and solve for g $TV_{t=10}^{t11-\infty} = \frac{FCFF_{10}(1+g)}{WACC-g}$ $\$13{,}720m = \frac{\$767m_{10}(1+g)}{7.57\%-g}$

Multiply both sides by (WACC-g) $TV_{t=10}^{t11-\infty}(WACC-g) = FCFF_{10}(1+g)$

Multiply out the brackets $TV_{t=10}^{t11-\infty}WACC - TV_{t=10}^{t11-\infty}g = FCFF_{10} + FCFF_{10}g$

Group terms with g together $TV_{t=10}^{t11-\infty}WACC - FCFF_{10} = FCFF_{10}g + TV_{t=10}^{t11-\infty}g$

$$TV_{t=10}^{t11-\infty}WACC - FCFF_{10} = (FCFF_{10} + TV_{t=10}^{t11-\infty})g$$

$$g = \frac{TV_{t=10}^{t11-\infty}WACC - FCFF_{10}}{(FCFF_{10} + TV_{t=10}^{t11-\infty})} \quad g = \frac{\$13{,}720m \, x \, 7.57\% - \$767m_{10}}{(\$767m_{10} + \$13{,}720m)}$$

$$g = 1.87\%$$

The growth rate therefore implied in Hershey's 10x EBITDA terminal value is 1.87%. This growth rate would be benchmarked against comparables and the Hershey visible and terminal growth rate assumptions.

Step 5: Discount the cash flows

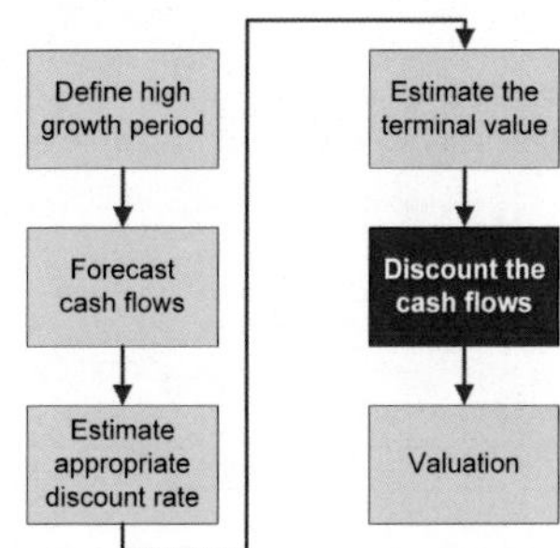

DCF is based on the premise that the value of a company is the sum of the present values of the cash flow streams generated by the company, discounted using an appropriate cost of capital.

Step 3 considered the calculation of an appropriate cost of capital.
Step 5 will now consider how to discount the cash flows using this cost of capital.

Typically DCF valuation models will discount the cash flows using one of two conventions:

- End of year discounting
- Mid year discounting

End of year discounting

The standard end of year discounting equation will discount a cash flow for full periods, assuming the cash flow occurs at the end of the period.

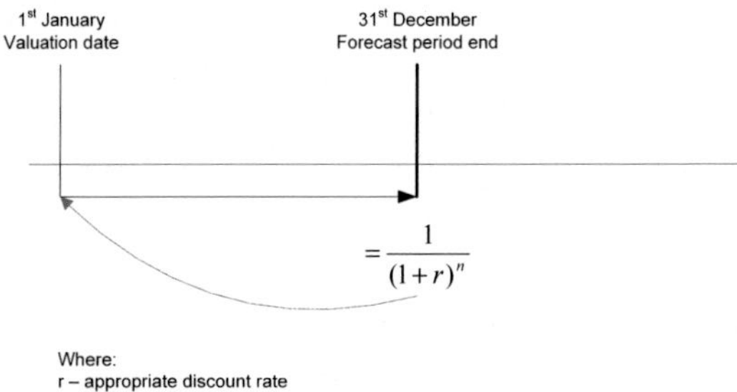

The calculation of EV for a DCF valuation using the end of year convention is therefore:

$$EV = \frac{FCF_1}{(1+r)} + \frac{FCF_2}{(1+r)^2} + ... + \frac{FCF_n}{(1+r)^n} + \frac{TV}{(1+r)^n}$$

Where:

FCF	=	Free cash flow	n	=	Number of periods
r	=	Appropriate discount rate	TV	=	Terminal value

Stub period valuation

The basic end of year discounting equation assumes that the first cash flow occurs exactly one year after the valuation date. However, this is an unrealistic assumption. Most Analysts will have to value companies on a valuation date that is part way through a period. Hence the initial period discounting (or stub period) equation will have to be amended to reflect a short first period.

For instance:

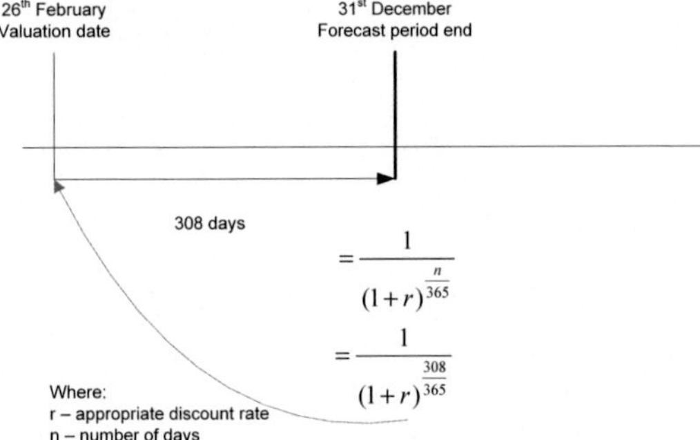

Subsequent period cash flows will then be assumed to occur full periods after the initial stub period.

Mid-year discounting

This convention assumes that the cash flows occur mid-way through the period. This is believed to provide a more accurate reflection of how the cash flows are generated over a period so most Analysts typically will apply the mid-year discounting convention to their cash flow forecasts.

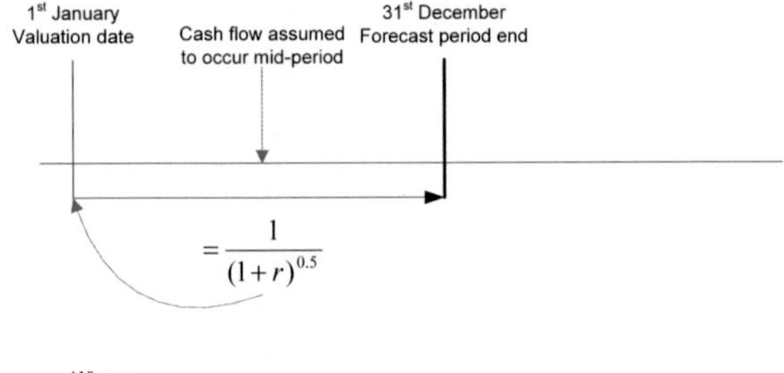

Where:
r – appropriate discount rate

The calculation of EV for a DCF valuation using the mid-year convention is therefore:

$$EV = \frac{FCF_1}{(1+r)^{0.5}} + \frac{FCF_2}{(1+r)^{1.5}} + \ldots + \frac{FCF_n}{(1+r)^{n-0.5}} + \text{PV of TV}$$

Where:

FCF = Free cash flow

r = Appropriate discount rate

n = Number of periods

TV = Terminal value

Mid-year discounting (stub period valuation)

Mid-year discounting of a stub period will assume that the cash flow occurs half way through the stub period. The example below illustrates a stub period valuation (26 February valuation date) for a 31 December period end. This is a 308 day stub period. The mid-year convention assumes that this cash flow occurs 154 days into the stub period.

The standard stub period discounting equation must be amended as follows:

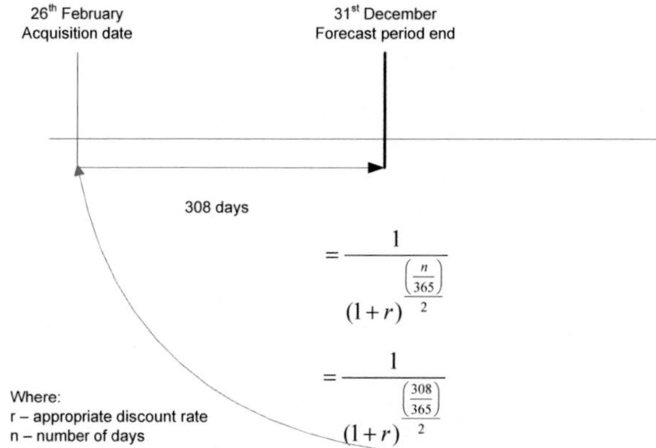

Mid-year discounting (cash flow perpetuity terminal value)

The mid-year discounting convention affects the terminal value discounting. The terminal value using the cash flow perpetuity method is calculated using the mid-point of the final forecast period and should be discounted for the period between the valuation date and the mid-point of the final forecast year.

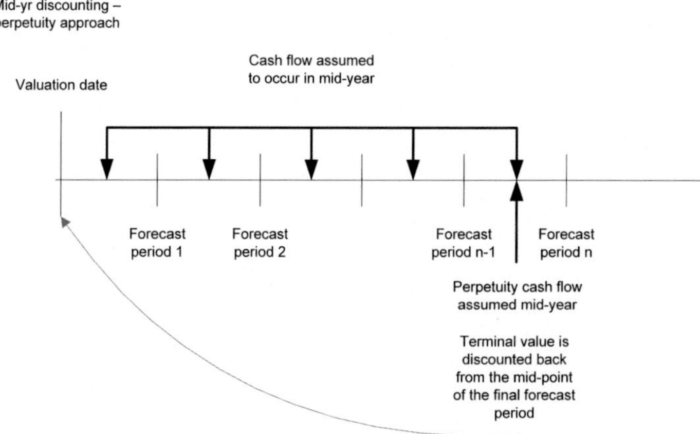

Mid-year discounting (multiple terminal value)

The terminal value using the terminal multiple method is calculated using the end-point of the final forecast period and should be discounted for the period between the valuation date and the end point of the final forecast year.

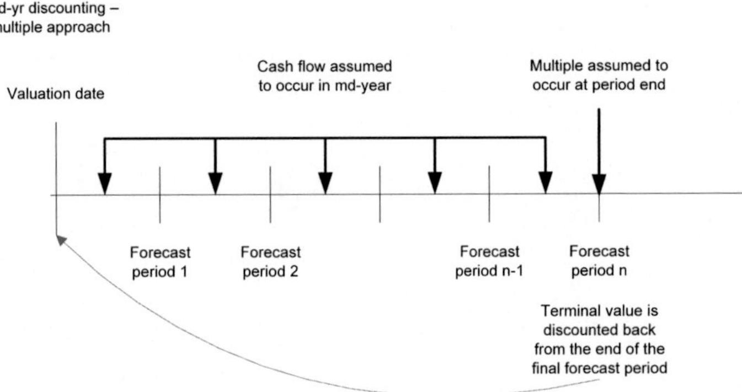

Step 6: Valuation

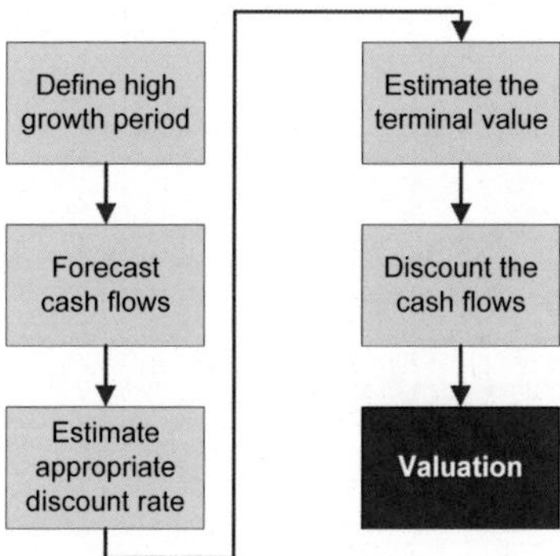

The valuation produced by the DCF method depends on the cash flows being discounted together with the discount rate.

- FCFF discounted with a WACC will produce an EV valuation
- FCFE discounted with a cost of equity will produce an equity valuation

The EV level valuation will need to be broken down to an equity value. The process is the same as discussed in the chapter on trading comps.

Breakdown enterprise value to equity value

The breakdown to equity value should be driven by fair values if available or if the breakdown component is material to the equity value derivation.

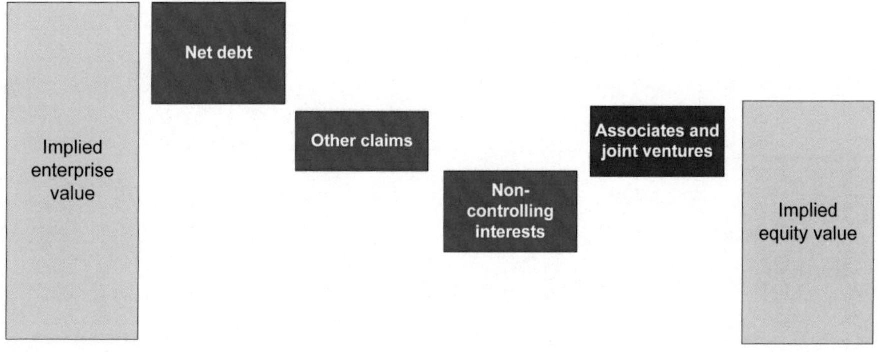

Hershey Full DCF

The DCF extract below brings together the FCFF forecasts for Hershey and the terminal value estimation. The terminal value has been calculated using the cash flow perpetuity method. All the cash flows are discounted using a WACC and a year-end discounting convention.

The EV is the present value of these cash flows.

The EV is broken down to equity value using fair values where appropriate and material.

DCF	31 Dec 10	31 Dec 11	31 Dec 12	31 Dec 13	31 Dec 14	31 Dec 15	31 Dec 16	31 Dec 17	31 Dec 18	31 Dec 19
Revenues	5,459	5,595	5,774	5,947	6,126	6,309	6,477	6,639	6,791	6,927
Operating costs	(4,559)	(4,666)	(4,807)	(4,940)	(5,087)	(5,228)	(5,361)	(5,489)	(5,602)	(5,714)
EBIT	900	929	967	1,008	1,039	1,081	1,116	1,150	1,189	1,213
DA	182	180	176	170	174	168	167	164	155	158
EBITDA	1,082	1,109	1,143	1,178	1,213	1,249	1,282	1,314	1,345	1,372
Decrease/(increase) in working capital	33	(96)	(54)	(42)	(36)	(33)	(27)	(23)	(18)	(14)
Capex (net)	(175)	(195)	(185)	(178)	(183)	(177)	(175)	(173)	(163)	(166)
Tax on operations	(314)	(325)	(339)	(353)	(364)	(378)	(391)	(403)	(416)	(425)
FCFF	626	493	566	605	631	661	690	717	747	767
Terminal value										14,045
Cash flows to be discounted	626	493	566	605	631	661	690	717	747	14,812
Discount factor	0.93	0.86	0.80	0.75	0.69	0.65	0.60	0.56	0.52	0.48
PV of cash flows	582	426	455	452	438	427	414	400	387	7,140

PV of visible cash flows	4,350	39.12%
PV of the terminal value	6,770	60.88%
Enterprise value	11,120	100.00%
Less: Net debt	(1,970)	
Less: Non-controlling interests	(32)	
Add: JVs and associates	63	
Equity value	9,181	
NOSH	241	
Equity value per share	38.10	

EV Breakdown (NCI, JVs and Associates)

Analysts must make sure they understand the components of the EV breakdown. The Analysts should investigate the components and know the information behind the non-controlling interest, associate and JV investments.

These components should be valued at fair value if material to the breakdown and provided that reliable information is available. If the investments are listed, the process is a straightforward percentage of the market capitalization. If the investments are unlisted, the Analyst will have to value the investment using DCF and trading comps.

Joint ventures (if equity accounted) and associates must be brought back into the equity value calculation as they are normally excluded from the FCFF derivation. Analysts must be confident of this statement, otherwise there is a risk that the value associated with these cash flows is double-counted.

FCFF derived from revenues or EBIT will normally exclude the results generated by JVs and associates as equity accounting will bring these numbers in below the EBIT line.

FCFF derived from net income however will include the JV and associate results as it is included in the net income figure. Most DCFs derived from net income will remove the JV and associate contribution and then value the JV and associate investments separately as components of the EV breakdown.

DCF Sensitivity Analysis

DCF is based on a number of sensitive assumptions. A DCF model will be built in an Excel environment that allows the sensitivity testing of these assumptions. It is this sensitivity analysis that will provide the DCF valuation range. The range captures the probable sensitivity in the DCF valuation.

Typical sensitive DCF assumptions are:

- Risk-free rates
- Betas
- Equity and credit market premiums
- Target capital structures
- Perpetuity growth rates
- Terminal exit multiples

Implied equity value per share sensitivity

Perpetuity growth rate					Beta
	0.606	0.656	0.706	0.756	0.806
3.00%	52.18	48.13	44.58	41.45	38.67
2.50%	47.37	44.00	41.02	38.35	35.95
2.00%	43.52	40.66	38.10	35.78	33.68
1.50%	40.38	37.90	35.66	33.62	31.75
1.00%	37.75	35.57	33.59	31.77	30.10

The extract above is a sensitivity table produced from the Hershey DCF model used as the background case study to this chapter. The equity value per share has been sensitized against the beta and the perpetuity growth rate used in the terminal value calculation. Using this information, the DCF valuation range is estimated as $33.62 to $44.00

Sanity Checking the DCF Output – EV Splits

The DCF output can be sanity checked in two main ways:

- EV splits
- Implied EV multiples

An EV split disaggregates the EV into two components – the amount of the EV derived from the present value of the terminal value and the amount generated by the present value of the high growth period cash flows. Both values are expressed in present value terms.

PV of high growth period cash flows	4,350	39.12%
PV of the terminal value	6,770	60.88%
Enterprise value	11,120	100.00%

The benchmark often used for the EV split by Analysts is the 30/70% split for ten year DCF models. The benchmark is applicable for mature companies only. EV splits that are not in the 30%/70% region may suggest that there is an underlying issue with the consistency of the valuation. For instance, if the EV is heavily dependent on the terminal value and the split is materially in excess of 70%, this may suggest:

- The high growth period is not long enough to allow an appropriate maturing of the cash flow profile
- The assumptions in the high growth period have not been profiled to hit maturity in the terminal year
- The terminal value drivers are too bullish (e.g. growth is too high or the multiples too large)
- A heavily weighted terminal value may suggest that the DCF model is not the most appropriate model to use to value the company and may be an alternative should be considered

A disproportionate split however does not provide answers – it merely suggests that there may be an issue and a need to review the underlying assumptions.

Sanity Checking the DCF Output – Implied EV Multiples

The DCF output produces an EV – this can be used to benchmark the valuation against peers. The implied EV multiples below have been calculated by dividing the DCF EV output by the EBITDA forecasts, to produce the EV/EBITDA multiples that are implied by the valuation. The implied multiples can then be benchmarked against trading comparables.

If the comparables are trading at a premium to the implied multiples generated by the DCF, this may suggest that the DCF drivers are too bearish. Likewise, if the comparables are trading at a discount to the DCF, this may suggest the DCF assumptions are not in line with the market and are too bullish.

	31 Dec 10	**31 Dec 11**	**31 Dec 12**
EBITDA	1,082	1,109	1,143
Enterprise value	11,120		

Implied EV/EBITDA multiples	
EV/EBITDA 2010	10.3x
EV/EBITDA 2011	10.0x
EV/EBITDA 2012	9.7x

Diluted equity value per share

The DCF valuation can be adjusted to produce a diluted equity value per share. The dilution anticipates the exercise of in-the-money (ITM) share options. The ITM calculation uses the implied equity value per share (undiluted) as the reference price to determine whether the share options are in or out of the money.

The dilution can be estimated using either the:

- Treasury method
- Net buyout method

Both methods are covered in detail in the chapter on trading comps.

The dilution however does create circularity in the DCF model as the dilution will increase in the NOSH used to calculate the equity value per share. The dilution in the share price will then impact the ITM options calculation. The dilution will then impact the NOSH and so the circularity is established.

Hershey Inc

The g assumption will be benchmarked against comparables and must be in line with the terminal high growth period assumptions

WACC calculation			
Risk free rate	3.646%	10yr US treasury	Bloomberg
Beta	0.706	2 yr weekly adjusted beta	Bloomberg
EMRP	6.82%	Bloomberg EMRP	Bloomberg
Cost of equity	8.46%		
Risk free rate	3.646%	10yr US treasury	Bloomberg
CRP	0.96%	Stable A	Bloomberg
Tax rate (marginal)	35.00%	US income tax rate	
Cost of debt	2.99%		
Target gearing (D/EV)	16.28%	Bloomberg WACC screen	Bloomberg
WACC	7.57% WACC		
Terminal growth rate	2.00% G		

All WACC assumptions are sourced. Hershey is a US listed company with a predominantly US shareholder base. Therefore the WACC components are US sources (risk free rates, EMRP, market index beta is regressed against the S&P 500

The initial forecasts can be sourced from broker research (and benchmarked against consensus). The broker research metrics must be consistent with the historic numbers.

DCF	31 Dec 07	31 Dec 08	31 Dec 09	31 Dec 10	31 Dec 11	31 Dec 12	31 Dec 13	31 Dec 14	31 Dec 15	31 Dec 16	31 Dec 17	31 Dec 18	31 Dec 19
Revenues	4,947	5,134	5,299	5,459	5,595	5,774	5,947	6,126	6,309	6,477	6,639	6,791	6,927
Operating costs	(4,489)	(4,544)	(4,438)	(4,559)	(4,666)	(4,807)	(4,940)	(5,087)	(5,228)	(5,361)	(5,489)	(5,602)	(5,714)
EBIT	458	590	861	900	929	967	1,008	1,039	1,081	1,116	1,150	1,189	1,213
DA	311	249	183	182	180	176	170	174	168	167	164	155	158
EBITDA	769	839	1,044	1,082	1,109	1,143	1,178	1,213	1,249	1,282	1,314	1,345	1,372
Decr/(incr) in w'cap	117	(133)	(90)	33	(96)	(54)	(42)	(36)	(33)	(27)	(23)	(18)	(14)
Capex (net)	(190)	(263)	(175)	(175)	(195)	(185)	(178)	(183)	(177)	(175)	(173)	(163)	(166)
Tax on operations	(170)	(217)	(305)	(314)	(325)	(339)	(353)	(364)	(378)	(391)	(403)	(416)	(425)
FCFF	526	226	474	626	493	566	605	631	661	690	717	747	767
Terminal value													14,045
Cash flows to be discounted				626	493	566	605	631	661	690	717	747	14,812
Discount factor				0.93	0.86	0.80	0.75	0.69	0.65	0.60	0.56	0.52	0.48
PV of cash flows				582	426	455	452	438	427	414	400	387	7,140

The cash flow profile has been profiled in order to achieve a steady mature growth rate by the end of the high growth period.

PV of visible cash flows	4,350	39.12%
PV of the terminal value	6,770	60.88%
Enterprise value	11,120	100.00%
Less: Net debt	(1,970)	
Less: Non-controlling interests	(32)	
Add: JVs and associates	63	
Equity value	9,181	
NOSH	241	
Equity value per share	38.10	
Current equity price	41.57	
Premium / (Discount)	(8.36%)	

The EV has been split between the EV derived from the terminal value and that derived from the high growth period

The terminal value has been calculated using a cash flow growth perpetuity, assuming at growth rate of 2% and a WACC of 7.57%

The NOSH can be diluted or undiluted

Implied EV/EBITDA multiples	
EV/EBITDA 2010	10.3x
EV/EBITDA 2011	10.0x
Implied EV/EBITDA terminal multiple	10.2x

The components of the EV breakdown are valued at fair value where material and when information is available

The implied EV multiples are derived from the DCF EV. They are used to benchmark the DCF against comparable multiples

Tick Sheet – DCF Valuation

DCF valuation – a six-step structured approach

- Define the high growth period
- Forecast the cash flows
- Estimate appropriate discount rates
- Estimate the terminal value
- Discount the cash flows
- Valuation

There are five key drivers of FCFF:

- Revenue growth rates
- EBITDA margins
- Changes in net working capital
- Capex (capital expenditure)
- Cash taxes on operations

The components of WACC:

- The cost of equity
- Risk-free rates
- Beta
- Equity market risk premiums
- The cost of debt
- Credit market risk premiums
- Interest tax shields
- Capital structure weightings

Terminal values can be calculated using:

- Cash flow growth perpetuities
- Reinvestment method
- Multiples

Sanity checks:

- EV splits
- Benchmarking against comparables
- Backing out growth rates from terminal multiples

Discounting

- End of year discounting
- Mid-year discounting
- Mid-year discounting and terminal value issues
- Stub periods

Valuation

- EV breakdown
- Implied multiples
- Diluted equity values (treasury method calculations)

Introduction

The valuation summary or Football Field summary as it is often known, is one of the most important parts of a pitch book presentation. It brings together all of the valuation techniques and their implied valuation ranges into one space. This summary will be scrutinized by senior bankers and clients alike. If the valuation summary does not stand up to this intense scrutiny, the whole presentation can lose its credibility.

The valuation summary will be used:

- To sanity check the individual valuation techniques
- To determine the indicative overall valuation range
- To justify the offer premium over and above the current or pre-announcement share price
- As a benchmark for bid negotiation
- To determine the offer premium for merger modeling purposes
- To formulate initial thoughts for transaction finance structures

A basic valuation summary would be presented as follows:

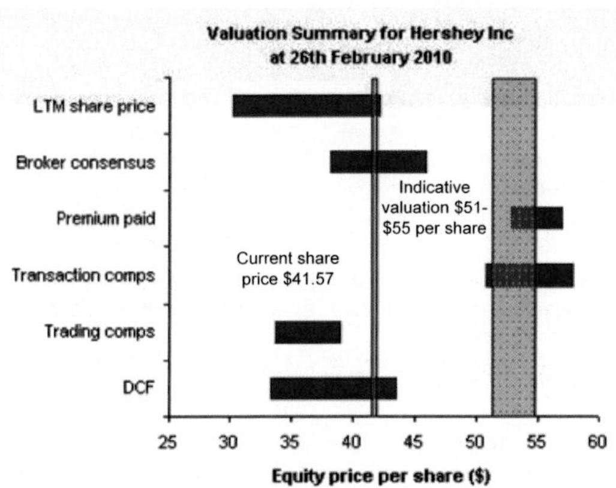

Valuation sanity check

Before any valuation summary is presented to senior bankers or clients, the summary must be sanity checked. The valuation summary is the first time that all the valuation technique results will have been brought together in one place.

There is a basic expectation that transaction comps and premium paid valuations will be at a premium to DCF and trading comps valuations as these techniques are inclusive of a control premium. However, a review of the valuation summary can identify anomalies and errors in the valuation process that can be missed when Analysts are focused on the detail of individual valuation techniques.

Valuation Summary

The valuation summary below would require further review before submitting to senior bankers or the client.

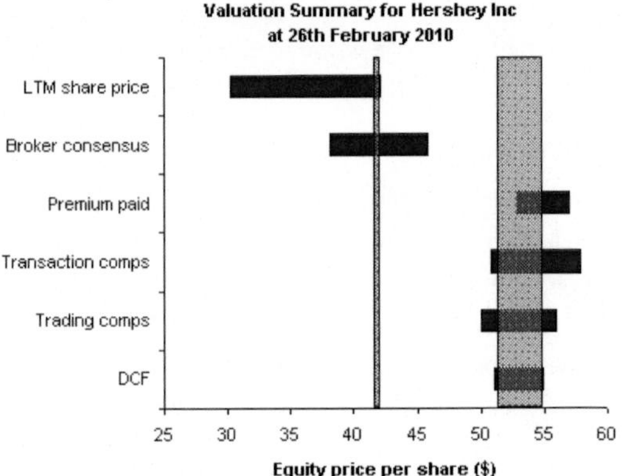

The valuations overall appear significantly inflated in relation to the LTM share prices and the broker consensus. The DCF and trading comps are falling within a similar region to the transaction comps and premium paid analysis.

The following issues may be relevant to this valuation summary:

- The transaction comps and premium paid analysis may be based on an inappropriate comparable universe. The current market may be strong, resulting in strong trading comps and DCF results, but the transaction comps and premium paid analysis may have been based on a comparable transaction universe that is dated and based within a bearish part of the economic cycle.
- The DCF and trading comps work appear to be inconsistent and significantly inflated in relation to the current market (as indicated by the current share price and the LTM data). Has the market got the valuation completely wrong?
- The DCF valuation may be based on overly bullish assumptions.
- The trading comps may be based on an unrepresentative universe. The universe may include outliers and/or trading comps that include bid speculation in the numbers.

The immediate issue that is highlighted by the valuation summary below is the width of the trading comps valuation range. The range is too wide and provides no focused analysis. The range may be too wide because:

- The Analyst has not analyzed the comps output sheet in sufficient detail to strip out outliers
- The trading comps valuation was based purely on high and low multiples in the comps sheet
- The comparable universe is inappropriate and too widely specified
- The comparable universe includes trading comps that capture bid speculation in the equity prices, thus inflating the multiples and valuations
- The Analysts may have made foreign currency translation errors when collecting or entering the data
- The wide range may just suggest that trading comps is not an appropriate valuation technique for the company under consideration

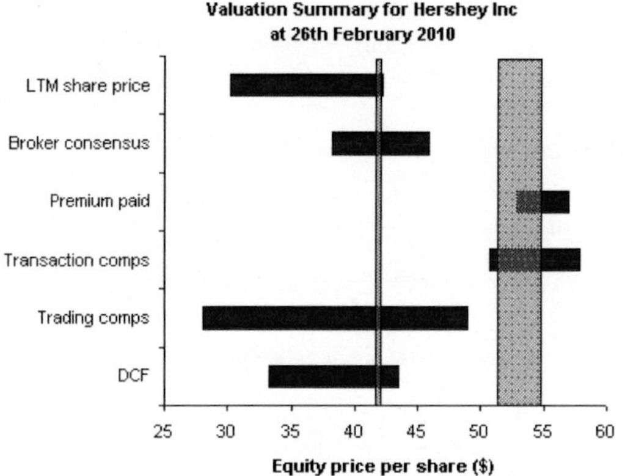

The valuation summary below highlights immediate issues as the valuation ranges do not support the indicative valuation range. The indicative valuation range is between $66 and $70.

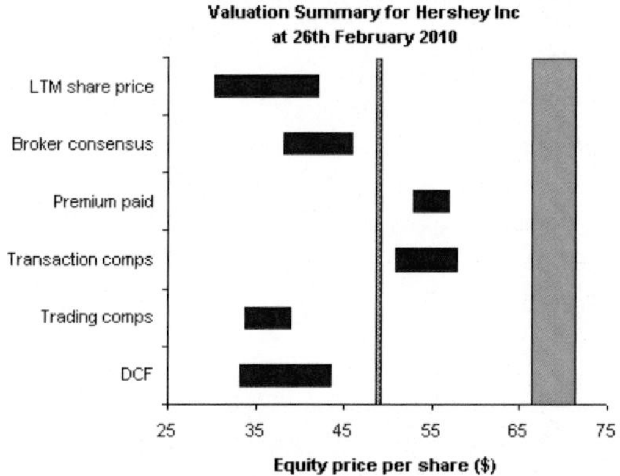

In fact, not one of the valuation technique ranges supports this level of valuation. Also the current share price of $48 lies outside the LTM share price range – again this is inconsistent.

Determining the overall valuation range

A valuation summary will initially only include the valuation ranges for each of the valuation techniques and benchmark LTM share prices and the consensus estimates. At this point an indicative valuation will need to be set.

The actual setting of the indicative price range will be influenced by:

- Which side of the deal is being advised – buy-side or sell-side
- Buyer and seller motivations
- Relative valuation ranges of each technique
- The extent to which a premium can be justified
- The ability of the bidding company to finance the transaction
- Pre-conceptions to a certain extent

The indicative valuation range must be supported by the individual valuation technique ranges and the premium over LTM equity prices must be justifiable.

Justifying the offer premium

The offer premium will be justified by the strategic rationale of the transaction and by the implied control premiums arising out of the transaction comps and premium paid analysis work, as well as the basic DCF and trading comps work.

Typical justifications of the offer premium will focus on:

- Previous transaction premiums
- Potential cost and revenue synergies
- Buyer and seller motivations
- Access to:
  - New markets and products
  - R&D pipelines
  - Distribution channels
  - Human capital
  - New capital markets

Offer premiums can range widely and are sector specific. Typically as a benchmark, offer premiums historically average between 30-40%.

The story supporting the justification must be built on a strong foundation of analysis.The Analyst is advising the client to pay what could be a significant premium over and above the pre-announcement share price. The argument must be strong as the client will need to carry this argument on to the shareholders. If the shareholders are not won over, there is no deal – there is no fee!

Benchmark for bid negotiation

The valuation summary will be one of the focuses when presenting to clients and when negotiating with the other side. Negotiation in most circumstances will be based on compromise. Buy-side advisors will pitch initially at the lower end of the valuation spectrum, whilst sell-side advisors will naturally gravitate towards the upper end of the range.

The valuation summary below illustrates possible buy vs. sell-side indicative valuation ranges. Ultimately where the valuation ends up will be due to the relative negotiating strengths of each side. The numbers generated by the valuation techniques provide only the initial benchmarks that kick start a negotiation. No deal has ever been completed on the basis of a number spat out by a financial valuation model. The models are just tools and are just one part of a larger process.

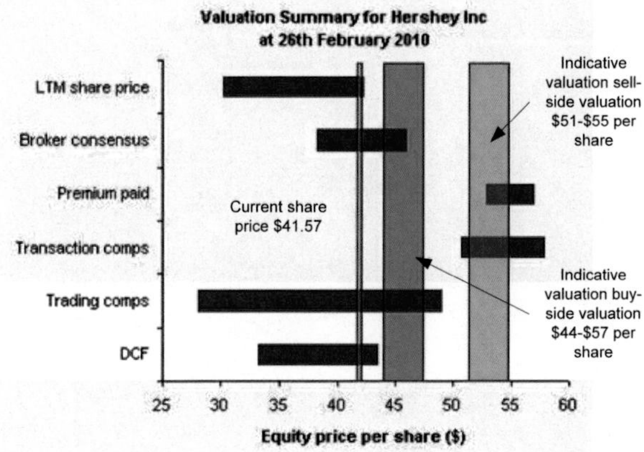

Offer premiums for the merger model

One of the key and sensitive inputs for the merger model is the offer premium. If the valuation summary is inconsistent or incorrect, the indicative valuation range and therefore the offer premiums will be incorrect. This will then distort the entire analysis generated by the merger model.

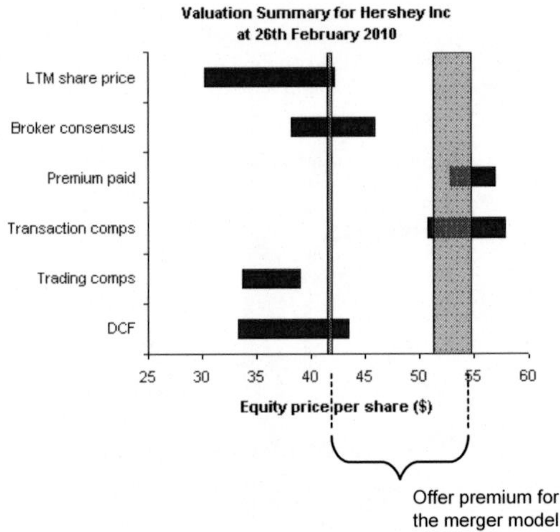

The offer premium drives the:

- Equity acquisition costs
- ITM option buy-out calculations
- Fees
- Size and structure of the sources of funds requirement
- EPS accretion/dilution analysis

What makes a good valuation summary?

Key components of a good summary:

- A current/pre-announcement equity price per share
- Valuation date
- Key valuation techniques included:
  - DCF
  - Trading comps
  - Transaction comps
  - Implied LBO valuation
- An indicative overall valuation range
- The indicative valuation range is consistent with the individual valuation ranges
- Implied multiples based on the valuation ranges
- Broker consensus benchmark
- LTM share price benchmark
- Implied multiples for the valuation ranges
- Clear annotations if required
- Annotated axes
- Clear currency denominations

Typical valuation summary issues:

- Too much detail included in the summary – the reader becomes distracted with the level of detail
- Valuation ranges too narrow – can make the valuation look too scientific
- Valuation ranges too wide – can make the valuation look spurious
- Ultimate valuation range not supported by valuation techniques
- Premium to current or pre-announcement price cannot be justified
- Transaction comps inconsistent with current market conditions
- Valuations inconsistent with the anticipated control premiums and synergies
- Valuation denominations missing
- Axes not defined

Analyzing Hershey Inc's valuation summary

The Hershey Inc valuation has been the background case study for the valuation work in this manual. The valuation ranges below are based on thorough valuation work.

What observations can be made?

- Hershey Inc is trading towards the higher end of the LTM range. The market seems to have a positive view of the stock. Recent earnings announcements had beaten broker estimates. However, the LTM price range must be considered in the context of the previous 12 months. Hershey is emerging (as all companies are) from a deep recession. Global confectionary was hit hard during the credit crunch and share prices reflected this. The LTM price and Hershey trading at the top end therefore is more a reflection of recovery than one of relative strength.
- Broker consensus is expecting that the share price will increase over the next 12 months to set a new 12 month high.
- The trading comps and DCF work barely support the current share price. This suggests that the share price again is trading beyond the true intrinsic value of the company. The global confectionary market is highly competitive, it is exposed to commodity price risk and the industry is consolidating.
- However, the transaction comps and premium paid work suggest that transactions in this industry attract significant control premiums in the region of 30% over pre-announcement prices. Most major global confectionary transactions are driven by the desire to acquire global market share and consumers have strong brand loyalties.

  The brand loyalty makes it hard for competitors to replicate these brands. Hence acquisition provides an effective way to acquire this brand loyalty and therefore market share. Size and economies of scale are also very important in this industry as they assist in supply chain negotiation, especially when these companies are trying to sell to the likes of Wal-mart and Tesco.
- The indicative overall valuation range was set at the lower end of the premium valuation range. This was an attempt to present a conservative valuation, given the views captured by the trading comps, DCF and broker consensus. Premiums are realized in this market, however, the economy is gently tip-toeing out of recession, financing is not as easy to structure as it has been in the past and the economy is a more conservative place. The lower end indicative valuation is also an acknowledgement of the fact that the majority of the transactions used in the premium paid analysis and transaction comps are dated prior to the credit crunch.

The above observations are based around the valuation summary. However, the background story is built on a thorough knowledge of the industry. Valuation summary analysis requires a mixture of valuation technical knowledge as well as practical industry knowledge and experience. Analysts must know their sector and transaction histories.

Presentational considerations

The valuation summary is a powerful tool and its impact in a presentation is significant.

A good valuation summary should contain four key elements:

- Rich content
- Inviting visuals
- Clean presentation
- Not cluttered with too much information

The valuation summary needs to speak for itself. Avoid using cheap graphical distractions. The reader of the summary will compare and contrast the valuations. A clear valuation summary then enables the reader to draw her own conclusions on the valuations.

Consider the two summaries below:

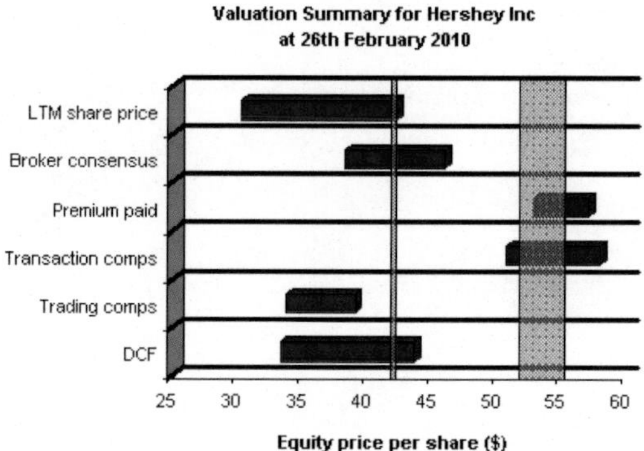

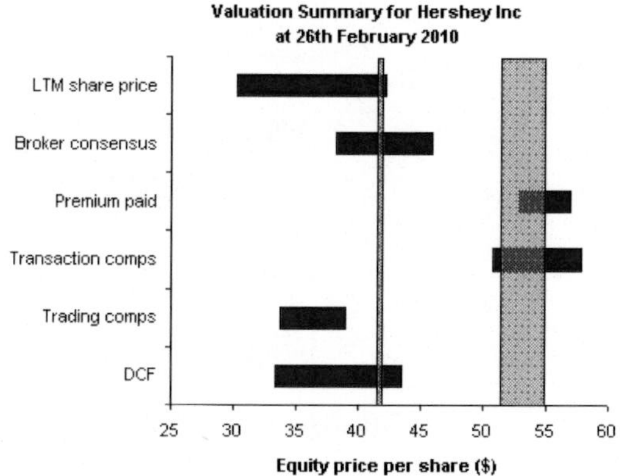

The first makes use of 3D bars and heavy gridlines. This makes it hard to read the data. The reader will have to concentrate harder to interpret the visual and will be drawn away from the content. In contrast, the second valuation summary is clean and easy to read – there are no artistic distractions; the data speaks for itself.

3D graphs should be avoided at all costs. They tend to be distracting, harder to read and ultimately they look amateur.

Valuation Summary

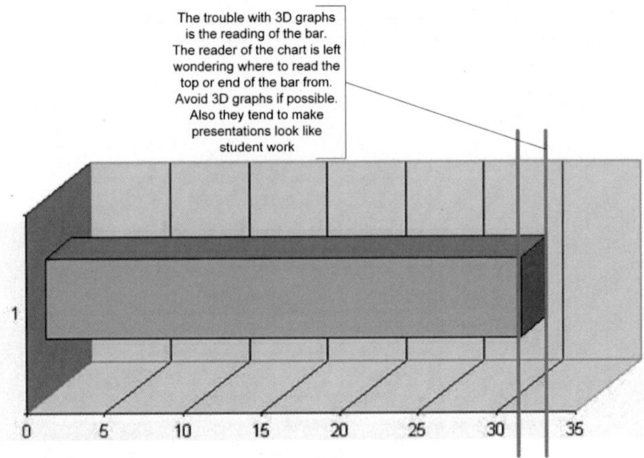

If gridlines are being used to frame and reference the data, keep the lines light. Vertical gridlines are normally used in conjunction with valuation summaries, as they can assist in the interpretation of the valuation ranges.

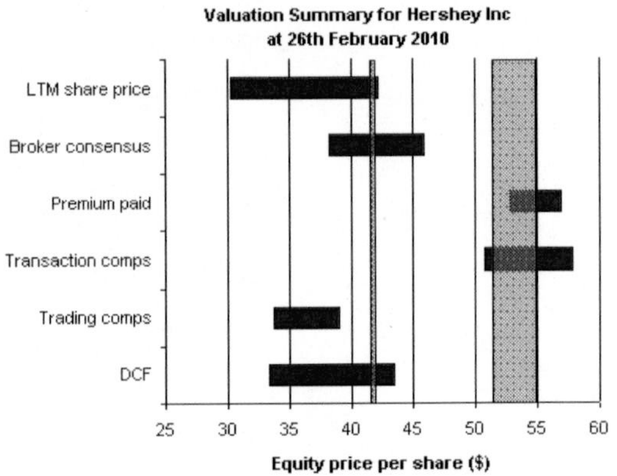

Tick Sheet – Valuation Summary

The valuation summary will be used:

- To sanity check the individual valuation techniques
- To determine the indicative overall valuation range
- To justify the offer premium over and above the current or pre-announcement share price
- As a benchmark for bid negotiation
- To determine the offer premium for merger modeling purposes
- To formulate initial thoughts for transaction finance structures

Key components of a good summary:

- A current/pre-announcement equity price per share
- Valuation date shown
- Key valuation techniques included:
  - DCF
  - Trading comps
  - Transaction comps
  - Implied LBO valuation
- An indicative overall valuation range
- The indicative valuation range is consistent with the individual valuation ranges
- Implied multiples based on the valuation ranges
- Broker consensus benchmark
- LTM share price benchmark
- Clear annotations if required
- Annotated axes
- Clear currency denominations

Typical valuation summary issues:

- Valuation ranges too narrow – can make the valuation look too scientific
- Valuation ranges too wide – can make the valuation look spurious
- Ultimate valuation range – not supported by valuation techniques
- Premium to current or pre-announcement price cannot be justified
- Transaction comps – inconsistent with the market
- Valuations inconsistent with the anticipated control premiums and synergies
- Valuation denominations missing
- Axes not defined